*Dialectics of
Third World
Development*

Dialectics
of Third World
Development

edited by

INGOLF VOGELER and
ANTHONY R. de SOUZA

ALLANHELD, OSMUN **Montclair**

ALLANHELD, OSMUN & CO. PUBLISHERS, INC.

Published in the United States of America in 1980
by Allanheld, Osmun & Co. Publishers, Inc.
(A Division of Littlefield, Adams & Co.)
81 Adams Drive, Totowa, New Jersey 07512

Copyright © 1980 by Ingolf Vogeler and Anthony de Souza

Second printing, 1982

Library of Congress Cataloging in Publication Data

Main entry under title:

Dialectics of Third World development.

   Includes bibliographical references and index.
   1. Underdeveloped areas—Addresses, essays, lectures.
I. Vogeler, Ingolf. II. De Souza, Anthony R.
HC59.7.D485   338.9′009172′4   79-53704
ISBN 0-916672-33-6
ISBN 0-916672-35-2 pbk.

Printed in the United States of America

*Written in the International Year of the Child,
this book is dedicated to the children of the world
in the hope that our better understanding
of global problems will lead to their liberation.*

Contents

Preface

This book is about ideas. Ideas help us understand our own lives and the world around us; and they have a way of staying around, regardless of how many people believe in them. This book presents the major classical and contemporary ideas which influence the way we think about the Third World—the countries of Latin America, Africa, the Middle East, and Asia. The purpose of this reader is to consider conflicting arguments and theories on six substantive topics related to Third World underdevelopment.

This book developed out of the editors inadequate academic training, which failed to consider *fundamentally* different ways of explaining the world. As teachers and researchers we have had to educate ourselves in these deficient areas in order to better prepare ourselves and our students for the present and the future.

Vogeler received his Ph.D. in geography in 1973 from the University of Minnesota, Minneapolis. In 1970 he was a cultural ecologist for the National Geographic Society-Tulane University archaeological expedition to the Yucatan peninsula, Mexico. His research interest in the Third World stems from this work. While teaching at St. Cloud State University, Minnesota, Julie Andrzejewski introduced him to many "new" ideas in and approaches to teaching human relations. He first incorporated these new ideas into a geography course on the dialectics of Third World development at Northwestern University, Illinois. This reader evolved from the experiences gained through that course. Student responses helped Vogeler compile a preliminary list of readings. The head of the geography department at Northwestern, Ed Espenshade, Jr., was interested in discussing controversial materials, even though he has a very different world view from Vogeler. His intellectual attitude was supportive of the teaching method presented in this book.

de Souza was trained in geography and economics at Reading University, England. After receiving his Ph.D. in 1968, he was hired as an urban-quantitative geographer at the University of Minnesota, Minneapolis. Within a few months, he left for Tanzania to work at the University of Dar es Salaam in both the Department of Geography and the Bureau of Resource Assessment and Land Use Planning. At this institution he came in contact with scientists from all over the world who held a variety of theoretical perspectives varying form free market economics to Third World socialism. Out of this experience grew an uneasiness about traditional science and its ability to explain the world. de Souza's new thinking was reflected in *The Underdevelopment and Modernization of the Third World*. The dialectical approach found in that monograph has been used in his teaching over the last seven years.

When we came to the University of Wisconsin-Eau Claire, we decided to compile a book on the Third World that reflected our similar but seperately developed dialecticism. Here, Brady Foust has been particularly supportive of our educational endeavors. We appreciate his wide-ranging intellectual curiosity and his friendship.

We express appreciation to the many organizations and individuals who freely shared their materials with us. However, we especially regret the absence of viewpoints from authors on five topics, which were excluded because the publisher thought the book would be too long. We wish to thank all those who helped put the book together: Steve Gosch for reviewing the contents of the three analytical perspectives; Robert Britton for writing an article on tourism and for recommending two of the readings; Crystal Blegen for her long hours of accurate typing; and Sharon Knopp for her insightful editing.

Ingolf Vogeler
Anthony R. de Souza

*Dialectics of
Third World
Development*

I

INTRODUCTION TO THE READINGS

1 Dialectics of Understanding the Third World

INGOLF VOGELER and *ANTHONY R. de SOUZA*

Almost every day we hear about Third World problems: overpopulation in the Sahel of Africa, high energy costs in India, massive urban unemployment in Brazil, and balance of payments difficulties in the banana republics of Central America. Yet there is little agreement on what causes and perpetuates these problems or how they might be eliminated.

The classic fable of five blind Indian gentlemen touching an elephant recalls this dilemma. Each gentleman feels a different part of the beast, and thinks that he can identify it correctly. The man who grabs the tail thinks it is a rope; the one who holds the leg believes it is a tree trunk; the one who touches the side of the elephant says it is a wall; the one who feels the ear proclaims it is a big leaf; and, the one who holds the trunk cries it is a snake. A concrete example will illustrate this dilemma. Consider the world food problem.[1] A hypothetical American resource pessimist declares: "Soaring numbers of people are over-running available food supplies. It seems to me that an acceptable solution to the world food supply situation is 'lifeboat ethics.' I believe that compassion is a luxury that we can no longer afford in this era of scarcity. Countries like Bangladesh are 'basket cases.' Their populations should not be recipients of American food aid, which will help only to maintain high population growth rates. We must learn to let the starving die for the survival of the human race." A United Nations adviser pipes up: "I think that high population growth rates and consequent population pressure, land fragmentation, poor soils, and unreliable rainfall keep people from feeding themselves. The best way to stabilize the overpopulation/food scarcity problem is to provide the poor with the contraceptive means to practice responsible parenthood." A World Bank official adds: "People are hungry because of insufficient food production. To solve the world food supply situation we must transform traditional agriculture which is inefficient. The only way to do this is for rich industrial countries to supply progressive farmers with imported technology, new seeds, artificial fertilizers, pesticides, irrigation, and machinery." A Marxist from Tanzania breaks in: "The cause of hunger is not the tropical environment, not too many people, not scarcity of available land, not lack of technology, and not overconsumption by greedy Americans. Every country has the capacity to feed itself. The real problem is the inequality generated by the world's political economy. The unequal distribution of global wealth is an historical product, the end result of the process by which the capitalist countries through colonialism and neo-imperialism gained control of the global economy. Today the hungry cannot be fed because of Third World elites and foreign corporations who benefit from the way things are. The only guarantee of long-term food security is for us Third World people to take control of our own food resources."

Box A
LABELING/LIBELING THE THIRD WORLD

The yawning chasm between prosperity and poverty in the world has created a language of its own. Or, is it in fact the rich person, not the yawning chasm, who has created this language? Author Göran Palm, writing for the Swedish International Development Authority (SIDA) journal *RAPPORT,* took a closer look at the vocabulary we use.

"The developed world" is contrasted to "the Third World." "Industrialized countries" are contrasted to "the poor in the South."

UN trade statistics commonly divide the world into three areas or "economic classes": industrialized countries or developed (Western) countries; developing countries or underdeveloped countries; socialist countries, Eastern bloc countries, or planned economies.

In addition to North America and Western Europe, the "industrialized countries" include Japan, Australia, New Zealand, South Africa, and sometimes Israel. The "developing countries" are mainly the nearly one hundred nations of Asia, Africa, Latin America, and Oceania which within the framework of the UN, form the Group of 77 (sometimes identified with the non-aligned states). This latter includes several nations with certain ties to the Soviet Union or China such as Guinea, Yugoslavia, India, Tanzania, but also members of the "Eastern bloc." Lastly, the "socialist countries" include all nations of Eastern Europe except Yugoslavia, a handful of countries in Asia and a single country in Latin America—Cuba.

This may seem like a good enough preliminary classification but on closer inspection, we find that the first group of countries is the only one to be given an indisputably positive label. To be labelled "underdeveloped" or to represent a "developing country" is less gratifying. Such labels imply that one is somehow a little inferior or backward, that one, say, lives in tribes, worships holy cows, is afraid of contraceptives, doesn't know one's own best interests.

To be reckoned a member of the "Eastern bloc" or one of the "communist countries" is not much better. It amounts to being excluded or discriminated against on political grounds. Such countries are not a part of the "development" and "industrialization" so craved throughout the southern hemisphere.

Labels like "socialist countries" and "planned economies" are in that case more accurate, but here, too, a different norm is applied to these countries than to the other groups. They are identified not according to their level of development, but according to ideology and the nature of their economic system.

If we take industrialization as the criterion, any differences between the Eastern and Western countries evaporate. A similar lexicographical justice might be extended to all the countries outside the industrial world. Most of the countries of Latin America, Africa, and Asia depend on the production of foodstuffs and primary materials for industry for their livelihood. To sidestep the problem of ideology we may conveniently categorize the world into "industrialized countries" versus "raw materials-producing countries."

It is perfectly acceptable to say "industrialized countries" just as long as they are not contrasted to "developing countries" but to "agrarian" or "raw materials-producing countries." It is fine to say "socialist countries" as long as they are contrasted to "capitalistic countries." Fine to say "underdeveloped" just as long as it is contrasted to "overdeveloped." The old terminology is perfectly admissible; the problem lies in the misleading pairs of opposites so frequently used.

Source: "Lexical Lapses on the Line," *Development Forum,* 6, no. 10 (November-December 1978): 6.

Different perspectives on the causes of world hunger lead to different solutions with profoundly different effects on Third World people. If human suffering and misery are to be eliminated as expediently as possible, then alternative world views must be understood and the best one must be selected to solve problems of underdevelopment. The question we invite you to consider is: What perspective provides the best explanation of the facts of underdevelopment? To answer this question we will have to become aware of the different theoretical and analytical frameworks scholars use to argue their cases. And such an awareness can only be achieved if we go beyond the usual level of learning common in Western educational institutions.

We can recognize four levels to the acquisition of knowledge.[2] First-level learning involves simple perception of fact. For example, we are hungry and are conscious of that fact. Second-level learning occurs when at least two facts are interrelated. When there is a drought we harvest less food per acre, and therefore, the likelihood of hunger increases. When we attain a higher level of performance within an existing system of understanding we are learning on the third level. Several options are possible: (1) If there is recurring drought, we can improve food yields either by planting drought resistant crops or by irrigating traditional crops. (2) If we choose not to change our traditional agricultural practices, we will be less well fed. When fourth-level learning is achieved, we are able to perceive the nature of existing systems and to re-examine them to discover how new options can be created by improving or changing *the system*. If we stay with the overpopulation/food scarcity issue, we can consider solutions beyond improved food yields if we evaluate the entire agricultural system. For instance, we could consider expropriating prime agricultural lands which are now used to produce exports crops such as coffee and cotton. This land could be given back to local farmers who could then produce food for their own needs instead of depending on purchased food and food aid from the industrialized countries.

Western educational systems are geared primarily to third-level learning. At this level, learning in the social sciences is synonymous with status quo theories supporting existing social systems. Consequently, most scientists stress *techniques* that permit them to optimize existing institutions rather than consider a wide range of alternative paradigms. In fourth-level learning the goal is to move beyond present perceptions of reality. This point may be illustrated with a simple problem. Connect the nine points drawn here with four continuous straight lines.

• • •

• • •

• • •

In looking for a solution you will find that there is none so long as you stay within the area limited by the points. But if you move outside the self-imposed square, a solution quickly springs to mind. (For the answer, see footnote 3 in the *NOTES AND REFERENCES*.) Similarly, if we are to understand the nature and causes of Third World underdevelopment, we must be willing to broaden the basis of our enquiry and examine alternative ideologies outside the ones currently limiting our perceptions of problems and solutions.

Most of us find it difficult to restructure the way we think and learn. Perspectives we hold about the world tend to persist. There is much danger that a perspective that subtly leads us to see the world in a particular way will prevent us from seeing the world in a more meaningful way. A drawing by Toulouse-Lautrec which is a perceptual illusion (Figure 1.1) illustrates this point. Those of us who see an old woman in the picture have difficulty seeing a young woman, and vice versa. To learn to see is to impose order on stimuli. The manner in which we impose that order is determined by our expectations and is therefore value-laden. If everything were as it seems then there would be no need for science.

In an ideological world value-free positions are impossible to maintain, even in

Figure 1.1

science. After all, science is as socially conceived and just as subject to bias and misinterpretation as all other forms of knowledge in society. To meet the challenge of Third World development problems we must become aware of alternative and competing world views. In order to select the best explanations and directions for solving Third World problems, we suggest the dialectical approach. Webster's Third International Dictionary defines "dialectic" as "The theory and practice of weighing and reconciling juxtaposed or contradictory arguments for the purpose of arriving at truth especially through discussion and debate." Not all theories can be compatible with each other, and hence scientists are forced to make difficult decisions about the adequacy and validity of competing paradigms. By affirming one paradigm, another one must be negated. In this way, the dialectical approach necessarily becomes synonymous with controversy, polemics, and challenge to status quo theories.

The dialectical approach adopted in this book provides a structure to help you determine which arguments are superior in terms of analytical strength and in terms of your own values. This book was designed as a reader because we wanted the authors to argue their own cases. To summarize or even to paraphrase the authors would prevent you from judging their arguments without distortion and bias. The readings have also been selected for their concise and well-reasoned positions on Third World problems. Individually and collectively, they are meant to be provocative, and designed to facilitate the evaluation of the presuppositions, the explanatory power, and the implications of alternative theoretical frameworks.

Analytically, the readings reflect three general perspectives: conservative, liberal, and radical.[4] These three paradigms rest on different assumptions about human nature, normative values, and social authority, and they employ different concepts to describe the nature and causes of underdevelopment.[5] A discussion of the major components of each paradigm will help you to begin to choose the perspective which you find most convincing.

ANALYTICAL CHOICES

The Conservative Perspective

The conservative view of the world is inherited from the ideas of Adam Smith, Ricardo, and their modern-day followers.[6] Conservatives assume that humans need positive (wage raises) *and* negative (threats of unemployment) material incentives to be productive. They are convinced that a capitalistic free enterprise economy based on competition and maximizing profits allows egoistic and calculating individuals to achieve maximum personal liberty and material well-being. Individual decision-making units (individuals, households, firms) act freely and rationally to produce a harmonious and moving equilibrium by means of market forces. Consequently, the process of social and economic change is a gradual cumulative and undirectional evolution. Faith in the efficiency and optimality of private market mechanisms, especially those of supply and demand, allows conservatives to postulate a limited role for governments. Probably, the single most important function of the State is to maintain social order, that is, provide national and international law and order through use of police and military forces, so that capitalism can operate freely. Given this view of the State, conservatives

Table 1.1   Alternative Explanations of Reality under Capitalism

Alternative Paradigms	Human Nature	Work Incentives	Unit of Analysis	Analysis Based on
Conservative	Humans are naturally unproductive and individualistic	Essentially material: 1) positive— raise in income 2) negative— unemployment	Individuals: persons or companies	Classical and neo-classical economics: competition and individuals maximizing profits
Liberal	Humans are naturally unproductive, but of goodwill	Essentially material: 1) positive— raise in income 2) negative— unemployment	Individuals and groups in society	Keynesian economics: competition and individuals maximizing profits with government assistance
Radicals	Humans are naturally productive and cooperative	None really necessary; socially valuable rewards	Classes in society	Marxist economics: labor theory of value, theory of surplus value, theory of class struggle and revolution

hold that government involvement in the economy usually causes more problems than it solves. They argue that many national and international problems are due to government interference and that the solutions to these problems lie in fewer government regulations and programs. Finally, conservatives believe that social change occurs gradually through the free actions of individuals in the market place.

The conservative approach to Third World development rests on two points. First, more participation by Third World countries in the world market economy, not less as some socialists argue, will assure faster and greater economic growth. Second, difficulties of economic growth can be traced to internal obstacles in the environment and culture (Table 1.1). The most dominant theory conservatives use to assert that underdeveloped countries will benefit from more interaction in the world economy is Ricardo's Theory of Comparative Advantage. Ricardo wrote, "It is quite important to the happiness of mankind that our enjoyments should be increased by a better division of labor, by each country producing those com-

Human Goals	Nature of Market Exchange Economy	Nature of Societal Problems	Role of State	Social Change
Maximum personal liberty and material well-being	Harmonious state of equilibrium: created by supply and demand forces	1) Individuals: lack of motivation, unrealistic demands, culture of poverty, racial inferiority 2) Government interference in the economy	Ideally, only police power to maintain law and order so that the market can work freely	Gradual change results from individual interactions in the market place
Individual equality and social justice (equal opportunity)	State of equilibrium, achievable with government involvement in the economy	1) Monopolistic tendencies in major economic sectors 2) Insufficient and inappropriate government programs	Police power and offsetting inadequacies in the economy whenever basic human needs and social justice are not achieved	Rapid change through government actions
Social equality: from each according to one's ability, to each according to one's need	Contradictions and crises of production and consumption; exploitation of workers; irrational allocation of natural and human resources	Private ownership of resources; production for profit rather than for human use; alienation; class conflict; unequal regional development	Police and economic power is used to maintain and enhance capitalism	Revolutionary change through mass movements to transform society's structure and values

modities for which by its situation, its climate and its other material or artificial advantages, it is adapted, and by their exchanging them for the commodites of other countries. . . . Under a system of perfectly free commerce, each country naturally devotes its capital and labor to such employments as are most beneficial to each. This pursuit of individual advantage is admirably connected with the universal good of the whole.'' Ricardo illustrated his trade theory by means of a two-nation labor-cost model. The theory holds that it is in the best interests of underdeveloped countries to exchange more labor for less. According to conservatives, this unequal division of labor works to the advantage of all, for it permits each country to make the best use of its natural resources, stock of skills, and infrastructures. Moreover, any deviation from free trade sacrifices efficiency and reduces world outputs and income. An example of a contemporary Ricardian is Henry Kissinger, former U.S. Secretary of State. At the Seventh Special Session of the United Nations General Assembly in 1975, he said, ''Comparative advantage and specialization, the exchange of technology and the movement of capital,

Table 1.2 Popular and Academic Examples of the Three Paradigms

Alternative Paradigms	Politicians	Entertainers	Popular Magazines	Classical Intellectuals	Contemporary Intellectuals	Academic Journals
Conservative	Amin Goldwater Kissinger Nixon Park Pinochets Schlafly Somoza Sukarno Vorster	S. Davis, Jr. B. Hope F. Sinatra J. Stewart J. Wayne	*Business Week* *National Review* *Spectator* *Wall Street Journal*	Darwin Durkheim Freud Malthus Ricardo Smith Spencer Toynbee	Berg (Econ.) Buckley Friedman (Econ.) Gourou (Geog.) Lewis (Anthro.) McClelland (Psych.) Parsons (Soc.) Ayn Rand (Lit.)	*American Economic Review* *American Historical Review* *American Sociological Review* *Annals of the Association of American Geographers* *Commentary* *Comparative Political Studies* *Comparative Politics* *Comparative Studies in Society and History* *Economic Development and Cultural Change* *Ekistics* *Foreign Affairs* *Foreign Policy* *International Journal of Comparative Sociology* *International Studies Quarterly* *Journal, American Institute of Planners* *Journal of Political Economy* *Journal of World History* *World Development*
Liberal	Echeverria Friedan I. Ghandi Humphrey Johnson Kennedy Nasser U. Thant	J. Baez J. Carson D. Cavett	*The Economist* *Ms.* *New Republic* *Newsweek* *Time*	Keynes Weber E. Howard	Black (Hist.) Berry (Geog.) Galbraith (Econ.) Mead (Anthro.) Mills (Soc.) Myrdal (Econ.) Nash (Anthro.) Rogers (Soc.) Samuelson (Econ.)	
Radical	Allende Brandt Castro Chavez Hayden Ho Chi Mihn Mao Tse Tung Nyerere	J. Fonda V. Redgrave P. Seeger	*In These Times* *Mother Jones* *New Internation-alist* *The Progressive*	Engles E. Goldman Lenin Luxemburg Marx G. Stein	Amin (Econ.) Casteus (Soc.) Chomski (Pol. Sci.) Fanon (Lit.) Harrington (Pol. Sci.) Harvey (Geog.) Howe (Hist.) O'Connor (Soc.) Stone S. Turkel (Lit.)	*Alternatives: A Journal of World Policy* *Antipode: A Radical Journal of Geography* *History Workshop: A Journal of Socialist Historians* *Insurgent Sociologist* *Latin American Perspectives* *Marxist Perspective* *Peace and Change* *Politics and Society* *Radical Historical Review* *Radical Philosophy* *Review of African Political Economy* *Review of Radical Political Economics* *Third World Forum*

the spur to productivity that competition provides—these are central elements of efficiency and progress. For developing nations, trade is perhaps the most important engine of development'' (Table 1.2).

Despite the advantages of free trade, conservatives recognize that many Third World countries have not yet developed. They explain this by considering internal obstacles in the form of local environments and indigenous cultures. The tropical environment, in particular, is viewed as a major obstacle to progress. Soils are poor and fragile; rainfall is unreliable; and numerous endemic, debilitating diseases reinforce low levels of productivity. Above all, conservatives hold that the traits of individuals, rather than international market forces, prevent the advancement of people in underdeveloped countries. They account for the lack of development on the basis of backward cultures: traditional religious beliefs, values, and habits of life, insufficient incentives and entrepreneurialship, ignorance of science and technology, and unstable political systems.

Box B

TONGUE-IN-CHEEK DEFINITIONS OF COMMON
IDEOLOGICAL PERSPECTIVES

Socialism: You have two cows, and you give one to your neighbor.

Communism: You have two cows, the government takes both of them, and gives you milk.

Fascism: You have two cows, the government takes both of them, and sells you milk.

Nazism: You have two cows, the government takes both of them, and shoots you.

Bureaucracy: You have two cows, the government takes both of them, shoots one of them, milks the other, and pours the milk down the drain.

Capitalism: You have two cows, you sell one of them, and buy a bull.

The Liberal Perspective

The liberal view of the world did not attract much attention until the depression of the 1930s. Keynes' General Theory analyzes the causes of unemployment and discredits the conservative belief that the capitalist economic system is self-righting. He did not think that a modern capitalist economy would sustain a high enough level of investment to maintain full employment. While advocating government control of the level of economic activity in the national interest (state capitalism), he advised that the economy in general be left free to respond to the decisions of welfare-maximizing consumers and profit-maximizing producers. Keynes presented an alternative to socialism. His theory, which permitted government to borrow and spend money to prevent economic depressions, did not amend the conservative paradigm to any great degree. It was designed less to alter market exchange economies than to preserve and revitalize them.

Like Keynes, liberals of the present day do not launch a thorough-going critique of either the conservative theory of human nature or the capitalist system (Table

1.1). Indeed, liberals share with conservatives the view that humans are naturally unproductive, and they share a faith in the capitalist system. Unlike conservatives, however, they place great emphasis on the goals of individual equality and social justice. To achieve these goals, government legislation and programs are necessary. Although liberals criticize inequality of opportunity based on wealth, position, and power, they understand that certain inequalities are based on inherited characteristics such as family structure or ethnic culture (e.g. "culture of poverty"). The State redistributes wealth by taxing the rich to assist the poor, and, therefore, societal changes can occur more rapidly than under the conservative laissez-faire model. Problems at national and international levels result from monopolistic tendencies in major economic sectors and insufficient and/or inappropriate government programs. The State must intervene on behalf of everyone whenever market mechanisms fail to satisfy consumer preferences and provide basic human needs (e.g. housing, health care, food, and adequate income). Galbraith's analyses of the industrial state and the affluent society reflect this perspective (Table 1.2).

Liberals share with conservatives many of the same assumptions about barriers to Third World development. They believe that traditional values and social institutions are the prime obstacles to development, and they are convinced that the town is the gateway for Third World innovations. As centers of innovation, large towns can transmit modern values and social institutions to smaller centers and rural areas. Although liberals also employ the "blaming the victim" approach (see Ryan's article in Section III) to explain the causes of world problems, they, unlike conservatives, are willing to provide governmental assistance to the world's needy. Consequently, liberal governments provide unilateral (e.g. U.S. Agency for International Development) and multilateral (e.g. World Bank) foreign aid, food aid (e.g. U.S. Food for Peace Program), volunteers (e.g. U.S. Peace Corps), and military and technical assistance.

The Radical Perspective

Conservative and liberal perspectives are widely accepted by social scientists, although at present the latter has more followers than the former.[7] They are not radical because their analyses do not go to the root or origin of problems. Radicals argue that the dynamics of socio-economic organization (mode of production, to use a Marxist term) in capitalist societies produce particular kinds of class and institutional structures. Classes and institutions formed by the capitalist mode of production explain a particular set of social problems that cannot be solved without changing the form of socio-economic organization at national and international levels (Table 1.1).

Contrary to conservatives and liberals, radicals assume that humans are naturally productive and cooperative and therefore, that material rewards are not really necessary. They argue that humans are not inherently passive beings at the mercy of their cultural and physical environments; rather they are active creatures of their own destiny. If we behave passively, unproductively, or uncooperatively, it is because our economic system demands such behaviors. They reject the liberal's belief that people can enjoy equality of opportunity in a class society when the majority produce the wealth and when power is in the hands of the few. In such a society, the pursuit of profit by the dominant class shapes all aspects of life, including the quality of personal relations. Under capitalism human needs are subordinated to the needs of the market place. Only commodities (goods and services) which have exchange value are produced, while other use values remain unmet. An illustration: The United States sells (exchange value) most of its food surpluses to countries who can afford to buy it rather than distributing food to countries on the basis of need (use value).

Radicals claim that in a market economy the State predominantly serves the interests of the ruling class—the capitalists—not the workers whose labor produces more wealth than is returned to them in the form of wages. Marx called this extra wealth "surplus value." Surplus value (or the product of exploitation) is the difference between the value produced by workers (value of units of labor produced) and workers' wage (value of labor power). Marx, in discussing the labor theory of value, asked: How can one class of people, capitalists, get something for nothing? How do they acquire a portion of produced value for themselves without contributing any labor in return? Marx defined labor as a commodity, and its value is determined in just the same way as the value of any other commodity, by the amount of socially necessary labor required to produce it. This is nothing more than workers' subsistence wages. For example, if laborers have to work six hours to obtain a subsistence income, then that is the socially necessary amount of labor time required to "produce" workers. If workers have to work 12 hours instead of six hours to hold a job in a factory, Marx said, workers create surplus value, or profit for capitalists. Workers labor six hours for themselves and another six hours for their masters, and the rate of surplus value or exploitation is six hours or 100 percent.

Exploitation of workers can be intensified, and the surplus value appropriated by capitalists increased when employers stretch the working day. If the work week were stabilized, employers could expand surplus value by substituting capital for labor. Marx argued that the process of introducing even more labor-saving equipment is inimical to workers. Displaced laborers form a reserve army of the unemployed, which keeps wages at minimal levels. The existence of a pool of unemployed workers means that employed workers know that others are available to take their jobs if productivity falls.

The essence of the radical argument is that the engine which drives economic growth is capital accumulation for its own sake. Economic growth is always unbalanced. The capitalist mode of production fails to achieve equilibrium as claimed by conservatives and liberals because of the contradictory nature of competitive production. As a result, there are short-run cyclical crises (unemployment and declining rates of profit) which are connected by increasing rates of accumulation through concentration (the trend toward larger, more efficient factories in each industry), and geographical extension (imperialism). Periodic crises become more frequent over time. In each crisis big capitalists devour little capitalists, and individual capitalism becomes corporate capitalism. Capitalists seek larger outputs and bigger profits, and they deploy bigger machines which replace more and more laborers, whose work generally consists of small, insignificant, and tedious operations that are repeated for hours. This expansion intensifies the misery and alienation of workers so that increasing class struggle charts the course of socio-economic development (Table 1.2).

From this sketch of Marxist theory, it is plain that radicals argue that inequality of wealth among classes originates in the capitalist system. Exploitation of one class by another is based on the private ownership of the means of production. Irreconcilable conflict between classes is the key to understanding the need for revolutionary change through mass movements.

Uneven development pertains not only to the unequal distribution of wealth among classes, but also to spatial dimensions of development: underdevelopment and dependence. Radicals argue that Third World countries have been underdeveloped first by the development and expansion of Europe, later neo-European countries (United States, Canada, Australia, and New Zealand), and most recently Japan. The capitalist world economy causes underdevelopment by generating and reinforcing an infrastructure of dependency which includes institutions, social classes, and processes such as urbanization and industrialization. Thus dependency is not merely an external matter. Foreign exploitation is possible only when it finds support among local elites who profit from it. To break out of dependency and to achieve development, Third World countries must go beyond capitalism to a collectively owned and collectively governed economic system. To achieve the goals of socialism different paths may be followed: in Cuba, Castro used a military approach; and in Tanzania, Nyerere uses an evolutionary approach (Table 1.2).

It is important to remember that each of the three perspectives lumps a great many different theories and models together. Traditional social science practices *splitting,* the art of ever-increasing articulation of minute theoretical and empirical details. On the other hand, in this reader we are interested in *lumping* broadly similar scientific arguments to facilitate the reexamination of existing theoretical positions. The labels conservative, liberal, and radical are not so important as the ideas behind them. Too often we reject views which we understand poorly and

---

Box C
THE THREE WORLDS

Westerners divide the countries of the world into three parts: the First World, Second World, and Third World. The First World includes the countries of Western Europe, North America, Israel, Australia, New Zealand, and Japan. Some would even include the Republic of South Africa and Argentina. The Second World is represented by the Soviet Union and Eastern Europe. The Third World consists of the remaining countries in Latin America, Africa, the Middle East, and Asia. Through the eyes of "the free world," the Second and Third Worlds are associated with negative and undesireable traits (Communism and poverty, respectively), while the First World countries reflect positive and desireable characteristics.

Many Third World people disagree with this ethnocentric view. Mao Tse-tung's Three World theory categorizes the world's people in very different terms. The First World consists of the superpowers, i.e. the Soviet Union and United States, with their negative military and economic influence on the rest of the world. The Second World includes the allies of the two superpowers—the remaining industralized countries. The Third World represents the underdeveloped countries and the hope for the *whole* world, not the dispair that most Westerners see. In dialectical fashion, Mao saw Third World "problems" as assets to create a better future for the masses everywhere.

libel them by labeling them. We should not dismiss any perspective because of its label but rather, we should judge it on the basis of its theoretical merits.

These viewpoints are most useful for providing alternative *explanations* of Third World problems, not in providing detailed and specific blueprints for the future. A great deal of dissent exists among the three groups on the specific directions change should take.

How can we choose among these different perspectives? From a scientific point of view, this question can be answered easily: That approach which most accurately and completely explains the past and present realities of the Third World. The readings are designed to provide an opportunity to answer this question. From our research and field experiences in Africa, Latin America, Western Europe, and North America, we are convinced that the radical paradigm provides the most complete explanation of conditions in the Third World. In other words, we believe it explains more of reality than the other two paradigms.

VALUE CHOICES

We stated earlier that one deficiency of most Western educational institutions is that they fail to train students in fourth-level learning—that of seeking solutions outside of status-quo frameworks. Another deficiency is that most schools fail to acknowledge the values that are both explicit and implicit in their teachings, and help students to recognize and judge those values along with their own. Such learning is essential for a full comprehension of this book and of Third World issues.

Values Clarification

Comprehensive understanding requires cognitive and affective learning. Determining the analytical power of the readings is part of the cognitive realm; judging their value content falls both within the cognitive and affective realms. Each realm is an important and necessary part of each person. We all hold implicit and explicit values on a whole range of issues, which we express in verbal and written communications and through actions. We need to distinguish between our espoused values and our innermost values, often unknown even to ourselves without reflection. Among the various approaches to teaching values—inculcation, moralization, laissez-faire attitudes, and action learning—we find the values clarification method the most useful.[8] This approach is not concerned with the content of people's values but with the processes of valuing.

What are the processes by which we develop values and decide what we stand for, and what we wish to live for? To discover the answer to these questions, we need to explore the values in our ideas, feelings, choices, and behavior. Hirschenbaum identifies five major valuing processes to achieve this goal (Table 1.3).[9]

Feelings have traditionally been avoided in schools, since educators believe that solutions to human problems are best solved through rational processes. The denial of feelings, however, deprives us of important information in making decisions which affect us and others. Our thinking, communicating, choosing, and acting processes all suffer as a result, particularly since on any given issue, these may derive from a feeling of which we are unaware. Humans *think* at various

Table 1.3 The Valuing Process[a]

I. <u>Feeling</u>

1. Being open to one's inner experience.
    a. awareness of one's inner experience
    b. acceptance of one's inner experience

II. <u>Thinking</u>

1. Thinking on all seven levels.
    a. memory
    b. translation
    c. application
    d. interpretation
    e. analysis
    f. synthesis
    g. evaluation
2. Critical thinking.
    a. distinguishing fact from opinion
    b. distinguishing supported from unsupported arguments
    c. analyzing propaganda, stereotypes, etc.
3. Logical thinking (logic).
4. Creative thinking.
5. Fundamental cognitive skills.
    a. language use
    b. mathematical skills
    c. research skills

III. <u>Communicating—Verbally and Nonverbally</u>

1. Sending clear messages.
2. Empathetic listening.
3. Drawing out.
4. Asking clarifying questions.
5. Giving and receiving feedback.
6. Conflict resolution.

IV. <u>Choosing</u>

1. Generating and considering alternatives.
2. Thoughtfully considering consequences, pros and cons.
3. Choosing strategically.
    a. goal setting
    b. data gathering
    c. problem solving
    d. planning
4. Choosing freely.

V. <u>Acting</u>

1. Acting with repetition.
2. Acting with a pattern and consistency.
3. Acting skillfully, competently.

[a]For further information on materials available in the values education field, write the National Humanistic Education Center, 110 Spring Street, Saratoga Springs, New York 12866.

levels, from memorization to synthesis and evaluation, and they usually progress, as Hirschenbaum says, "to higher, more flexible levels of thinking," given the right environment. Ultimately, the level of our thinking will determine the kinds of cognitive and emotive decisions we make.

Learning *communication* skills is critical in the valuing and understanding processes. Making clear statements, drawing people out, asking clarifying questions, and listening to arguments empathetically are the essence of basic communication skills. In the values clarification approach, choices are based on freely *choosing* from alternatives, after thoughtful consideration has been given to the possible consequences.[10] Again, the kinds of choices made depend on the earlier processes of feeling, thinking, and communicating. Existentialists point out that we define ourselves through our *actions*. The more we act on what we feel and think, the more we value these particular emotions and thoughts.[11]

Hirschenbaum's valuing processes can be applied to the articles in this book. When reading the selections, try to answer each of the following questions.

(1) *Feeling*. Try to recognize the feelings you are experiencing as you consider each author's arguments. Are they positive or negative feelings?

(2) *Thinking*. What values can you identify in the articles and how do they compare with your own values?

(3) *Communicating*. What clarifying questions would you like to ask the authors, before you could fully determine their values and your reactions to them?

(4) *Choosing*. After reading the alternative viewpoints in each topic section, which perspective most closely matches your values?

(5) *Acting*. Is the perspective you have choosen one you would be willing to

Some additional questions may help you to develop your own thinking process. Given what we have said earlier in this chapter on the three analytical frameworks, you should also be able to answer the following analytical questions for each selection.

(1) What overall questions are asked?
(2) What specific questions are asked?
(3) What concepts are used? (e.g. life-boat analogy)
(4) What evidence and/or data are used to answer the questions?
(5) What conclusions are drawn?
(6) Are you convinced by the data and arguments that the specific and general questions are answered?
(7) Which theoretical framework is employed?

Moral Development

Another aspect of critical thinking is to assess the moral content of arguments. Kohlberg presents a developmental sequence of moral thinking which is based on a long series of studies with children and adults in the United States and was consequently tested in other countries (Mexico, Turkey, and Taiwan).[12] He has found that we develop through some or all of these stages in a generally linear manner as our reasoning matures, and that any moral argument can be assessed by

Figure 1.2   Kohlberg's Stages of Moral Development

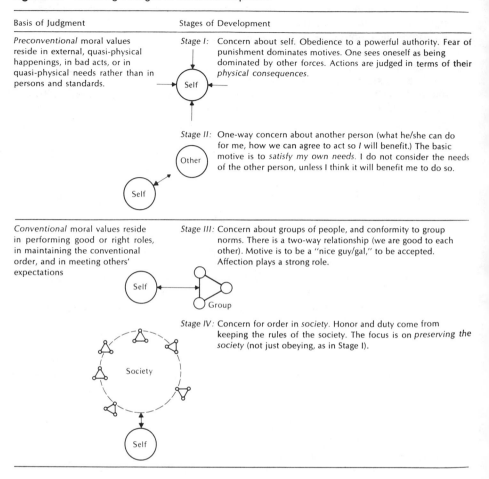

Basis of Judgment	Stages of Development
Preconventional moral values reside in external, quasi-physical happenings, in bad acts, or in quasi-physical needs rather than in persons and standards.	*Stage I:* Concern about self. Obedience to a powerful authority. Fear of punishment dominates motives. One sees oneself as being dominated by other forces. Actions are judged in terms of their *physical consequences.*
	Stage II: One-way concern about another person (what he/she can do for me, how we can agree to act so *I* will benefit.) The basic motive is to *satisfy my own needs.* I do not consider the needs of the other person, unless I think it will benefit me to do so.
Conventional moral values reside in performing good or right roles, in maintaining the conventional order, and in meeting others' expectations	*Stage III:* Concern about groups of people, and conformity to group norms. There is a two-way relationship (we are good to each other). Motive is to be a "nice guy/gal," to be accepted. Affection plays a strong role.
	Stage IV: Concern for order in *society.* Honor and duty come from keeping the rules of the society. The focus is on *preserving the society* (not just obeying, as in Stage I).

its stage of development. According to Kohlberg's research, the basic set of moral stages are not significantly affected by widely varying socioeconomic, cultural, or religious conditions. Only the rate at which individuals progress through the sequence is different.

For Kohlberg, a moral stage does not represent a type of person, but a way of thinking. People usually use more than one stage of moral thinking for any particular topic, and certainly employ different stages for different topics. In other words, people are rarely morally and intellectually consistent. Kohlberg points out that at each stage individuals see themselves as being "honest," "fair," and "descent," within their own terms of reference. Consequently, moral judgments are, first, judgments of value, not of fact. They are also social judgments about people. "Third, they are prescriptive or normative judgments, judgments of ought, of rights and duties, rather than value judgments of liking and preference."[13]

Basis of Judgment	Stages of Development
Postconventional moral values are derived from principles which can be applied universally	*Stage V:* Social contract, legalistic orientation. What is right is what the whole society decides. There are no legal absolutes. The society can *change standards* by everyone agreeing to the change. Changes in the law are usually made for reasons of the greatest good for the greatest number of people. Where law is not affected, what is right is a matter of personal opinion and agreement between persons. The U.S. Constitution is written in Stage 5 terms.
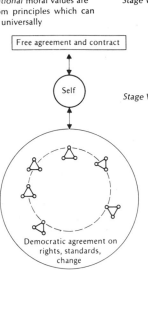	*Stage VI:* Universal ethical principles. What is right is a decision of one's conscience, based on ideas about rightness that apply to *everyone* (all nations, people, etc.). These are called *ethical principles*. An ethical principle is different from a rule. A rule is specific (Thou shalt not kill). An ethical principle is *general* (All persons are created equal). The most important ethical principles deal with justice, equality, and the dignity of all people. These principles are *higher* than any given law.

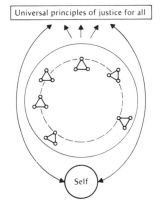

Kohlberg identifies three levels, each with two stages, of moral development (Figure 1.2).[14]

(1) At the preconventional level individual decisions are based on physical power and physical consequences (punishment and reward). Stage 1 moral thinking corresponds to "might makes right" and "survival of the fittest." Avoidance of *phyiscal punishment* and unquestioning *obedience* of power are valued for their own sake. Morality does not play a large part in a person's life. Stage-2 behavior conforms to obtain rewards and have favors returned: "Look out for number one" and "You scratch my back and I'll scratch yours." Fairness and *reciprocity* are evaluated only in concrete and pragmatic ways.

(2) Within the conventional level of moral development, identification with and maintainence of the dominant social order prevails. At this level, two stages emerge. Stage 3 is the "good boy, good girl" or a limited conformity orientation. Morality is seen in terms of *helping* and *pleasing* a limited group of people whose

well-being and approval is valued. At this stage stereotypical images of conventional wisdom or "natural" behavior determine moral thinking. Stage 4 is a *law-and-order* orientation. Right behavior consists of conforming to fixed rules, respecting established authority, and maintaining the given social order for its own sake.

(3) Postconventional or autonomous moral thinking rests on moral values which are valid apart from the authority of the groups who hold them and apart from one's identification with these groups. In Stage 5 *social contracts* expressed in legal terms are the guiding principle. Laws are understood to be constitutionally and democratically agreed upon, yet individual opinions can differ with established laws and practices. Hence, emphasis is also placed on changing laws to serve greater social needs. This is the official morality of the United States government and the United States Constitution. Stage-6 persons behave according to "self-chosen ethical principles appealing to logical comprehensiveness, universality, and consistence." Abstract and *ethical principles,* such as the Golden Rule, are dominant, not concrete moral ones, like the Ten Commandments.[15] For Stage-6 persons the sole purpose of morality is to serve fundamental life goals, such as freedom, justice, equality, happiness, and self-respect. Moral values are *means* to maximize ultimate life goals for one's self and for humanity. Gandhi, Socrates, Thoreau, and Martin Luther King are among the relatively few people to attain Stage-6 moral thinking.

Moral thinking and judgments are complex and diverse. To better understand and appreciate Kohlberg's stages of moral thinking, a concrete example might be helpful.[16] Let us use our earlier example of world hunger. The possible responses given below might be those of middle class North Americans.

Since no coercive force exists to make people help the hungry of the world, Stage-1 people fail to be interested in the topic. However, if such people perceived an invasion from a hungry country as a possible retribution, they would be willing to send food aid. Stage-2 people do not consider the needs of others unless they benefit from such actions. If we want fuels and minerals from a particular Third World country, we will then provide food assistance. If, on the other hand, they have nothing that we want, there is no reason to help them.

In Stage 3, other people's points of view are usually taken, regardless of individual self-interest for the sake of social self-interest. Individuals recognize shared social interests and expectations with particular groups, such as religious organizations. Going along with the group facilitates social approval, and being called a "nice" person. By giving food aid, the United States will be seen as a "moral nation" or a "Christian country." Others might phrase it as "the White man's burden" to help the less fortunate nations. If the group that people identify with does not believe in food aid (such as the John Birch Society), they will gain social approval by not supporting assistance to the Third World.

Stage-4 people have a societal identification which is defined by and restricted to absolute rules which come either from government or God. Any proposals to expand current policies and practices to help the hungry are rejected because of the strong adherence to "law and order." In religious terms, God may command us to help starving people; in legal terms, the United States should provide food assistance if Congress mandates it. On the other hand, we may not help the hungry of a particular nation because we have a defense treaty with their political enemy.

Stage-5 people believe that the rules identified by Stage-4 people are not absolute and can be changed to reflect a particular universal issue. A Stage-5 person may believe that the world's hungry should be fed regardless of our current laws, and would support legislative change. But a Stage-5 person could also argue that we should not feed the hungry of a particular nation because their government is communist. Stage-6 people deal with a holistic range of universal ethical principles—justice, equality, and freedom, including freedom from hunger—which allows them to change current laws, and also obligates them, when necessary, to break the laws through civil disobedience. Stage-6 people would be willing to support private agencies who send food to a country with which the United States was at war.[17]

Each of the three analytical perspectives can operate at this highest stage of moral development. Conservatives would make voluntary, individual donations to local churches or to world organizations, such as CARE or UNESCO. Liberals would want the government to tax the population at large so that "giving" would become official policy and not dependent on the occassional good intentions of a few persons or organizations. Individually, then, liberals would do all the things conservatives do, plus help to mandate and subsequently, to expand, foreign aid, particularly food relief. At Stage 6 radicals would add yet another layer of activism; boycotting certain companies like Nestlé for selling formula milk to poor mothers in the Third World, and/or contributing resources and energy to organizations such as the World Council of Churches or national liberation groups in various Third World countries. At this stage radicals would work towards major global structural changes to eliminate the root causes of hunger for all times.

Research on the age and stage of moral development shows that under current conditions in the United States, moral maturity stabilizes by late adolescence and early adulthood, between the ages of 16 and 25. Indeed, very little moral growth occurs after age 25. In their research Kohlberg and Kramer found that 13 percent of the 25 year olds used preconventional levels (Stages 1 and 2) of thinking; 51 percent used conventional levels (Stages 3 and 4) of thinking; and 35 percent adhered to postconventional (Stages 5 and 6) moral thinking. Relating these findings to the three analytical frameworks presented earlier in this chapter, we would argue that although all three perspectives can be found in several of the six stages, each perspective by its very definition would tend to be concentrated more at some stages than at others. The moral content of the conservative framework corresponds largely to Stages 1, 2, 3, and 4; the liberal perspective is concentrated mostly in Stages 3, 4, and 5; and the radical framework tends to be located in Stages 5 and 6.

In a culturally universal sense, Kohlberg's stages lead toward an expanded conception of moral judgment. At each stage, the same basic moral issue is defined, but at each higher stage this definition becomes differentiated, more integrated, and more universal. This is illustrated by an experimental study.[18] Undergraduate subjects were ordered by an experimenter to administer increasingly more severe electric shock punishment to a stooge victim in the guise of a learning experiment. In this case, the principles of justice involved in the Stage-5 social contract orientation do not clearly prescribe a decision. The victim had voluntarily agreed to participate in the experiment and the subjects had contractually committed themselves to perform the experiment. Only Stage-6 thinking clearly defined the situation as one in which the experimenter did not have the moral right to ask them to inflict pain on another person. Accordingly, 75 per cent of the Stage-6 subjects quit or refused to shock the victim as compared to only 13 per cent of all the subjects at lower stages.

Kohlberg maintains that individuals comprehend all stages up to their own, but not more than one stage beyond their own. And significantly, they prefer this next stage. Moral development can be facilitated by identifying people's moral stage and through subsequent reinforcement and discussion expose them to the next highest stage.

Perry provides further evidence of personal intellectual and ethical development.[19] He shows that college students develop from positions of "simple dualism" (e.g. good vs. bad) through various stages of "relativism" to final stages of "commitment in relativism." Perry found that students did not remain in the second stage, characterized by kaleidoscopic possibilities, for more than a year before proceeding to some kind of affirmation of values or escape from further growth, at least for awhile. The dialectic approach used in this book encourages students to take risks, to explore the meanings of explanations, and to dare to make commitments to clarified values. Simultaneously, teachers need to provide support and encouragement to students regardless of their stages of intellectual and moral development. Clearly, for educators to facilitate cognitive and affective learning processes, they need to realize that "it is no longer tenable for an educator to take the position that what a person does with his [or her] intellectual skills is a moral rather than intellectual problem and therefore none of the scholar's business."[20]

You are therefore urged to determine your own stage of moral development in response to the selected readings and to analyze carefully your objections to the moral stage presented in the readings. In the introduction to each section, only the analytical differences will be outlined; the ideological and value statements are left for readers to determine. Hopefully, teachers will assist students in this task.

OUTLINE OF THE BOOK

In the next article, the Third World is defined and delineated. Through text and maps Buchanan shows that the countries of the Third World are distinctive from the industrialized countries. Although he uses data from the 1950s and 1960s, his statistics are merely illustrative and later data would make little difference to the dimensions of the problems discussed. The Third World still has the same characteristics Buchanan identified almost two decades ago: low rates of GNP per capita, calorie and protein intake; high rates of employment in the farm and tertiary sectors; and high rates of urbanization, illiteracy, infant mortality, population growth, and resource exports.

How can these conditions be explained? In which directions do the solutions lie? One way of answering the above questions is to consider a number of empirical topics. The remaining readings have been grouped under six possible causes of Third World underdevelopment. Each section has several articles which reflect alternative points of view. Although each perspective tends to stress certain causes and omit others, among the six topics the three analytical perspectives present a vast range of explanations (Table 1.4).

Table 1.4   Authors in the Reader Grouped by the Three Paradigms

Alternative Paradigms	Climate and Resources	Cultural Traditions	Plantation Agriculture	Population	Tourism	Imperialism
	Topic Sections in the Reader					
Conservative	Huntington	Heston	May and Plaza	Hardin	Bond and Ladman	
Liberal	Hodder	Harris Ryan	Beckford	Ritchie-Calder	Britton	
Radical	Szentes	Dorfman and Mattelart	Tobis	Commoner Harvey	Pérez	Galtung Chilcote Harvey

Environmental factors are discussed in Section II. The emphasis on the environment to account for underdevelopment is a characteristically conservative approach. Although the older climatic determinism is now out of fashion, particularly among geographers, many liberal social scientists still consider the presence of tropical climates and the absence of certain natural resources in a country to be of major importance to its economic development. In the radical paradigm, environmental conditions are essentially irrelevant to explain the present level of development.

In Section III cultural traditions in the Third World are examined as possible causes of underdevelopment. Anthropologists, geographers, psychologists, and economists have written about the inferiority of "non-western" cultures to explain the lack of incentives and institutions that allow nations to prosper. The blatant racism of the past is now modified to blaming the victim, which is another important conservative concept in explaining Third World poverty. To cite one specific example: many of India's population and food problems are often linked to the Hindu practice of revering cattle. The conservative approach sees this non-western religion as a barrier to economic progress. The liberal perspective, on the other hand, argues that the Indian sacred cattle practice performs positive functions for small-scale farmers, but it fails to examine the national and international economic institutions (e.g. landlordism, money lenders, merchants, and international oil companies), which radicals argue can best explain India's underdevelopment. Disney comic books in South America still show evidence of racism and cultural imperialism, which facilitates the exploitation of these Third World people.

Developments in agriculture are of utmost importance to Third World people because so many work in this sector and so many are hungry. In Section IV one aspect of this vast topic is examined. Colonial rule provided the means for Europeans to establish plantation agriculture. The conservative viewpoint argues that plantations were and remain beneficial to tropical countries and foreign countries alike. The profits of foreign companies were and are more than offset by providing local employment, social services, taxes, and the transfer of technology. But the liberal perspective points out that while plantations enhance private commercial interests, they distort, if not retard, the national development of Third World economies. From the radical perspective plantations have had and continue to have mostly negative consequences. Colonialism with its plantation crops underdeveloped these countries and this process explains Third World poverty.

For most Westerners the single most important cause of problems in the Third World is the high rate of population growth. In Section V the ideological basis for the scientific study of the relationship between population and resources is exposed. Three specific approaches to "overpopulation" can then be assessed: lifeboat ethics (conservative); family planning programs (liberal); and political and economic revolutions (radical). From the conservative perspective, the world already has too many people, all of whom cannot be fed. Some will have to perish. The liberal perspective agrees that the population/food supply relationship is unbalanced, but Third World and First World governments can temporarily alleviate these problems with food aid and permanently solve overpopulation through birth control programs. Within the radical paradigm several kinds of explanations exist, but they all agree that "overpopulation" is the result of exploitation. The poor have large families because this is *their* best way of safeguarding their survival. Furthermore, such large families are only perceived as overpopulation when they exist at the poor end of the economic distribution.

Social scientists have also considered Rostow's stages of economic growth, and the role of transnational corporations and foreign aid to explain underdevelopment. The capitalist analysis concludes that poor countries are only at a lower economic stage than rich countries at the present time, and that eventually the current poor countries will develop, if they follow the Western model of economic growth. While geocentric mining, manufacturing, and service corporations diffuse modern technology and provide revenue for national development, foreign aid may actually do more harm than good in the short-term and long-run.

The liberal perspective prefers to curb some of the more blatant abuses of multinationals, such as bribing and blackmailing foreign governments and avoiding their full share of taxes. This viewpoint sees foreign aid from industrial countries in conjunction with multinational corporations as the means of helping developing countries. The radical view is fundamentally different. Marxists maintain that underdevelopment is caused by the exploitative relations between capitalist and Third World countries in the past and in the present. Hence, transnational corporations take advantage of their monopoly position to extract more capital in the form of profits from underdeveloped countries than they invest. Indeed, foreign aid, like multinational and international trade in general, benefits the donor countries more than the recipient countries, thus perpetuating the economic and political power of privileged elites in the Third World. The length of the original manuscript precluded the inclusion of reading selections for these topics. Since Rostow's stages of economic growth, the debate about multinationals, and foreign aid are well known, we decided to exclude these topics in favor of a less recognized topic—tourism.

Tourism is another path towards economic development. Or is it? In Section VI the conservative perspective holds that tourism avoids many of the problems associated with mineral and luxury crop exports. Foreign capital and ideas provide the necessary engine and steam for development. The benefits of international tourism, from the liberal viewpoint, go to multinationals and Third World elites. The indigeneous populations gain only seasonal and menial jobs and lose their culture and resources in return. From the radical perspective tourism is another form of exploitation and imperialism, which drains and concentrates Third World wealth primarily among the elites of the First World.

In Section VII the radical paradigm employs the concept of imperialism as a primary explanation for Third World material poverty. To account for global and national inequalities, the radical analysis, depending on its specific formulation, employs such concepts as center-periphery relations, dependency, and the theory of capitalist accumulation. Within both the conservative and liberal frameworks, the importance radicals place on the concept of imperialism is discounted. The conservative perspective dismisses the concept altogether and its value in explaining current Third World conditions. The liberal perspective sees no casual correlation between capitalism and imperialism, but it does recognize that governments use their political and military power to expand geographically.

Before reading the articles, we recommend that you turn to the awareness exercises in the Appendix. The first exercise allows you to compare your own view of the Third World with those of others. In Exercise 2 you can assess your knowledge about some of the attributes of underdeveloped countries. The remaining exercises help you to get in touch with the ideological nature of description and explanation with reference to Third World issues.

Table 1.5   Concepts and Terms Used by the Three Paradigms for the Six Topics

Alternative Paradigms	Topic Sections in the Reader					
	Climate and Resources	Cultural Traditions	Plantation Agriculture	Population	Tourism	Imperialism
Conservative						
Liberal						
Radical						

Starting with Section II, we suggest that you note the important concepts and terms presented by the three analytical perspectives under each of the six substantative topics. The completion of Table 1.5 will allow you to choose intelligently the analytical framework which provides the best explanation of Third World underdevelopment.

NOTES AND REFERENCES

1. For commonly asked questions about world hunger and for well-documented answers, see Frances Moore Lappe and Joseph Collins, *Food First: Beyond the Myth of Scarcity* (Boston: Houghton Mifflin Company, 1977).

2. Based on the theories of Gregory Bateson.

3.

4. Each perspective is given a generic term rather than labeled after a particular person. Many present and past scholars, besides Milton Friedman, John Kenneth Galbraith, and Michael Harrington, employ a conservative, liberal, or radical paradigm.

5. David Gordon in *Problems in Political Economy* (Lexington, Mass.: D.C. Heath, 1971) employs this trichotomy to examine U.S. urban problems, and Alison M. Jaggar and Paula Rothenberg Stuhl in *Feminist Frameworks* (New York: McGraw-Hill, 1978) use a similar approach to explore feminist issues.

6. For various definitions of who is a conservative and who is a liberal, see *Commentary*, 62, no. 3 (September 1976): 31–113.

7. For substantiation, see Anthony R. de Souza and Philip W. Porter, *The Underdevelopment and Modernization of the Third World* (Washington, D.C.: Association of American Geographers, Commission on College Geography, Resource Paper No. 28, 1974), pp. 20–23 and 69–82.

8. For an overview of various approaches to values education, see Douglas P. Superka, Christine Ahrens, and Judith E. Hedstrom, *Values Education Sourcebook: Conceptual Approaches, Material Analyses, and an Annotated Bibliography* (Boulder, Col.: Social Science Education Consortium, 1976). For a discussion of some of the problems associated with values education, see Alan L. Lockwood, "Values Education and the Right to Privacy," *Journal of Moral Education*, 7, no. 1: pp. 9–26. For a standard treatment of values clarification, see Sidney B. Simon, Howe Leland, and Howard Hirschenbaum, *Value Clarification* (New York: Hart Publishing, 1972).

9. Howard Kirschenbaum, "Beyond Values Clarification," in Sidney B. Simon and Howard Kirschenbaum, eds., *Readings in Values Clarification* (Minneapolis: Winston Press, 1973), pp. 92–110. The approach in this book emphasizes broader and more generalized processes than traditional values clarification.

10. For a general critique of the traditional values clarification approach, see Alan L. Lockwood, "A Critical View of Values Clarification," *Teachers College Record*, 77, no. 1 (September 1975).

11. For a discussion of the limitations of the valuing processes, see Kirschenbaum, "Beyond Values Clarification," pp. 106–109.

12. Lawrence Kohlberg, "Development of Moral Character and Moral Ideology," in Martin L. Hoffman and Lois Wladis Hoffman, eds., *Review of Child Development Research*, Vol. 1 (New York: Russell Sage Foundation, 1964), pp. 383–431; and "Stage and Sequence: The Cognitive Developmental Approach to Socialization," in David Goslin, ed., *Handbook of Socialization Theory and Research* (Chicago: Rand McNally, 1969), pp. 347–480.

13. Some psychologists criticize Kohlberg's last two stages because of their rarity and the claim that they represent morally higher forms of reasoning. See John C. Gibbs, "Kohlberg's Stages of Moral Judgment: A Constructive Critique," *Harvard Educational Review*, 47, no. 1 (February 1977): 43–61.

14. This figure is from Richard C. Sprinthall and Norman A. Sprinthall, *Educational Psychology: A Development Approach*, second edition (Reading, Mass.: Adison-Wesley Publishing Co., 1977), Table 10.1, pp. 240–241. Reprinted by permission of publisher.

15. L. Kohlberg and R. Kramer, "Continuities and Discontinuities in Childhood and Adult Moral Development," *Human Development*, 12 (1969): 93–120.

16. For some theoretical background in moral education, including Kohlberg's developmental stages, and ideas for mini-courses and classroom discussions of values, see Clive Beck, *Moral Education in the Schools: Some Practical Suggestions,* Profiles in Practical Education No. 3 (Toronto: Ontario Institute for Studies in Education, 1971). Another useful book is by Miriam Wolf-Wasserman and Linda Hutchinson, *Teaching Human Dignity: Social Change Lessons for Everyteacher* (Minneapolis: Education Exploration Center, 1978).

17. We want to thank Doug Risberg, St. Cloud State University, for his assistance in applying Kohlberg's stages of moral development to the world hunger example.

18. Stanley Milgram, "Behavioral Study of Obedience," *Journal of Abnormal and Social Psychology,* 67, no. 4 (1963): 371–378; and "Some Conditions of Obedience and Disobedience to Authority," *Human Relations,* 8 (1965): 57–76.

19. William G. Perry, Jr., *Forms of Intellectual and Ethical Development in the College Years* (New York: Holt, Rinehart and Winston, 1970).

20. Ibid., p. 212.

2 Delineation of the Third World

KEITH BUCHANAN*

The maps presented here, with a brief commentary, give a series of profiles of the social and economic geography of the Third World.[1] This "immense community of newly or imminently independent nations" forms the third element in a world power structure dominated up to the present by the technologically more advanced nations of the Atlantic bloc or the European Communist bloc. Its muted or passive role in world affairs has been due to its technological backwardness, and to the colonial control, overt or concealed, which was both a cause and a consequence of this backwardness. This passive role is increasingly a thing of the past for, among at least the elites of the Third World, there is an emerging and increasingly focused awareness of their potential strength. This awareness is not entirely the product of an opportunism which has flourished in the genial climate provided by the manoeuvres of two opposing power blocs, each desperately striving to win friends and influence nations; it is ultimately much more solidly based. For two out of every three men on our globe are citizens of a Third World country (and by the end of the century it will be three out of every four) and these countries, in spite of present poverty, have a rich resource endowment. They have the immense resource represented by two thousand million human beings, often technologically undeveloped but capable of acquiring all the skills and the techniques to build great cities, convert bushland into farmland, to convert matter into energy—and maybe destruction. Many of them are heirs of rich and complex cultures, cultures which perhaps have been less gutted of human content and purpose than has our own; this psychic wealth may be their greatest asset. In spite of stark and abject poverty they yet possess, collectively, great riches—for this Third World contains much of the world's metallic minerals, its water power and oil and coal, its timbers and its potential cropland. Because of this wealth these countries have in the past been an important source of strength to the colonial countries of the West; the drive towards total national independence, involving real economic independence and a possible withdrawing of many of these resources from the unfettered control of the West, could, under these conditions, significantly change the world power pattern. In the next decade or so we may therefore expect a continuing drive to win over the hearts and minds of these dwellers in the world's slums, and, perhaps even more important, the weaving of "subtler nets to enmesh the new countries" to counter this potentially

*Keith Buchanan, "Profiles of the Third World," *Pacific Viewpoint*, 5, no. 2 (September 1964): 97–126. Reprinted by permission of author and publisher.

disastrous loss of an extremely important resource base.[2] Whichever way we look at it, these Third World countries are going to be of critical importance in the years ahead.

DEFINITION

The congealment of political blocs resulting from the Cold War has given us a clear picture of the location, on the world's political map, of the crevasse which separates the Western bloc from the Soviet bloc. The unremitting and indefatigable industry of the propagandists may, indeed, have resulted in a dangerous and misleading exaggeration of the differences which divide the two great groups of developed countries; we tend too easily to overlook the increasing similarity of conditions of material life, even of details such as industrial organisation, between the affluent nations of the West and those of the socialist bloc.[3] And while we are vaguely aware of the *other* split in our world society—of the Iron Curtain of poverty which separates the "haves" and the "have nots"—we are not always aware of the content, in terms of countries or hundreds of millions of human beings, of the world behind *this* Iron Curtain.

We are aware that this shadowy world of half-life exists, just as in the past it was possible to be aware of the squalid and shadowy slums in which many millions of citizens of a wealthy and imperial Britain lived and died. We know that from time to time desperate groups rise in despair against the desperate conditions of their day to day life—the Rastafarians in Jamaica, the Africans in Angola, the peasants of South Vietnam or Brazil or Peru—but we see these as merely isolated episodes, not as the first twisting birth pangs of the world's hungry and half-human masses as they struggle to be born as full men. Yet, if over the years we plot on a map these peasant uprisings, guerilla wars, anti-colonial struggles—if we plot all these we get emerging a coherent pattern, a geo-political unity, which stretches from the Andes, across Latin America and Africa and South Asia towards the rainforests of Borneo and the tawny steppe lands of Mongolia.

We can define this Third World, this "commonwealth of poverty," then, by mapping the symptoms of its unease, by mapping the world's "trouble spots." We can dissect in more clinical fashion and map the individual conditions giving rise to unease, to the rapidly festering tensions. The contours of poverty, for example, define it clearly, for in contrast to the affluent nations of the "white north," most of the rest of the world's peoples exist on incomes of under £100 [U.S. $200] a year; if we reduce the other social and economic conditions of the world's population also to a series of indices we get emerging again and again the same pattern of shading, the same shadowed world of poverty and deprivation, contrasting sharply with the neon-lit garishness of the other world—the world of those who are prosperous or who are attaining prosperity.

The northern margins of this Third World are sharp enough [Figure 2.1]. They run along the southern frontier of the United States, along the Mediterranean and along the north of Turkey and Iran, and then follow the widening split which separates the European and Asian communist countries. China, North Vietnam, North Korea, these are included in the Third World for their past experience and the character of their present problems—and the fashions in which they are seeking to solve these problems—align them much more closely with the

Figure 2.1

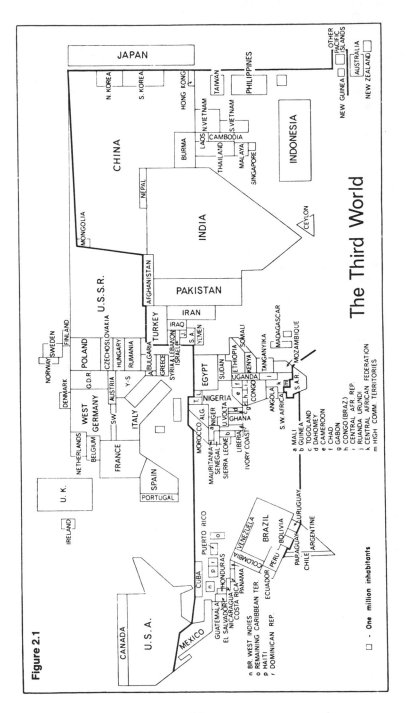

The Third World

□ - **One million inhabitants**

"damned of the earth," the coloured and mestizo masses of Asia, Africa and Latin America, than with the developed nations of the "white north". The southern boundary is more debatable; we follow French workers in this field and exclude from the Third World the relatively developed white nations of Chile and Argentina (Chile is especially controversial but the convenience of following United Nations population groupings which include Chile in "Temperate South America" is a strong argument for its exclusion in any statistical examination of the Third World), the white racialist society of South Africa, and the developed capitalist society of Japan.

The definition is of necessity based on a grouping of political units and this has some very obvious weaknesses in detail. In most of their essential social and economic features, for example, the Bantu areas of South Africa belong to the Third World; so, too, does the Mezzogiorno of Italy, much of the Iberian Peninsula, possibly, too, the American South. Israel, on the other hand, represents a wedge of prosperity driven deep into one of the poorest and most backward parts of the world.

The Third World, within the boundaries shown on the map, contains two-thirds of the world's population.

"A UNIVERSE OF RADICAL SCARCITY"

"The Third World is a universe of radical scarcity. Defining and determining every dimension of men's relationship to each other . . . the inadequacy of the means of livelihood is the first and distinguishing truth of this area."[4]

We can measure this scarcity, and map its areal pattern in several ways. In Figure 2.2 the real G.N.P. per capita is shown; over much of the Third World it is under $200 per capita; only in one or two areas does it exceed $500 and here the wealth is a precarious one, based either on a highly specialized export economy (Malaya) or the feverish exploitation of fugitive resources such as oil (Venezuela). Per capita income figures follow the same general pattern; over much of Africa and Asia they are below $100 per capita; this is the *annual* income and it is an *average* figure inflated by the incomes of the affluent few.[5] And, as Robert Heilbroner observes, "This is a standard which in fact defies numerical treatment; it means existence at the borderline of animal needs."[6]

This "borderline" quality of life for hundreds of millions of human beings is emphasized by the extent of the dark-hatched areas on Figures 2.3 and 2.4; these indicate, in the impersonal language of statistics, how heavily hunger weighs on the world's peoples. While in the developed areas of the West food intake exceeds requirements by about 20 per cent, while tens of millions of Europeans or Americans are endangering their health by overeating, while millions of tons of unsaleable food grains accumulate in the United States, hundreds of millions of people in South and East Asia, in parts of Africa and in the Andean republics of Latin America (and in *relatively* wealthy Venezuela) are existing on diets whose calorie content is below the critical minimum, *for the average adult at rest,* of 2,200 calories. Just what the total of the world's hungry is, is difficult to establish; a recent evaluation of the food situation by Professor Michel Cépède states: "more than one-third and no doubt nearly one-half of mankind suffers from under-nutrition due to lack of calories, that is hunger in the strictest sense of the

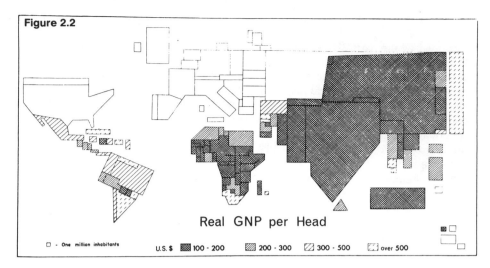

Figure 2.2

Real GNP per Head

□ - One million inhabitants   U.S. $ ▨ 100 - 200   ▨ 200 - 300   ▨ 300 - 500   ▨ over 500

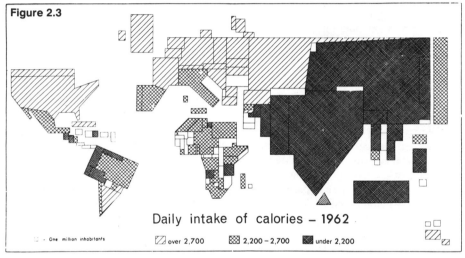

Figure 2.3

Daily intake of calories – 1962

□ - One million inhabitants   ▨ over 2,700   ▨ 2,200 – 2,700   ■ under 2,200

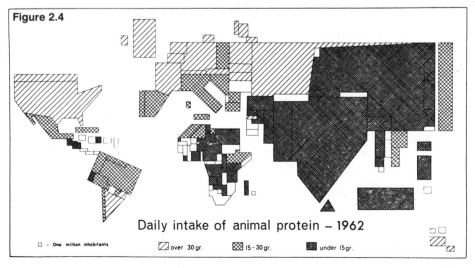

Figure 2.4

Daily intake of animal protein – 1962

□ - One million inhabitants   ▨ over 30 gr.   ▨ 15 - 30 gr.   ■ under 15 gr.

word"—in short, perhaps between one billion and one and a half billion people.[7] Moreover, in addition to this generalized hunger, there are the "specific hungers," resulting from the shortages of essential food elements such as vitamins, minerals or protein, which may sap the health of those whose diet, measured in energy-giving (calorie) terms, appears adequate.[8] Protein deficiency, in particular, has been described as "without a doubt the most serious of all the diseases which afflict mankind"; in its acute form, *kwashiorkor,* it affects some four-fifths of the children in parts of the tropical world, killing, or leaving those who survive crippled for life.

It will be seen from Figure 2.4 that low protein intake is more widely distributed than low calorie intake but these two indices define clearly the shape of the Third World, overlapping on to the poorer countries of Southern Europe and the Balkans. These hungers, as Michel Cépède rightly affirms, "are the scandal of our time for which ignorance is responsible and not the ungenerosity of nature or the number of people on earth—ignorance and the problems of economics"—and this scandal, as the maps show, is one with a clearly defined pattern.

A LEGACY OF WARPED ECONOMIES

The hunger of so great a proportion of the world's population is not in any way predestined, determined by a relentless and hostile environment. Many countries of the Third World *do* face environmental difficulties—poor soils, erratic climatic regimes which bring drought or flood, devastating human diseases and pest and predators which ravage the food crops. But the control exercised by these influences is by no means absolute, rather, does it depend on the level of technology and the material resources of the groups concerned; many tropical diseases, which are killing or crippling diseases to the African, are of minor importance to immigrant groups possessed of the means, in the shape of prophylactics or immunisation, to effectively counter them. Poverty and underdevelopment give rise to a vicious circle in which poverty means helplessness in the face of the problems posed by a particular environment—and this helplessness leads to ill health, inefficient farming, hunger, and back to poverty. And this poverty and underdevelopment has been perpetuated, even aggravated, by generations of Western exploitation which have distorted and twisted the economies of the dependent territories.

This Western impact, says Che Guevara, "has produced a monstrously distorted economy that has been described by economists of the imperialist regimes with an innocuous phrase, demonstrating the profound charity that they feel for us. . . . They give us, the peoples of America, [a] decorous and inoffensive name: the 'underdeveloped.'

"What is underdevelopment?"

"A dwarf with an enormous head and a swollen chest is 'underdeveloped' in the sense that his weak legs and short arms do not correspond to the rest of his anatomy; he is the monstrous product of a malformation that distorted his development. That is what we, the kindly named 'underdeveloped' countries, are in reality, countries that are colonial, semi-colonial or dependent. Ours are countries with distorted economies, distorted by imperialist policy, which has abnormally developed the industrial or agricultural branches that complement the imperialists' own complex economies. 'Underdevelopment' or distorted development brings a dangerous specialization in raw materials that keeps all our people in peril of hunger. We, the underdeveloped, are also the countries of monoculture, of the single product, of the single market.''[9]

Over most of the Third World over one-half of the population is engaged in agriculture (Figure 2.5), and over most of Africa and southern Asia the proportion is between 70 and 90 per cent; this compares with under 30 per cent in most of the advanced countries of the West, dropping to under 15 per cent in countries such as the United States or the United Kingdom. Over wide areas the agriculture remains a grubbing subsistent type; in Africa such subsistent economies occupy between one-quarter and four-fifths of the land, according to territory, and even in the case of a relatively market-oriented economy such as that of Nigeria, subsistence crops represent three-quarters of the agricultural output by value. Export production takes the form of small islands of market-oriented production set in the midst of a sea of stagnating peasant economies; it is, moreover, highly specialized in terms of crops grown—three-fifths of Ghana's exports consist of cocoa, nine-tenths of Gambia's exports of ground nuts, three-fifths of Malaya's of rubber.

The economies of the Third World countries are thus misshapen, with a grossly inflated agricultural sector (Figure 2.5) polarised between inefficient production of food for local consumption and the production of export crops for a world market. Moreover, given the stagnation (or in some territories the actual deterioration) in levels of food production, these countries, in spite of the size of their agricultural sector, are heavy importers of foodstuffs (Figure 2.6). In the cases of Malaya and Pakistan, Indonesia and Egypt, to mention only a few, the proportion of total imports represented by foodstuffs is higher than in some of the industrialized nations of northwest Europe. This fact helps to set China's recent grain imports into something like a correct perspective; it also underlines the precarious character of the Third World economies, especially when seen against their rapid rates of population increase, and emphasizes the difficulties they face in reaching the point of economic ''take-off'' (for the necessity to use scarce overseas funds to purchase food means a corresponding reduction in the amount available to purchase capital equipment for industry).

The warped, and consequently highly vulnerable, character of the economies of the Third World countries is highlighted by Figure 2.7 which shows the dependence of their export trade, and thus of their overall prosperity, on the sale of a very limited group of primary products.[10] This degree of export specialization, as Beguin remarks, "constitutes a supplementary index of dependency."[11] In some countries, such as Malaya, most of West Africa and the Andean republics of Latin America, over 90 per cent of their exports are accounted for by three commodities, and in the case of certain smaller countries such as Jamaica, Panama and Fiji, this specialization has increased in the last decade. A high degree of specialization and hence of vulnerability is especially typical of oil-producing countries such as Iraq and Venezuela. Such patterns of specialization are the result of the abnormal development of certain sectors of the economy which complement the industrial economies of the West and this "colonial hangover" seems likely to be perpetuated by agreements which tie in the economies of the emergent countries to neo-capitalist groupings such as the E.E.C.[12]

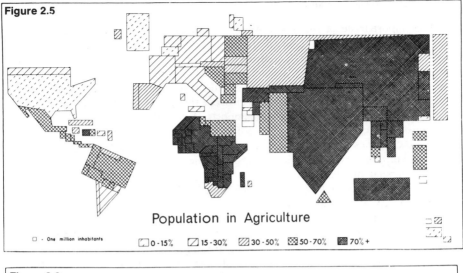

Figure 2.5

Population in Agriculture

□ - One million inhabitants   ▢ 0 - 15%   ▨ 15 - 30%   ▨ 30 - 50%   ▨ 50 - 70%   ▨ 70% +

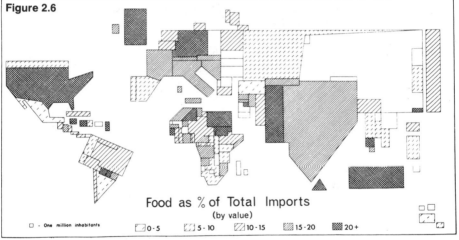

Figure 2.6

Food as % of Total Imports
(by value)

□ - One million inhabitants   ▢ 0 - 5   ▨ 5 - 10   ▨ 10 - 15   ▨ 15 - 20   ▨ 20 +

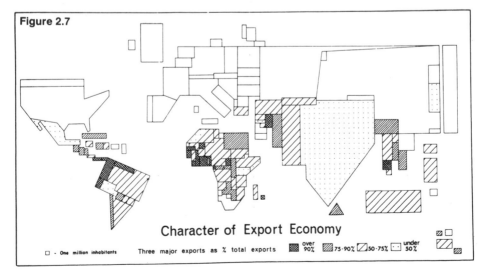

Figure 2.7

Character of Export Economy

□ - One million inhabitants   Three major exports as % total exports   ▨ over 90%   ▨ 75 - 90%   ▨ 50 - 75%   ▢ under 50%

The import trade of the Third World countries shows an equally distinctive quality. Some 70–80 per cent of the imports consist of manufactured goods, especially consumer goods; in contrast to the developed countries the imports of primary products and fuels represent only a small proportion of total imports. As far as imports of capital goods are concerned, the contrast between the developed and underdeveloped countries is less clearcut though it may be noted that in the case of countries in the first group the imports of capital goods are on a small scale because these countries supply most of their own needs; in the case of underdeveloped countries such as Afghanistan or Niger they are negligible simply because these countries are not equipping their economies to any significant degree.[13]

The dependent character of these "semi-economies" in the Third World countries is underlined by the "polarisation" of trade on a limited group of developed countries and particularly on the former metropolitan power. Beguin has attempted to measure this "polarisation of trade" between what he terms the pays-foyers and the pays-affiliés (dependent countries). It is strongest in the case of the French African colonies and the trading agreements which create this "polarisation" are excellent examples of the "subtler nets" which are being woven to enmesh the newer countries. The formerly British colonies and the countries of South and South-East Asia show a more diversified pattern of trade, with a higher Third World component. The Latin American countries are "polarised" largely on the United States, the degree of "polarisation" increasing northwards; it has tended to decrease in recent years as a result of the swing of trade towards the Common Market countries. Summarizing the trade situation, it is clear from the maps that there is a sharp contrast in the composition and character of trade between the Third World and the countries of the "white north"; it is also clear that within the Third World a certain regional diversity can be discerned, a diversity due to factors such as proximity, colonial history or the heterogeneity or complementarity of certain regions.[14]

The distortion of the economies of the Third World countries manifests itself in another significant fashion—the gross inflation of the tertiary sector. This is due to many factors: to the proliferation of the bureaucracy which has been one of the infantile disorders of new nationalism, to the high profits offered by commerce as contrasted with the lower, less certain, profit offered by secondary industry, to the migration of the unemployed and underemployed from the rural areas towards the cities to find semi-employment as white collar workers, petty traders, servants and the like.[15] The result is that those employed in the tertiary sector outnumber those employed in secondary industry by 2:1 in many parts of the Third World and the ratio exceeds 2.5:1 in parts of Central America, in some of the newly emergent countries of Africa and parts of South-East Asia (Figure 2.8). It is largely this rapid expansion of the tertiary sector of the economy which explains the rapid growth of the capital cities and large towns of the Third World. Great-city growth rates have been considerably higher than the growth rates of the population as a whole (Figure 2.9) and this has been due, not to any great increase in the productive sector of the city's economies, but rather to an accentuation of their "parasitic" function. The city is a centre of consumption rather than of production and the misery of the stagnating countryside siphons off into the cities to create an impoverished and explosive *lumpen-proletariat*. Lack of structural change in agriculture is thus intimately related to the mushroom growth of

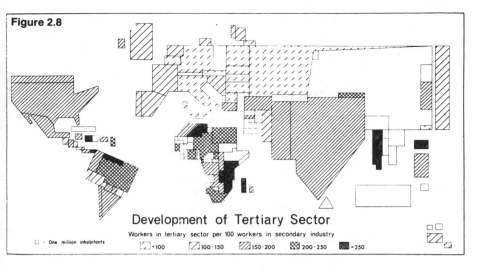

Figure 2.8

Development of Tertiary Sector

Workers in tertiary sector per 100 workers in secondary industry

☐ - One million inhabitants   ☐ <100   ☐ 100·150   ☐ 150·200   ☐ 200·250   ☐ >250

Figure 2.9 Growth of National and Great-City Populations, 1940–41—1959–60. Base year 1940–41 = 100.

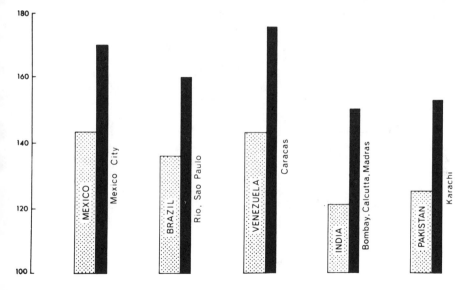

parasitic *megalopoli* in which "the gulf between excess of luxury and excess of misery shatters the human dimension."[16]

"ULTIMATES IN POVERTY AND DEGRADATION"

The long, and continuing, exploitation of the colonial and semi-colonial territories led to what have been aptly described as "the ultimates in poverty and degradation.'' It produced a world (a world containing two-thirds of humanity) whose existence was that of, at the best, half men, living poorly and living briefly, living in the twilight world of the illiterate, living in the brutalising certainty that half their children would perish of hunger or preventable disease before adolescence. Living alongside the West somewhat as Dickens, in *A Tale of Two Cities*, describes the Parisian crowds faced with the Marquis: "So cowed was their condition, and so long and hard their experience of what such a man could do to them, within the law and beyond it, that not a voice, or a head or even an eye was raised. . . .''

China, Vietnam, Cuba, these countries and others suggest that this long nightmare of humanity is drawing to a close and, indeed, perhaps the most striking feature of the contemporary world is not the much talked-of emergence of *new nations* as the emergence of *humanity*—as two-thirds of mankind struggle upwards to assert themselves as full men. Such a full human stature is not acquired automatically as a result of the granting or the winning of political independence; this may be only the first and possibly easiest step forward. Far more important is the wiping out of the conditions which political dependence created or prolonged, such as illiteracy and the short and brutish quality of life for the majority.

The size of this problem, and the gradients between the countries of the Third World and the ''white north'' in such fields as literacy, infantile mortality or death rates, are illustrated in Figures 2.10-2.12.

Except in limited parts of Latin America and South-East Asia illiteracy rates in the Third World are everywhere over 50 per cent; even in these countries cited which have a lower figure, whole groups, such as the Andean Indians or the hill tribes of South-East Asia, remain largely illiterate. Over much of Black Africa and much of colonial South Asia over four-fifths of the population were illiterate in 1950. It is scarcely necessary to stress that any real economic breakthrough is made immeasurably more difficult if to the purely economic barriers there are added the deadweights of illiteracy and ignorance. The vulgarisation of even simple agricultural techniques must then depend on word of mouth, the creation of any real political awareness is hampered and the masses exposed to the influence of rumour and of demagogues, the problem of enlarging a group's awareness beyond the limits of the clan, the tribe or the village is almost insuperable. The mass education drive is thus of critical importance in consolidating any real national unit in an emergent country; moreover, it not only removes a major obstacle to modernization but also offers, as in China and Cuba, a field in which the idealism of the young, and of the student group in particular, can find expression.

One of the greatest resources of the ''underdeveloped'' countries is their people and as China has illustrated, the mass mobilization of millions of hands can be used as a partial substitute for machinery and capital to begin the leap from poverty to decency; this ''turning of labour into capital'' is, indeed, one of the lessons of Chinese experience most widely applicable to other countries of the Third World. But this population resource is at present only partially utilized. Preventable disease leaches away the energies of hundreds of millions of people; death rates are often higher than in the West, in spite of the fact that the Third World's population is demographically a much younger one; reduced expectation of life means for hundreds of millions a working life of 15-20 years as against a

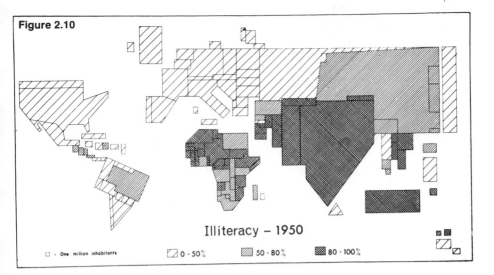

Figure 2.10

Illiteracy – 1950

□ - One million inhabitants   ▨ 0 - 50%   ▨ 50 - 80%   ▨ 80 - 100%

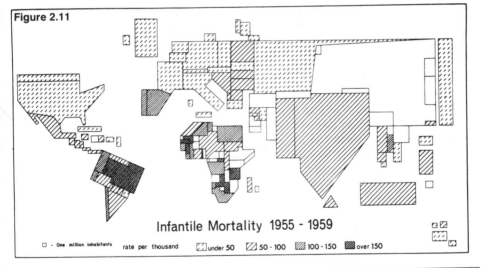

Figure 2.11

Infantile Mortality 1955 - 1959

□ - One million inhabitants   rate per thousand   ▨ under 50   ▨ 50 - 100   ▨ 100 - 150   ▨ over 150

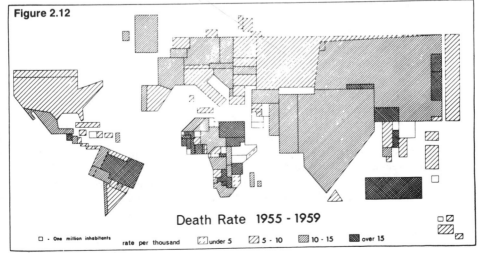

Figure 2.12

Death Rate 1955 - 1959

□ - One million inhabitants   rate per thousand   ▨ under 5   ▨ 5 - 10   ▨ 10 - 15   ▨ over 15

working life of 35-40 years in the advanced countries. The most savage losses are in the younger age groups. In Brazil "every 42 seconds a child dies, that is 85 every hour, 2,040 every day. Every year, 6 million Brazilians aged under 16 are taken to the cemetery. Of each 1,000 children, 350 and even 400 die before reaching one year of age. . . ."[17] In many of the so called "underdeveloped" countries, more than one-half of the child population dies before adolescence and in infantile mortality rate is between five and eight times that of the developed countries of the West. And, while we may attempt to assess the economic wastage, the wastage of a precious human resource, which these cold and impersonal statistics convey, it is fitting that we should not lose sight of what is ultimately of much greater human significance—the anguished deprivation, the shattered hopes and personal sufferings which lie behind the statistical measure.

EXPLOITATION AND CALCULATING CHARITY

At a time like the present, when the talk is all of international aid and of uplift schemes, of the World Bank and the Colombo Plan and the Alliance for Progress, it seems almost churlish to introduce the word "exploitation" or to even suggest that our aid is a charity carefully calculated, calculatedly meted out, a soup-kitchen sort of aid which keeps peoples on their feet—and often in order to fight the battles we have convinced ourselves (but not always those aided, as South Vietnam illustrates) have to be fought. But behind the banner headlines and the pious declarations which launch our aid schemes the old techniques of exploitation are refurbished, face-lifted, and the lineaments of the "new imperialism" have begun to emerge: "the tactics of the economic loan, the Aid Plan, and the blocked sterling balance; the proliferation of trade union advisers despatched to promote tame and non-political unionism in the colonies; and the education of an indigenous intelligentsia in the cautious liberalism of the English intellectual and in the mythology of the New, benevolent Post-capitalism."[18]

Let us put the *volume* of aid into some sort of perspective. American bilateral assistance to underdeveloped countries is estimated at 0.4 per cent of her gross national product; that of Britain at 0.3 per cent.[19] A homely measurement of the magnitude of Britain's aid effort is given by the fact that she spends annually about as much on football pools as on aid to the underdeveloped countries. If we set the amounts allocated in aid against the needs of the billion and quarter people in the non-Communist sector of the Third World (Figure 2.13) it becomes evident that the dollars (at least in the late 1950s) were being spread pretty thinly; annual aid to India, for example, worked out at less than a dollar a head—and even though dollars are mighty useful, doled out at this rate they won't help initiate much real economic development. Jordan, Libya, South Korea, these fortunate few were getting 10 times as much aid and here at least there's today something to show for the lavish expenditure—Hussein is still in possession of his throne and South Korea still without any sort of democratic government. But, by and large, the pattern of aid shows little relation to the capability of the affluent nations to help and even less relation to the desperate human needs of much of the Third World.

Soviet aid is likewise on a small scale in relation to both the resources of the Soviet bloc and the needs of the underdeveloped world. An American analysis

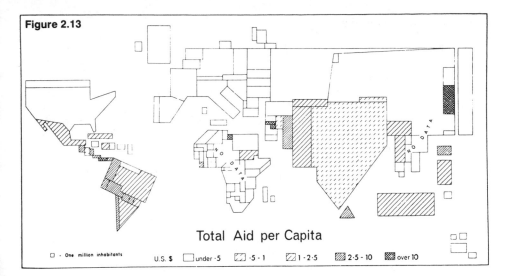

Figure 2.13

Total Aid per Capita

☐ - One million inhabitants   U.S. $ ☐ under ·5   ◢ ·5 - 1   ◪ 1 - 2·5   ◪ 2·5 - 10   ▨ over 10

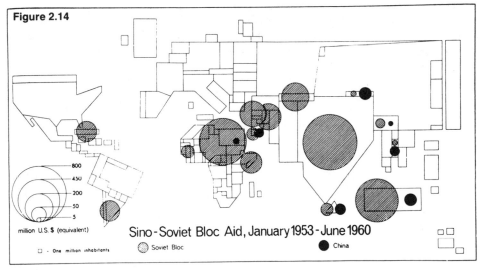

Figure 2.14

800
450
200
50
5

million U.S. $ (equivalent)

Sino - Soviet Bloc Aid, January 1953 - June 1960

☐ - One million inhabitants   ⬤ Soviet Bloc   ● China

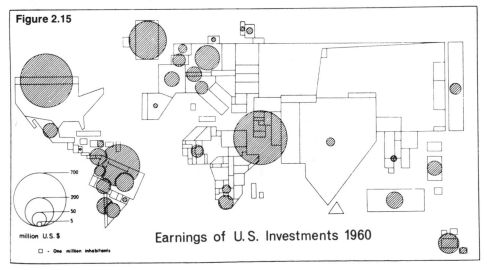

Figure 2.15

700
200
50
5

million U.S. $

Earnings of U.S. Investments 1960

☐ - One million inhabitants

comments that "the outlays of the Bloc for foreign aid [are] only a tiny fraction of the Bloc's total output." It estimates that "Russia alone has the capacity to devote $1 billion or more to programmes of foreign credit aid" and that the then current commitment to external economic development was about one-half this figure.[20] The aid is heavily concentrated (Figure 2.14)—six countries, Yugoslavia, Egypt, Afghanistan, India, Indonesia and Syria, received 95 per cent of the credits granted up to the end of 1957—and approximately one-fifth was represented by military assistance.

The effectiveness of this trickle of aid is reduced by the inability of some of the traditional structures to absorb aid without disastrous inflation (cf. Laos) and above all, by the declining price of primary products. Peter Worsley comments that "the equivalent of six years' lending by the International Bank was lost to the underdeveloped world through the driving-down of raw materials prices because of recession in the advance industrial countries"[21] and, taking a more specific example, Carlos Fuentes points out that in 1961 the Alliance for Progress gave Colombia $150 million—but that in the same year the decrease in coffee prices cost the country the equivalent of three times this aid.[22]

Meanwhile, even though the Third World countries remain poor, or are getting poorer, they remain a major field for Western investors. The general pattern of earnings from American investments overseas is shown in Figure 2.15. The importance of investment in oil comes out clearly, as does the relevance of Latin America to the United States business economy; equally striking is the relatively small scale of investment in Africa and Monsoon Asia. That these investments, however massive they may appear, bring only "fringe" benefits to the underdeveloped countries is illustrated by American investments in Latin America, where, in 1959, United States firms "made 775 million [dollars], only reinvested 200 million and sent 575 back to the United States. In the last seven years, Latin America lost, because of these shipments of money, $2,679,000,000."[23] Under these conditions, overseas investment is a powerful factor making for a widening gap between the rich nations and the poor, rather than a factor making for real economic progress.

THE SEARCH FOR IDENTITY

The Third World countries are differentiated from the old-developed countries of the "white north" not only in economic terms but also in sociopolitical terms. Most of them are engaged in a search for identity—national identity in the shape of an integrated and purposeful national structure, international identity in the sense of a place in relation to the great power blocs which dominate the world scene. And given the shifting balance of classes or even of ethnic groups within national boundaries, given the shifting pressures of the international scene, this search for identity may be accompanied by protean changes in the world's political map.

The striving towards an integrated national structure is closely bound up with the whole process of economic development for, as Robert Heilbroner points out, *economic development is not primarily an economic process in the Third World but a social and political process.* In the Euro-American world (and including, to some extent, the U.S.S.R. in this context) economic development took place within existing societies which had been created over a relatively long period of time. In the Third World, by contrast, such national societies do not exist and here a prime essential is the "creation, forcibly or otherwise, of workable institutional structures."[24] Such a process must inevitably be revolutionary in character for the necessary reorganization involves, in a backward nation, a reorganization of its class structure. The extent of the problem posed is indicated by Figure 2.16, which attempts to show, in the very broadest of terms, the degree of national integration. In contrast to the developed nation-state of Euro-America the Third World shows a range of national structures: the traditional societies of Black Africa consisting of a loosely-structured aggregate of tribal groups set within often arbitrary colonial-inherited boundaries; the colony-derived states of Latin America, controlled by a small "white" *élite,* with a dominantly *mestizo* population and with large and compact Indian communities existing largely outside the political or social framework of the state; and the new nations of Southern Asia which contain uncomfortably within their frontiers advanced "lowland" cultures and backward hill peoples, together with sizeable Asian immigrant groups (such as the Chinese) whose role in the country's economic life may be out of all proportion to their numbers. The Communist nationalities policy, as exemplified by China, or North Vietnam, offers one solution to this problem of integration; the alternatives are the nation-wide political party as in Guinea, or the charismatic ruler as in Cambodia.

THE GEOPOLITICAL PERSONALITY OF THE THIRD WORLD

Speaking of the Afro-Asian bloc, Samaan Boutros Farajallah says: "Elements of both an objective and subjective character . . . the fruits of a long and painful history and skillfully exploited by the Great Powers, intervene to fragment the emergent geopolitical unity constituted by the Afro-Asiatic world . . . they reduce it, at the best, to more or less limited and unstable regional structures . . . at the worst, they threaten to pulverise it into a multitude of 'micro-nations' which take the form of miniature states, fiercely jealous of their nominal independence, the latter freshly acquired at a period when only the large units have a chance of survival and progress."[25] These remarks are no less valid if extended to the countries of the Third World as a whole; within this extended grouping the same play of centripetal and centrifugal forces can be discerned.

Two themes dominate the policies of the emergent countries: their refusal to be any longer the *objects* of world diplomacy and their aspirations to assume a positive role, the role of *active subjects,* on the international scene.[26] This twofold, negative and positive, aspect of their policies expresses itself clearly in their role in the United Nations; together with the pressures exerted by the United States and the other great powers on these economically vulnerable "micro-nations," or, more precisely, on the *élites* who hold the reins of power, it explains what appears to be a bewildering mixture of principles and opportunism in the voting pattern of the Third World countries.[27]

The cohesion of the group varies (Figure 2.17). On the general issue of anti-colonialism the Third World countries, and especially the Afro-Asian bloc, have shown a high degree of solidarity as far as *general declarations of principle* are concerned. On *specific issues* in this field many of the countries with special ties with the colonial powers or the United States have shown themselves very vulnerable to great power pressures; these became particularly marked after the

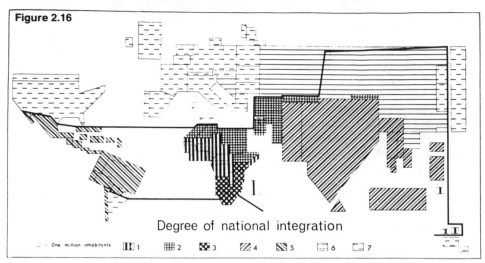

Figure 2.16

Degree of national integration

One million inhabitants ⊞ 1 ⊞ 2 ▨ 3 ▨ 4 ▨ 5 ▭ 6 ▭ 7

Key: (1) Traditional societies lacking political integration. (2) Partially integrated traditional societies. (3) Traditional societies with considerable settler groups. (4) Asian societies with substantial indigenous minorities. (5) Colony-derived societies with marginal indigenous populations. (6) Socialist multi-national states. (7) European-type national states.

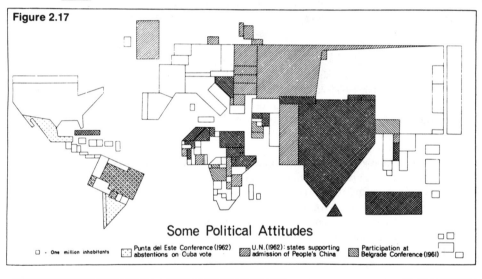

Figure 2.17

Some Political Attitudes

□ - One million inhabitants | Punta del Este Conference (1962) abstentions on Cuba vote | U.N. (1962): states supporting admission of People's China | Participation at Belgrade Conference (1961)

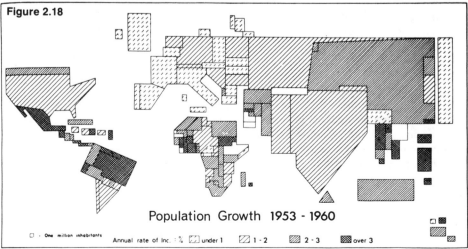

Figure 2.18

Population Growth 1953 - 1960

□ - One million inhabitants | Annual rate of Inc. : % ▨ under 1 ▨ 1 - 2 ▨ 2 - 3 ▨ over 3

Cold War extended to Asia in 1949-50 and produced a fragmentation of the Third World bloc in United Nations.[28] In the socio-economic field there is the same solidarity with regard to many of the general measures discussed by the Economic and Social Committee of United Nations (indeed, largely because many of the suggested measures were the result of extensive compromises, they were often adopted virtually unanimously); discussions on the allocation of financial and technical assistance, however, revealed cleavages between the African bloc and the Latin American and Asian blocs who feared increased aid to Africa would reduce the aid they were receiving. On the relative merits of the policy of channeling all such aid through United Nations or seeking bilateral or multi-lateral aid outside the machinery of United Nations there has again been little unanimity; certain states, such as Thailand and the members of the U.A.M., for example, express a strong preference for the latter policy.[29] Most of the Third World countries are agreed on the vital need for stabilizing the prices of raw materials, more especially for prices determined not so much by the operations of world markets but by reference to the price of manufactured goods; on the need for freedom of trade there is less unanimity, for countries such as the African states associated with the E.E.C. show little inclination to forego any advantages such association may bring in order to present a united front to those who seek tropical raw materials. As Farajallah observes: "Their reactions, indeed, are those of underdeveloped *countries* and not those of an *organized group;* national egoism and competition between countries have not yet given place to an Afro-Asian solidarity (and not even to any real *regional* solidarity)."[30]

Confronted with the problem of the Cold War the countries of the Third World have shown much less solidarity than is sometimes imagined. Changing local or regional pressures have, indeed, given a protean quality to the voting pattern on critical issues such as the admission of the Chinese People's Republic to United Nations. Two major groups may be distinguished: first, a pro-Western bloc consisting of countries tied in to the policies of the West by military or economic agreements; these countries include the participants in SEATO, CENTO and OAS and countries heavily dependent on Western aid such as the Lebanon or Morocco; secondly, a neutralist group generally favourably disposed towards People's China. The first grouping, cemented by treaty obligations, is the most rigid but even states in this group may be strongly influenced by local conditions. The best example of this is Pakistan, a member of SEATO and CENTO and which opposed the admission of People's China as long as Chinese-Indian relations were amicable; deteriorating relations between these two countries after the Tibetan affair led to a Sino-Pakistani *rapprochement* and Pakistani support of the proposal to admit the Chinese People's Republic to United Nations in 1961-62. A third, rather indeterminate, group is represented by countries striving for a policy of "non-alignment" but whose history or economic need pushes them towards the Western bloc. The attitudes of the U.A.M. towards the problem of China illustrate admirably this condition of political schizophrenia.[31]

As a geopolitical entity, then, the Third World demonstrates an inchoate quality. This derives in part from the very number of nation-states which it comprises, but more powerful influences are the diversity of political regimes, the economic orientation of the component states, the variety of conditions under which they attained national status (and thus the strength of ties which still bind them to the former metropolitan power), the character and dedication of their *élite* groups, above all, the susceptibility of these groups to outside pressures. Under these conditions, while the coalition of the Latin American and Afro-Asian blocs gives the countries of the Third World an *ad hoc* unity when confronted by socio-economic problems in United Nations, the achievement of any wider unity, of any unifying sense of purpose, among the proletarian nations is dependent upon internal political changes. Such changes and such a realignment are likely to be slow; the process is likely to begin in the U.A.M. group of states whose pro-Western orientation is largely determined by the francophile character of the *élites* and the personal influence of de Gaulle; it is likely to be delayed longest in the Latin American satellites of the United States. But whatever its timing, this "revolution of the Third World" will decisively transform the character of the United Nations; for this reason alone, it will mark a turning point in human history.

THE DEMOGRAPHIC LEAP

The contrast between the unintegrated "primitive" political structures of the countries of the Third World and the developed nation or multi-national states of the "white north" focuses attention on the fact that one of the outstanding features of the underdeveloped world is retardation in a historical sense. Largely because of the degree of outside control which irradiated it, the Third World was bypassed by many of the great economic and socio-political changes which transformed the rest of the globe. The fluid conditions within it today are thus in large measure the result of the sudden involvement of its countries in a series of changes which in Europe were spread out over generations or even centuries, but which in the Third World are being compressed into decades. The outstanding example of this is the demographic revolution.[32]

In eighteenth century Europe the expectation of life did not exceed 30 years and one out of every two men died before the age of 20. The revolutions in hygiene and medicine which accompanied the Industrial Revolution in Europe gradually eliminated the epidemics and infectious diseases which each year had erased millions of lives; Europe went through a period of explosive population increase. This "demographic revolution" has, after a delay of a century or so, reached the countries of the Third World. Moreover, it has reached them in an accelerated form, for the new techniques of death control make possible a much more rapid drop in mortality rates; in Ceylon [Sri Lanka], for example, the elimination of malaria resulted in a drop in the death rate of from 22 per thousand to 12 per thousand in seven years—the achievement of a comparable reduction in England and Wales took a century. And, what is even more important, this explosive growth of population in the Third World is not being accompanied by any great expansion of the economy, as was the case in Western Europe during *its* period of greatest population growth. Such a rapidly expanding economy (based in part on the exploitation of overseas territories and the possibility of relieving population pressure by migration) just does not exist in the case of the Third World countries.

A general picture of the world's population growth rates is given in Figure 2.18. While the world's population is growing at the rate of 1.8 per cent annually, growth rates in many parts of the Third World are as high as 3.5 per cent, which means the population is doubling every 21 years—and with increasing control over infantile mortality rates and the gradual increase of the at present shockingly low expectation of life, we may expect this rate to increase rather than diminish. It is hardly necessary to add—for this is abundantly emphasized by a comparison of Figure 2.18 with, say Figures 2.2, 2.3, 2.4 and 2.10—that this increase is greatest in those countries which at present are the most impoverished and marginal. By the end of the century the underdeveloped countries, most of which already have a large "surplus" or underemployed population, will have increased their total population from the present figure of 2,000 million to some 4,900 million, of these, some 2,000 million will be in the under-15 age group, so the Third World's age structure will be a relatively "young" one, with potentialities for continuing rapid growth.

The shape of the world our children will live in is suggested graphically in Figure 2.19; here the size of countries is proportional to area, and both maps are constructed on the same scale. If, instead of the medium growth assumptions used here, we adopt the United Nations "high" assumption (which seems increasingly the most likely) a Europe of probably 592 million people, a North America of 544

Figure 2.19 The size of the various countries or groups of countries is proportional to the population at the appropriate period. The massive population increase of the Third World is dramatically highlighted by a comparison of these two maps.

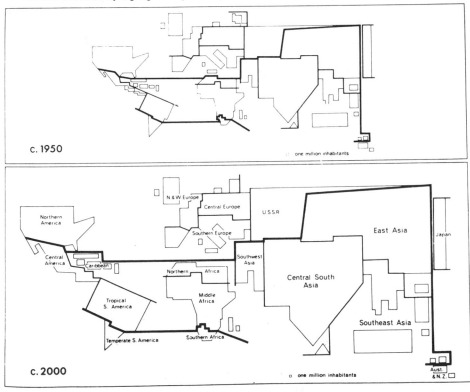

Figure 2.20   Estimated per capita income in dollars.

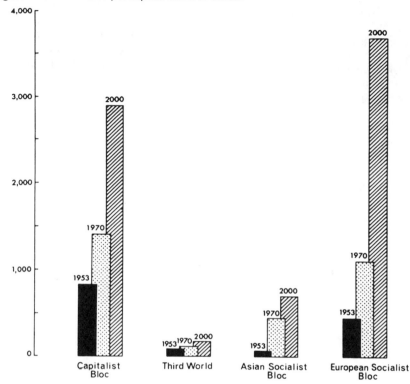

million, are going to be dwarfed by an East Asia of 2,000 million, a South Asia of 1,440 million, by Africa and Latin America which together will have a total of over 1,200 million people. Geographically, politically, the future of the white nations of the north threatens to be that of a wealthy but small minority group cramped and confined on the northernmost margins of the American and Eurasian continental masses; cut off from the impoverished and coloured majority of mankind by the alienating influence of their own affluence.

"REDUCING EVEN THE IRREDUCIBLE"

This alienation of the "white north" from the rest of mankind is perhaps the most critical challenge confronting the advanced countries, for the forces which are producing it—the lagging growth and continuing exploitation of the Third World, the swiftly elaborated and increasingly sophisticated strategies of neo-capitalism and neo-imperialism, the defection of some of the Third World's political leaders—these are a challenge to men of goodwill whatever their political or religious affiliations.

The maps presented here are intended to bring this challenge into some sort of focus; the *size* of the problem, and the *increasing* size of the problem, is suggested in Figure 2.20. These estimates of the probable trends in per capita income are based on the work of Robert Fossaert; like all such estimates they must be used as, at the best, a scale of relative magnitudes.[33] Detailed analysis is unnecessary; we have only to ask ourselves what sort of world solidarity is likely if Fossaert's projections prove accurate, if the ratio between the living levels of the "white north" and the great mass of the underdeveloped countries—*even after almost half a century of "development"*— is of the order of 20:1, on a world increasingly crowded, a world of which wealth is white and poverty wears a dark skin. What is the answer of our affluent societies to the problem thus posed?

NOTES AND REFERENCES

1. The base map used in this series is purely diagrammatic, with the size of the countries proportional to their population in the mid-1950s. Certain smaller island territories are grouped together.

2. P. Worsley, "Imperial Retreat" in *Out of Apathy*, ed. E. P. Thompson (London, 1960), p. 139.

3. See, for example, D. Granick, *The Red Executive* (New York, 1961). The same topic is dealt with by F. Zweig, "The Use of Models for Economic Structures," *The Sociological Review*, 5, 1 (1975): 65-73, especially 70-71.

4. *New Left Review*, 1963, p. 4.

5. For example, Malaya's per capita income was $(U.S.) 275 in 1957, which was among the highest in Asia. The country's wealth, however, is highly concentrated in the hand of a relatively small and in part non-resident group. Tjoa Soei Hock (*Institutional Background to Modern Economic & Social Development in Malaya*. Kuala Lumpur, 1963), comments: "If $(M) 1,500 (approximately $(U.S.) 500) per year is taken as a subsistence level for Malaya, then the great majority of the Malayan people (about 98 per cent)—Malays, Indians and Chinese—live on the verge of subsistence" (p. 77). He adds: "The concept of per capita income should be scrutinised more, especially in the so-called underdeveloped countries where income is much less equally distributed than in Western countries."

6. R. Heilbroner, *The Future as History* (New York, 1960), p. 84.

7. M. Cépède, "Hidden Hunger," *Courier* (UNESCO) (Paris, July-August 1962), p. 20.

8. To produce one calorie of animal products, 7 calories of vegetable origin must be fed to the animal. A diet of 2,200 calories, of which 600 come from animal products, corresponds thus to a figure of 5,800 "initial" calories (1,600 calories + 600 calories × 7). Cépède, "Hidden Hunger," *Courier*, p. 22.

9. Che Guevara, "Cuba: Exceptional Case," *Monthly Review*, New York (July-August 1961): 61-62.

10. To take a single example, the drop in coffee prices in Latin America over the last 10 years has cost the continent $10 billion—which more than cancels out all aid received.

11. H. Beguin, "Aspects structurels du commerce exterieur des pays sousdéveloppés," *Tiers-Monde*, Paris (January-June 1963): 6.

12. Thus Carlos Fuentes observes: "A good part of the Latin American economy is not serving its own development, but is nothing more than an extension of foreign economies. . . . Iron and oil in Venezuela, copper in Chile, Peruvian minerals . . . are a possession of the American economy and benefit only that economy." Carlos Fuentes, "The Argument of Latin America" in *Whither Latin America?* eds. P. Sweezy and L. Huberman (New York, 1963), p. 13.

13. Beguin, "Aspects structurels du dommerce exterieur des pays soudéveloppés," *Tiers-Monde*, p. 91.

14. Examined more fully by Beguin, ibid., pp. 114-116.

15. Dealt with by J. Cheverny, *Eloge de colonialisme* (Paris: 1961) and R. Dumont, *L'Afrique noire est mal partie* (Paris, 1962).

16. C. Lévi-Strauss, "Crowds," *New Left Review*, London, 15 (May-June 1962): 6.

17. F. Juliao, "Brazil: A Christian Country" in *Whither Latin America?* eds. P. Sweezy and L. Huberman (New York, 1963), p. 106.

18. Worsley, "Imperial Retreat" in *Out of Apathy*, ed. E. P. Thompson, p. 121.

19. United Nations Economic and Social Council, *Economic Development of Underdeveloped Countries* (E. 3395), 1960, p. 97.

20. M. Sapir, *The New Role of the Soviets in the World Economy* (New York, 1958), pp. 30-31.

21. Worsley, "Imperial Retreat" in *Out of Apathy*, ed. E. P. Thompson, p. 129.

22. Fuentes, "The Argument of Latin America" in *Whither Latin America?* eds. P. Sweezy and L. Huberman, p. 15.

23. Ibid., p. 18.

24. R. Heilbroner, *Great Ascent* (New York, 1963), p. 24.

25. Samarn Boutrous Farajallah, *Le groupe afro-asiatique dans le cadre des Nations Unies* (Geneva, 1963), pp. 413-414 (freely translated).

26. Ibid., p. 417.

27. See, for example, C. C. O'Brien, *To Katamga and Back* (London, 1962), pp. 22-29.

28. Farajallah, *Le groupe afro-asiatique dans le cadre des Nations Unies,* pp. 433-434.

29. Union africaine et malgache.

30. Farajallah, *Le groupe afro-asiatique dans le cadre des Nations Unies,* p. 448. (free translation, emphasis mine, K.B.).

31. The U.A.M. coupled lip-service to the admission of People's China with two conditions which deprived this token gesture of any meaning, viz: that the Taiwan regime should retain its seat in United Nations *and* its permanent membership of the Security Council. . . .!

32. See, for example, J. Lenica and A. Sauvy, *The Population Explosion* (New York, 1962).

33. R. Fossaert, *L'Avenir du capitalisme* (Paris, 1961).

ACKNOWLEDGEMENTS

The writer acknowledges with gratitude the assistance of Mrs. Margaret Carr who helped in the compilation of the statistics and of Mrs. B. M. Winchester who draughted the maps.

STATISTICAL SOURCES USED IN PREPARATION OF CARTOGRAMS

Figure 2.2: Based on P. N. Rosenstein-Roden, "International Aid for Underdeveloped Countries" in *Review of Economics and Statistics,* May 1961.

Figure 2.3-2.4: Based on F.A.O. data given in *Courier* (UNESCO) July-August 1962.

Figure 2.5: Based on data from *United Nations Demographic Yearbook* (1956); *International Yearbook of Labour Statistics* (1961); *African Labour Survey* (I.L.O., 1958).

Figure 2.6: *United Nations Yearbook of International Statistics,* 1959.

Figure 2.7: As Figure 6, with addition of *Economic Survey of Africa since 1950* (U.N., 1958) and *United Nations Economic Bulletin for Africa,* January 1962.

Figure 2.8: Based on *Yearbook of Labour Statistics* (I.L.O., 1962) and African sources cited above.

Figure 2.9, 2.11, 2.12, 2.18: *United Nations Demographic Yearbooks 1960 and 1961.*

Figure 2.10: Based on *World Illiteracy at Mid-Century* (UNESCO, 1957).

Figure 2.13: Based on *Economic Development of Underdeveloped Countries* (United Nations Economic and Social Council (E. 3395, July 1960) Table 11-4).

Figure 2.14: Based on K. Billerbeck, 1960, *Soviet Bloc Foreign Aid to the Underdeveloped Countries,* (Hamburg, 1960), p. 53.

Figure 2.15: Based on *Survey of Current Business* (United States Department of Commerce, August 1962).

Figure 2.19: Based on estimates give in *The Future Growth of World Population* (United Nations, Population Studies No. 28, New York, 1958).

Figure 2.20: Based on estimates given by R. Fossaert, *L'avenir du capitalisme*.

Additional Readings

Anderson, James. "Ideology in Geography: An Introduction," *Antipode*, 5, no. 3 (December 1973): 1–6.

Brewer, M. and Campbell, D. T. *Ethnocentrism and Intergroup Attitudes: East African Evidence.* New York: Halsted Press, 1976.

Cirino, Robert. *Don't Blame the People.* Los Angeles: Diversity Press, 1971.

Damachi, Ukandi G., Routh Guy, and E. Abdel-Rahman, Ali Taha, eds., *Development Paths in Africa and China.* Boulder: Westview Press, 1976.

Dowd, D. F. "Thorstein Veblen and C. Wright Mills: Social Science and Social Criticism," in I. L. Horowitz, ed., *The New Sociology: Essays in Social Science and Social Theory in Honor of C. Wright Mills.* New York: Oxford University Press, 1964, pp. 54–65.

Folke, Steen. "First Thoughts on the Geography of Imperialism," *Antipode*, 5, no. 3 (December 1973): 16–20.

Ginsburg, Norton. *Atlas of Economic Development.* Chicago: University of Chicago Press, 1961.

Gregory, Derek. *Science and Human Geography.* Agincourt, Ontario: G. L. C. Publishers, 1978.

Goulet, Denis. *A New Moral Order: Studies in Development Ethics and Liberation Theology.* New York: Orbis Books, 1974.

King, L. J. "Alternatives to a Positive Economic Geography," *Annals of the Association of American Geographers*, 66 (1976): 293–308.

Magubane, Bernard. "A Critical Look at Indices Used in the Study of Social Change in Colonial Africa," *Current Anthropology*, 12, no. 4–5 (October–December 1971): 419–430.

Mall, R. A. "Marxism and Gandhism: Two Challenging Ideologies in the So-Called Third World, *Die Dritte Welt*, 4, no. 2 (1974): 115–127.

McGee, T. G. "In Praise of Tradition: Towards a Geography of Anti-Development," *Antipode*, 6, no. 3 (December 1974): 30–47. .

Mercer, D. and J. M. Powell. "Phenomenology and Related Non-Positivitic Viewpoints in the Social Sciences," *Monash University Publications in Geography.* Clayton, Australia: Monash University Department of Geography, 1972.

Mills, C. Wright. "The Professional Ideology of Social Pathologists," *American Journal of Sociology*, 49, no. 2 (September 1943): 165–180.

Ray, D. M. "The Role of Ideology in Development," *International Journal of Comparative Sociology*, 11, no. 4 (1970), 306–316.

Santos, Milton. "Geography, Marxism and Underdevelopment," *Antipode*, 6, no. 3 (December 1974): 1–9.

Slater, David. "Contributions to a Critique of Development Geography," *Canadian Journal of African Studies*, 8, no. 2 (1974): 325–354.

Steel, R. W. "The Third World—Geography in Practice," *Geography*, 59, Part 3 (July 1974): 189–207.

World Atlas of the Child. Washington, D. C.: World Bank, 1979.

World Bank Atlas. Washington, D. C.: World Bank, 1978. Each year the Bank issues a new atlas, which graphically and cartographically illustrates population, per capita product, and growth rates.

II

CLIMATE AND RESOURCES

Five years of subnormal rainfall have brought severe drought to the Sahelian region of Africa. The effects of hunger can be seen in the faces and bodies of these destitute nomads from Mali. In 1973 they came to northern Upper Volta in search of food and water for themselves and their cattle, but all they found was a wasteland. Are human tragedies caused by environmental conditions, like droughts? Or are they orchestrated by national elites and international organizations including transnationals? The answer to these questions will determine the effectiveness of the 450,000 tons of food sent to the Sahel by the European Economic Community. United States and Canada. (Source: F. Botts for FAO)

Many environmental theories have been advanced to explain the low GNP of Third World countries. Environmental theories go back to the Greeks, who divided the world into three parts: frigid, temperate, and torrid. Climatic conditions in these different zones either retarded or encouraged the development of civilization. Toynbee's theory of Challenge and Response continued this very old tradition. He argued that in the Arctic climatic conditions were so severe that cultural development was retarded; the environmental challenges were too great for the advancement of civilization. In the Tropics, the environment was so generous that there was insufficient incentive for humans to advance. People could live off the fruits of nature rather than the fruits of their labor. Only in the Temperate zone was there an adequate mixture of *challenge* from and *response* to the environment (allowing for the growing of crops in the summer but requiring the storage of food for the winter), which enabled humans to most effectively utilize resources, and consequently to advance their culture.

Like Toynbee, Huntington also contributed to this environmental tradition. In the 1920s and 1930s, he and others were responsible for the reemergence and the academic importance of environmental determinism in North America. Of particular significance was Huntington's Climatic Theory which argued that certain climates are more stimulating for human efficiency than others. The industrial countries, in Huntington's view, have the most "stimulating climate," whereas most Third World countries have "difficult climates."

Although most economists have dismissed the significance of climate on economic development, a few, like Kamarck, continue the belief that climate and resources are important to Third World development. Hodder, a geographer, also criticizes economists for neglecting to consider environmental conditions. However, at the same time, he is critical of other geographers who have explained Third World underdevelopment solely in terms of unfavorable climates and resource endowments. He proposes a middle ground: physical factors are not deterministic, but should be included within a broad analysis of Third World development. Contrary to conservatives like Huntington, Hodder argues that physical factors cannot be used as an excuse "for the present relatively low standard of living" in the tropics. Instead, he recommends more research to overcome our ignorance of the interplay between people and their environment.

Szentes and other radicals rarely consider environmental conditions to be fundamental, because for them these are passive attributes of place which are molded to suit human needs. They criticize conservative and liberal perspectives which argue that climate and resources are either deterministic or even significant. For radicals the question regarding the physical environment is: why have problems of climate and resource utilization been overcome in the rich industrial countries but not in most of the underdeveloped ones?

3 Huntington's Climatic Theory of Underdevelopment

*ELLSWORTH HUNTINGTON**

REGIONS OF HIGH EFFICIENCY

North America and Europe share the climatic supremacy of the world so far as our particular stage of civilization is concerned. The northeastern quarter of the United States, together with a strip of southern Canada, excels from the standpoint of storms and polar infalls. Western Europe excels from that of temperature. Both continents owe a great deal to their location in the main storm belt which circles around the earth's northern magnetic (not geographic) pole. The corresponding southern belt lies too far south to have much effect on man. Although extremes of temperature cause climatic efficiency to decline toward the interior in both continents, cyclonic storms keep all parts of the northern United States and southern Canada well within the limits of the high or highest level of climatic efficiency. In the eastern United States cyclonic storms sweep into relatively low latitudes more often than in any other part of the world. This is one reason why the American South has a more stimulating climate than the corresponding Asiatic region in China. Some of the North American storms, with their meeting of polar and tropical air masses, sweep inward from the North Pacific Ocean but more originate in North America. The extremes of temperature accompanying some of these storms lower human efficiency, but the net effect is to give the United States what appears to be the world's most stimulating climate.

This cyclonic climate may be too stimulating. We have seen that it apparently has much to do with American traits, such as excessive eagerness for action without due planning, boisterousness among children, and the prevalence of degenerative diseases among other people. These handicaps are accentuated by the urban type of life, which in turn is in part a response to the activity stimulated by the highly cyclonic type of climate, as well as to abundant resources and the temperament arising from selective migration. Herrington and Moriyama have shown statistically that the correlation between degenerative diseases and the degree of urbanization is close, but the correlation between such diseases and climatic efficiency is closer. The overstimulation indicated by the degenerative diseases represents, so to speak, the wearing out of imperfect human machinery

*Ellsworth Huntington. *Mainsprings of Civilization*. New York: Mentor Books, New American Library, 1962. Chapter 20, "The Distribution of Civilization," pp. 391-408. Reprinted by permission of Anna Huntington Deming.

which is run too fast. It is apparently a price paid for the kind of energy which enabled the United States to do a colossal job of manufacturing in a very short time during World War II. It is quite possible that innate ability, natural resources, and the cultural endowment derived from earlier generations are more important than climatic efficiency as primary conditions of civilization, but in the United States, as in the entire world, the broad *geographic pattern* of civilization conforms more closely to climatic efficiency and the weather than to any other factor.

The effect of storms in setting this geographic pattern is so great that we may well follow the American storms eastward and see what happens. The low barometric pressure arising from the tropical water that sweeps northward from the West Indies toward Iceland and Scandinavia provides a pathway, so to speak, whereby many American storms cross the Atlantic to Europe. There they join with prevailing westerly winds in giving western Europe a stimulating climate with frequent changes of weather and yet with relatively few extremes of heat and cold such as are the worst climatic feature of the area of highest climatic efficiency in North America. This European cyclonic climate, as experienced within six or seven hundred miles of the Strait of Dover, does not stimulate activity so much as the American cyclonic type. In this respect it is the better of the two. In fact, for all-round permanent efficiency among modern civilized people, the world's best climate is apparently found in a rough rectangle with corners near Liverpool, Copenhagen, Berlin, and Paris.

Other candidates for the first place climatically include the American region from New Hampshire to New Jersey, and the Puget Sound region. A very narrow strip along the California coast, although relatively deficient in cyclonic storms, is also a candidate for high honors, as are New Zealand and the southeastern coast of Australia. None of these climates is so stimulating as that of the Great Lakes region of North America, but there the stimulus seems to be too great. When size as well as quality is considered, the stormy part of western Europe seems to be the most favored of all regions for climatic efficiency in our stage of civilization. The northeastern United States from southern New England to the Great Lakes and beyond probably stands second.

THE ASIATIC HANDICAP

In Europe and especially Asia the value of the climate as an aid to civilization declines quite steadily eastward. The general level of progress falls off similarly. The North Sea portion of Germany is more advanced than East Prussia. The Baltic States stand ahead of western Siberia. Poland and the Ukraine surpass Central Asia, Mongolia, and the region east of Lake Baikal. Sheer distance from advanced countries helps to keep the more remote regions backward, but the handicap of remoteness and isolation would largely vanish if the climate were good, as is well seen in New Zealand. Omitting other factors, which undoubtedly play a large part, let us concentrate on the relation of climate to the backwardness of Asia. The main factor is Eurasia's sheer size, which injures both climatic efficiency and agriculture in three chief ways: (1) by extremes of temperature; (2) by scarcity of storms and rain; (3) by contrasts in rainfall from season to season and year to year with consequent droughts, floods, and famines.

In summer, masses of polar air can settle southward over northern Asia, thus helping to give southern Siberia an admirable climate for a few months. Even in summer, however, when heat and consequent low atmospheric pressure open a path for cyclonic storms, oceanic air masses can rarely bring much moisture to the interior from the west because of distance, from the south because of mountains, and from the east because air masses in middle latitudes normally move eastward rather than westward. Hence both rain and the stimulus of changing air masses are scanty over most of the interior of Asia even in summer. Only a narrow strip of Siberia extending from the southern Urals to Lake Baikal has summer temperatures and rainfall well adapted to both agriculture and human efficiency. Farther north and in the highlands farther east the temperature is too low. Farther south extreme dryness, great heat, and the absence of storms combine to give the lowlands a disadvantage, and the highlands, such as Tien Shan and Tibet, are generally too lofty.

In winter the disadvantages of the entire Asiatic interior north of the main mountains are aggravated. All continents tend to become warm or cold much faster than oceans. This is especially important in large continents and in latitudes high enough so that the days are long in summer and short in winter. Accordingly, eastern Russia, and still more the vast Asiatic regions farther east, become relatively hot for their latitude in summer and extremely cold in winter. These extremes in themselves, especially the prolonged low temperature, are unfavorable to health and efficiency. The extreme cold of winter also does harm by causing the air to contract and become heavy, so that a vast area of very high pressure is formed. This acts as a buffer, barring out storms that might enter from the west. Some such storms follow the belt of open water and low atmospheric pressure that extends into polar latitudes along the coast of Norway. Some swing along the Baltic Sea, where the presence of open water well into the winter creates a slight trough of low atmospheric pressure. In this connection it is interesting to note the high cultural level of the Finns and the Baltic States, as well as of Norway. Russians say that their countrymen in the Leningrad region are the "Yankees of Russia."

Some of the winter storms from the Atlantic cross Germany north of the Alps, but in winter they usually fade away in Russia and never reach Central Asia. Others cross southern France, or even Spain, and bring winter rains and the stimulus of storms to the Mediterranean, especially north Italy. They give the Gulf of the Lion south of Marseille a reputation for storminess in winter. They make the Po Valley, more markedly than the Leningrad area, a relatively "cyclonic" and active region that contrasts favorably with a less cyclonic and less active region in the south of the same country. Northern Italy gets some storms and rain in summer as well as winter, but in Sicily the long summer is practically stormless. Waterpower from the Alps now encourages industrial activity in the Po Valley, but north Italy was outstandingly active industrially in the great mercantile days of Venice and Genoa.

In winter the Mediterranean storms sometimes cross Turkey, or even Palestine, and reach Iran. Some, indeed, in an attenuated form, persist into northern India, but here their influence falls to a minimum. Farther east some cross the Burmese mountains into China. There they revive somewhat and are re-enforced by new storms, thus bringing a mild degree of storminess to central and southern China.

It is obvious from all this that Asia as a whole gets little of the benefit to agriculture and health that comes from cyclonic storms. Some storms, to be sure, penetrate Siberia in summer and a few traverse the southern countries in winter. The few that penetrate the interior in winter are generally accompanied by such violent winds and intense cold waves that they do more harm than good. Such conditions join with extremes of temperature and rainfall in placing most of Asia under the handicap of low efficiency, both agricultural and human. Out of Asia's seventeen million square miles about three fourths (four times the size of the United States) are agriculturally almost useless because of aridity of low temperature. A level of climatic efficiency above the medium grade is rarely exceeded even in latitudes where North America and Europe reach the highest level. The quarter of Asia where agriculture is feasible is also subject to great handicaps. In the best parts of Siberia, along the western section of the transcontinental railway, the summers are so short and cool that relatively few crops can mature. Elsewhere, from the Amur River in Siberia around through China, Indo-China, India, and Persia, to Turkey the rainfall is everywhere highly seasonal. Consequently the average yield of crops per acre is limited, and danger from drought, flood, crop failure, and famine is frequent. From China to India this marginal part of Asia also suffers from extremes of humid heat. Nowhere does climatic efficiency rise much above medium, and in many regions it falls lower.

The reader does not need to be reminded that . . . differences in civilization arise from the combined effect of biological inheritance, physical environment, and cultural endowment. Any one of these, if strong enough, may largely overcome the others. For example, New England stands high in climate and culture, but certain villages fall far below the normal level of progress. The reason seems to be lack of innate ability. Many inhabitants are mentally subnormal. In the Heartland, on the contrary, natural selection appears to have given the nomads a biological inheritance which more or less compensates for climatic handicaps so far as alertness and military capacity are concerned.

LIMITATIONS OF THE CLIMATIC THEORY

Several objections have been raised to the theory that climatic efficiency is basic in setting the geographical pattern of civilization. It is said, for example, that the climatic pattern is frequently overshadowed by isolation, as in Tibet and the southern Appalachians; by innate biological traits, as in Iceland and among the Parsis; by overpopulation, as in Japan; by recent migration within the limits of a single culture, as in Florida; and by the introduction of an advanced culture, as in tropical Hawaii and northern Australia.

This objection disappears when two essential points are remembered. First, climatic efficiency, as we have seen again and again, is only one of the many agencies which influence the geographic pattern of civilization. Indeed it is only a single phase of climate, and its effect is modified by the other phases as well as by soil, minerals, and other physical conditions. The geographic factor, in turn, ranks with heredity and cultural endowment as only one among three major factors that influence the level of civilization. Such being the case, the outstanding fact is not local departures from the cultural level that would be expected on the basis of climatic efficiency, but the broad geographical agreement between the patterns of civilization and climate.

The other essential point is that the theory of climatic efficiency must not be stretched to cover non-climatic matters. High climatic efficiency does not provide inventive brains; it merely stimulates such brains. It does not supply natural resources, even though the climates that are best for human energy are also admirable for agriculture and animal husbandry, and happen in some cases to be located in regions well supplied with minerals. Climates which promote efficiency merely help in developing the possibilities provided by the geographical environment. In short, not even the most stimulating climate insures the presence of a high civilization. It merely aids in the attainment of such a civilization.

This last point deserves amplification. The Indians of New York State, for example, the famous Five Nations, had merely the rude culture of the Stone Age, although they lived in one of the world's most stimulating climates. In spite of their low culture, however, they were notable for their activity and alertness. The climate, although not the optimum for their stage of culture, apparently stimulated them much as it stimulates the present inhabitants of the same region. The absence of civilization was due to a variety of reasons, some of which can only be guessed. We do not know, for example, whether the absence of iron tools among the American Indians was due to innate lack of inventive ability or to mere accident. We do know, however, that in their rainy, forested environment the absence of such tools and the consequent difficulty in felling trees and digging up grass or the weedy sod of old fields made agriculture very difficult except in especially favorable spots such as the flood plains of rivers. We also know that the Indians of New York could not possibily use domestic animals for wool, milk, plowing, and transport, because no wild animals fit for these purposes existed anywhere near them. Even if the bison had not lived far away, it was too big and stupid.

On the other hand, in spite of the limitations of agriculture, the Indians of the Five Nations showed remarkable advancement in social, military, and political organization, and in those handicrafts for which they had both the need and the raw materials. In these respects, as well as in energy, they surpassed the Indians of less stimulating climates. Many of these others, however, such as the Aztec and Pueblo tribes, had a higher civilization because they lived in a milder climate more closely approaching the optimum for their stage of culture. Agriculture by means of irrigation was there possible, and the climate was dry enough so that good protection from the weather could be secured by means of easily constructed houses of adobe. Thus the American Indians seem to be in harmony with the theory of climatic efficiency.

The fact that in Hawaii and tropical Queensland the white people preserve the highest type of civilization in climates which are relatively unstimulating illustrates another type of evidence which is sometimes presented that climatic efficiency has little to do with level of civilization. The first thing to understand about this is that such climates are not typically tropical. They represent the best type found anywhere in tropical lowlands aside from the cool coastal variety of Peru. In their effect on human efficiency they probably stand not far from midway between the North Sea type, which our stage of civilization seems to find most favorable, and the worst type as found in steadily hot, humid, equatorial rain forests. A careful examination of the culture of Queensland and Hawaii makes the effect of this intermediate climate clear, provided the biological and social endowments of the people are also considered. Biologically the "British" population of Queensland, and still more the "American" population of Hawaii, has been highly selected through migration. Culturally both groups have been constantly in touch with Europe and America. Hence, if such conditions as climate and contact with more backward cultures did not intervene, we should expect the highest level of activity and progress in both places.

What we actually find in Hawaii and northern Queensland differs from this expectation. Among the really permanent residents of these regions, that is, those who do not go "South" or to "the mainland" for education, vacations, general recuperation, and the benefit of a stimulating climate, the pace of life is leisurely compared with that of San Francisco or Melbourne, let us say. This is not due to differences in stage of civilization or innate capacity, but mainly to diminished energy because of the less stimulating climate. This climatic difference is reflected in the social system. Leisurely rest and social amenities get more time than in more bracing climates, whereas such matters as serious reading, inventions, new projects, and the promotion of education, health, and good government get less. Activities of this latter type are by no means absent, but they proceed more slowly than among people of similar ability, character, and training in more stimulating climates. Moreover, they are largely led by people who frequently go to the more bracing climates for education, recuperation, and stimulus.

Then, too, the basic needs of life—food, clothing, shelter—can be satisfied with less work in the tropical climates than in the cooler ones. Thus lowered energy is accompanied by a lower demand for that same energy wherewith to maintain a reasonable standard of living. This difference in degree of activity has not yet had time to produce any great cleavage between the tropical and the cooler types of European culture. The growth of such cleavage is retarded by constant interchange of populations. Nevertheless, the difference in tempo is clear. In spite of the high qualities sorted our by selective migration, the social system in both Queensland and Hawaii is assuming a character appropriate to a climate that is not particularly stimulating. If these regions were left entirely to themselves for generations, the distinctive quality of their culture would doubtless became more conspicuous. Thus the life and character of these modern migrants of European stock are in harmony with the theory of climatic efficiency, just as are those of the American Indians in their stimulating climate, the British in their "efficient" climate, and the Pygmies in a climate at the opposite extreme.

TROPICAL CIVILIZATIONS

Another objection sometimes urged against the climatic part of the efficiency theory of civilization is that notable civilizations have existed for centuries in tropical climates that are comparatively unstimulating. Evidences of such civilizations are found in regions of three main types: (1) tropical highlands, such as Mexico with its Aztecs, Peru with its Incas, Yemen in southern Arabia, and Zimbabwe in Rhodesia; (2) cool westcoast deserts, of which the only conspicuous example is the Pacific Coast of Peru; (3) warm, rainy forested lowlands, such as northern Ceylon, Cambodia in Indo-China, Java, Guatemala, and Yucatan.

All of these civilizations were located in places that are geographically more favored than the average within the tropics. The highland civilizations of Yemen,

Rhodesia, and Mexico occur in climates where the temperature never departs far from the optimum. The Andean civilization had its center in a somewhat cooler and more stimulating climate. At Quito, on the equator, 9,400 feet above the sea, the average temperature is practically 55° at all seasons. At Cuzco, the ancient Inca capital, 13° farther south and 11,000 feet above the sea, the warmest month (November) also averages 55°, but the coolest is 47°. Still farther south, but lower down (8,000 feet), the monthly averages of Arequipa range only from 56° to 58°. Such temperatures impel people to be active. That is presumably one reason why the Indians of the Andean plateau run so constantly when they carry loads on their backs with straps over the forehead.

The relatively low temperature of the Andean highland stimulates invention, as well as activity. People have to make inventions or suffer from the cold. The agriculture of South America apparently arose in the lowlands or foothills east of the Andes in the general region where Argentina, Paraguay, and Brazil come fairly close together about 20° or 25° south of the equator. From there it was presumably carried equatorward and upward by migrants who moved slowly forward from generation to generation. As they went north the altitude at which their corn would grow best naturally became higher. Finally, however, the migration took these pre-Inca people into such high country that the temperature was too low for comfort and health. Then there occurred one of those significant combinations of climate, natural resources, human ability, and cultural inventions which seem to be at the basis of all great progress in civilization. The climate apparently stimulated both bodily and mental activity. That, however, would not have made such a cold place as Cuzco highly favorable for a relatively advanced stage of civilization unless there had been some means of keeping warm. Such a means was present on the high, cold grassy uplands of the Andean plateau. It took the form of two wool-bearing animals of the camel family, the llama and alpaca. Nowhere else in America was there any easily tamed animal which could be kept in herds and used as a source of wool. Moreover, the llama could also be used as a pack animal.

Before wool could be made into clothing someone had to make some extremely important inventions. The incentive to do so was there in the chilly evenings. The challenge to do so was present in the woolly animals, but these two conditions were not enough. People with alert, inventive minds were also needed. At some stage of their progress the old Peruvians must have been of high quality for otherwise they could scarcely have made so many of the most fundamental inventions—first, the domestication of animals, then spinning, weaving, and the fashioning of warm clothes, also the art of loading and driving animals, and afterward that of making trails for them and carrying on trade by their means.

Other conditions also combined with the climate and the llamas to hasten the progress of Andean civilization. When the migrants came to the higher levels of the plateau, they found conditions under which irrigation was much more necessary than lower down because the climate was drier. It was also more difficult than in the gentler topography that they had previously been accustomed to. Irrigation canals that required high engineering ability were constructed, winding along steep mountain sides. Terraces, too, were needed on the hillsides. Still another condition joined with the presence of wool in enabling the migrants to protect themselves against low temperature. In the regions of relatively mild rainfall to which they had come, dried mud can be used not only to plaster dwellings made of branches or stones but to build entire houses. This is a great advantage because clay of reasonably good consistency is widely distributed and can easily be used. Moreover, adobe walls of dried clay are especially good as a means of keeping out both the cold at night and the heat of a vertical sun. A new and valuable crop, the potato, played a semi-climatic part in encouraging civilization in Peru, for it is found wild only on the high, cool Andean plateau. It must have added considerably to the security of the population against crop failures and famine.

From the standpoint of direct as well as indirect effects on human efficiency, the climate of tropical highlands has advantages in other respects as well as temperature. First, the updraft of air under the warm tropical sun and the corresponding downdraft at night make mountain climates more variable and to that extent more stimulating than those of neighboring lowlands. Second, if either atmospheric ozone or atmospheric electricity is a stimulant, highlands have an advantage which is largely independent of temperature. The amount of ozone in the air and the potential gradient of electric currents increase steadily upward. In places as high as Cuzco or Mexico City they are relatively large compared with sea level. Even if ozone and electricity are not factors, tropical highlands have a kind of climate close to the best for a certain stage of cultural progress, although it is not the best when a higher stage is reached.

The second, or cool, dry lowland, type of tropical civilization also has special advantages. Its temperature is close to the optimum all the time. At the port of Callao in Peru, near Lima, oceanic currents cause the coolest month to average only 62° and the warmest 71°. These are almost ideal temperatures. The development of the lowland Peruvian civilization in this extremely dry desert was also helped by the fact that numerous small and easily handled streams from the high Andes favor irrigation. The temperature is never too hot or too cold for corn. Cotton grows wild, thus helping to provide material for clothing. Means describes the coastal valleys as having one of the best diets in the world by reason of potatoes, maize, squash, beans, sweet potatoes, peppers, and many fruits, nuts, and spices, together with an abundance of varied seafood as well as game birds, deer, and other wild animals in higher valleys.[1]

The location of the third, or wet lowland, type of tropical civilization, depends largely on soil, as well as on seasons of rainfall. The majority of tropical soils are so badly leached that they have lost most of their soluble minerals. Hence they are not good for cereals. Crops grown in them tend to be deficient in minerals, vitamins, and fats, so that they provide a poor diet. The Cambodian region, where the magnificent ruins of Angkor Wat are located, and the lowlands of northern Ceylon, which also once supported a relatively high civilization, are favored with alluvial soils or with muddy streams for irrigation whereby the soil is renewed. New alluvial soils and a limestone type not badly weathered are found in the Maya region of Guatemala and Yucatan. Java is especially favored with rich volcanic soils, as is Guatemala. In both Java and Guatemala ancient civilizations existed in the highlands, as well as the lowlands. Another important factor in the location of lowland tropical civilization is a rainfall of the "plantation" type, abundant but not excessive. Its chief advantage, as we have already seen, is a good amount of rain most of the year, combined with a dry season not severe enough to injure moisture-loving crops but long enough to favor their ripening and to make cultivation and weeding practicable. Climates with this kind of favorable combination of moderately wet and dry seasons are rare in the tropics. They are especially important because they favor the growing of rice or corn, which forms the basis of the kinds of agriculture most favorable to tropical civilizations.

THE HUMAN FACTOR IN TROPICAL CIVILIZATIONS

From the human, as well as the physical, standpoint all three types of tropical civilization have common characteristics which differentiate them from non-tropical civilizations, such as those of Egypt, Mesopotamia, and northwestern India. First, they all appear to be intrusive, that is, we have not yet found evidence of a gradual development from more primitive stages, such as are found beneath the Asiatic and Egyptian types. This suggests that their early stages of development took place elsewhere. When they arrived at the locations where we now find their ruins their bearers had already attained at least the rudiments of civilization. For example, according to Means, both the highland and lowland civilizations of early South America were founded by people who already understood the rudiments of agriculture, pottery making, and weaving.[2] This seems to have been true of the founders of all tropical civilizations.

If the cultures that blossomed into tropical civilizations were intrusive, it is practically certain that they must have been brought by migrants from some other region. This is the second great human fact that seems to be common to all tropical civilizations. The story of the coming of such migrants to Ceylon is well known, and practically the same general set of events occurred also in Cambodia and Java. For example, in the fifth century A.D. Java began to be the goal of voyagers, traders, and bold adventurers from India. According to Kennedy, the typical "procedure was for a prince of some Indian ruling house to come to the Indies [Java] and there insinuate himself into the graces of a native chieftain. Acting as advisor, oftentimes marrying the chief's daughter, the Hindu would then establish . . . a state government copied after the Indian model."[3] This quotation oversimplifies the matter, but it suggests what must have happened, namely, a vigorous selective migration. The famous pyramidal temple of Boro Budur, the most impressive memorial of this period, was built about the time of Charlemagne (A.D. 742–814). Episodes from the life of Buddha are carved in stone along nearly three miles of terraced walls rising tier after tier to a small lofty dome. The greatest political period came later, in the fourteenth and fifteenth centuries, when the empire of Modjopahit, with its capital in eastern Java, ruled most of the Dutch East Indies, Philippines, and Malay Peninsula. The overthrow of this empire is usually ascribed to the introduction of Mohammedanism.

A third characteristic common to all three types of tropical civilization is that they perish through senescence, giving birth to no surviving successors that surpass them, and leaving scarcely a trace in any later civilization. They perished thus in spite of a rather long life in certain cases. The Mayan civilization probably lasted at least fifteen hundred years, if we include both its earlier stage in Guatemala and its later stages in Yucatan with its medieval revival. Nevertheless, when the white man arrived in America, the distinctive arts and social habits of the Mayas had practically vanished. The Indians of Yucatan scarcely had any traditions of their people's ancient grandeur. The Inca civilization was already decadent when the white man arrived. All tropical civilizations have disappeared in a way that suggest premature senescence. None has passed on the torch of culture to other civilizations. Even in Java, where Europeans found a kind of gentle, decayed culture, analogous in this respect to that of modern Iran, the present natives show little of the originality and industry which gave rise to magnificent temples such as that of Boro Budur. Contrast all this with the way in which Babylonia transmitted civilization to Assyria and Syria, Egypt to Palestine and Crete, the Indus region (non-tropical) to modern India, Greece to Rome and western Europe, and China to Korea and Japan. Today none of the leading types of civilization owes more than a few minor items of its culture to any of the three types of tropical civilization.

We are now ready for a tentative final conclusion as to tropical civilizations. We have seen that in every instance the geographical location of such civilizations has special advantages of climate, soil, native plants, or native animals. Climatically, however, there is a wide range from warm, moist, unstimulating lowlands, such as those of Ceylon, Java, Cambodia, and the lower parts of Guatemala, to the cool and relatively stimulating, although monotonous, highlands. We have also seen that all the tropical civilizations are alike in being intrusive, in being due to immigrants from some other region, and in disappearing without leaving progressive successors or exerting any appreciable influence on the rest of the world. The lowland cultures show these last three qualities with special strength. Every one of them had progressed far toward its highest stage when it first appeared within the tropics. The earliest traces of the Mayas indicate that they had already developed their marvelous calender through generations of accurate observation. They also had made one of the world's small handful of supreme inventions, namely, the art of writing. The people of Ceylon, Cambodia, and Java merely took the culture that had originally evolved in northern India outside the tropics and added a few relatively minor items of their own. On the other hand, the civilization of Peru went through many stages of growth after it reached the highlands. Thus, in general, the amount of development of these civilizations after they reached their tropical homes was least in the unstimulating lowlands and greatest in the relatively stimulating highlands.

The course of events becomes clearer when we take account not only of the climate and resources, but of the quality of the people. In fact the principles of biological selection go far toward solving the mystery of tropical civilization. Means puts his finger on the crux of the problem when he says that in order to attain civilization people need not only a stimulating climate and raw materials well fitted to their work, but also "an indefinable factor" which is "apparently psychological."[4] The Incas, who were the latest native rulers to dominate Peru, apparently possessed this unknown quality. It seems quite likely that the Incas were a kith that had acquired especially strong qualities during an unknown period of migration, mountaineering, and wandering with their herds of llama. As described by Means, they had a character and played a part like that of the Mongols in China, the Moguls in India, and the Turks in Asia Minor.

Going back to tropical civilizations as a whole, we may inquire as to the place of origin of the migrant groups which brought their primitive culture to low latitudes. The culture of the peninsulas and islands of southeastern Asia appears to have had its origin in the Indus region, where the record of human progress is almost complete from primitive times. For Yemen the corresponding location was presumably north of the Arabian Desert. Little is known as to the exact place of origin of the Mayan and Peruvian civilizations. A final conclusion can be reached only after there is agreement as to where corn (maize) was first cultivated. It was formerly supposed that this occurred in Mexico, but Mangelsdorf and Reeves, . . . favor a location east of the Andes and 20–25° from the equator. From there the art of agriculture may have been carried across the Andes to the dry coast and even through Ecuador and Colombia to Central America and finally to the Maya region of Guatemala. This suggests great possibilities for selective migration and for the evolution of a kith such as the Mayas.[5]

It is probable that migration was at the basis of all tropical civilizations. Migrations are practically always selective. The more difficult they are, the greater is the probability that people of unusually high quality, physically, temperamentally, and intellectually will be segregated. If migration brings such people to the more favored parts of the tropics, as it presumably did in the cases now under consideration, the stage is set for a sudden outburst of civilization. This might last hundreds of years if the competent invaders retained their biological inheritance unmixed, if new migrants of the same type arrived, or if some other selective process was in operation. On the other hand, degeneration and the decline of civilization would normally result from intermarriage with less competent people, from the gradual weakening effect of the climate, or from the growth of luxury and licentiousness.

The Parsis illustrate the extraordinary way in which high ability and achievement may persist in a tropical environment if a high biological inheritance is strictly maintained. The British in India and the Dutch in Java illustrate the way in which a high culture from a more bracing climate may enter a country and create buildings and engineering works utterly beyond the power of the indigenous peoples. If the Dutch should die out in Java and that country should cease to have contact with the rest of the world for centuries, the ruins of Dutch structures might be as outstanding as are those of the Mayas in Yucatan or the Khmers in Cambodia. Thus tropical cultures, as a whole, whether ancient or modern, harmonize with the conclusion that there is a strong relation between climatic efficiency and civilization, but allowance must always be made for natural resources, heredity, biological selection, and the stage of culture which migrants bring with them. All this is merely another way of stating the basic fact that civilization depends on the combined effect of heredity, physical environment, and cultural history.

NOTES AND REFERENCES

1. Philip Ainsworth Means, *Ancient Civilizations of the Andes* (New York: Chas. Scibner's, 1931), p. 11.

2. Ibid.

3. Raymond Kennedy, *The Ageless Indies* (New York: John Day, 1942), p. 33.

4. Means, *Ancient Civilizations of the Andes*, p. 25.

5. Ellsworth Huntington, *The Climatic Factor as Illustrated in Arid America* (Washington: Carnegie Inst., 1914), p. 184.

4 A Liberal Critique of Environmental Determinism

B. W. HODDER*

THE SIGNIFICANCE OF NATURAL RESOURCES

In assessing the role of natural resources in economic development, a number of writers strongly criticize the "geographical school" (by which is meant the "natural resource" school) of economic development studies for its crude determinism, its tendency to discuss physical factors at length but non-physical and especially economic factors hardly at all, and for appearing to ignore altogether the theoretical framework of economic development studies. Examples of this "natural resource" school of thought can be found in the work of Semple, Huntington and Parker.[1]

Some authorities would go so far as deliberately to disregard the role of natural or physical resources in economic development. It is argued, for instance, that economic growth is determined by capital—"the engine of growth"—and is thus largely the result of an interaction between savings and the capital-output ratio.[2] Analyses such as this leave nature out of explicit consideration and give little if any attention to the role of natural resources, either qualitatively or quantitatively. While natural resources may receive some mention in theoretical analyses, their explicit consideration is commonly believed to be unnecessary.[3] It is argued not only that land is a fixed factor but also that the old Ricardian model in which economic growth is limited by land—and especially by the poverty of natural resources—has been completely disproved by the experiences of nineteenth-century Europe and North America. Increasing returns and technical progress have always upset the Ricardian model. Even where countries have resource deficiencies, it would be possible for them to draw upon the resources of other countries, for instance by trade. Trade clearly opens up the possibility of breaking through any constraints imposed by natural resource deficiencies and links growth more intimately and directly to population and capital accumulation, both of which leave a continuing potential for economic expansion.[4] Again, it is possible to compensate for lack of natural resources by the substitution of capital or labour skills and by social and economic improvements, including education—"investment in human capital"—managerial capacity, and economies of scale.[5]

*B. W. Hodder, *Economic Development in the Tropics*. (London: Methuen, 1968), Chapter 1, "Natural Resources and Tropical Development," pp. 8–11 and 13–14. Reprinted by permission of Methuen & Co. Ltd.

Even the most cursory glance at natural resources—water, forests, soils, minerals, or power—reveals that there is indeed little correlation between the occurrence of these resources and the level of economic development in any particular tropical country. The presence or absence of naturally occurring material resources in no way immutably determines the economic development of a country. "Since the changing fortunes of many countries and regions have not been connected with the discovery or exhaustion of natural resources within their territories, the fortuitous distribution of these resources certainly does not provide the only, and probably not even the principal, explanation of differences in development and prosperity."[6] High productivity and prosperity can be achieved without abundant natural resources. While their possession may give certain initial advantages, plentiful natural resources are not necessarily associated with prosperity, nor are they a precondition for economic development.

It is true that many analyses grossly exaggerate the role of natural resources in economic development; and this is perhaps especially true of the work of geographers. In spite of his interest in the physical environment and in the broader aspects of man-environment relationships in specific areal settings, the geographer cannot afford to argue the overriding importance of the physical factors in development; he cannot associate himself with the school of thought which puts the emphasis upon natural resources and claims that the level of economic development in a country is somehow causally connected with its natural resource endowment; nor can the geographer afford to view economic development simply in terms of how far the natural resources in a country are developed or utilized. To abstract the purely physical factors in applied development studies is to falsify as surely as is to abstract the purely economic, political, or social factors.

On the other hand, it can be argued that there is no justification for ignoring natural resources altogether in any development analysis, and that there are real dangers in any tendency to under-estimate the role of natural resources in tropical development. That any analysis of the applied problems of economic development cannot afford to accept natural resources as "given" or "fixed" is clear from the widely accepted need for the conservation of resources, both exhaustible and renewable: the problems of soil erosion and forest degeneration, for example, vividly illustrate the consequences of neglecting the utilization and conservation of resources. In recent years, too, a great deal of public attention has been focused on the dangers of exhausting many of the world's mineral, power and water resources; and considerable concern is being expressed over the way in which ecological systems are being disturbed or destroyed. Again, the theoretical arguments for giving scant attention to natural resources in tropical development studies may fall down in practice: for while in theory tropical low-income countries can make up for the lack of certain natural resources by trade, capital, and skills substitution, in practice most of these countries do not have the external trading potential, capital, or labour skills to enable them to make up for limited natural resources in this way.[7] Furthermore, a good deal of the available empirical evidence supports the contention that natural resources are by no means an irrelevance, especially in the early stages of development. In Venezuela the *per capita* income is higher than in most other tropical countries, and this fact is clearly and causally connected with the exploitation of rich oil resources in that country.

Thus while the relative lack or abundance of natural resources is never a determining factor in economic development, and while the natural endowment is usually less important to this process than is the human contribution, natural resources may constitute an important factor in planning and decision-making as far as economic development in low-income tropical countries is concerned. . . . The importance of natural resources to developing countries is relatively greater than to the developed countries of the world. In low-income tropical countries rich natural resources can have great significance as sources of exports and foreign investments, while poor resources may form some limitation to growth. The quantity and character of natural resources may well have an important initial effect on patterns of production and levels of income.[8]

THE STUDY OF NATURAL RESOURCES

Perhaps the most striking impression received from any study of the natural resources of the tropical world is the urgent need for more information about those resources. Such an impression remains true, not only for the assessment of mineral and power resources but also for the quantitative and qualitative analysis of moisture resources, vegetation, and soils. This point . . . is underlined by the reading of the current development plans of any tropical country. It is now widely realized that not enough is known about most of the natural resources of countries in the tropics, and that topographical, geological, hydrological, soil, and ecological surveys are vital prerequisites to any successful attempt at resource utilization. Though precise, accurate data are often very difficult and expensive to obtain, and though, also, it is true that these resources cannot easily acquire commercial value, further research into the various natural resources and their utilization is an immediate and basic need everywhere. Without such information, as has been abundantly proved on a number of occasions over the last two decades or so, all development schemes can be undertaken only with a serious risk of failure.

Yet even though it is necessary to emphasize our ignorance rather than our knowledge about the physical factors and natural resources of the tropics, it is also necessary to emphasize that there are no grounds for assuming that natural resources are anywhere a limitation to economic development or an excuse for the present relatively low standard of living in any part of the tropics: "the Creator has not divided the world into two sectors, developed and under-developed, the former being more richly blessed with natural resources than the latter."[9] The early traditional viewpoint of the tropics as having exceptionally rich natural resources and the "modern" view of the tropics as poor or inferior in natural resources are equally false. The problem of natural resources is not that they are especially poor or inadequate in tropical countries but rather that the facts about these resources are little known and that their significance for economic development in any specific area is not fully understood. . . . [A]ny realistic analysis of an applied situation in tropical economic development must start from the assumption that the natural resource base is potentially adequate for substantial development, given sufficient knowledge about these resources and a ready adaptation of planning to the opportunities and limitations set by them.

NOTES AND REFERENCES

1. E. C. Semple, *Influences of Geographic Environment* (New York, 1911); E. Huntington, *Civilization and Climate* (New Haven, 1915); and H. H. Parker, comment in J. J. Spengler, ed. *Natural Resources and Economic Growth* (Washington, 1961), p. 190.

2. R. J. Harrod, *Towards a Dynamic Economics* (London, 1948).

3. S. Kuznets, *Six Lectures on Economic Growth* (New York, 1959), and J. E. Meade, *Trade and Welfare* (Fair Lawn, 1955).

4. H. J. Barnett and C. Morse, *Scarcity and Growth: The Economics of Natural Resource Availability* (Baltimore, 1963).

5. C. P. Kindleberger, *Economic Development* (New York, 1966), pp. 53–4.

6. P. T. Bauer and B. S. Yamey, *The Economics of Underdeveloped Countries* (Cambridge, 1957), pp. 46–7.

7. Barnett and Morse, *Scarcity and Growth*.

8. Chenery in K. Berrill, ed. *Economic Development with Special Reference to East Asia* (London; 1965).

9. Bauer and Yamey, *The Economics of Underdeveloped Countries*, p. 46.

5 The Political Economy of Resource Exploitation

TAMAS SZENTES*

In addition to the high rate of population growth as a limiting factor, Jacob Viner also points to the low level of productivity which he traces back partly to unfavourable natural endowments (poor-quality soil, virgin forests, lack of mineral resources, and waterpower, unfavourable climatic and precipitation conditions, poor transport facilities, unfavourable geographical situation with respect to its opportunities for profitable foreign trade, etc.), and partly to the poor quality of the working population (in respect of culture and education, health and nutrition).

No doubt, the low level of productivity is a characteristic of the economy of underdeveloped countries, but not even Viner says that low productivity is attributable simply to the lack of natural resources. A case in point is Switzerland whose unfavourable natural conditions have not proved to be a fatal obstacle to development.

As a matter of fact, the natural conditions and resources of underdeveloped countries can hardly be regarded as unfavourable *in general* when it is common knowledge that there are countries in Africa, Latin America and Asia which are very rich in mineral resources.[1] Some of them have very high potentials of water power, and, though the climatic conditions are disadvantageous in a number of countries, they are definitely favourable in others.[2]

The *geographical situation* may, of course, be of primary importance in transport and foreign trade. The backwardness of transport and/or the high cost of its development, as well as the great distance from international trade routes, are indeed considerable obstacles to development. At the same time the expansion and standard of the transport system itself is dependent on economic development. Its course is determined by the centres of economic growth, and natural obstacles are no longer unsurmountable barriers today. Therefore the inadequate standard of transport may be an obstacle to a more rapid economic development but it is only a concomitant symptom of underdevelopment, not a determining factor by any means. At the present stage of the development of international trade and transport one must not lay too much importance on the geographical situation as even the remotest parts of the world have already been brought into the blood circulation of international trade, and it is precisely in the economies of

*Tamás Szentes, *The Political Economy of Underdevelopment*. (Budapest: Akadémiai Kiadó, 1971), Chapter 2, "Underdevelopment as the aggregate of certain and limiting factors," Part 2, pp. 36–41. Reprinted by permission of author and publisher.

the excolonial and dependent countries that international trade plays a decisive role.

Meier and Baldwin also point to the state of natural resources as one of the factors of underdevelopment.[3] But, as Meier himself asserts in another study of his, however popular it is to refer to the lack of resources, and however evident it is that the possibilities of development are highly restricted where natural resources are lacking, in 1870 very few countries could have been said to be poor in them. "The present phenomenon of a low amount of resources per head is the result of either the exhaustion of resources or such a rapid growth in population that overpopulation now puts pressure on the available resources."[4]

Thus Meier only accepts the abundance or shortage of natural resources as a *relative* phenomenon—a standpoint we readily agree with—and he also points out that the position of the developing countries today is more unfavourable in respect of natural resources than it was in 1870. In the end, however, he seems to return to the idea of the scarcity of natural resources. The fact that the resources that had existed earlier were "exhausted" so soon and turned out to be scarce due to a rapid growth of population, might prove that they had been considerably limited in an absolute sense, too. If resources did not represent a bottleneck earlier (but only since they became exhausted and scarce in relation to the number of population), the question ought to be answered why they did not promote development to a greater or lesser extent when and where they were still available in abundance? There is convincing evidence that it is no good just pointing to the exhaustion of natural resources without bringing it out clearly: by whom and for what purposes the resources were exploited. Did the given national economy benefit from the exhaustion of its resources or not? And was the exploitation of the resources justified *at that time* and *to such an extent* from the point of view of the development of this economy? It is not necessary to develop this train of thought further. It is obvious that what is needed here too, is a genuinely historical answer and not a type of explanation based on demographic trends or the "natural" exhaustion of resources.

It should be noted that as regards the scarcity or abundance of natural resources it is not scientific to speak of the "drying up" of resources because geological explorations can never be regarded as finished (they are in fact still in the initial stage in the underdeveloped countries), and because science and technology are developing continuously.[5] Indeed, the more unfavourable situation which in fact exists today as compared with 1870 is due less to the diminishing volume of natural resources than to the impact of changes in world trade and the international division of labour. (Meier and Baldwin also point to the problem of the trends of the terms of trade.)

Thus it is hardly acceptable to regard the underdeveloped countries as *generally poor* in mineral and power resources. And to talk about the "drying up" of natural resources is not only unjustified but it would require answering further questions. As regards the abundance and state of natural resources, the scale of variants is even wider than in respect of the demographic situation, and the differences within the underdeveloped world are considerably larger than between the underdeveloped groups of countries.

There is, no doubt, one natural-geographical endowment which seems to be a more or less common feature: "almost all the newly developing countries are *tropical countries*."[6] In this connection it is usual to refer partly to the unfavourable psychological effect of the hot climate which "does not encourage hard work and makes a primitive way of life bearable in many respects"[7] and partly to the poor quality of the tropical soil which prevents any considerable agrarian, and thereby also industrial development.

The fact that physical work under tropical conditions is more difficult is realized by everybody. It is also self-evident that the lack of that system of work involving regularly repeated and constant efforts, which is objectively required by agriculture in the temperate zone, and the objectively greater possibility of a mere reliance on the mercy of Nature in the tropical zones: all these may have at least a curbing effect on development. Marx, too, referred to these factors when he called the temperate zone the natural father-land of capital. At a certain stage of the development of productive forces, natural conditions have an increased importance in social development, and there is no doubt that these and similar factors still largely determine the living conditions and the development of certain tribes inhabiting the depths of the forests. But, on the other hand—as Tinbergen also mentions—it was just in the tropical belt that the great ancient cultures developed, while primitive tribes of that time lived in the temperate zone.[8] Thus, even if in a certain period some zones are more favourable to socio-economic development than others, this does not preclude the possibility of the opposite in another period. And as to the recent historical period, it is in the underdeveloped countries that the most "sweating" methods of exploitation were (and in many places still are) applied, such as a long working day, low wages, various penalties, poor mechanization where hard manual work is done, etc., which are the characteristic phenomena of colonial capitalism.[9]

A realistic assessment of the quality of tropical soil still needs considerable scientific work and research.[10] It seems to be certain, however, that the transplantation of some crops to tropical soil proves unsuccessful, and certain methods of cultivation used in the temperate zone (e.g. deep ploughing) may be definitely harmful in the tropics. It is also an established fact that the qualititive deterioration of the tropical soil (mechanical disintegration and erosion) may be very rapid if it is not protected against the sun which "would burn away the organic matter and kill the micro-organisms" and the heavy rainfall which "would crush the structure of the soil, seal off the underlying soil from the air, and leach out the minerals or carry them so far into the earth that the plant roots cannot reach them."[11] All this, however, is a long way from the proof that the quality of the soil is a determining factor concerning the state of underdevelopment. A great dependence on weather, a high degree of exposure to natural disasters (flood, drought), uncertainty of the marketable surplus and even the danger of erosion, etc. used to be typical of European agriculture, too. The solution of these problems is to a great extent a social and technical question and is, in this respect, the function of economic development. The considerable share of the underdeveloped countries in the world production of a great number of agricultural products must make us careful in making negative statements about their natural endowments and soil quality.[12] The difficulties in marketing these products call our attention to the fact that the problems of the development of agriculture are not primarily connected with natural factors. It is even less admissible to link up economic development as a whole with the blessings of soil and climate. As B.

Higgins writes: "The soil and climate of Japan did not suddenly change in the latter part of the nineteenth century when its transformation to an industrialised country began."[13]

According to H. Leibenstein, the low agricultural yields of underdeveloped countries can be explained, in principle, by three factors: "(1) some of the capital found in advanced agricultural countries may not be of a kind for which we can substitute labor; (2) advanced countries may utilize superior agricultural techniques; and (3) on the average, the quality of the cultivated land may be superior in the advanced countries." As far as the former two points are concerned, they are obviously the functions of economic development, and not the other way round. About the third factor Leibenstein writes the following: "Certainly, persistently low yields cannot be ascribed to climatic characteristics since these are often more favourable to high yields in the underdeveloped countries than in the developed ones. But the *average quality* of the land may be inferior for two reasons. First, because incomes are low, the margin of cultivation is carried much further in the direction of poorer land. . . . But, second, and more to the point, there may be an inherent dynamic process in the utilization of the land that keeps yields low." And this is because as a result of certain "counterforces" "an improvement in the quality of the land generates a more intensive utilization of that land." "Increased current yields imply improved nutrition, a diminution of periodic starvation, and consequent diminished mortality rates, resulting in an increased population and necessary further subdivision of holdings . . ."; ". . .there is now little room for quality-maintenance measures that imply a diminution in the current yield."[14]

Though this explanation is in perfect consonance with Leibenstein's "quasi-stable equilibrium" idea, it is at the same time completely devoid of any genuine historical factor.[15] The fact that the acceleration of population growth in underdeveloped countries is *de facto* not a consequence of improved soil and higher yields, is so evident that there is no need to prove it. But the further subdivision of holdings is a fairly general phenomenon, and so is the gradual disuse of the traditional quality-maintenance measures. But is it possible not to see behind these phenomena the spreading of the big monocultural plantations and the growing of export crops?[16]

The question of natural resources is dealt with by several economists, *including* H. Myint, not as an absolute or relative plenty or poverty, but as the measure of the utilization of potentials (which theoretically may mean the utilization of mineral resources as well as soil potentials).[17] Myint indicates "underdevelopment of natural resources" (in connection with "backward people")[18] as one of the factors of underdevelopment.[19]

The term "underdeveloped resources" means, in fact, the underutilization of potential resources or the non-optimum allocation of the given resources to possible uses, i.e. "a species of deviation from the productive optimum." Thus the factor "unfavourable natural endowments" is replaced by the factor "underutilization of existing natural resources" (available perhaps in abundance) as a criterion of underdevelopment or obstacle to development. This is, no doubt, more realistic than the generalizing criterion of unfavourable natural endowments though it does not reveal more about the roots, the deep-lying causes of underdevelopment either. Here, too, quite a number of questions remain unanswered:

What is the yardstick by which the inadequate utilization of potential resources can be measured? What are the causes of underutilization? Why did even those colonial countries in which a part of the resources was exploited intensively—according to Meier perhaps even exhaustively—not achieve a higher level of development, i.e. the phase of "self-sustained growth."

NOTES AND REFERENCES

1. Latin America possesses one third of the total copper and iron resources of the world, one tenth of the crude oil, zinc, tin and lead resources, one sixth of the nickel and manganese resources, two fifths of the bauxite resources and stands first in the capitalist world production of 22 important minerals. In Africa, Ghana, Guinea and the Congo due to their rich bauxite resources could produce aluminium amounting to three times the quantity of the present world production. Zambia has one fourth of all the copper reserves and Gabon the second largest manganese ore deposit in the world, etc. India's iron ore reserves amount to about five or six times those of Britain or West Germany. The oil wealth of the Near East countries amounts to one fourth of the crude oil production of the capitalist world.

2. Africa's water power potential amounts to about 40-50 percent of the potential hydraulic power of the entire world. In Latin America there are immense areas of virgin land which could yield three crops annually if they were cultivated.

3. G. M. Meier and R. E. Baldwin, *Economic Development: Theory, History Policy* (New York, 1957), pp. 291–303.

4. G. M. Meier, "The Problem of Limited Economic Development," in G. M. Meier and R. E. Baldwin, eds., *The Economics of Underdevelopment*, p. 56.

5. The book of J. Barnett and C. Morse, *Scarcity and Growth, The Economics of Natural Resource Availability* (Johns Hopkins Press, Baltimore, 1963), set this problem in its proper light.

6. J. Tinbergen, *Lessons from the Past* (Elsevier Publishing Company, 1963), p. 85.

7. Ibid.

8. Ibid.

9. For further details see J. Woodis, *Africa, The Roots of Revolt* (London, 1961); *Economic Survey of Africa Since 1950* (U.N., 1958); W. A. Hunton, *Decision in Africa* (1956); and F. Fanon, *Les damnes de la terre* (Maspers, Paris, 1961).

10. "Little is known about how best to exploit and improve tropical soils." A. M. Kamarck, *The Economics of African Development* (F. A. Praeger, 1967), p. 92.

11. Ibid. p. 93.

12. Africa supplies, e.g. 82 per cent of the palm oil, 26 per cent of the groundnut, 64 per cent, meat 16 per cent, cotton 15 per cent, flax 25 per cent. (*Production Yearbook 1961*, Vol. world. (*Africa v tsifrah*. Moscow, 1963, p. 38.) The share of Latin America in the world production of sugar cane is 50 per cent, coffee 75 per cent, cocoa 30 per cent, bananas 67 per cent, meat 16 per cent, cotton 15 per cent, flax 25 per cent. (*Production Yearbook 1961*, Vol. 15, 1962).

13. B. Higgins, *Economic Development* (New York: W. W. Norton and Co., 1959), p. 273.

14. H. Leibenstein, *Economic Backwardness and Economic Growth* (New York, 1957), pp. 48–51.

15. Tamás Szentes, *The Political Economy of Underdevelopment* (Budapest: Akadémiai Kiadó, 1971), pp. 55–60.

16. Instances of and references to the harmful effects of monocultural plantation farming (depletion of land, increased sensitivity to plant diseases and insects) and its drawbacks, as opposed to traditional cultivation methods can be found in a great number of books, official reports and studies. See: Higgins, *Economic Development*, p. 270; Woddis, *Africa. The Roots of Revolt;* K. Brown, *Land in Southern Rhodesia* (London: Africa Bureau, 1959); *Special Study on Economic Conditions in Non-Self-Governing Territories* (U.N., 1958); and T. R. Batten, *Problems of African Development* (London, 1947), p. 54.

17. Viner, too, stresses the utilization of potentials when he defines the concept of

underdeveloped countries by declaring that an underdeveloped country is one "which has good *potential prospects* for using more capital or more labour or *more available natural resources,* to support its present population on a higher level of living or if its per capita income level is already fairly high to support a larger population on a not lower level of living." (*The Economics of Underdevelopment,* p. 12.)

18. In this context underdevelopment theories apply an interesting terminological distinction between the concepts "underdeveloped resources" and "backward people."

19. H. Myint, "An Interpretation of Economic Backwardness," in A. N. Agarwala and S. P. Singh, eds., *The Economics of Underdevelopment* (New York: Oxford University Press, 1963), pp. 93–96.

Additional Readings

Bryan, P. W. *Man's Adaption to Nature*. London: University of London Press, 1933.

Bryson, Reid A. and Murray, Thomas J. *Climates of Hunger*. Madison: University of Wisconsin Press, 1979.

Campbell, I. A. "Human Mismanagement as a Factor in the Sahelian Tragedy," *Ekistics*, 38 (1975): 26–30.

Chappell, J. E. Jr., "Climatic Change Reconsidered: Another Look at the Pulse of Asia," *Geographical Review*, 60 (1970): 347–373.

Eckholm, Erik P. *Losing Ground*. New York: W. W. Norton & Co., 1976.

Febvre, L. A. *Geographical Introduction to History*. London: Routledge & Kegan Paul, 1950.

Ginsburg, Norton. "Natural Resources and Economic Development," *Annals of the Association of American Geographers*, 47 (September 1957): 196–212.

Gourou, P. *The Tropical World: Its Social and Economic Conditions and Its Future Status*. New York: John Wiley, 1953.

Kamarck, Andrew M. *Climate and Economic Development*. New York: International Bank for Reconstruction and Development, 1972.

Lambert, L. D. "The Role of Climate in the Economic Development of Nations," *Land Economics*, 47, no. 4 (November 1974): 339–44.

Lewthwaite, G. R. "Environmentalism and Determinism: A Search for Clarification," *Annals of the Association of American Geographers*, 56 (1966): 1–23.

Matley, I. M. "The Marxist Approach to the Geographic Environment," *Annals of the Association of American Geographers*, 56 (1966): 97–111.

Owen, D. F. *Man in Tropical Africa: The Environmental Predicament*. New York: Oxford University Press, 1975.

Porter, P. W. "Environmental Potentials and Economic Opportunities: A Background for Cultural Adaptation," *American Anthropologist*, 67 (1965): 409–420.

Ridker, Ronald G. *Changing Resource Problems of the Fourth World*. New York: Resources for the Future by John Hopkins Press, 1976.

Semple, E. C. *The Influences of Geographic Environment*. New York: Henry Holt, 1911.

Spate, O. H. K. "Toynbee and Huntington: A Study in Determinism," *Geographical Journal*, 118 (1952): 406–428.

Tatham, G. "Environmentalism and Possibilism," in G. T. Taylor, ed., *Geography in the Twentieth Century*. London: Methuen, 1957.

Taylor, G. T. *Environment and Nation: Geographical Factors in the Cultural and Political History of Europe*. Toronto: University of Toronto Press, 1936.

Tosi, Joseph A. and Voertman, Robert F. "Some Environmental Factors in the Economic Development of the Tropics," *Economic Geography*, 40, no. 3 (July 1964): 189–205.

III

CULTURAL TRADITIONS

One of the world's oldest civilizations was located in Central America. The Mayans constructed elaborate cities with massive temples, while Europeans lived in the Dark Ages. Directed by foreign archaeologists, Mayan descendants in Mexico help to uncover their own past.

In Guatemala, Mayan Indians celebrate Easter. Roman Catholism has been grafted onto the indigenous culture. The sounds, smells, and materials in this procession are characteristic of what some anthropologists call the "Little Tradition." As Third World people give up their "traditional" religions for European ones, is their economic development facilitated? Why do they retain elements of their own culture? In Guatemala City, Easter is celebrated as it is in Spain. The "Great Tradition" is practiced by the European descendants who identify more with industrialized countries than with local Indian cultures. How would members of the Great Tradition explain poverty among the Indians?

Culture is *learned* behavior. People learn to eat only certain foods, dress in certain ways, speak in certain languages and dialects, assign various roles and statuses to women and men, and hold certain concepts about life and death. Social scientists frequently identify positive characteristics of culture to explain the development of the industrialized countries. Weber's concept of the Protestant work ethic to explain the rise of industrial capitalism in Western Europe is such an example. By contrast, social scientists commonly assign negative attributes of culture to explain Third World underdevelopment. They and the general public have often seized upon the example of India's sacred cattle to illustrate the irrationality of "backward" cultures.

Harris, however, shows systematically that contrary to popular belief the sacred cow concept in Hinduism protects small-scale farmers from starvation. The prohibition of slaughtering cows allows these farmers to use cattle as draught animals, as dung producers for fuel and fertilizer, as milk providers, and as sources of beef and hides for the untouchables and non-Hindus. Harris, a cultural anthropologist, finds the "sacred cow complex" a *rational* economic device.

Heston, an economist, argues that the sanctity of the cow for Hindus prevents the rational allocation of scarce agricultural resources. Contrary to Harris, he argues that the particular religious beliefs and practices of Hinduism cause backwardness. Interestingly the anthropologist rejects culture whereas the economist accepts culture as explaining India's population-resource problem.

Ryan's article critiques the conservative kind of argument made by Heston. When cultural or personal traits are used to explain social problems, Ryan labels such explanations "blaming the victim." Liberals are quick to point out the inadequacies of the conservative explanation which blames individuals for their own shortcomings. Accordingly, liberals see individuals largely as *victims* of their societal position, hence not totally responsible for their personal predicaments.

Dorfman and Mattelart analyze one of the most powerful media for inculcating cultural values in children and adults: comic books. Their analysis of Disney comics in Latin America shows that blaming Third World people for their cultural "backwardness" has been used to explain foreign intrusion, exploitation, and domination. When reading Dorfman and Mattelart, try to recognize examples of blaming the victim.

6 India's Sacred Cattle: Rational Management Under Hinduism

MARVIN HARRIS*

In this paper I attempt to indicate certain puzzling inconsistencies in prevailing interpretations of the ecological role of bovine cattle in India. My argument is based upon intensive reading—I have never seen a sacred cow, nor been to India. As a non-specialist, no doubt I have committed blunders an Indianist would have avoided. I hope these errors will not deprive me of that expert advice and informed criticism which alone can justify so rude an invasion of unfamiliar territory.

I have written this paper because I believe the irrational, non-economic, and exotic aspects of the Indian cattle complex are greatly overemphasized at the expense of rational, economic, and mundane interpretations.

My intent is not to substitute one dogma for another, but to urge that explanation of taboos, customs, and rituals associated with management of Indian cattle be sought in "positive-functioned" and probably "adaptive" processes of the ecological system of which they are a part, rather than in the influence of Hindu Theology.[1]

Mismanagement of India's agricultural resources as a result of the Hindu doctrine of *ahimsa*, especially as it applies to beef cattle, is frequently noted by Indianists and others concerned with the relation between values and behavior.[2] Although different anti-rational, dysfunctional, and inutile aspects of the cattle complex are stressed by different authors, many agree that *ahimsa* is a prime example of how men will diminish their material welfare to obtain spiritual satisfaction in obedience to nonrational or frankly irrational beliefs.

A sample opinion on this subject is here summarized: According to Simoons, "irrational ideologies" frequently compel men "to overlook foods that are abundant locally and are of high nutritive value, and to utilize other scarcer foods of less value."[3] The Hindu beef-eating taboo is one of Simoons' most important cases. Venkatraman claims, "India is unique in possessing an enormous amount

*Marvin Harris, "The Cultural Ecology of India's Sacred Cattle," *Current Anthropology,* 7, no. 1 (February 1966): 51–59. Reprinted by permission of author and The University of Chicago Press. Copyright 1966 The Wenner-Gren Foundation for Anthropological Research. In the original publication, comments were made about the article by Nirmal K. Bose, Morton Klass, Joan P. Mencher, Kalervo Oberg, Marvin K. Opler, Wayne Suttles, and Andrew P. Vayda, including a reply by the author.

of cattle without making profit from its slaughter."[4] The Ford Foundation reports "widespread recognition not only among animal husbandry officials, but among citizens generally, that India's cattle population is far in excess of the available supplies of fodder and feed. . . At least ⅓, and possibly as many as ½, of the Indian cattle population may be regarded as surplus in relation to feed supply."[5] Matson writes it is a commonplace of the "cattle question that vast numbers of Indian cattle are so helplessly inefficient as to have no commercial value beyond that of their hides."[6] Srinivas believes "Orthodox Hindu opinion regards the killing of cattle with abhorrence, even though the refusal to kill the vast number of useless cattle which exist in India today is detrimental to the nation."[7]

According to the Indian Ministry of Information, "The large animal population is more a liability than an asset in view of our land resources."[8] Chatterjee calculates that Indian production of cow and buffalo milk involves a "heavy recurring loss of Rs 774 crores. This is equivalent to 6.7 times the amount we are annually spending on importing food grains."[9] Knight observes that because the Hindu religion teaches great reverence for the cow, "there existed a large number of cattle whose utility to the community did not justify economically the fodder which they consumed."[10] Das and Chatterji concur: "A large number of cattle in India are old and decrepit and constitute a great burden on an already impoverished land. This is due to the prejudice among the Hindus against cow killing."[11] Mishra approvingly quotes Lewis: "It is not true that if economic and religious doctrines conflict the economic interest will always win. The Hindu cow has remained sacred for centuries, although this is plainly contrary to economic interest."[12] Darling asserts, "By its attitude to slaughter Hinduism makes any planned improvement of cattle-breeding almost impossible."[13] According to Desai, "The cattle population is far in excess of the available fodder and feeds."[14]

In the Report of the Expert Committee on the *Prevention of Slaughter of The Cattle in India,* the Cattle Preservation and Development Committee estimated "20 million uneconomic cattle in India."[15] Speaking specifically of Madras, Randhawa insists, "Far too many useless animals which breed indiscriminately are kept and many of them are allowed to lead a miserable existence for the sake of the dung they produce. Sterility and prolonged dry periods among cows due to neglect add to the number of superfluous cattle. . ."[16] Mamoria quotes with approval the report of the Royal Commission of Agriculture: ". . . religious susceptibilities lie in the way of slaughter of decrepit and useless cattle and hence the cattle, however weak and poor are allowed to live . . . bulls wander about the fields consuming or damaging three times as much fodder as they need. . . Unless the Hindu sentiment is adjured altogether the Indian cultivators cannot take a practical view of animal keeping and will continue to preserve animals many of which are quite useless from birth to death."[17] Despite his own implicit arguments to the contrary, Mohan concludes, "We have a large number of surplus animals."[18] The National Council of Applied Economic Research notes in Rajasthan: "The scarcity of fodder is aggravated by a large population old and useless cattle which share scant feed resources with working and useful cattle."[19]

The Food and Agriculture Organization reports, "In India, as is well-known, cattle numbers exceed economic requirements by any standard and a reduction in the number of uneconomic animals would contribute greatly to the possibilities of improving the quality and condition of those that remain."[20] Kardel reported to the International Cooperation Administration, "Actually, India's 180 million cattle and 87 million sheep and goats are competing with 360 million people for a scant existence."[21] According to Mosher, "There are thousands of barren heifers in the Central Doab consuming as much feed as productive cows, whose only economic produce will be their hides, after they have died of a natural cause."[22] Mayadas insists "Large herds of emaciated and completely useless cattle stray about trying to eke out an existence on wholly inadequate grazing."[23] Finally, to complete the picture of how, in India, spirit triumphs over flesh, there is the assertion by Williamson and Payne: "The . . . Hindu would rather starve to death than eat his cow."[24]

In spite of the sometimes final and unqualified fashion in which "surplus," "useless," "uneconomic," and "superfluous" are applied to part or all of India's cattle, contrary conclusions seem admissible when the cattle complex is viewed as part of an *eco-system* rather than as a sector of a national price market. Ecologically, it is doubtful that any component of the cattle complex is "useless," i.e., the number, type, and condition of Indian bovines do not per se impair the ability of the human population to survive and reproduce. Much more likely the relationship between bovines and humans is symbiotic instead of competitive.[25] It probably represents the outcome of intense Darwinian pressures acting upon human and bovine population, cultigens, wild flora and fauna, and social structure and ideology. Moreover presumably the degree of observance of taboos against bovine slaughter and beef-eating reflect the power of these ecological pressures rather than *ahimsa;* in other words, *ahimsa* itself derives power and sustenance from the material rewards it confers upon both men and animals. To support these hypotheses, the major aspects of the Indian cattle complex will be reviewed under the following headings: (1) Milk Production, (2) Traction, (3) Dung, (4) Beef and Hides, (5) Pastures, (6) Useful and Useless Animals, (7) Slaughter, (8) Anti-Slaughter Legislation, (9) Old-Age Homes, and (10) Natural Selection.

MILK PRODUCTION

In India the average yield of whole milk per Zebu cow is 413 pounds, compared with the 5,000-pound average in Europe and the U.S.[26] In Madhya Pradesh yield is as low as 65 pounds, while in no state does it rise higher than the barely respectable 1,455 pounds of the Punjab.[27] According to the 9th Quinquennial Livestock Census (1961) among the 47,200,000 cows over three years old, 27,200,000 were dry and/or not calved.[28]

These figures, however should not be used to prove that the cows are useless or uneconomic, since milk production is a minor aspect of the sacred cow's contribution to the *eco-system*. Indeed, most Indianists agree that it is the buffalo, not the Zebu, whose economic worth must be judged primarily by milk production. Thus, Kartha writes, "the buffalo, and not the Zebu, is the dairy cow."[29] This distinction is elaborated by Mamoria:

> Cows in the rural areas are maintained for producing bullocks rather than for milk. She-buffaloes, on the other hand, are considered to be better dairy animals than cows. The male buffaloes are neglected and many of them die or are sold for slaughter before they attain maturity.[30]

Mohan makes the same point:

> For agricultural purposes bullocks are generally preferred, and, therefore, cows in rural areas are primarily maintained for the production of male progeny and incidentally only for milk.[31]

It is not relevant to my thesis to establish whether milk production is a primary or secondary objective or purpose of the Indian farmer. Failure to separate emics from etics contributes greatly to confusion surrounding the Indian cattle question.[32] The significance of the preceding quotations lies in the agreement that cows contribute to human material welfare in more important ways than milk production. In this new context, the fact that U.S. cows produce 20 times more milk than Indian cows loses much of its significance. Instead, it is more relevant to note that, despite the marginal status of milking in the symbiotic syndrome, 46.7% of India's dairy products come from cow's milk.[33] How far this production is balanced by expenditures detrimental to human welfare will be discussed later.

TRACTION

The principle positive ecological effect of India's bovine cattle is in their contribution to production of grain crops, from which about 80% of the human calorie ration comes. Some form of animal traction is required to initiate the agricultural cycle, dependent upon plowing in both rainfall and irrigation areas. Additional traction for hauling, transport, and irrigation is provided by animals, but by far their most critical kinetic contribution is plowing.

Although many authorities believe there is an overall surplus of cattle in India, others point to a serious shortage of draught animals. According to Kothavala, "Even with . . . overstocking, the draught power available for land operations at the busiest season of the year in inadequate . . ."[34] For West Bengal, the National Council of Applied Economic Research reports:

> However, despite the large number of draught animals, agriculture in the State suffers from a shortage of draught power. There are large numbers of small landholders entirely dependent on hired animal labour.[35]

Spate makes the same point, "There are too many cattle in the gross, but most individual farmers have too few to carry on with."[36] Gupta and Lewis and Barnouw say a pair of bullocks is the minimum technical unit for cultivation, but in a survey by Diskalkar, 18% of the cultivators had only one bullock or none.[37] Nationally, if we accept a low estimate of 60,000,000 rural households and a high estimate of 80,000,000 working cattle and buffaloes,[38] we see at once that the allegedly excess number of cattle in India is insufficient to permit a large portion, perhaps as many as ⅓, of India's farmers to begin the agricultural cycle under conditions appropriate to their techno-environmental system.

Much has been made of India's having 115 head of cattle per square mile, compared with 28 per square mile for the U.S. and three per square mile for Canada. But what actually may be most characteristic of the size of India's herd is the low ratio of cattle to people. Thus, India has 44 cattle per 100 persons, while in the U.S. the ratio is 58 per 100 and in Canada, 90.[39] Yet, in India cattle are employed as a basic instrument of agricultural production.

Sharing of draught animals on a cooperative basis might reduce the need for additional animals. Chaudhri and Giri point out that the "big farmer manages to cultivate with a pair of bullocks a much larger area than the small cultivators."[40] But, the failure to develop cooperative forms of plowing can scarcely be traced to *ahimsa*. If anything, emphasis upon independent, family-sized farm units follows intensification of individual and tenure patterns and other property innovations deliberately encouraged by the British.[41] Under existing property arrangements, there is perfectly good economic explanation of why bullocks are not shared among adjacent households. Plowing cannot take place at any time of the year, but must be accomplished within a few daylight hours in conformity with seasonal conditions. These are set largely by summer monsoons, responsible for about 90% of the total rainfall.[42] Writing about Orissa, Bailey notes:

> As a temporary measure, an ox might be borrowed from a relative, or a yoke of cattle and a ploughman might be hired . . . but during the planting season, when the need is the greatest, most people are too busy to hire out or lend cattle.[43]

According to Desai:

> . . . over vast areas, sowing and harvesting operations, by the very nature of things, begin simultaneously with the outbreak of the first showers and the maturing of crops respectively, and especially the former has got to be put through quickly during the first phase of the monsoon. Under these circumstances, reliance by a farmer on another for bullocks is highly risky and he has got, therefore, to maintain his own pair.[44]

Dube is equally specific:

> The cultivators who depend on hired cattle or who practice cooperative lending and borrowing of cattle cannot take the best advantage of the first rains and this enforced wait results in untimely sowing and poor crops.[45]

Wiser and Wiser describe the plight of the bullock-short farmer as follows, "When he needs the help of bullocks most, his neighbors are all using theirs."[46] And Shastri points out, "Uncertainty of Indian farming due to dependence on rains is the main factor creating obstacles in the way of improvements in bullock labor."[47]

It would seem therefore, that this aspect of the cattle complex is not an expression of spirit and ritual, but of rain and energy.

DUNG

In India cattle dung is the main source of domestic cooking fuel. Since grain crops cannot be digested unless boiled or baked, cooking is indispensable. Considerable disagreement exists about the total amount of cattle excrement and its uses, but even the lowest estimates are impressive. An early estimate by Lupton gave the BTU equivalent of dung consumed in domestic cooking as 35,000,000 tons of coal or 68,000,000 tons of wood.[48] Most detailed appraisal is by National Council of Applied Economic Research, which rejects J. J. Bhabha's estimate of 131,000,000 tons of coal and the Ministry of Food and Agriculture's 112,000,000 tons. The figure preferred by the NCAER is 35,000,000 tons anthracite or 40,000,000 tons bituminous, but with a possible range of between 35–45,000,000 of anthracite dung-coal equivalent. This calculation depends upon indications that only 36% of the total wet dung is utilized as fuel, a lower estimate than any reviewed by Saha.[49] These vary from 40% (Imperial Council on Agricultural Research) to 50% (Ministry of Food and Agriculture) to 66.6% (Department of Education, Health and Lands). The NCAER estimate of a dung-coal equivalent of 35,000,000 tons is therefore quite conservative; it is nonetheless an impressive amount of BTU's to be plugged into an energy system.

Kapp, who discusses at length the importance of substituting tractors for bullocks, does not give adequate attention to finding cooking fuel after the bullocks are replaced.[50] The NCAER conclusion that dung is cheaper than coke seems an understatement.[51] Although it is claimed that wood resources are potentially adequate to replace dung the measures advocated do not involve *ahimsa* but are again an indictment of a land tenure system not inspired by Hindu tradition.[52] Finally, it should be noted that many observers stress the slow burning qualities of dung and its special appropriateness for preparation of *ghi* and deployment of woman-power in the household.[53]

As manure, dung enters the energy system in another vital fashion. According to Mujumdar, 300,000,000 tons are used as fuel, 340,000,000 tons as manure, and 160,000,000 tons "wasted on hillsides and roads."[54] Spate believes that 40% of dung production is spread on fields, 40% burned, and 20% "lost."[55] Possibly estimates of the amount of dung lost are grossly inflated in view of the importance of "roads and hillsides" in the grazing pattern (see Pasture). Similarly artificial and culture- or even class-bound judgments refer to utilization of India's night soil. It is usually assumed that Chinese and Indian treatment of this resource are radically different, and that vast quantities of nitrogen go unused in agriculture because of Hindu-inspired definitions of modesty and cleanliness. However, most human excrement from Indian villages is deposited in surrounding fields; the absence of latrines helps explain why such fields raise 2 and 3 successive crops each year.[56] More than usual caution, therefore, is needed before concluding that a significant amount of cattle dung is wasted. Given the conscious premium set on dung for fuel and fertilizer, thoughtful control maintained over grazing patterns (see Pasture), and occurrence of specialized sweeper and gleaner castes, much more detailed evidence of wastage is needed than is now available. Since cattle graze on "hillsides and roads," dung dropped there would scarcely totally be lost to the *eco-system*, even with allowance for loss of nitrogen by exposure to air and sunlight. Also, if any animal dung is wasted on roads and hillsides it is not because of *ahimsa* but of inadequate pasturage suitable for collecting and processing animal droppings. The sedentary, intensive rainfall agriculture of most of the subcontinent is heavily dependent upon manuring. So vital is this that Spate says substitutes for manure consumed as fuel "must be supplied, and lavishly, even at a financial loss to government."[57] If this is the case, then old, decrepit, and dry animals might have a use after all, especially when, as we shall see, the dung they manufacture employs raw materials lost to the culture-energy system unless processed by cattle, and especially when many apparently moribund animals revive at the next monsoon and provide their owners with a male calf.

BEEF AND HIDES

Positive contributions of India's sacred cattle do not cease with milk-grazing, bullock-producing, traction, and dung-dropping. There remains the direct protein contribution of 25,000,000 cattle and buffalo which die each year.[58] This feature of the *eco-system* is reminiscent of the East African cattle area where, despite the normal taboo on slaughter, natural deaths and ceremonial occasions are probably frequent enough to maintain beef consumption near the ecological limit with dairying as the primary function.[59] Although most Hindus probably do not consume beef, the *eco-system* under consideration is not confined to Hindus. The human population includes some 55,000,000 "scheduled" exterior or untouchable groups, many of whom will consume beef if given the opportunity, plus several million more Moslems and Christians.[60] Much of the flesh on the 25,000,000 dead cattle and buffalo probably gets consumed by human beings whether or not the cattle die naturally. Indeed, could it be that without the orthodox Hindu beef-eating taboo, many marginal and depressed castes would be deprived of an occasional, but nutritionally critical, source of animal protein?

It remains to note that the slaughter taboo does not prevent depressed castes from utilizing skin, horns and hoofs of dead beasts. In 1956 16,000,000 cattle hides were produced.[61] The quality of India's huge leather industry—the world's largest—leaves much to be desired, but the problem is primarily outmoded tanning techniques and lack of capital, not *ahimsa*.

PASTURE

The principle positive-functioned or useful contributions of India's sacred cattle to human survival and well-being have been described. Final evaluation of their utility must involve assessment of energy costs in terms of resources and human labor input which might be more efficiently expended in other activities.

Direct and indirect evidence suggests that in India men and bovine cattle do not compete for existence. According to Mohan:

> . . . the bulk of the food on which the animals subsist . . . is not the food that is required for human consumption, i.e., fibrous fodders produced as incidental to crop production, and a large part of the crop residues or by-products of seeds and waste grazing.[62]

On the contrary, "the bulk of foods (straws and crop residues) that are ploughed into the soil in other countries are converted into milk."[63]

> The majority of the Indian cattle obtain their requirements from whatever grazing is available from straw and stalk and other residues from human food-stuffs, and are starved seasonally in the dry months when grasses wither. . .
> In Bengal the banks and slopes of the embankments of public roads are the only grazing grounds and the cattle subsist mainly on paddy straw, paddy husks and . . . coarse grass . . .[64]

According to Dube, ". . . the cattle roam about the shrubs and rocks and eat whatever fodder is available there."[65] This is confirmed by Moomaw: "Cows subsist on the pasture and any coarse fodder they can find. Grain is fed for only a day or two following parturition."[66] The character of the environmental niche reserved for cattle nourishment is described by Gourou, based on data furnished by Dupuis for Madras:

> Il faut voir clairement que le faible rendement du bétail indien n'est pas un

gaspillage: ce bétail n'entre pas en concurrence avec la consommation de produits agricoles . . . ils ne leur sacrifient pas des surfaces agricoles, ou ayant un potential agricole.[67]

NCAER confines this pattern for Tripura: "There is a general practice of feeding livestock on agricultural by-products such as straw, grain wastes and husks;"[68] for West Bengal: "The state has practically no pasture or grazing fields, and the farmers are not in the habit of growing green fodders . . . livestock feeds are mostly agricultural by-products;"[69] and for Andhra Pradesh: "Cattle are stall fed, but the bulk of the feed consists of paddy straw. . . ."[70]

The only exceptions to the rural pattern of feeding cattle on waste products and grazing them on marginal or unproductive lands involve working bullocks and nursing cows:

> The working bullocks, on whose efficiency cultivation entirely depends, are usually fed with chopped bananas at the time of fodder scarcity. But the milch cows have to live in a semi-starved condition, getting what nutrition they can from grazing on the fields after their rice harvest.[71]
>
> At present cattle are fed largely according to the season. During the rainy period they feed upon the grass which springs up on the *uncultivated* hill-sides. . . . But in the dry season there is hardly any grass, and cattle wander on the *cropless* lands in an often half-starved condition. True there is some fodder at these times in the shape of rice-straw and dried copra, but it is not generally sufficient, and is furthermore given mainly to the animals actually *working* at the time.[72]

There is much evidence that Hindu farmers calculate carefully which animals deserve more food and attention. In Madras, Randhawa, et al. report: "The cultivators pay more attention to the male stock used for ploughing and for draft. There is a general neglect of the cow and the female calf even from birth . . ."[73] Similar discrimination is described by Mamoria:

> Many plough bullocks are sold off in winter or their rations are ruthlessly decreased whenever they are not worked in full, while milch cattle are kept on after lactation on poor and inadequate grazing . . . The cultivator feeds his bullocks better than his cow because it pays him. He feeds his bullocks better during the busy season, when they work, than during the slack season, when they remain idle. Further, he feeds his more valuable bullocks better than those less valuable . . . Although the draught animals and buffaloes are properly fed, the cow gets next to nothing of stall feeding. She is expected to pick up her living on the bare fields after harvest and on the village wasteland. . . .[74]

The previously cited NCAER report on Andhra Pradesh notes that "Bullocks and milking cows during the working season get more concentrates . . ."[75] Wiser and Wiser sum up the situation in a fashion supporting Srinivas' observation that the Indian peasant is "nothing if he is not practical";[76]

> Farmers have become skillful in reckoning the minimum of food necessary for maintaining animal service. Cows are fed just enough to assure their calving and giving a little milk. They are grazed during the day on lands which yield very little vegetation, and are given a very sparse meal at night.[77]

Many devout Hindus believe the bovine cattle of India are exploited without mercy by greedy Hindu owners. *Ahimsa* obviously has little to do with economizing which produces the famous *phooka* and *doom dev* techniques for dealing with dry cows. Not to Protestants but to Hindus did Gandhi address lamentations concerning the cow:

> How we bleed her to take the last drop of milk from her, how we starve her to emaciation, how we ill-treat the calves, how we deprive them of their portion of milk, how cruelly we treat the oxen, how we castrate them, how we beat them, how we overload them . . . I do not know that the condition of the cattle in any other part of the world is as bad as in unhappy India.[78]

USEFUL AND USELESS ANIMALS

How then, if careful rationing is characteristic of livestock management, do peasants tolerate the widely reported herds of useless animals? Perhaps "useless" means one thing to the peasant and quite another to the price-market-oriented agronomist. It is impossible at a distance to judge which point of view is ecologically more valid, but the peasants could be right more than the agronomists are willing to admit.

Since non-working and non-lactating animals are thermal and chemical factories which depend on waste lands and products for raw materials, judgment that a particular animal is useless cannot be supported without careful examination of its owner's household budget. Estimates from the cattle census which equate useless with dry or non-working animals are not convincing. But even if a given animal in a particular household is of less-than-marginal utility, there is an additional factor whose evaluation would involve long-range bovine biographies. The utility of a particular animal to its owner cannot be established simply by its performance during season or an animal cycle. Perhaps the whole system of Indian bovine management is alien to costing procedures of the West. There may be a kind of low-risk sweepstakes which drags on for 10 or 12 years before the losers and winners are separated.

As previously observed, the principal function of bovine cows is not their milk-producing but their bullock-producing abilities. Also established is the fact that many farmers are short of bullocks. Cows have the function primarily to produce male offspring, but when? In Europe and America, cows become pregnant under well-controlled, hence predictable, circumstances and a farmer with many animals, can count on male offspring in half the births. In India, cows become pregnant under quite different circumstances. Since cows suffer from malnutrition through restriction to marginal pasture, they conceive and deliver in unpredictable fashion. The chronic starvation of the inter-monsoon period makes the cow, in the words of Mamoria, "an irregular breeder."[79] Moreover, with few animals, the farmer may suffer many disappointments before a male is born. To the agriculture specialist with knowledge of what healthy dairy stock look like, the hot weather herds of walking skeletons "roaming over the bare fields and dried up wastes" must indeed seem without economic potential.[80] Many of them, in fact, will not make it through to the next monsoon. However, among the survivors are an unknown number still physically capable of having progeny. Evidently neither the farmer nor the specialist knows which will conceive, nor when. To judge from

Bombay city, even when relatively good care is bestowed on a dry cow, no one knows the outcome: "If an attempt is made to salvage them, they have to be kept and fed for a long time. Even then, it is not known whether they will conceive or not."[81]

In rural areas, to judge a given animal useless may be to ignore the recuperative power of these breeds under conditions of erratic rainfall and unpredictable grazing opportunities. The difference of viewpoint between the farmer and the expert is apparent in Moomaw's incomplete attempt to describe the life history of an informant's cattle. The farmer in question had 3 oxen, 2 female buffaloes, 4 head of young cattle and 3 "worthless" cows.[82] In Moomaw's opinion, "The three cows . . . are a liability to him, providing no income, yet consuming feed which might be placed to better use." Yet we learn, "The larger one had a calf about once in three years:" moreover 2 of the 3 oxen were "raised" by the farmer himself. (Does this mean that they were the progeny of the farmer's cows?) The farmers tells Moomaw, "The young stock get some fodder, but for the most part they pasture with the village herd. The cows give nothing and I cannot afford to feed them." Whereupon Moomaw's *non sequitur:* "We spoke no more of his cows, for like many a farmer he just keeps them, without inquiring whether it is profitable or not."[83]

The difficulties in identifying animals that are definitely uneconomic for a given farmer are reflected in the varying estimates of the total of such animals. The Expert Committee on the Prevention of Slaughter of Cattle estimated 20,000,000 uneconomic cattle in India.[84] Roy settles for 5,500,000, or about 3.5%.[85] Mamoria, who gives the still lower estimate of 2,900,000, or 2.1%, claims most of these are males.[86] A similarly low percentage—2.5%—is suggested for West Bengal.[87] None of these estimates appears based on bovine life histories in relation to household budgets; none appears to involve estimates of economic significance of dung contributions of older animals.

Before a peasant is judged a victim of Oriental mysticism, might it not be well to indicate the devastating material consequences which befall a poor farmer unable to replace a bullock lost through disease, old age, or accident? Bailey makes it clear that in the economic life of the marginal peasantry, "Much of the most devastating single event is the loss of an ox (or a plough buffalo)."[88] If the farmer is unable to replace the animal with one from his own herd, he must borrow money at usurious rates. Defaults on such loans are the principal causes of transfer of land titles from peasants to landlords. Could this explain why the peasant is not overly perturbed that some of his animals might turn out to be only dung-providers? After all, the real threat to his existence does not arise from animals but from people ready to swoop down on him as soon as one of his beasts falters. Chapekar's claim that the peasant's "stock serve as a great security for him to fall back on whenever he is in need" would seem to be appropriate only in reference to the unusually well-established minority.[89] In a land where life expectancy at birth has only recently risen to 30 years, it is not altogether appropriate to speak of security.[90] The poorest farmers own insufficient stock. Farm management studies show that holdings below ⅔ of average area account for ⅖ of all farms, but maintain only ¼ of the total cattle on farms. "This is so, chiefly because of their limited resources to maintain cattle."[91]

SLAUGHTER

Few, if any, Hindu farmers kill their cattle by beating them over the head, severing their jugular veins or shooting them. But to assert that they do not kill their animals when it is economically important for them to do so may be equally false. This interpretation escapes the notice of so many observers because the slaughtering process receives recognition only in euphemisms. People will admit that they "neglect" their animals, but will not openly accept responsibility for the *etic* effects, i.e., the more or less rapid death which ensues. The strange result of this euphemistic pattern is evidenced in the following statement by Moomaw: "All calves born, however inferior, are allowed to live until they die of neglect."[92] In the light of many similar but, by Hindu standards, more vulgar observations, it is clear than this kind of statement should read, "Most calves born are not allowed to live, but are starved to death."

This is roughly the testimony of Gourou, "Le paysan conserve seulement les veaux qui deviendront boeufs de labour ou vaches laitières; les autres sont écartés . . . et meurent d'epuisement."[93] Wiser and Wiser are even more direct:

Cows and buffaloes too old to furnish milk are not treated cruelly, but simply allowed to starve. The same happens to young male buffaloes. . . . The males are unwanted and little effort is made to keep them alive.[94]

Obviously, when an animal, undernourished to begin with, receives neither food nor care, it will not enjoy a long life.[95] Despite claims that an aged and decrepit cow "must be supported like an unproductive relative, until it dies a natural death,"[96] ample evidence justifies the belief that "few cattle die of old age."[97] Dandekar makes the same point: "In other words, because the cows cannot be fed nor can they be killed, they are neglected, starved and left to die a 'natural' death."[98]

The farmer culls his stock by starving unwanted animals and also, under duress, sells them directly or indirectly to butchers. With economic pressure, many Indians who will not kill or eat cows themselves:

are likely to compromise their principles and sell to butchers who slaughter cows, thereby tacitly supporting the practice for other people. Selling aged cows to butchers has over the centuries become an accepted practice alongside the *mos* that a Hindu must not kill cattle.[99]

Determining the number of cattle slaughtered by butchers is almost as difficult as determining the number killed by starvation. According to Dandekar, "Generally it is the useless animals that find their way to the slaughter house."[100] Lahiry says only 126,900 or .9% of the total cattle population is slaughtered per year.[101] Darling claims:

All Hindus object to the slaughter and even to the sale of unfit cows and keep them indefinitely . . . rather than sell them to a cattle dealer, who would buy only for the slaughter house, they send them to a *gowshala* or let them loose to die. Some no doubt sell secretly, but this has its risks in an area where public opinion can find strong expression through the *panchayat*.[102]

Such views would seem to be contradicted by Sinha: "A large number of animals are slaughtered privately and it is very difficult to ascertain their numbers."[103] The difficulty of obtaining accurate estimates is also implied by the comment of the Committee on the Prevention of Slaughter that "90% of animals not approved for slaughter are slaughtered stealthily outside of municipal limits."[104]

An indication of the propensity to slaughter cattle under duress is found in connection with the food crisis of World War II. With rice imports cut off by Japanese occupation of Burma, increased consumption of beef by the armed forces, higher prices for meat and foodstuffs generally, and famine conditions in Bengal, the doctrine of *ahimsa* proved to be alarmingly ineffectual.[105] Direct military intervention was required to avoid destruction of animals needed for plowing, milking, and bullock-production:

> During the war there was an urgent need to reduce or to avoid the slaughter for food of animals useful for breeding or for agricultural work. For the summer of 1944 the slaughter was prohibited of: 1) Cattle below three years of age; 2) Male cattle between two and ten years of age which were being used or were likely to be used as working cattle; 3) All cows between three and ten years of age, other than cows which were unsuitable for bearing offspring; 4) All cows which were pregnant or in milk.[106]

Gourou, aware that starvation and neglect are systematically employed to cull Indian herds, nonetheless insists that destruction of animals through starvation amounts to an important loss of capital.[107] This loss is attributed to the low price of beef caused by the beef-eating taboo, making it economically infeasible to send animals to slaughter. Gourou's appraisal, however, neglects deleterious consequences to the rural tanning and carrion-eating castes if increased numbers of animals went to the butchers. Since the least efficient way to convert solar energy into comestibles is to impose an animal converter between plant and man,[108] it should be obvious that without major technical and environmental innovations or drastic population cuts, India could not tolerate a large beef-producing industry. This suggests that insofar as the beef-eating taboo helps discourage growth of beef-producing industries, it is part of an ecological adjustment which maximizes rather than minimizes the calorie and protein output of the productive process.

ANTI-SLAUGHTER LEGISLATION AND GOWSHALAS

It is evident from the history of anti-slaughter agitation and legislation in India that more than *ahimsa* has been required to protect Indian cattle from premature demise. Unfortunately, this legislation is misinterpreted and frequently cited as evidence of the anti-economic effect of Hinduism. I am unable to unravel all the tangled economic and political interests served by the recent anti-slaughter laws of the Indian states. Regardless of the ultimate ecological consequences of these laws, however, several points deserve emphasis. First it should be recalled that cow protection was a major political weapon in Ghandi's campaign against both British and Moslems. The sacred cow was the ideological focus of a successful struggle against English colonialism; hence the enactment of total anti-slaughter legislation obviously had a rational base, at least among politicians who seized and retained power on anti-English and anti-Moslem platforms. It is possible that the legislation will now backfire and upset the delicate ecological balance which now exists. The Committee on the Prevention of Slaughter claimed that it actually saw in Pepsu (where slaughter is banned completely) what a menace wild cattle can be. Conditions have become so desperate there, that the State Government have got to spend a considerable sum for catching and redomesticating wild animals to save the crops.[109]

According to Mayadas:

The situation has become so serious that it is impossible in some parts of the country to protect growing crops from grazing by wandering cattle. Years ago it was one or two stray animals which could either be driven off or sent to the nearest cattle pound. Today it is a question of contantly being harrassed day and night by herds which must either feed on one's green crops, or starve. How long can this state of affairs be allowed to continue?[110]

Before the deleterious effects of slaughter laws can be properly evaluated, certain additional evolutionary and functional possibilities must be examined. For example, given the increasing growth rate of India's human population, the critical importance of cattle in the *eco-system,* and the absence of fundamental technical and environmental changes, a substantial increase in cattle seems necessary and predictable, regardless of slaughter legislation. Furthermore, there is some indication, admittedly incomplete but certainly worthy of careful inquiry, that many who protest most against destructiveness of marauding herds of useless beasts may perceive the situation from very special vantage points in the social hierarchy. The implications of the following newspaper editorial are clear:

The alarming increase of stray and wild cattle over wide areas of Northern India is fast becoming a major disincentive to crop cultivation . . . Popular sentiment against cow slaughter no doubt lies at the back of the problem. People prefer to let their aged, diseased, and otherwise useless cattle live at the expense of *other people's crops.*[111]

Evidently we need to know something about whose crops are threatened by these marauders. Despite post-Independence attempts at land reform, 10% of the Indian agricultural population still owns more than ½ the total cultivated area and 15,000,000, or 22%, of rural households own no land at all.[112] Thorner and Thorner call the land reform program a failure, and point out how "the grip of the larger holder serves to prevent the lesser folk from developing the land . . ."[113] Quite possibily, in other words, the anti-slaughter laws, insofar as they are effective, should be viewed as devices which, contrary to original political intent, bring pressure to bear upon those whose lands are devoted to cash crops of benefit only to narrow commercial, urban, and landed sectors of the population. To have one's cows eat other people's crops may be a very fine solution to the subsistence problem of those with no crops of their own. Apparently, in the days when animals could be driven off or sent to the pound with impunity, this could not happen, even though *ahimsa* reigned supreme then as now.

Some form of anti-slaughter legislation was required and actually argued for, on unambiguously rational, economic, and material grounds. About 4% of India's cattle are in the cities.[114] These have always represented the best dairy stock, since the high cost of feeding animals in a city could be offset only by good milking qualities. A noxious consequence of this dairy pattern was the slaughter of the cow at the end of its first urban lactation period because it was too expensive to maintain while awaiting another pregnancy. Similarly, and by methods previously discussed, the author calf was killed after it had stimulated the cow to "let down." With the growth of urban milk consumption, the best of India's dairy cattle were thus systematically prevented from breeding, while animals with progressively poorer milking qualities were preserved in the countryside.[115] The Committee on the Prevention of Slaughter of Cattle claimed at least 50,000 high-yielding cows and she-buffaloes from Madras, Bombay, and Calcutta were "annually sent to premature slaughter" and were "lost to the country."[116] Given such evidence of waste and the political potential of Moslems being identified as cow-butchers and Englishmen as cow-eaters, the political importance of *ahimsa* becomes more intelligible.[117] Indeed, it could be that the strength of Gandhi's *charisma* lay in his superior understanding of the ecological significance of the cow, especially in relation to the underprivileged masses, marginal low caste and out caste farmers. Gandhi may have been closer to the truth than many a foreign expert when he said:

> Why the cow was selected for apotheosis is obvious to me. The cow was in India the best companion. She was the giver of plenty. Not only did she give milk but she also made agriculture possible.[118]

OLD-AGE HOMES

Among the more obscure aspects of the cattle complex are bovine old-age homes, variously identified as *gowshalas, pinjrapoles,* and, under the Five-Year Plans, as *gosadans.* Undoubtedly some of these are "homes for cows, which are supported by public charity, which maintain the old and derelict animals till natural death occurs."[119] According to Gourou, however, owners of cows sent to these religious institutions pay rent with the understanding that if the cows begin to lactate they will be returned.[120] The economics of at least some of these "charitable" institutions is, therefore, perhaps not as quaint as usually implied. It is also significant that, although the First Five-Year Plan called for establishment of 160 *gosadans* to serve 320,000 cattle, only 22 *gosadans* servicing 8,000 cattle were reported by 1955.[121]

NATURAL SELECTION

Expert appraisers of India's cattle usually show little enthusiasm for the typical undersized breeds. Much has been made of the fact that one large animal is a more efficient dung, milk, and traction machine than two small ones. "Weight for weight, a small animal consumes a much larger quantity of food than a bigger animal."[122] "More dung is produced when a given quantity of food is consumed by one animal than when it is shared by two animals."[123] Thus it would seem that India's smaller breeds should be replaced by larger, more powerful, and better milking breeds. But once again, there is another way of looking at the evidence. It might very well be that if all of India's scrub cattle were suddenly replaced by an equivalent number of large, high-quality European or American dairy and traction animals, famines of noteworthy magnitude would immediately ensue. It is not possible that India's cattle are undersized precisely because other breeds never could survive the atrocious conditions they experience most of the year? I find it difficult to believe that breeds better adapted to the present Indian *eco-system* exist elsewhere.

> By nature and religious training, the villager is unwilling to inflict pain or to take animal life. But the immemorial grind for existence has hardened him to an acceptance of survival of the fittest.[124]

Not only are scrub animals well adapted to the regular seasonal crises of water and forage and general year-round neglect, but long-range selective pressures may be even more significant. The high frequency of drought-induced famines in India places a premium upon drought-resistance plus a more subtle factor: A herd of smaller animals dangerously thinned by famine or pestilence, reproduces faster than an equivalent group of larger animals, despite the fact that the larger animal consumes less per pound than two smaller animals.[125] This is because there are two cows in the smaller herd per equivalent large cow. Mohan is one of the few authorities to have grapsed this principle, including it in defense of the small breeds:

> Calculations of the comparative food conversion efficiency of various species of Indian domestic livestock of the writer has revealed, that much greater attention should be paid to small livestock than at present, not only because of their better conversion efficiency for protein but also because of the possibilities of bringing about a rapid increase in their numbers.[126]

CONCLUSION

The probability that India's cattle complex is a positive-functioned part of a naturally selected *eco-system* is at least as good as that it is a negative-functioned expression of an irrational ideology. This should not be interpreted to mean that no "improvements" can be made in the system, nor that different systems may not eventually evolve. The issue is not whether oxen are more efficient than tractors. I suggest simply that many features of the cattle complex have been erroneously reported or interpreted. That Indian cattle are weak and inefficient is not denied, but there is doubt that this situation arises from and is mainly perpetuated by Hindu ideology. Given the techno-environmental base, Indian property relationships, and political organization, one need not involve the doctrine of *ahimsa* to understand fundamental features of the cattle complex. Although the cattle population of India has risen by 38,000,000 head since 1940, during the same period, the human population has risen by 120,000,000. Despite the anti-slaughter legislation, the ratio of cattle to humans actually declined from 44:100 in 1941 to 40:100 in 1961.[127] In the absence of major changes in environment, technology or property relations, it seems unlikely that the cattle population will cease to accompany the rise in the human population. If *ahimsa* is negative-functioned, then we must be prepared to admit the possibility that all other factors contributing to the rapid growth of the Indian human and cattle populations, including the germ theory of disease, are also negative-functioned.

NOTES AND REFERENCES

1. The author (1960) suggested that the term "adaptive" be restricted to traits, biological or cultural, established and diffused in conformity with the principle of natural selection. Clearly, not all "positive-functioned," i.e., useful, cultural traits are so established.

2. *Ahimsa* is the Hindu principle of unity of life, of which sacredness of cattle is principal sub-case and symbol.

3. F. J. Simmons, *Eat Not This Flesh* (Madison: University of Wisconsin Press, 1961), p. 3.

4. R. B. Venkatraman, "The Indian Village, Its Past, Present, Future," *Agriculture and Livestock in India* (1938), p. 706.

5. Ford Foundation, *Report on India's Food Crises and Steps to Meet It* (New Delhi: Government of India, Ministry of Food and Agriculture and Ministry of Community Development and Cooperation, 1959), p. 64.

6. J. Matson, "Inefficiency of Cattle In India through Disease," *Agriculture and Livestock in India,* 1 (1933), p. 227.

7. M. N. Srinivas, *Religion and Society Among the Coorgs of South India* (Oxford: Oxford University Press, 1952), p. 222.

8. Government of India, *India* (New Delhi: Ministry of Information and Broadcasting, 1957), p. 243.

9. I. Chatterjee, "Milk Production in India," *Economic Weekly* (1960), pp. 1347–1348.

10. Henry Knight, *Food Administration in India, 1939–47* (Stanford: Stanford University Press, 1954), p. 1941.

11. A. B. Das and M. N. Chatterji, *The Indian Economy* (Calcutta: Bookland Private, 1962), p. 120.

12. W. A. Lewis, *The Theory of Economic Growth* (Homewood, Ill.: R. D. Irwin, 1955), p. 105.

13. M. L. Darling, *Wisdom and Waste in a Punjab Village* (London: Oxford University Press, 1934), p. 158.

14. M. D. Desai, "India's Food Crises," *The Indian Journal of Agricultural Economics,* 14 (1959): 36.

15. P. N. Nandra, et al., *Report of the Expert Committee on the Prevention of Slaughter of Cattle in India* (New Delhi: Government of India Press, 1955), p. 62.

16. M. S. Randhawa, et al., *Farmers of India,* 2 vols. (New Delhi: Indian Council of Agricultural Research, 1961), p. 118.

17. C. B. Mamoria, *Agricultural Problems of India* (Allahabad: Kitab Mahal, 1953), pp. 268–269.

18. S. N. Mohan, "Animal Husbandry in the Third Plan," *Bulletin of National Institute of Sciences of India,* 20 (1962): 54.

19. National Council of Applied Economic Research, *Techno-Economic Survey of Rajasthan* (New Delhi, 1963), p. 51.

20. Food and Agriculture Organization, *Agriculture in Asia and the Far East: Development and Outlook* (Rome: FAO, 1953), p. 109.

21. Hans Kardel, *Community Development in Agriculture: Mysore State, India* (Washington D.C.: International Cooperation Administration, 1956), p. 19.

22. Arthur T. Mosher, *The Economic Effect of Hindu Religion and Social Traditions on Agricultural Production by Christians in North India.* Ph.D. dissertation (University of Chicago, 1946), p. 124.

23. C. Mayadas, *Between Us and Hunger* (London: Oxford University Press, 1954), p. 28.

24. G. Williamson and W. J. A. Payne, *An Introduction to Animal Husbandry in the Tropics* (London: Longmans Green, 1959), p. 137.

25. F. E. Zeuner, "Domestication of Animals," in *A History of Technology,* ed. C. Singer, et al., pp. 327–52 (New York: Oxford University Press, 1954), p. 328.

26. K. P. R. Kartha, "A Note on the Comparative Economic Efficiency of the Indian Cow, the Half Breed Cow, and the Buffalo as Producers of Milk and Butter Fat," *Agriculture and Livestock in India,* 4 (1936): 607. The U.S. Census of Agriculture (1954) showed milk production averaging from a low of 3,929 pounds per cow in the Nashville Basin sub-region to 11,112 pounds per cow in the Southern California sub-region.

27. I. Chatterjee, "Milk Production in India," p. 1347.
28. S. C. Chaudhri and R. Giri, "Role of Cattle in India's Economy," *Agricultural Situation in India,* 18 (1963): 598.
29. K. P. R. Kartha, "Buffalo" in *An Introduction to Animal Husbandry in the Tropics,* ed. G. Williamson and W. J. A. Payne (London: Longmans, Green, 1959), p. 225.
30. C. B. Mamocia, *Agricultural Problems of India,* p. 255.
31. S. N. Mohan, "Animal Husbandry in the Third Plan," *Bulletin of the National Institute of Sciences of India,* 20 (1962): 47.
32. Marvin Harris, *The Nature of Cultural Things* (New York: Random House, 1964).
33. I. Chatterjee, "Milk Production in India," p. 1347.
34. Zal R. Kothavalia, "Milk Production in India," *Agriculture and Livestock in India* (1934), p. 122.
35. National Council of Applied Economic Research, *Techno-Economic Survey of West Bengal* (New Delhi, 1962), p. 56.
36. Oskar Hermann Spate, *India and Pakistan: A General and Regional Geography* (London: Methuen, 1954), p. 36.
37. S. C. Gupta, *An Economic Survey of Shamaspur Village* (New York: Asia Publishing House, 1959), p. 42; Oscar Lewis and Victor Barnouw, *Village Life in Northern India* (Urbana: University of Illinois Press, 1958), p. 102; and P. D. Diskalkar, *Resurvey of a Deccan Village Pimple Sandagar* (Bombay: The Indian Society of Agricultural Economics, 1960), p. 87.
38. Ashok Mitra, "Tax Burden for Indian Agriculture," in *Traditions, Values, and Socio·Economic Development,* ed. R. Braibanti and J. J. Spengler (Durham: Duke University Press, 1963), p. 298, and Government of India, *Statistical Abstract of the Indian Union,* 11 (Cabinet Secretariat, New Delhi, 1967), p. 76.
39. C. B. Mamoria, *Agricultural Problems of India,* p. 256.
40. S. C. Chaudhri and R. Giri, "Role of Cattle in India's Economy," p. 596.
41. B. M. Bhatia, *Famines in India* (New York: Asia Publishing House, 1963), p. 18ff.
42. Ibid., p. 4.
43. F. G. Bailey, *Caste and the Economic Frontier* (Manchester: University of Manchester Press, 1957), p. 74.
44. M. B. Desai, *The Rural Economy of Gujarat* (Bombay: Oxford University Press, 1948), p. 86.
45. S. C. Dube, *Indian Village* (Ithaca: Cornell University Press, 1955), p. 84.
46. William H. Wiser and C. V. Wiser, *Behind Mud Walls: 1930-1960* (Berkeley: University of California Press, 1963), p. 62.
47. C. P. Shastri, "Bullock Labour Utilization in Agriculture," *Economic Weekly,* 12 (1960): 1592.
48. Arnold Lupton, *Happy India* (London: G. Allen and Unwin, 1922), p. 60.
49. National Council of Applied Economic Resarch, *Domestic Fuels in India* (New York: Asia Publishing House, 1959), pp. 3 and 14; and M. N. Saha, "Fuel in India," *Nature,* 177 (1956): 923.
50. K. W. Kapp, *Hindu Culture, Economic Development and Economic Planning in India* (New York: Asia Publishing House, 1963), p. 144ff.
51. National Council of Applied Economic Research, *Domestic Fuel in India,* p. 20.
52. Ibid., p. 20 ff and P. C. Bansil, *India's Food Resources and Population* (Bombay: Vora, 1958), p. 97ff.
53. Lewis and Barnouw, *Village Life in Northern India,* p. 40, and Mosher, *The Economic Effect of Hindu Religion and Social Traditions on Agricultural Production by Christians in North India,* p. 153.
54. N. A. Mujumdar, "Cow Dung as Manure," *Economic Weekly,* 12 (1960): 743.
55. Spate, *India and Pakistan: A General and Regional Geography,* p. 238.
56. Mosher, *The Economic Effect of Hindu Religion and Social Traditions on Agricultural Production by Christians in North India,* pp. 154 and 33, and Bansil, *India's Food Resources and Population,* p. 104.
57. Spate, *India and Pakistan: A General and Regional Geography,* p. 239.
58. Mohan, "Animal Husbandry in the Third Plan," *Bulletin of the National Institute of Sciences of India,* p. 54.

59. Harold Schneider, "The Subsistence Role of Cattle Among the Pakot and in East Africa," *American Anthropologist*, 59 (1957): 278ff.

60. J. H. Hutton, *Caste in India* (London: Oxford University Press, 1961), p. vii, and Dube, *Indian Village*, pp. 68–69.

61. M. S. Randhawa, *Agriculture and Animal Husbandry in India* (New Delhi: Indian Council of Agricultural Research, 1962), p. 322.

62. Mohan, "Animal Husbandry in the Third Plan," p. 43 ff.

63. Ibid., p. 45.

64. Mamoria, *Agricultural Problems of India,* pp. 263–264.

65. Dube, *Indian Village,* p. 84.

66. I. W. Moomaw, *The Farmer Speaks* (London: Oxford University Press, 1949), p. 96.

67. Pierre Gourou, "Civilization et economie pastorale," *L'Homme* (1963), p. 123, and J. Dupuis, *Madras et le nord du coromandel; etude des conditions de la vie indienne dans un cadre geografigue* (Paris: Maisonneuve, 1960).

68. National Council of Applied Economic Research, *Techno-Economic Survey of Tripura* (New Delhi, 1961), p. 57.

69. National Council of Applied Economic Research, *Techno-Economic Survey of West Bengal,* p. 59.

70. National Council of Applied Economic Research, *Techno-Economic Survey of Andhra Pradesh* (New Delhi, 1962), p. 52.

71. N. Gangulee, *The Indian Peasant and His Environment* (London: Oxford University Press, 1935), p. 17.

72. Adrian Mayer, *Land and Society in Malabar* (Bombay: Oxford University Press, 1952), p. 70, italics added.

73. Randhawa et al., *Farmers of India,* p. 117.

74. Mamoria, *Agricultural Problems of India,* p. 263ff.

75. National Council of Applied Economic Research, *Techno-Economic Survey of Andhra Pradesh,* p. 52.

76. Srinivas, "India's Cultural Values and Economic Development," *Economic Development and Cultural Change,* p. 4.

77. Wiser and Wiser, *Behind Mud Walls,* p. 71.

78. M. K. Gandhi, *How to Serve the Cow,* ed. Bharaton Kumarappa (Ahmedabad: Navajivan Publishing House, 1954), p. 7.

79. Mamoria, *Agricultural Problems of India,* p. 263.

80. Martin H. Leake, *The Foundations of Indian Agriculture* (Cambridge: W. Heffer, 1923), p. 267.

81. Nandra, *Slaughter of Cattle in India,* p. 9.

82. Moomaw, *The Farmer Speaks,* p. 23.

83. Ibid., p. 25.

84. Nandra, et al., *Slaughter of Cattle in India,* p. 62.

85. Prodipto Ray, "The Sacred Cow in India," *Rural Sociology,* 20 (1955): 14.

86. Mamoria, *Agricultural Problems of India,* p. 257.

87. National Council of Applied Economic Research, *Techno-Economic Survey of West Bengal,* p. 56.

88. Bailey, *Caste and the Economic Frontier,* p. 73.

89. L. N. Chapekar, *Thakurs of the Sabyachi* (Oxford: Oxford University Press, 1960), p. 27.

90. John D. Black, "Supplementary to the Ford Foundation Team's Report: India's Food Crises and Steps to Meet it," *The Indian Journal of Agricultural Economics,* 14 (1959): 2.

91. Chaudhri and Giri, "Role of Cattle in India's Economy," p. 598.

92. Moomaw, *The Farmer Speaks,* p. 96.

93. Gourou, "Civilization et economie pastorale," p. 125.

94. Wiser and Wiser, *Behind Mud Walls,* p. 70.

95. Gourou, "Civilization et economie pastorale," p. 124.

96. Mosher, *The Economic Effect of Hindu's Religion and Social Traditions on Agricultural Production by Christian in North India,* p. 124.

97. Bailey, *Caste and the Economic Frontier,* p. 75. Srinivas (*Caste in Modern India,* New York: Asia Publishing House, 1962, p. 126.) declared himself properly skeptical in this matter: "It is commonly believed that the peasant's religious attitude to cattle comes in the

way of the disposal of useless cattle. Here again, my experience of Rampura makes me skeptical of the general belief. I am not denying that cattle are regarded as in some sense sacred, but I doubt whether the belief is as powerful as it is claimed to be. I have already mentioned that bull-buffaloes are sacrificed to village goddesses. And in the case of the cow, while the peasant does not want to kill the cow or bull himself he does not seem to mind very much if someone else does the dirty job out of his sight."

98. U. M. Dandekar, "Problem of Numbers in Cattle Development," *Economic Weekly,* 16 (1964): 352.

99. Roy, "The Sacred Cow in India," p. 15.

100. Dandekar, "Problem of Numbers in Cattle Development," p. 35.

101. N. L. Lahiry, "Conservation and Utilization of Animal Food Resources," in Proceedings of Symposium on Food Needs and Resources, *Bulletin of the National Institute of Sciences of India,* 20 (n.d.): 140.

102. Darling, *Wisdom and Waste in a Punjab Village,* p. 158.

103. R. R. Sinkha, *Food in India* (London: Oxford University Press, 1961), p. 95.

104. Nandra, et al., *Slaughter of Cattle in India,* p. 11.

105. Shri Thirumalai, *Post-War Agricultural Problems and Policies in India* (New York: Institute of Pacific Relations, 1954), p. 38, and Bhatia, *Famines in India,* p. 309 ff.

106. Knight, *Food Administration in India,* p. 141.

107. Gourou, "Civilization et economie pastorale," pp. 124–125.

108. Fred Cottrell, *Energy and Society* (New York: McGraw-Hill, 1955).

109. Nandra, et al., *Slaughter of Cattle in India,* p. 11.

110. Mayadas, *Between Us and Hunger,* p. 29.

111. *Indian Express* (New Delhi, February 7, 1959), italics added.

112. Mitra, "Tax Burden for Indian Agriculture," p. 298.

113. Daniel Thorner and Alice Thorner, *Land and Labour in India* (New York: Asia Publishing House, 1962), p. 3.

114. Mohan, "Animal Husbandry in the Third Plan," p. 48.

115. Ibid.; Mayadas, *Between Us and Hunger,* p. 29; and Gandhi, *How to Serve the Cow,* p. 13 ff.

116. Nandra, et al., *Slaughter of Cattle in India,* p. 2.

117. Gandhi, *How to Serve the Cow,* p. 16.

118. Ibid., p. 3.

119. Kothavala, "Milk Production in India," p. 123.

120. Gourou, "Civilization et economie pastorale," p. 125.

121. Government of India, *Second Five-Year Plan.* Planning Commission (New Delhi, 1956), p. 283.

122. Mamoria, *Agricultural Problems of India,* p. 268.

123. Ford Foundation, *Report on India's Food Crisis and Steps to Meet It,* p. 64.

124. Wiser and Wiser, *Behind Mud Walls.*

125. Bhatia, *Famines in India.*

126. Mohan, "Animal Husbandry in the Third Plan," p. 45.

127. Government of India, *Statistical Abstract of the India Union,* p. 74, and Government of India, *India* (New Delhi: Ministry of Information and Broadcasting, 1963), p. 6.

7 India's Sacred Cattle: Irrational Management Under Hinduism

ALAN HESTON*

The large cattle population of India has long interested travelers, social reformers, district officers, commissions of inquiry, orthodox Hindus, nonvegetarians, and the Editors of *Life*. To many, reverence for the cow is the "one thing" that has led to the impoverishment of India (though to others the "one thing" is land fragmentation, caste, use of ghi, or, recently, human population). While most Western observers and many Indians view the cattle population as excessive, expert groups, like the Ford Foundation team, have argued that any policy must take account of the strong religious attitudes which have affected the cow population.[1] In contrast, Harris has made a strong attack on both the view that cattle are in excess and the view that religious attitudes towards cattle are useful in explaining characteristics of the Indian cattle population.[2] Harris attempts to show that, viewed in the large context of the balance between cattle, land and crops, and humans, most features of the cow population in India can be explained in terms of adjustment to their environment. To him, the "cultural ecology of India's sacred cattle" does not appear out of balance.[3]

Although he argues that India's cattle economy is in ecological balance, Harris vehemently denies that this balance produces optimal results.[4] Evolutionary development in Indian agriculture, he asserts, will lead to better uses of cattle. He does not deny, however, and apparently affirms, that the Indian cattle population is the best possible configuration under present conditions. If his argument is an empirical assertion about the Indian economy, then he must consider the possibility that alternative cattle complexes might exist under present conditions; that the present cattle population might be in some way poorly adapted to the environment and the goals of Indians; and that the present population might be explained in part by religion. If for Harris there is one and only one adaptation of the cattle population to present ecological conditions, then of course his is not an empirical assertion, since the circumstances under which it would be false can never be realized. While much of Harris' discussion sounds deterministic, and indeed he

*Alan Heston, "An Approach to the Sacred Cow of India," *Current Anthropology*, 12, no. 2 (April 1971): 191–197. Reprinted by permission of author and The University of Chicago Press. Copyright 1971 by The Wenner-Gren Foundation for Anthropological Research. In the original publication, comments were made about the article by John W. Bennett, James W. Hamilton, Marvin Harris, Michael M. Horowitz, Joan Mencher, Moni Nag, Manning Nash, H. K. Schneider, and Imre Wellmann, including a reply by the author.

says that it is, I cannot accept this interpretation.[5] It would, for one thing, make his article unnecessary, since there could never have been doubt about whether the Indian cattle population was in balance. Secondly, it would leave no grounds upon which economists and cultural ecologists could carry on discussion; and since I feel that they have much to learn from each other I would like to believe that there is a basis for a meaningful exchange of ideas.

My own approach to the cattle question in India is an economic one and is, I believe, more useful than that of Harris. What Harris does is find that for most aspects of the Indian cattle population there are sensible explanations that do not need to fall back on custom or religion. Most of these observations, while not generally wrong, are either not specific enough or not relevant to the question of whether the cattle population is in excess. An illustration of the lack of specificity is the fact that Harris makes no real attempt to discuss the relative numbers of males and females, which, as I will show, is at the center of the problem. The lack of relevance of most of Harris' remarks is due to his particular framework. It is perfectly possible that individual peasants are sensible in their handling of cattle and that the sum of their individual actions nevertheless adds up to a poor allocation of cattle for the economy as a whole. Since Harris does not look at the specific facts at the farm level, let alone the overall figures for India, he is evidently led to believe that because the peasant has reasons for what he does with cattle, the existing number of cattle is appropriate for present conditions.

The approach of the economist to the question is to ask whether alternative cattle populations (or alternative uses of the resources embodied in the population) under the present rural conditions could increase the satisfaction of the society.[6] I argue that in India, if cow slaughter were allowed, the cattle population could be substantially reduced, the output of the cattle could be increased, and land would be freed for production of other crops. Further, I show that even with no cow slaughter at all (this is not a part of Harris' argument; he apparently believes that the appropriate number are slaughtered), the cattle allocation under existing institutions could be improved by presently known methods. As a part of this presentation I also show that the present Indian cattle complex appears to be definitely influenced by the Indian tradition of *ahimsa* (nonviolence) and the Hindu reverence for the cow.

I

Cattle, while producing power, milk, and other products, are also competitors with humans for land. If cattle did not compete for land or other resources with man or with other productive animals (as may be the case in hilly tracts), they could not be in excess from the economic point of view. On this point Harris makes what I think is a major misinterpretation of the Indian scene. He says: "Direct and indirect evidence suggests that in India men and bovine cattle do not compete for existence."[7] He goes on to say that most cattle feed in India comes from grain by-products, for which the alternative is not human consumption but, at best, mulch. He points out, further, that many of India's scrawniest cattle are not fed at all, but are left to chew stubble remaining in the field or otherwise scrounge for their feed. Harris notes that for the individual cultivator it may make sense to let females, which might possibly breed sometime, scrounge for their feed. It costs the peasant nothing, and the gains are some dung, a hide, and perhaps a work animal—or the cow might perchance be hit by a car, and the driver, Indian or foreigner, made to compensate the owner for the loss of such a valuable animal.

While none of what Harris says about feed and use of waste products by cattle is wrong, it does not follow that cattle do not compete with humans. India devotes 5% of her acreage to fodder crops. Feed for all livestock was valued in 1958–59 at Rs. 5.74 billion. Stalks, straw, husk, sugarcane tufts, and bran represented slightly more than half of this amount, Rs. 2.93 billion.[8] These feeds are by-products of grain, sugar, and other crops, and while they have alternative uses, including export, they are not directly consumed by humans. The remaining feed is fodder crops, cereals, pulses, and concentrates that directly use land that could be planted to crops for human consumption. In addition, several rotations of Indian crops include grains with a large amount of feed by-products—because people will pay for rice bran or jowar grass. The value of the milk and power of bullocks and cows justifies spending money to feed some fraction of the cattle population, but another significant proportion is left to graze where it can. Because pasture for grazing is in short supply, many of the animals left to themselves die off, though not from old age.

If a large fraction of the cattle population were not allowed to graze freely but were somehow (to be discussed below) removed, there would be more cattle feed available to the remaining cattle. Less land would be needed for fodder crops, and hence more land would be available for human uses. It is in this sense that the cattle population compete with the human population. It is not that the marginal cow is eating feed that humans want, but that she eats feed that other productive animals could eat, and these latter animals are using resources, like fodder acreage, in direct competition with humans. However, competition of cattle with man for land need not imply that the cattle population is in excess; to deal with this question we must turn to a discussion of cattle, both male and female.

II

The cow in India is worshipped as a symbol of warmth and moisture, as earth mother, and as producer of milk and indirectly ghi, so essential in sacrifices. She is also protected because of the principle of nonviolence to living things (*ahimsa*). The Indian respect for the cow has many specific characteristics, but also shows similarities to beliefs found in some African societies, where cattle are sometimes called the "gods with the wet noses."[9] Though cow protection in India refers to the "cow and her progeny," and Nanda and other bulls are important minor deities, there are additional sanctions which single out the female cow for special consideration. *Go*, "cow," refers to both male and female, but when a Hindu says, "*Go hamārie mātā hai*," he is likening the female cow, not the bull or bullock, to our mother. The special consideration shown females, which as we shall see, are in excess if any cattle are, is illustrated by the slaughterhouse statistics. In 1958–59, for example, 122,000 bullocks and only 10,000 cows were slaughtered in Maharashtra State.[10] Even if sex is grossly misreported, this shows less reluctance to slaughter, or report the slaughter of, the economically valuable bullock than the cow. Similarly, in 1952–53, of the licensed slaughterhouses in

Uttar Pradesh none could slaughter youngstock, one could slaughter cows, and five could slaughter bullocks.[11]

The Indian buffalo is not considered sacred. Rather, to the ardent cow protectionist the buffalo is a target for criticism because the female is a better milker than the cow. Both cattle and buffaloes adapt to most of the subcontinent, though their relative distribution is uneven, depending in part on local breeds and the type of agricultural work to be done. The male buffalo is used as a work animal, particularly in wet paddy cultivation, except in eastern India and East Pakistan [Bangladesh]. He is also adaptable to heavy tasks like pressing bales of hay or turning a wheel. However, the bullock is the predominant work animal, because he can do dry and wet ploughing and pull a cart. In India in 1956, 88.4% of the working cattle and buffaloes were bullocks, 2.6% cows, and 9% buffaloes (90% of these male), while in Pakistan buffaloes account for under 6% of the bovine work animals. For milk, however, the buffalo is often preferred. Thus for all of India in 1956, buffaloes were 14% of all cattle and buffaloes, but buffaloes in milk were as much as 37% of all female cattle and buffaloes. Since the average yield of milk per buffalo is about double that of cows, buffaloes provide India over half its milk.[12]

Because the buffalo is a better milker, there is discrimination against the cow. Table 7.1, which gives the age and sex distribution of cattle in India for the last two censuses, shows the effects of this discrimination. In the age groups up to three years, the ratio of the sexes is about equal; after that, the ratio of females to males declines markedly. If there were no discrimination among the sexes, we would expect the ratio of females over three to males over three to be 1.0. Only in Rajasthan, Jammu and Kashmir, Himachal Pradesh, and Kerala, however, does this ratio exceed 1.0, whereas for all India it was .77 in 1956.[13] Ironically, the state

---

Table 7.1   Indian Cattle Population, 1956 and 1961, by Age and Sex[a] (figures in millions)

	1961	1956
Cattle over three years	126.7	114.8
Males	72.5	64.9
Females	54.2	49.9
Youngstock one to three years old	25.9	23.0
Males	12.3	11.2
Females	13.6	11.8
Youngstock under one year	22.9	20.8
Males	11.5	10.5
Females	11.4	10.3

[a]Figures for 1956 are from the *Indian Livestock Census, 1956, Vol. 1: Summary Tables* (New Delhi: Economic and Statistical Adviser to the Government of India, Directorate of Economics and Statistics, Ministry of Food and Agriculture, 1960); figures for 1961 are from Chaudhuri and Girl (S.C. Chaudhuri and R. Giri, "Role of Cattle in India's Economy," *Agricultural Situation in India,* Vol. 18 (1963), pp. 591-599). The two sets of figures are not strictly comparable, the increase from 1956 to 1961 being probably in part due to improved coverage. The National Sample Survey (No. 25: *Sample Verification of Livestock Census: 1956.* Delhi: The Cabinet Secretariat, Government of India, 1960) conducted a sample verification of the 1956 census and found that total cattle were under-reported by 3.7%, total males by 4.4%, though cows in milk were over-estimated somewhat.

with the lowest ratio of females to males, .49, is Uttar Pradesh, which generates the most rhetoric about cow protection but apparently neglects them most. (It can be assumed that the low ratio is explained not by export or import of cattle or slaughter, but by neglect of females and their premature death.)

Given the desire to preserve cows, a major dilemma is posed in the areas where both buffaloes and cows can thrive. The peasant wants bullocks and female buffaloes; or, to put the matter negatively, cows are needed principally to produce bullocks, and male buffaloes are needed even less. A commonly offered solution to this problem is to breed cows that are better milkers. This, for example, was a hope of the Gosamvardhan (cow protection) Enquiry Committee of Uttar Pradesh in 1955 in its discussion "Cow versus Buffalo."[14] But even if the cow were to become the preferred milker, there would remain, as Dandekar has so clearly pointed out a problem of numbers in Indian cattle development.[15]

The problem is this: To stay in milk, a cow must calve every one or two years, so that in her lifetime a cow with normal feeding would produce, say, six adults. If only two-thirds of the adult females (a low rate) could successfully breed, each adult female and male would be replaced by four ($\frac{2}{3} \times 6$) new adults, a doubling of the cattle population every 10–15 years. (India has clearly not allowed this situation.) If it is desired to maintain a given number of bullocks, the ratio of adult breeding females to bullocks must be one-third or less. That is, two of every three females born must (1) never reach maturity, or (2) never reproduce, if allowed to mature. This particular case, which is an equilibrium of sorts, I would like to refer to as the *stationary bullock solution*. If it should be desired to maintain a bullock population of 300 and at the same time to have more than 100 females, say 150, as milch animals, there would be even more surplus animals to be disposed of; for 150 females in milk will produce 450 males and 450 females, resulting in 150 extra males and 300 extra females.

If, on the other hand, the main purpose of the cattle population is milk production (and here I assume, contrary to fact for India, that the cow is the superior milker, for if only milk were desired, India could just use the buffalo), then 100 milk cows, who must be breeding, will produce 300 males, an excess of 500 animals, give or take a prize bull or two. Under the *stationary milch cow solution*, typical of countries using considerable mechanical power in agriculture, the surplus animals are usually bred for slaughter. If slaughter is unacceptable, tremendous conflict results, since five of every six cattle are surplus and competing for scarce food.

India sits somewhere between these two extremes, allowing most adult females to procreate, as in the stationary milch cow case, but desiring a given stock of bullocks for agricultural work. The problem of numbers is inevitable, then, even without the buffalo. It might be argued that the competition of the buffalo as a milker leads to more neglect of cows and therefore less progeny, creating less conflict over surplus cattle than would otherwise exist. A final point about our examples: if it is desired that the cattle population grow each year the situation is not basically changed, though it is eased the higher the growth rate desired.

III

In what sense is the Indian cattle population in excess? Let us consider first the case in which the slaughter of females is culturally acceptable and the goal is to maintain a given stock of bullocks, as in the stationary bullock solution. India has excess cattle in the sense that the present adult population of 72.5 million would require for maintenance only 24 million breeding females, as opposed to the actual 54 million. The extra 30 million females could be slaughtered or, as is now being suggested, exported to other countries without reducing the output of milk and other products; for one cow fed on the feed that would keep two cows alive produces more than twice the milk, more than twice the dung, and probably a hide of more value than the hides of two poorly fed cows.

The argument here is in part based on the fact that larger animals use feed more efficiently. Harris has argued against applying this idea to Indian cattle on the grounds that emaciated Indian breeds may be particularly well adapted in their metabolism to scrounging for feed.[16] No evidence is offered for this. Evidence is available, on the other hand, for the position taken here. Estimated responses of milk yield to increased feeding are given for 12 milk production areas in different parts of India by Whyte and Mathur.[17] Milk yield per lactation for a cow is held to vary from 750 to 3,000 lbs. with various combinations of concentrates, green fodder, and hay. In general, milk yield rises proportionately or more than proportionately with feed. For example, in the Maharashtra Deccan, milk yield doubles (from 1,000 to 2,000 lbs. per lactation) when groundnut cake and other concentrates rise 50% (from 800 to 1,200 lbs. per year) and when green fodder and hay rise 70% (from 19,200 to 32,500 lbs. per year).[18] This means that one cow will produce a given amount of milk for less feed than it would take to maintain two cows that together would produce the same amount of milk. Furthermore, during youth and periods not in milk, one well-fed cow will require even less feed than that. Dung output will probably be higher from the one cow. The quality of the hide might also be improved, since it depends partly on timely removal from the animal and better-fed animals tend to be skinned sooner than neglected ones. If slaughter were allowed, then, or cattle were exported, India could have all the products it now has (except the presence of those slaughtered) and free land for other uses. All of this could be done with existing breeds of cattle.

Thus far, I have argued that the number of cattle in India is in excess because there are more females than necessary to maintain the present (and, I assume, needed) male population and to produce the present milk, hide, and dung supply. I have further shown that extra cattle are a real cost to the economy because the use of land for cattle feed competes with alternative human uses. In other words, and still assuming slaughter is culturally acceptable, there are alternative cattle populations that would better use India's resources, given the present technology. Or, in Harris' terms, the cultural ecology of India's sacred cattle is not in balance.

Let us turn to the more realistic case, namely that a significant group within Indian society values positively the presence of cows and negatively their slaughter. Harris has argued that the sacredness of Indian cattle is not important in explaining the Indian cattle population; I shall argue that he is wrong here. The case I now discuss assumes, contrary to Harris, that cattle are valued in part as pets, so that one cannot summarily slaughter 30 million cows and leave Indian welfare unchanged. The following exercise will in part show that the present cattle population of India is in excess in terms of "the system's own objectives."[19]

These objectives could be better served by allowing fewer cattle to be born. The institutions for this control exist in many localities: all but breeding males are castrated, and the service of bulls can be, and often is regulated. The advantage of lowering cattle births is that the feed now used to support those cattle which eventually die of starvation could be transferred to milking and work cattle.

The practice of allowing surplus cattle to starve to death is reflected in Table 7.1, which shows, in addition to high mortality of females after age three, high mortality among the youngstock of both sexes. Rather than being close to double the number of cattle under one year, the number in the one- to three-year age group is just slightly greater, indicating that almost half the one-year-olds die in the next two years. I suspect that the age reporting may produce some of this high mortality, since it seems surprising that females in the one- to three-year age group exceed males, only to drop so drastically after age three. However, the general pattern of high mortality of youngstock of both sexes occurs in all states and territories, and the high mortality of females after three years occurs in most states, lending broad support to this pattern.

In Figure 7.1, the broken line indicates the age and sex distribution of cattle that would be necessary to maintain the bullock population at the 1961 figure, 70 million, under the assumption of no slaughter or neglect of females. I estimate that the maintenance of this population would require that 8 million males (and 8 million females) be born each year. Assuming adequate feed for these cattle (though the 30 or so million breeding or working females would, of course, get more feed than the 35 million or so idle adult females), the number of males and females at all ages would be the same, as is indicated by the solid line.

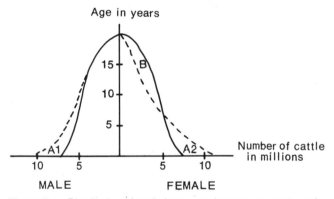

Figure 7.1　Distribution of cattle by age and sex necessary to maintain the bullock population at the 1961 figure, 70 million, assuming no slaughter or neglect of females, with adequate feed for all cattle (solid line) and without it (broken line). Since there is no data on the year-by-year age distribution of cattle in India and not much is known about mortality at a given level of food intake at various ages, the distribution is conjectural; it is based on what is known about the age and sex distribution of Indian cattle (shown in Table 7.1) and on some crude demographic considerations.

The area within the solid line, representing the model population, may be contrasted with the area within the broken line. As drawn—and again I emphasize the conjectural nature of the figure—there are three areas of overlap, labeled A1, A2, and B. In A1 and A2, the model population is less than the actual population, indicating that at present there is an excess of cattle births and very high mortality in the early years. In area B, the model population exceeds the actual population, because the model does not allow females to die prematurely of neglect and starvation.

Under the model regime, the cattle in areas A1 and A2 would not need to be fed. On the other hand, since the model regime provides green pastures, or at least a maintenance ration for nonbreeding and nonworking adult females, the cows in area B would require feed (and yield welfare) beyond that at present. Would enough feed be freed by the cattle in areas A1 and A2 to provide for the cattle in area B, allowing for the fact that many of the former are young and require less feed than the latter? Assuming that the ration for animals in area A1 and A2 is 60% of that of nonworking and nonbreeding females in area B, it would seem that the answer is yes, and further that there would be feed left over for use by cattle in all age classes. The 60% figures is calculated on the basis of data from a survey conducted by Panse, Singh, and Murty, which shows that milk cows consume 23 lbs. of fodder per day, cows not in milk 14 lbs. per day, and youngstock about 8 lbs. per day, and the fact that there are 13 to 14 million animals in area B compared to about 25 million in areas A1 and A2 taken together.[20]

This means that with its present feed, India could support a cattle population that better fulfilled its objectives of better feeding the existing cattle population and feeding all adults. Since dung production from one animal weighing 500 lbs. is greater than from two animals each weighing 250 lbs. and requires less feed, the model population in the figure produces more organic manure and fuel. As discussed earlier, milk production too would tend to be higher, and hide quality would be improved. This exercise, then, has suggested a regime in which, with the present use of resources, India could have more physical output from its cattle without slaughter and without neglect of useless cattle. Such a regime would operate to improve welfare.

IV

While a religious belief may sanction or be consistent with a set of practices, it need not be seen as *explaining* those practices where other explanations—such as rational self-interest—are available. This view is consistent with the idea that religious belief is a projection of the social structure and practices of a society. Morris has examined the Hindu value system in this respect and found that, contrary to Weberian tradition, religion and values were unnecessary as an explanatory device for, or were even at odds with, the reality of economic change in India in the 19th century.[21] In this context one might argue, as does Harris, that one need not have recourse to the beliefs of Hindus in explaining the cattle complex of India. This argument against invoking religion as an explanatory variable might be extended to the 1966–67 demonstrations and agitation against cow slaughter in New Delhi and elsewhere. These demonstrations might be considered as political, not religious, movements employing certain convenient symbols. In this view cow slaughter was one of a number of symbols that could be used against those in power; the fact that it was chosen over the others is unimportant.

I maintain, nevertheless, that the composition of the cattle population of India is affected by the high regard given to the cow by Hindus, Jains, and other groups in

India. If my view is correct, we can expect that if one of two adjacent areas with similar physical environments has a large number of Hindus, it will have a higher ratio of adult female to adult male cattle. India and Pakistan naturally recommend themselves as suitable areas for testing this hypothesis, because in Pakistan the proportion of Hindus is very low, and in India very high. I shall compare parts of East Pakistan with Assam and West Bengal, West Punjab with East Punjab, and Sind with Rajasthan and Gujarat. The test is not as simple as it may at first appear, because the proportion of female to male cattle also varies with other factors, including the use of females for work and the extent to which an area exports cattle.[22]

In the comparison of the predominantly Muslim Chittagong and Dacca Divisions of East Pakistan with the State of Assam, we are faced with three problems. First, in these East Pakistan areas adult female (3.37 million) outnumber adult male cattle (2.98 million) because female animals are used for work (1.77 million females work versus 1.60 million milch). In the previous section I did not consider the case in which the female is a work animal, and indeed this is not the usual case in the subcontinent. But where it is possible the problem of cattle slaughter or neglect need rarely arise.[23] Second, the feed situation for cattle is very much better in Assam than other areas so there is less likelihood that the excess females will die in early adulthood. Finally, Assam is not in the mainstream of movements for cow protection because of its very heterogeneous population and fairly independent past. Thus, although in the Muslim areas of East Pakistan the ratio of females to males is 1.13 while in Assam the ratio is .93, this seems best explained by the use in East Pakistan of the female as a work animal, and does not bear on the issue of religion and cattle.

Similarly, in West Bengal adult females are .82 of adult males, while in the Rajshahi and Khulna Divisions of East Pakistan the figure is .96, but the main reason is that in Rajshahi and Khulna 30% of the adult females are used as work animals, while only 1% are so used in West Bengal. One might argue that use of females as work animals is in itself evidence that Muslims use their cattle more rationally than Hindus. I know of no evidence that would confirm or negate this argument. Of using female cattle as work animals, the *Indian Livestock Census* of 1956 says,

> Cows are generally not put under yoke. For reasons of economy this is, however, done in areas where milk yield is very poor. The largest number of such cows is found in Madras (558 thousand) followed by Bihar and Mysore with 300 thousand and 267 thousand respectively.[24]

My source for Pakistan, the 1960 Agricultural Census, does not discuss the subject.[25] My own conclusion is that comparisons of Assam and West Bengal with East Pakistan offer no evidence bearing on religion and the cattle complex, though they raise questions of the circumstances in which the female will be used for work.

In the western portion of the subcontinent, on the other hand, the comparison produces remarkably clear results. In the predominantly Muslim districts in West Pakistan bordering on East Punjab we find that the adult females total only .33 of adult male cattle, while in Hindu and Sikh East Punjab adult females are .76 of the adult male cattle.[26] Although both divisions of the Punjab have been leading areas of growth for India and Pakistan, and the Punjabi farmer, whether Hindu, Muslim, or Sikh, is noted as a rational sort, there appears to be only one explanation of the high proportion of female cattle in East Punjab: the Hindu regard for the cow. This comparison is the more convincing when we contrast individual adjacent districts in Pakistani and Indian Punjab. In all Pakistani districts the ratio of female to male adult cattle is lower than its Indian counterpart and lower than in any district in East Punjab.

A comparison of Sind districts of West Pakistan with equivalent districts in Rajasthan and Gujarat yields similar results.[27] The Sind-Rajasthan comparison is not as helpful as it might be because the Rajasthan districts of Barmer, Bikaner, Ganganagar, Jaisalmer, and Jodpur all export cattle, and would be expected to have more adult female than adult male cattle for that reason alone.[28] A better comparison is provided by the Sind districts, where adult females are .60 of adult males, and the Rajkot division of Gujarat, where adult females are .79 of adult males. Even stronger support for the hypothesis may be seen in the fact that two of the Sind districts involved, Thatta and Tharparkar (the name is also a cattle breed), are famous for the cattle they export. Thus beliefs about cow slaughter in Gujarat seem a reasonable explanation for the higher ratio of female to male cattle in Gujarat than in Sind.

V

I have provided evidence that the sanctity of the cow for Hindus is a belief that is useful in explaining the composition of the Indian cattle population. I have argued that to the extent that India does try both to prevent cow slaughter and to produce livestock products it does not do so very well. I have said that changes within the present institutions of rural India could produce more output than is now obtained from the resources devoted to cattle. If we are willing to follow Harris and ignore the sanctity of the cow, then the Indian cattle complex is even more decidedly out of balance. In supporting the use of traditional economic analysis, it has not been my intention to deny either the contributions of cultural ecology or its comparative advantage in dealing with some problems of peasant and other economies.[29] However, I would also insist that the traditional tools of economic analysis will provide for certain problems—including the sacred cattle of India—at least as useful a framework.

NOTES AND REFERENCES

1. Ford Foundation *Report on India's Food Problem and Steps to Meet It* (New Delhi: Government of India, Ministry of Food and Agriculture and Ministry of Community Development and Cooperation, 1959).

2. Marvin Harris, "The Cultural Ecology of India's Sacred Cattle," *Current Anthropology*, 7 (1966): 51–60.

3. Harris' article received a number of responses; I have relied on several of these, particularly that of Bennett (John W. Bennett, "On the Cultural Ecology of India Cattle," *Current Anthropology*, 8 (1967): 251–252). I also acknowledge a large intellectual debt to Brown (W. Norman Brown, "The Sanctity of the Cow in Hinduism," *Economic Weekly* (Bombay), 16 (1964): 245–255) for his doctrinal article on the cow, to Dandikar (V. M. Dandikar, "Problem of Numbers in Cattle Development," *Economic Weekly* (Bombay), 16 (1964): 351–356) for his paper on what might be called cow economics, and to Arnold Green for very useful comments on an earlier draft of the paper.

4. Marvin Harris, reply to: "On the Cultural Ecology of Indian Cattle," by John W. Bennett, *Current Anthropology,* 8 (1967): 252–253.

5. Marvin Harris, *The Rise of Anthropological Theory* (New York: T. Y. Crowell, 1968).

6. Satisfaction here is measured by the money value of goods and services produced in a given time period. Clearly, in treating cattle in India the outputs should go beyond power, milk, and hides, since part of the production is the presence of cows themselves. Conventionally, for instance, the output of pets and zoos, in the United States can only be approximated by the expenditure on cat food, fish tanks, zoo keepers, etc. With productive animals, however, the cost of their feed is customarily subtracted from the gross value of milk and other agricultural products to arrive at output net of the cost of maintaining milk and work animals. To the extent that cattle are also maintained partly as pets, the value of their presence, as approximated by the cost of their feed, might be included in national income, contrary to present practice.

7. Marvin Harris, "The Cultural Ecology of India's Sacred Cattle," p. 55.

8. Government of India, *National Income Statistics. Proposals for a Revised Series of National Income Estimates for 1955–56 to 1959–60* (New Delhi: Central Statistical Organization, Department of Statistics, Government of India, 1961), pp. 61–63.

9. H. M. Southworth and E. F. Johnson, eds., *Agricultural Development and Economic Growth* (Ithaca: Cornell University Press, 1967), p. 217. Although one associates the sacred cow with India, it is doubtful whether the like of the Indian peasant is nearly as involved with cattle as the life of an African Pastoralist. Judging by the accounts of Evans-Pritchard (E. E. Evans-Pritchard. *The Nuer.* Oxford: Oxford University Press, 1940) or Dupire (Marguerite Dupire, "The Fulani—Peripheral Markets of a Pastoral People," in *Markets in Africa,* ed. Paul Bohannan and George Dalton. Garden City: Doubleday, 1965, pp. 93–129), for example, cattle play a much larger role in Africa than in India.

10. Dandekar, "Problem of Numbers in Cattle Development," (Bombay) p. 35.

11. Government of Uttar Pradesh, *Report of the Gosamvardhan Enquiry Committee* (Allahabad: Animal Husbandry, State of Uttar Pradesh, 1955), p. 38.

12. The National Sample Survey (National Sample Survey. *Sample Verification of Livestock Census* (Delhi: The Cabinet Secretariat, Government of India, 1960) No. 25, p. 24.) estimates production of buffalo milk at 29,000 tons and cow milk at 20,000 tons per day, though other estimates put cow milk relatively higher. Per animal, the daily yield of buffaloes is around twice that of a cow, but they lactate more days; buffaloes are estimated to produce 1,018 lbs. of milk per lactation, and cows 428 lbs. (Ibid., p. 11) Estimates of profitability vary widely by region, but usually the most per pound of buffalo milk (which usually commands a slightly higher price per pound) is less than that of cow milk. It is often argued that improvements in treatment of cows could improve their yield to compete with the buffalo, but it is not clear in these comparisons whether the conditions, such as feed, of the buffalo are also a change. Chatterjee (I. Chatterjee, "Towards a Single Species Cattle Economy," *Agricultural Situation in India,* 17 (1962): 764–784) and Chaudhuri and Giri (S. C. Chaudhuri and R. Giri, "The Role of Cattle in India's Economy," *Agricultural Situation in India,* 18 (1963): 591–599.)

13. Adult females exceed males in Rajasthan probably because it is a cattle-exporting area. In mountainous areas like Jammu and Kashmir and Himachal Pradesh, the noncultivated area is sufficient to allow all cattle enough pasture.

14. Government of Uttar Pradesh, *Report of the Gosamvardhan Enquiry Committee,* pp. 10–15.

15. V. M. Dandekar, "Problem of Numbers in Cattle Development."

16. Marvin Harris, "The Cultural Ecology of India's Sacred Cattle," p. 59.

17. R. O. Whyte and M. L. Mathur. *The Planning of Milk Production in India* (Calcutta: Orient Longmans, 1968), pp. 155–212.

18. Ibid., pp. 192–93.

19. Bennett, "On the Cultural Ecology of Indian Cattle."

20. While I think these calculations are reasonable, it is not essential to my main position that areas A1 and A2 are nearly twice as large as area B. The fact that areas A1 and A2 exist and could be eliminated within the existing rural framework is sufficient to indicate that the present cattle population represents a nonoptimal arrangement.

21. Morris D. Morris, "Values as an Obstacle to Economic Growth in South Asia: An Historical Survey," *Journal of Economic History,* 27 (1967): 588–607.

22. After completing this paper, I learned of an excellent discussion by Raj (K. N. Raj, "Investment in Livestock in Agrarian Economics: A Theoretical and Empirical Analysis," paper prepared for the Graduate Economics Association Seminar at the Massachusetts Institute of Technology, Cambridge, Mass., December 14, 1967) of some of the issues raised in the first two sections of this paper. Raj also argues that religion is unimportant in explaining the Indian cattle composition. His international analysis is less detailed than the above. His interstate analysis for India cites Kashmir, with its large Muslim population, and Kerala, with its sizable Christian and Muslim population, both areas having ratios of females to adult male cattle greater than the Indian average, as indication that religion plays no role. The case of Kerala is special, but I would guess it is the cropping pattern that leads to the female/male composition there. Kashmir is a hill area; all hill areas tend to have more grazing area, so adult females do not easily starve. Finally, Raj analyses eight districts of the state of Uttar Pradesh, including traditionally Hindu districts like Benares and traditionally Muslim districts like Aligarh, showing there is little difference in the ratio of females to males. In this case, I believe Raj is misled by the districts chosen. My own analysis of all 54 districts of Uttar Pradesh shows that the correlation between the percent of total population Muslim in 1961 and the ratio of adult female to adult male cattle in 1961 was −.48. The obverse of this correlation is that in highly Hindu districts in Uttar Pradesh more females are retained relative to males than in other districts. But I would qualify this finding by stating that many of the hill districts of U.P., which as I argued for Kashmir would have a high proportion of females to males because they are hill districts, happen to have few Muslims, which in this case provides spurious support for our hypothesis.

23. Returning to the model, we see that if, say, 500 male and female animals are desired for work, this may be achieved by 100 females producing 600 animals, of which 200 females and 300 males work, and 100 females breed and give milk. This would be an equilibrium with no surplus animals. However, in most of the subcontinent the female is not desired as a work animal, so this solution is unavailable.

24. Government of India, *Indian Livestock Census, 1956, Vol. I: Summary Tables* (New Delhi: Economic and Statistical Adviser to the Government of India, Directorate of Economics and Statistics, Ministry of Food and Agriculture, 1960), p. vii.

25. Government of Pakistan, *Pakistan Census of Agriculture, 1960, Vol. I: Final Report, East Pakistan; Vol. II: West Pakistan Report 3* (Karachi: Agricultural Census Organization, Ministry of Agriculture and Works, Government of Pakistan, 1962).

26. The districts compared in West Pakistan were Gujarat, Lyllapur, Sialkot, Gujranwala, Sheikhupur, Lahore, and Montgomery. If Multan is added to this group, the relation is not affected. The Indian districts considered were Amritsar, Ferozepur, Gurdaspur, Bhatinda, Kapurthala, Jullundur, Hissar, and Ludhiana (Government of Punjab, *Punjab Livestock Census of 1961.* Chandigarh: Department of Land Records, Punjab State, 1964).

27. Ratios were calculated for the districts of Dadu, Larkana, Sukkur, Bahawalpur, Bahawalanagar, Rahimya Khan, Khairpur, Nawabshah, Sanghar, Hyderabad, Tharparkar, and Thatta in Pakistan (Government of Pakistan, *Pakistan Census of Agriculture 1960, Vol. I: Final Report, East Pakistan; Vol. II: West Pakistan Report 3*) and for Gujarat (Government of Gujarat, *Season and Crop Report, Gujarat State, 1960–61.* Baroda: Government Press, 1964).

28. Government of Rajasthan, *Statistical Abstract, Rajasthan, 1961* (Jaipur: Directorate of Economics and Statistics, Rajasthan State, 1963), p. 100.

29. Clifford Geertz, *Agricultural Involution* (Berkeley: University of California Press, 1963).

8 The Art Of Savage Discovery: Blaming the Victim

WILLIAM RYAN*

I

Twenty years ago, Zero Mostel used to do a sketch in which he impersonated a Dixiecrat Senator conducting an investigation of the origins of World War II. At the climax of the sketch, the Senator boomed out, in an excruciating mixture of triumph and suspicion, "What was Pearl Harbor *doing* in the Pacific." This is an extreme example of Blaming the Victim.

Twenty years ago, we could laugh at Zero Mostel's caricature. In recent years, however, the same process has been going on every day in the arena of social problems, public health, anti-poverty programs, and social welfare. A philosopher might analyze this process and prove that, technically, it is comic. But it is hardly ever funny.

Consider some victims. One is the miseducated child in the slum school. He is blamed for his own miseducation. He is said to contain within himself the causes of his inability to read and write well. The shorthand phrase is "cultural deprivation," which, to those in the know, conveys what they allege to be inside information: that the poor child carries a scanty pack of cultural baggage as he enters school. He doesn't know about books and magazines and newspapers, they say. (No books in the home: the mother fails to subscribe to *Reader's Digest*.) They say that if he talks at all—an unlikely event since slum parents don't talk to their children—he certainly doesn't talk correctly. (Lower-class dialect spoken here, or even—God forbid!—Southern Negro.) (*Ici on parle nigra.*) If you can manage to get him to sit in a chair, they say, he squirms and looks out the window. (Impulse-ridden, these kids, motoric rather than verbal.) In a word he is "disadvantaged" and "socially-deprived," they say, and this, of course, accounts for his failure (*his failure*, they say) to learn much in school.

Note the similarity to the logic of Zero Mostel's Dixiecrat Senator. What is the culturally deprived child *doing* in the school? What is wrong with the victim? In pursuing this logic, no one remembers to ask questions about the collapsing buildings and torn textbooks, the frightened, insensitive teachers, the six additional desks in the room, the blustering, frightened principals, the relentless

*William Ryan, *Blaming the Victim*. (New York: Vintage Books, Division of Random House, 1972.) Chapter 1, "The Art of Savage Discovery," pp. 3–29. Copyright © 1971 by William Ryan. Reprinted by permission of Pantheon Books, a Division of Random House, Inc.

segregation, the callous administrator, the irrelevant curriculum, the bigoted or cowardly members of the school board, the insulting history book, the stingy taxpayers, the fairy-tale readers, or the self-serving faculty of the local teachers' college. We are encouraged to confine our attention to the child and to dwell on all his alleged defects. Cultural deprivation becomes an omnibus explanation for the educational disaster area known as the inner-city school. This is Blaming the Victim.

Pointing to the supposedly deviant Negro family as the "fundamental weakness of the Negro community" is another way to blame the victim. Like "cultural deprivation," "negro family" has become a shorthand phrase with stereotyped connotations of matriarchy, fatherlessness, and pervasive illegitimacy. Growing up in the "crumbling" Negro family is supposed to account for most of the racial evils in America. Insiders have the word, of course, and know that this phrase is supposed to evoke images of growing up with a long-absent or never-present father (replaced from time to time perhaps by a series of transient lovers) and with bossy women ruling the roost, so that the children are irreparably damaged. This refers particularly to the poor, bewildered male children, whose psyches are fatally wounded and who are never, alas, to learn the trick of becoming upright, downright, forthright all-American boys. Is it any wonder the Negroes cannot achieve equality? From such families! And, again, by focusing our attention on the Negro family as the apparent *cause* of racial inequality, our eye is diverted. Racism, discrimination, segregation, and the powerlessness of the ghetto are subtly, but thoroughly, downgraded in importance.

The generic process of Blaming the Victim is applied to almost every American problem. The miserable health care of the poor is explained away on the grounds that the victim has poor motivation and lacks health information. The problems of slum housing are traced to the characteristics of tenants who are labeled as "Southern rural migrants" not yet "acculturated" to life in the big city. The "multiproblem" poor, it is claimed, suffer the psychological effects of impoverishment, the "culture of poverty," and the deviant value system of the lower classes; consequently, though unwittingly, they cause their own troubles. From such a viewpoint, the obvious fact that poverty is primarily an absence of money is easily overlooked or set aside.

The growing number of families receiving welfare are fallaciously linked together with the increased number of illegitimate children as twin results of promiscuity and sexual abandon among members of the lower orders. Every important social problem—crime, mental illness, civil disorder, unemployment—has been analyzed within the framework of the victim-blaming ideology. . . .

It would be possible for me to venture into other areas—one finds a perfect example in literature about the underdeveloped countries of the Third World, in which the lack of prosperity and technological progress is attributed to some aspect of the national character of the people, such as lack of "achievement motivation"—but I plan to stay within the confines of my own personal and professional experience, which is, generally, with racial injustice, social welfare, and human services in the city.

I have been listening to the victim-blamers and pondering their thought processes for a number of years. That process is often very subtle. Victim-blaming is cloaked in kindness and concern, and bears all the trappings and statistical furbelows of scientism; it is obscured by a perfumed haze of humanitarianism. In observing the process of Blaming the Victim, one tends to be confused and disoriented because those who practice this art display a deep concern for the victims that is quite genuine. In this way, the new ideology is very different from the open prejudice and reactionary tactics of the old days. Its adherents include sympathetic social scientists with social consciences in good working order, and liberal politicians with a genuine commitment to reform. They are very careful to dissociate themselves from vulgar Calvinism or crude racism; they indignantly condemn any notions of innate wickedness or genetic defect. "The Negro is *not born* inferior," they shout apoplectically. "Force of circumstance," they explain in reasonable tones, "has *made* him inferior." And they dismiss with self-righteous contempt any claims that the poor man in America is plainly unworthy or shiftless or enamored of idleness. No, they say, he is "caught in the cycle of poverty." He is trained to be poor by his culture and his family life, endowed by his environment (perhaps by his ignorant mother's outdated style of toilet training) with those unfortunately unpleasant characteristics that make him ineligible for a passport into the affluent society.

Blaming the Victim is, of course, quite different from old-fashioned conservative ideologies. The latter simply dismissed victims as inferior, genetically defective, or morally unfit; the emphasis is on the intrinsic, even hereditary, defect. The former shifts its emphasis to the environmental causation. The old-fashioned conservative could hold firmly to the belief that the oppressed and the victimized were born that way—"that way" being defective or inadequate in character or ability. The new ideology attributes defect and inadequacy to the malignant nature of poverty, injustice, slum life, and racial difficulties. The stigma that marks the victim and accounts for his victimization is an acquired stigma, a stigma of social, rather than genetic, origin. But the stigma, the defect, the fatal difference—though derived in the past from environmental forces—is still located *within* the victim, inside his skin. With such an elegant formulation, the humanitarian can have it both ways. He can, all at the same time, concentrate his charitable interest on the defects of the victim, condemn the vague social and environmental stresses that produced the defect (some time ago), and ignore the continuing effect of victimizing social forces (right now). It is a brilliant ideology for justifying a perverse form of social action designed to change, not society, as one might expect, but rather society's victim.

As a result, there is a terrifying sameness in the programs that arise from this kind of analysis. In education, we have programs of "compensatory education" to build up the skills and attitudes of the ghetto child, rather than structural changes in the schools. In race relations, we have social engineers who think up ways of "strengthening" the Negro family, rather than methods of eradicating racism. In health care, we develop new programs to provide health information (to correct the supposed ignorance of the poor) and to reach out and discover cases of untreated illness and disability (to compensate for their supposed unwillingness to seek treatment). Meanwhile, the gross inequities of our medical care delivery systems are left completely unchanged. As we might expect, the logical outcome of analyzing social problems in terms of the deficiencies of the victim is the development of programs aimed at correcting those deficiencies. The Formula for action becomes extraordinarily simple: change the victim.

All of this happens so smoothly that it seems downright rational. First, identify a social problem. Second, study those affected by the problem and discover in what ways they are different from the rest of us as a consequence of deprivation and injustice. Third, define the differences as the cause of the social problem itself. Finally, of course, assign a government bureaucrat to invent a humanitarian action program to correct the differences.

Now no one in his right mind would quarrel with the assertion that social problems are present in abundance and are readily identifiable. God knows it is true that when hundreds of thousands of poor children drop out of school—or even graduate from school—they are barely literate. After spending some ten thousand hours in the company of professional educators, these children appear to have learned very little. The fact of failure in their education is undisputed. And the racial situation in America is usually acknowledged to be a number one item on the nation's agenda. Despite years of marches, commissions, judicial decisions, and endless legislative remedies, we are confronted with unchanging or even widening racial differences in achievement. In addition, despite our assertions that Americans get the best health care in the world, the poor stubbornly remain unhealthy. They lose more work because of illness, have more carious teeth, lose more babies as a result of both miscarriage and infant death, and die considerably younger than the well-to-do.

The problems are there, and there in great quantities. They make us uneasy. Added together, these disturbing signs reflect inequality and a puzzlingly high level of unalleviated distress in America totally inconsistent with our proclaimed ideals and our enormous wealth. This thread—this rope—of inconsistency stands out so visibly in the fabric of American life, that it is jarring to the eye. And this must be explained, to the satisfaction of our conscience as well as our patriotism. Blaming the Victim is an ideal, almost painless, evasion.

The second step in applying this explanation is to look sympathetically at those who "have" the problem in question, to separate them out and define them in some way as a special group, a group that is *different* from the population in general. This is a crucial and essential step in the process, for that difference is in itself hampering and maladaptive. The Different Ones are seen as less competent, less skilled, less knowing—in short, less human. The ancient Greeks deduced from a single characteristic, a difference in language, that the barbarians—that is, the "babblers" who spoke a strange tongue—were wild, uncivilized, dangerous, rapacious, uneducated, lawless, and, indeed, scarcely more than animals. Automatically labeling strangers as savages, weird and inhuman creatures (thus explaining difference by exaggerating difference) not infrequently justifies mistreatment, enslavement, or even extermination of the Different Ones.

Blaming the Victim depends on a very similar process of identification (carried out, to be sure, in the most kindly, philanthropic, and intellectual manner) whereby the victim of social problems is identified as strange, different—in other words, as a barbarian, a savage. Discovering savages, then, is an essential component of, and prerequisite to, Blaming the Victim, and the art of Savage Discovery is a core skill that must be acquired by all aspiring Victim Blamers.

They must learn how to demonstrate that the poor, the black, the ill, the jobless, the slum tenants, are different and strange. They must learn to conduct or interpret the research that shows how "these people" think in different forms, act in different patterns, cling to different values, seek different goals, and learn different truths. Which is to say that they are strangers, barbarians, savages. This is how the distressed and disinherited are redefined in order to make it possible for us to look at society's problems and to attribute their causation to the individuals affected.

II

Blaming the Victim is an ideological process, which is to say that it is a set of ideas and concepts deriving from systematically motivated, but *unintended,* distortions of reality. In the sense that Karl Mannheim used the term, an ideology develops from the "collective unconscious" of a group or class and is rooted in a class-based interest in maintaining the *status quo* (as contrasted with what he calls a *utopia,* a set of ideas rooted in a class-based interest in *changing* the *status quo*).[1] An ideology, then, has several components: First, there is the belief system itself, the way of looking at the world, the set of ideas and concepts. Second, there is the systematic distortion of reality reflected in those ideas. Third is the condition that the distortion must not be a conscious, intentional process. Finally, though they are not intentional, the ideas must serve a specific function: maintaining the *status quo* in the interest of a specific group. Blaming the Victim fits this definition on all counts. . . . Most particularly, it is important to realize that Blaming the Victim is not a process of *intentional* distortion although it does serve the class interests of those who practice it. And it has a rich ancestry in American thought about social problems and how to deal with them.

Thinking about social problems is especially susceptible to ideological influences since, as John Seeley has pointed out, defining a social problem is not so simple.[2] "What is a social problem?" may seem an ingenuous question until one turns to confront its opposite: "What human problem is *not* a social problem?" Since any problem in which people are involved is social, why do we reserve the label for some problems in which people are involved and withhold it from others? To use Seeley's example, why is crime called a social problem when university administration is not? The phenomena we look at are bounded by the act of definition. They become social problems only by being so considered. In Seeley's words, "*naming* it as a problem, after naming it as a *problem.*"

It is only recently, for example, that we have begun to *name* the rather large quantity of people on earth as the *problem* of overpopulation, or the population explosion. Such phenomena often become proper predicaments for certain solutions, certain treatments. Before the 1930's, the most anti-Semitic German was unaware that Germany had a "Jewish problem." It took the Nazis to *name* the simple existence of Jews in the Third Reich as a "social problem," and that act of definition helped to shape the final solution.

We have removed "immigration" from our list of social problems (after executing a solution—choking off the flow of immigrants) and have added "urbanization." Nowadays, we define the situation of men out of work as the social problem of "unemployment" rather than, as in Elizabethan time that of "idleness." (The McCone Commission, investigating the Watts Riot of 1966, showed how hard old ideologies die; it specified both unemployment and idleness as causes of the disorder.) In the near future, if we are to credit the prophets of automation, the label "unemployment" will fade away and "idleness," now renamed the "leisure-time problem," will begin again to raise its lazy head. We have been comfortable for years with the "Negro problem," a term that clearly implies that the existence of Negroes is somehow a problematic fact. *Ebony* Magazine turned the tables recently and renamed the phenomenon as "The White Problem in America," which may be a good deal more accurate.

We must particularly ask, "To whom are social problems a problem?" And usually, if truth were to be told, we would have to admit that we mean they are a problem to those of us who are outside the boundaries of what we have defined as the problem. Negroes are a problem to racist white, welfare is a problem to stingy taxpayers, delinquency is a problem to nervous property owners.

Now, if this is the quality of our assumptions about social problems, we are led unerringly to certain beliefs about the causes of these problems. We cannot comfortably believe that *we* are the cause of that which is problematic to us; therefore, we are almost compelled to believe that *they*—the problematic ones— are the cause and this immediately prompts us to search for deviance. Identification of the deviance as the cause of the problem is a simple step that ordinarily does not even require evidence.

C. Wright Mills analyzed the ideology of those who write about social problems and demonstrated the relationship of their texts to class interest and to the preservation of the existent social order.[3] In sifting the material in thirty-one widely used textbooks in "social problems," "social pathology," and "social disorganization," Mills found a pervasive, coherent ideology with a number of common characteristics.

First, the textbooks present material about these problems, he says, in simple, descriptive terms, with each problem unrelated to the others and none related in any meaningful way to other aspects of the social environment. Second, the problems are selected and described largely according to predetermined norms. Poverty is a problem in that it deviates from the standard of economic self-sufficiency; divorce is a problem because the family is supposed to remain intact; crime and delinquency are problematic insofar as they depart from the accepted moral and legal standards of the community. The norms themselves are taken as givens, and no effort is made to examine them. Nor is there any thought given to the manner in which norms might themselves contribute to the development of the problems. (In a society in which everyone is assumed and expected to be economically self-sufficient, as an example, doesn't economic dependency almost automatically mean poverty? No attention is given to such issues.)

Within such a framework, then, deviation from norms and standards comes to be defined as failed or incomplete socialization—failure to learn the rules or the inability to learn how to keep to them. Those with social problems are then viewed as unable or unwilling to adjust to society's standards, which are narrowly conceived by what Mills calls "independent middle class persons verbally living out Protestant ideas in small town America." This, obviously, is a precise description of the social origins and status of almost every one of the authors.

In defining social problems in this way, the social pathologists are, of course, ignoring a whole set of factors that ordinarily might be considered relevant—for instance, unequal distribution of income, social stratification, political struggle, ethnic and racial group conflict, and inequality of power. Their ideology concentrates almost exclusively on the failure of the deviant. To the extent that society plays any part in social problems, it is said to have somehow failed to socialize the individual, to teach him how to adjust to circumstances, which, though far from perfect, are gradually changing for the better. Mills' essay provides a solid foundation for understanding the concept of Blaming the Victim.

This way of thinking on the part of "social pathologists," which Mills identified as the predominant tool used in *analyzing* social problems, also saturates the majority of programs that have been developed to *solve* social problems in America. These programs are based on the assumption that *individuals* "have" social problems as a result of some kind of unusual circumstances—accident, illness, personal defect or handicap, character flaw or maladjustment—that exclude them from using the ordinary mechanisms for maintaining and advancing themselves. For example, the prevalent belief in America is that, under normal circumstances, everyone can obtain sufficient income for the necessities of life. Those who are unable to do so are special deviant cases, persons who for one reason or another are not able to adapt themselves to the generally satisfactory income-producing system. In times gone by these persons were further classified into the worthy poor—the lame, the blind, the young mother whose husband died in an accident, the aged man no longer able to work—and the unworthy poor—the lazy, the unwed mother and her illegitimate children, the malingerer. All were seen, however, as individuals who, for good reasons or bad, were personal failures, unable to adapt themselves to the system. . . .

Elsewhere I have proposed the dimension of *exceptionalism-universalism* as the ideological underpinning for these two contrasting approaches to the analysis and solution of social problems.[4] The *exceptionalist* viewpoint is reflected in arrangements that are private, voluntary, remedial, special, local, and exclusive. Such arrangements imply that problems occur to specially-defined categories of persons in an unpredictable manner. The problems are unusual, even unique, they are exceptions to the rule, they occur as a result of individual defect, accident, or unfortunate circumstance and must be remedied by means that are particular and, as it were, tailored to the individual case.

The *universalistic* viewpoint, on the other hand, is reflected in arrangements that are public, legislated, promotive or preventive, general, national, and inclusive. Inherent in such a viewpoint is the idea that social problems are a function of the social arrangements of the community or the society and that, since these social arrangements are quite imperfect and inequitable, such problems are both predictable and, more important, preventable through public action. They are not unique to the individual, and the fact that they encompass individual persons does not imply that those persons are themselves defective or abnormal.

Consider these two contrasting approaches as they are applied to the problem of smallpox. The medical care approach is exceptionalistic; it is designed to provide remedial treatment to the special category of persons who are afflicted with the disease through a private, voluntary arrangement with a local doctor. The universalistic public health approach is designed to provide preventive inoculation to the total population, ordered by legislation and available through public means if no private arrangements can be made. . . .

The similarity between exceptionalism and what Mills called the "ideology of social pathologists" is readily apparent. Indeed, the ideological potential of the exceptionalist viewpoint is unusually great. If one is inclined to explain all instances of deviance, all social problems, all occasions on which help is provided to others as the result of unusual circumstances, defect or accident, one is unlikely to inquire about social inequalities....

The danger in the exceptionalistic viewpoint is in its impact on social policy when it becomes the dominant component in social analysis. Blaming the Victim occurs exclusively within an exceptionalistic framework, and it consists of applying exceptionalistic explanations to universalistic problems. This represents an illogical departure from fact, a method, in Mannheim's words, of systematically distorting reality, of developing an ideology.

Blaming the Victim can take its place in a long series of American ideologies that have rationalized cruelty and injustice.

Slavery, for example, was justified—even praised—on the basis of a complex ideology that showed quite conclusively how useful slavery was to society and how uplifting it was for the slaves.[5] Eminent physicians could be relied upon to provide the biological justification for slavery since after all, they said, the slaves were a separate species—as, for example, cattle are a separate species. No one in his right mind would dream of freeing the cows and fighting to abolish the ownership of cattle. In the view of the average American of 1825, it was important to preserve slavery, not simply because it was in accord with his own group interests (he was not fully aware of that), but because reason and logic showed clearly to the reasonable and intelligent man that slavery was good. In order to persuade a good and moral man to *do* evil, then, it is not necessary first to persuade him to *become* evil. It is only necessary to teach him that he is doing good. No one, in the words of a legendary newspaperman, thinks of himself as a son of a bitch.

In late-nineteenth-century America there flowered another ideology of injustice that seemed rational and just to the decent, progressive person. But Richard Hofstadter's analysis of the phenomenon of Social Darwinism shows clearly its functional role in the preservation of the *status quo*.[6] One can scarcely imagine a better fit than the one between this ideology and the purposes and actions of the robber barons, who descended like piranha fish on the America of this era and picked its bones clean. Their extraordinarily unethical operations netted them not only hundreds of millions of dollars but also, perversely, the adoration of the nation. Behavior that would be, in any more rational land (including today's America), more than enough to have landed them all in jail, was praised as the very model of a captain of modern industry. And the philosophy that justified their thievery was such that John D. Rockefeller could actually stand up and preach it in church. Listen as he speaks in, of all places, Sunday school:

> The growth of a large business is merely a survival of the fittest.... The American Beauty rose can be produced in the splendor and fragrance which bring cheer to its beholder only by sacrificing the early buds which grow up around it. This is not an evil tendency in business. It is merely the working-out of a law of nature and a law of God.[7]

This was the core of the gospel, adapted analogically from Darwin's writings on

evolution. Herbert Spencer and, later, William Graham Summer and other begin-
ners in the social sciences considered Darwin's work to be directly applicable to
social processes: ultimately as a guarantee that life was progressing toward
perfection but, in the short run, as a justification for an absolutely uncontrolled
laissez-faire economic system. The central concepts of "survival of the fittest,"
"natural selection," and "gradualism" were exalted in Rockefeller's preaching to
the status of laws of God and Nature. Not only did this ideology justify the
criminal rapacity of those who rose to the top of the industrial heap, defining them
automatically as naturally superior (this was bad enough), but at the same time it
also required that those at the bottom of the heap be labeled as potently *unfit*—a
label based solely on their position in society. According to the law of natural
selection, they should be, in Spencer's judgment, eliminated. "The whole effort of
nature is to get rid of such, to clear the world of them and make room for better."

For a generation, Social Darwinism was the orthodox doctrine in the social
sciences, such as they were at that time. Opponents of this ideology were shut out
of respectable intellectual life. The philosophy that enabled John D. Rockefeller to
justify himself self-righteously in front of a class of Sunday school children was
not the product of an academic quack or a marginal crackpot philosopher. It came
directly from the lectures and books of leading intellectual figures of the time,
occupants of professorial chairs at Harvard and Yale. Such is the power of an
ideology that so neatly fits the needs of the dominant interests of society.

If one is to think about ideologies in America in 1970, one must be prepared to
consider the possibility that a body of ideas that might seem almost self-evident is,
in fact, highly distorted and highly selective; one must allow that the inclusion of a
specific formulation in every freshman sociology text does not guarantee that the
particular formulation represents abstract Truth rather than group interest. It is
important not to delude ourselves into thinking that ideological monstrosities were
constructed by monsters. They were not; they are not. They are developed
through a process that shows every sign of being valid scholarship, complete with
tables of numbers, copious footnotes, and scientific terminology. Ideologies are
quite often academically and socially respectable and in many instances hold
positions of exclusive validity, so that disagreement is considered unrespectable
or radical and risks being labeled as irresponsible, unenlightened, or trashy.

Blaming the Victim holds such a position. It is central in the mainstream of
contemporary American social thought, and its ideas pervade our most crucial
assumptions so thoroughly that they are hardly noticed. Moreover, the fruits of
this ideology appear to be fraught with altruism and humanitarianism, so it is hard
to believe that it has principally functioned to block social change.

IV

We come finally to the question, Why? It is much easier to understand the process
of Blaming the Victim as a way of thinking than it is to understand the motivation
for it. Why do Victim Blamers, who are usually good people, blame the victim?
The development and application of this ideology, and of all the mythologies
associated with Savage Discovery, are readily exposed by careful analysis as
hostile acts—one is almost tempted to say acts of war—directed against the
disadvantaged, the distressed, the disinherited. It is class warfare in reverse. Yet

those who are most fascinated and enchanted by this ideology tend to be progressive, humanitarian, and, in the best sense of the word, charitable persons. They would usually define themselves as moderates or liberals. Why do they pursue this dreadful war against the poor and the oppressed?

Put briefly, the answer can be formulated best in psychological terms—or, at least, I, as a psychologist, am more comfortable with such a formulation. The highly-charged psychological problem confronting this hypothetical progressive, charitable person I am talking about is that of reconciling his own self-interest with the promptings of his humanitarian impulses. This psychological process of reconciliation is not worked out in a logical, rational, conscious way; it is a process that takes place far below the level of sharp consciousness, and the solution—Blaming the Victim—is arrived at subconsciously as a compromise that apparently satisfies both his self-interest and his charitable concerns. Let me elaborate.

First, the question of self-interest or, more accurately, class interest. The typical Victim Blamer is a middle-class person who is doing reasonably well in a material way; he has a good job, a good income, a good house, a good car. Basically, he likes the social system pretty much the way it is, at least in broad outline. He likes the two-party political system, though he may be highly skilled in finding a thousand minor flaws in its functioning. He heartily approves of the profit motive as the propelling engine of the economic system despite his awareness that there are abuses of that system, negative side effects, and substantial residual inequalities.

On the other hand, he is acutely aware of poverty, racial discrimination, exploitation, and deprivation, and, moreover, he wants to do something concrete to ameliorate the condition of the poor, the black, and the disadvantaged. This is not an extraneous concern; it is central to his value system to insist on the worth of the individual, the equality of men, and the importance of justice.

What is to be done, then? What intellectual position can he take, and what line of action can he follow that will satisfy both of these important motivations? He quickly and self-consciously rejects two obvious alternatives, which he defines as "extremes." He cannot side with an openly reactionary, repressive position that accepts continued oppression and exploitation as the price of a privileged position for his own class. This is incompatible with his own morality and his basic political principles. He finds the extreme conservative position repugnant.

He is, if anything, more allergic to radicals, however, than he is to reactionaries. He rejects the "extreme" solution of radical social change, and this makes sense since such radical social change threatens his own well-being. A more equitable distribution of income might mean that he would have less—a smaller or older house, with fewer yews or no rhododendrons in the yard, a less enjoyable job, or, at the least, a somewhat smaller salary. If black children and poor children were, in fact, reasonably educated and began to get high S.A.T. scores, they would be competing with *his* children for the scarce places in the entering classes of Harvard, Columbia, Bennington, and Antioch.

So our potential Victim Blamers are in a dilemma. In the words of an old Yiddish proverb, they are trying to dance at two weddings. They are old friends of both brides and fond of both kinds of dancing, and they want to accept both invitations. They cannot bring themselves to attack the system that has been so good to them, but they want so badly to be helpful to the victims of racism and economic injustice.

Their solution is a brilliant compromise. They turn their attention to the victim in his post-victimized state. They want to bind up wounds, inject penicillin, administer morphine, and evacuate the wounded for rehabilitation. They explain what's wrong with the victim in terms of social experiences *in the past,* experiences that have left wounds, defects, paralysis, and disability. And they take the cure of these wounds and the reduction of these disabilities as the first order of business. They want to make the victims less vulnerable, send them back into battle with better weapons, thicker armor, a higher level of morale.

In order to do so effectively, of course, they must analyze the victims carefully, dispassionately, objectively, scientifically, empathetically, mathematically, and hardheadedly, to see what made them so vulnerable in the first place.

What weapons, now, might they have lacked when they went into battle? Job skills? Education?

What armor was lacking that might have warded off their wounds? Better values? Habits of thrift and foresight?

And what might have ravaged their morale? Apathy? Ignorance? Deviant lower-class cultural patterns?

This is the solution of the dilemma, the solution of Blaming the Victim. And those who buy this solution with a sigh of relief are inevitably blinding themselves to the basic causes of the problems being addressed. They are, most crucially, rejecting the possibility of blaming, not the victims, but themselves. They are all unconsciously passing judgments on themselves and bringing in an unanimous verdict of Not Guilty.

If one comes to believe that the culture of poverty produces persons *fated* to be poor, who can find any fault with our corporation-dominated economy? And if the Negro family produces young men *incapable* of achieving equality, let's deal with that first before we go on to the task of changing, the pervasive racism that informs and shapes and distorts our every social institution. And if unsatisfactory resolution of one's Oedipus complex accounts for all emotional distress and mental disorder, then by all means let us attend to that and postpone worrying about the pounding day-to-day stresses of life on the bottom rungs that drive so many to drink, dope, and madness.

That is the ideology of Blaming the Victim, the cunning Art of Savage Discovery. The tragic, frightening truth is that it is a mythology that is winning over the best people of our time, the very people who must resist this ideology temptation if we are to achieve nonviolent change in America.

NOTES AND REFERENCES

1. Karl Mannheim, *Ideology and Utopia,* trans. Louis Wirth and Edward Shils (New York: Harcourt, Brace & World, Harvest Books, 1936). First published in German in 1929.

2. John Seeley, "The Problem of Social Problems," *Indian Sociological Bulletin,* 2, no. 3 (April, 1965). Reprinted as Chapter Ten in *The Americanization of the Unconscious* (New York: International Science Press, 1967), pp. 142–48.

3. C. Wright Mills, "The Professional Ideology of Social Pathologists," *American Journal of Sociology,* 49, no. 2 (September, 1943), pp. 165–80.

4. William Ryan, "Community Care in Historical Perspective: Implications for Mental Health Services and Professionals," *Canada's Mental Health,* supplement No. 60

(March–April, 1969). This formulation draws on, and is developed from the *residual-institutional* dimension outlined in H. L. Wilensky and C. N. Lebeaux, *Industrial Society and Social Welfare,* paperback ed. (New York: The Free Press, 1965). Originally published by Russell Sage Foundation, 1958.

5. For a good review of this general ideology, see I. A. Newby, *Jim Crow's Defense* (Baton Rouge: Louisiana State University Press, 1965).

6. Richard Hofstadter, *Social Darwinism in American Thought.* Revised ed. (Boston: Beacon Press, 1955).

7. William J. Ghent, *Our Benevolent Feudalism* (New York: The Macmillan Co., 1902), p. 29.

9 The Noble Savage: Cultural Imperialism in the Disney Comics

ARIEL DORFMAN and ARMAND MATTELART*

Donald (talking to a witch doctor in Africa): "I see you're an up to date nation! Have you got telephones?"

Witch doctor: "Have we gottee telephones! . . . All colors, all shapes . . . only trouble is only one has wires. It's a hot line to the world loan bank.[1]

Where is Aztecland? Where is Inca-Blinca? Where is Unsteadystan?

There can be no doubt that Aztecland is Mexico, embracing as it does all the prototypes of the picture-postcard Mexico: mules, siestas, volcanoes, cactuses, huge sombreros, ponchos, serenades, machismo, and Indians from ancient civilizations. The country is defined primarily in terms of this grotesque folklorism. Petrified in an archetypical embryo, exploited for all the superficial and stereotyped prejudices which surround it, "Aztecland," under its pseudo-imaginary name becames that much easier to Disnify. This is Mexico recognizable by its commonplace exotic identity labels, not the real Mexico with all its problems.

Walt took virgin territories of the U.S. and built upon them his Disneyland palaces, his magic kingdoms. His view of the world at large is framed by the same perspective; it is a world already colonized, with phantom inhabitants who have to conform to Disney's notions of it. Each foreign country is used as a kind of model within the process of invasion by Disney-nature. And even if some foreign country like Cuba or Vietnam should dare to enter into open conflict with the United States, the Disney Comics brand-mark is immediately stamped upon it, in order to make the revolutionary struggle appear banal. While the Marines make revolutionaries run the gauntlet of bullets, Disney makes them run a gauntlet of magazines. There are two forms of killing; by machine guns and saccharine.

Disney did not, of course, invent the inhabitants of these lands; he merely forced them into the proper mold. Casting them as stars in his hit-parade, he made them into decals and puppets for his fantasy palaces, good and inoffensive savages unto eternity.

According to Disney, underdeveloped peoples are like children, to be treated as

*Reprinted from Ariel Dorfman and Armand Mattelart, *How to Read Donald Duck: Imperialist Ideology in the Disney Comics*, David Kunzle, translator. (New York: International General, 1975.) Copyright I. G. Editions, 1975. Reprinted by permission of the publisher.

such, and if they don't accept this definition of themselves, they should have their pants taken down and be given a good spanking. That'll teach them! When something is *said* about the child/noble savage, it is really the Third World one is *thinking* about. The hegemony which we have detected between the child-adults who arrive with their civilization and technology, and the child-noble savages who accept this alien authority and surrender their riches, stands revealed as an exact replica of the relations between metropolis and satellite, between empire and colony, between master and slave. Thus we find the metropolitans not only searching for treasures, but also selling the native *comics* (like those of Disney), to teach them the role assigned to them by the dominant urban press. Under the suggestive title "Better Guile Than Force," Donald departs for a Pacific atoll in order to try to survive for a month, and returns loaded with dollars, like a modern business tycoon. The entrepreneur can do better than the missionary or the army. The world of the Disney comic is self-publicizing, ensuring a process of enthusiastic buying and selling even within its very pages.

Enough of generalities. Examples and proofs. Among all the child-noble savages, none is more exaggerated in his infantilism that Gu, the Abominable Snow Man: a brainless, feeble-minded Mongolian type (living by a strange coincidence, in the Himalayan Hindu Kush mountains among yellow peoples).[2] He is treated like a child. He is an "*abominable* housekeeper," living in a messy cave, "the worst of taste," littered with "cheap trinkets and waste." Hats etc., lying around which he has no use for. Vulgar, uncivilized, he speaks in a babble of inarticulate baby-noises: "Gu." But he is also witless, having stolen the golden jewelled crown of Genghis Khan (which belongs to Scrooge by virtue of certain secret operations of his agents), without having any idea of its value. He has tossed the crown in a corner like a coal bucket, and prefers Uncle Scrooge's watch: value, one dollar ("It is his favorite *toy*"). Never mind, for "his stupidity makes it easy for us to get away!" Uncle Scrooge does indeed manage, magically, to exchange the cheap artifact of civilization which goes tick-tock, for the crown. Obstacles are overcome once Gu (innocent child-monstrous animal—underdeveloped Third Worldling) realizes that they only want to take something that is of no use to him, and that in exchange he will be given a fantastic and mysterious piece of technology (a watch) which he can use as a plaything. What is extracted is gold, a

Figure 9.1 Walt Disney Productions

raw material; he who surrenders it is mentally underdeveloped and physically overdeveloped. The gigantic physique of Gu, and of all the other marginal savages, is the model of a physical strength suited only for physical labor.[3]

Such an episode reflects the barter relationship established with the natives by the first conquistadors and colonizers (in Africa, Asia, America and Oceania): some trinket, the product of technological superiority (European or North American) is exchanged for gold (spices, ivory, tea, etc.). The native is relieved of something he would never have thought of using for himself or as a means of exchange. This is an extreme and almost anecdotic example. The common stuff of other types of comic book (e.g. in the internationally famous *Tintin in Tibet* by the Belgian Hergé) leaves the abominable creature in his bestial condition, and thus unable to enter into any kind of economy.

Figure 9.2 Walt Disney Productions

But this particular victim of infantile regression stands at the borderline of Disney's noble savage cliche. Beyond it lies the foetus-savage, which for reasons of sexual prudery Disney cannot use.

Lest the reader feel that we are spinning too fine a thread in establishing a parallel between someone who carries off gold in exchange for a mechanical trinket, and imperialism extracting raw material from a mono-productive country, or between typical dominators and dominated, let us now adduce a more explicit example of Disney's strategy in respect to the countries he caricatures as "backward" (needless to say, he never hints at the causes of their backwardness).

The following dialogue (taken from the same comic which provided the quotation at the beginning of this chapter) is a typical example of Disney's colonial attitudes, in this case directed against the African independence movements. Donald has parachuted into a country in the African jungle. "Where am I," he cries. A witch doctor (with spectacles perched over his gigantic primitive mask) replies: "In the new nation of Kooko Coco, fly boy. This is our capital city." It consists of three straw huts and some moving haystacks. When Donald enquires after this strange phenomenon, the witch doctor explains: "Wigs! This be hairy idea our ambassador bring back from United Nations." When a pig pursuing Donald lands and has the wigs removed disclosing the whereabouts of the enemy ducks, the following dialogue ensues:

Pig: "Hear ye! hear ye! I'll pay you kooks some hairy prices for your *wigs!* Sell me all you have!"

Native: "Whee! Rich trader buyee our old head hangers!"

Another native: "He payee me six trading stamps for my beehive hairdo!"

Third native (overjoyed): "He payee me two Chicago streetcar tokens for my Beatle job."

To effect his escape, the pig decides to scatter a few coins as a decoy. The natives are happy to stop, crouch and cravenly gather up the money. Elsewhere, when the Beagle Boys dress up as Polynesian natives to deceive Donald, they mimic the same kind of behavior: "You save our lives . . . We be your servants for ever." And as they prostrate themselves, Donald observes: "They are natives too. But a little more civilized."

Figure 9.3 Walt Disney Productions

Another example: Donald leaves for "Outer Congolia," because Scrooge's business there has been doing badly.[4] The reasons is the "the King ordered his subjects not to give Christmas presents this year. He wants everyone to hand over this money to him." Donald comments: "What selfishness!" And so to work. Donald makes himself king, being taken for a great magician who flies through the skies. The old monarch is dethroned because "he is not a wise man like you [Donald]. He does not permit us to buy presents." Donald accepts the crown,

intending to decamp as soon as the stock is sold out: "My first command as king is
. . . buy presents for your families and don't give your king a cent!" The old king
had wanted the money to leave the country and eat what he fancied, instead of the
fish heads which were traditionally his sole diet. Repentant, he promises that
given another chance, he will govern better, "and I will find a way somehow to
avoid eating that ghastly stew."

Donald (to the people): "And I assure you that I leave the throne in good hands.
Your old king is a good king . . . and wiser than before." The people: "Hurray!
Long live the King!"

The king has learned that he must ally himself with foreigners if he wishes to
stay in power, and that he cannot even impose taxes on the people, because this
wealth must pass wholly out of the country to Duckburg through the agent of
McDuck. Furthermore, the strangers find a solution to the problem of the king's
boredom. To alleviate his sense of alienation within his own country, and his
consequent desire to travel to the metropolis, they arrange for the massive
importation of consumer goods: "Don't worry about that food," says Donald, "I
will send you some sauces which will make even fish heads palatable." The king
stamps gleefully up and down.

The same formula is repeated over and over again. Scrooge exchanges with the
Canadian Indians gates of rustless steel for gates of pure gold.[5] Moby Duck and
Donald, captured by the Aridians (Arabs), start to blow soap bubbles, with which
the natives are enchanted.[6] "Ha, ha. They break when you catch them. Hee,
hee." Ali-Ben-Goli, the chief says "it's real magic. My people are laughing like
children. They cannot imagine how it works." "It's only a secret passed from
generation to generation," says Moby, "I will reveal it if you give us our
freedom." (Civilization is presented as something incomprehensible, to be ad-
ministered by foreigners). The chief, in amazement, exclaims "Freedom? That's
not all I'll give you. Gold, Jewels. My treasure is yours, if you reveal the secret."
The Arabs consent to their own despoliation. "We have jewels, but they are of no
use to us. They don't make you laugh like magic bubbles." While Donald sneers
"poor simpleton," Moby hands over the Flip Flop detergent. "You are right, my
friend. Whenever you want a little pleasure, just pour out some magic powder and
recite the magic words." The story ends on the note that it is not necessary for
Donald to excavate the Pyramids (or earth) personally, because, as Donald says,
"What do we need a pyramid for, having Ali-Ben-Goli?"

Figure 9.4 Walt Disney Productions.

Each time this situation recurs, the natives' joy increases. As each object of their own manufacture is taken away from them, their satisfaction grows. As each artifact from civilization is given to them, and interpreted by them as a manifestation of magic rather than technology, they are filled with delight. Even our fiercest enemies could hardly justify the inequity of such an exchange; how can a fistful of jewels be regarded as equivalent to a box of soap, or a golden crown equal to a cheap watch? Some will object that this kind of barter is all imaginary, but it is unfortunate that these laws of the imagination are tilted unilaterally in favor of those who come from outside, and those who write and publish the magazine.

But how can this flagrant despoliation pass unperceived, or in other words, how can this inequity be disguised as equity? Why is it that imperialist plunder and colonial subjection, to call them by their proper names, do not appear as such?

"We have jewels, but they are of no use to us."

There they are in their desert tents, their caves, their once flourishing cities, their lonely islands, their forbidden fortresses, and they *can never leave them.* Congealed in their past-historic, their needs defined in function of this past, these underdeveloped peoples are denied the right to build their own future. Their crowns, their raw materials, their soil, their energy, their jade elephants, their fruit, but above all, their gold, can never be turned to any use. For them the progress which comes from abroad in the form of multiplicity of technological artifacts, is a mere toy. It will never penetrate the crystallized defense of the noble savage, who is forbidden to become civilized. He will never be able to join the Club of the Producers, because he does not even understand that these objects have been produced. He sees them as magic elements, arising from the foreigner's mind, from his word, his magic wand.

Since the noble savage is denied the prospect of future development, plunder never appears as such, for it only eliminates that which is trifling, superfluous, and dispensable. Unbridled capitalist despoliation is programmed with smiles and coquetry. Poor native. How naive they are. And since they cannot use their gold, it is better to remove it. It can be used elsewhere.

Scrooge McDuck gets hold of a twenty-four carat moon in which "the gold is so pure that it can be molded like butter."[7] But the legitimate owner appears, a Venusian called Muchkale, who is prepared to sell it to Scrooge for a fistful of earth. "Man! That's the biggest *bargain* I ever heard of in all history," cries the miser as he closes the deal. But Muchkale, who is a "good native," magically transforms the fistful of earth into a planet, with continents, oceans, trees, and a whole environment of nature, "Yessir! I was quite impoverished here, with only atoms of *gold* to work with!" he says. Exiled from his state of primitive innocence, longing for some rain and volcanoes, Muchkale rejects his gold in order to return to the land of his origin and content himself with life at subsistence level. "Skunk Cabbage! [his favorite dish on Venus] I live again . . . Now I have a world of my own, with food and drink and life!" Far from robbing him, Scrooge has done Machkale a favor by removing all that corrupt metal and facilitating his return to primitive innocence. "He got the dirt he wanted, and I got this fabulous twenty-four carat moon. Five hundred miles thick! Of *solid gold!* But doggoned if I don't think he got the *best* of the bargain!" Poor, but happy, the Venusian is left devoting himself to the celebration of the simple life. It's the old aphorism, the poor have no worries; it is the rich who have all the problems. So let's have no qualms about plundering the poor and underdeveloped.

Conquest has been purged. Foreigners do no harm, they are building the future, on the basis of a society which cannot and will not leave the past.

But there is another way of infantilizing others and exonerating one's own larcenous behavior. Imperialism likes to promote an image of itself as being the impartial judge of the interests of the people, and their liberating angel.

The only thing which cannot be taken from the noble savage is his subsistence living, because losing this would destroy his natural economy, forcing him to abandon Paradise for Mammon and a production economy.

Donald travels to the "Plateau of Abandon" to look for a silver goat, which his Problem Solving Agency has contracted to find for a rich customer. He finds the goat, but breaks it while trying to ride it, and then discovers that this animal—and nothing else—stands between life and death by starvation (forbidden word) for the primitive people who live near the plateau. What had brought this to pass? Some time ago, an earthquake cut off the people and their flocks from their ancient pasturelands. "We would have died of hunger in this patch of earth if a generous white man had not arrived here in that mysterious bird over there (i.e. an aircraft) . . . and made a white goat with the metal from our mine." It is this mechanical goat which leads the flocks of sheep through the dangerous ravine to pasture in the outlying plains, and without it, the sheep get lost. The natives admire the way Donald & Co. decide to venture back through perilous precipices "which only you and the sheep have the courage to cross. Our people have never had a head for heights." Once through the ravine, Donald and nephews mend the goat and bring the sheep safely back to their owners.

Enter at this point the villains: the rich Mr. Leech and his spoiled son who had contracted and sent Donald off in search of the goat. "You signed the contract and must hand over the goods." But the evil party is defeated and the ducks reveal themselves as disinterested friends of the natives. Trusting the ducks as they did their Duckburg predecessor, the natives enter into an alliance with the good foreigners against the bad foreigners. The moral Manichaeism serves to affirm foreign sovereignty in its authoritarian and paternalist role. Big Stick and Charity.[8] The good foreigners, under their ethical cloak, win with the native's confidence, the right to decide the proper distribution of wealth in the land. The villains, coarse, vulgar, repulsive, out-and-out thieves, are there purely and simply to reveal the ducks as defenders of justice, law, and food for the hungry, and to serve as a whitewash for any further action. Defending the only thing that the noble savages can use (their food), the lack of which would result in their death (or rebellion, either of which would violate their image of infantile innocence), the big city folk establish themselves as the spokesman of these submerged and voiceless peoples.

The ethical division between the two classes of predators, the would-be robbers working openly, and the actual ones working surreptitiously, is constantly repeated. In one episode, Mickey and company search for a silver mine and unmask two crooks.[9] The crooks, disguised as Spanish conquistadors, who had originally stolen the mineral, are terrorizing the Indians, and are now making great profits from tourists by selling them "Indian ornaments." The constant characteristic of the natives—irrational fear and panic when faced with any phenomenon which disrupts their natural rhythm of life—serves to emphasize their cowardice (rather like children afraid of the dark), and to justify the necessity that some superior being come to their rescue and bring daylight. As reward for catching the crooks, the heroes are given ranks within the tribe: Minnie, princess; Mickey and Goofy, warriors; and Pluto gets a feather. And, of course, Duckburg gets the "Indian ornaments." The Indians have been given the "freedom to sell their goods on the foreign market." It is only direct and open robbery without offering a share in the profits, which is to be condemned. Mickey's imperialist despoliation is a foil for that of the Spaniards and those who, in the past, undeniably robbed and enslaved the native more openly.

Things are different nowadays. To rob without payment is robbery undisguised. Taking with payment is no robbery, but a favor. Thus the conditions for the sale of the ornaments and their importation into Duckburg are never in question, for they are based on the supposition of equality between the two negotiating partners.

An isolated tribe of Indians find themselves in a similar situation.[10] They "have declared war on all Ducks" on the basis of a previous historical experience. Buck Duck, fifty years before (and nothing has changed since then) gypped them doubly: first stealing the natives' land, and then, selling it back to them in a useless condition. So it is a matter of convincing them that not all ducks (white men) are evil, that the frauds of the past can be made good. Any history book—even Hollywood, even television—admits that the natives were violated. The history of fraud and exploitation of the past is public knowledge and cannot be buried any longer, and so it appears over and done with. But the present is another matter.

In order to assure the redemptive powers of present-day imperialism, it is only necessary to measure it against old-style colonialism and robbery. Example: Enter a pair of crooks determined to cheat the natives of their natural gas resources. They are unmasked by the ducks, who are henceforth regarded as friends.

"Let's bury the hatchet, let's collaborate, the races can get along together." What a fine message! It couldn't have been said better by the Bank of America, who, in sponsoring the minicity of Disneyland in California, calls it a world of peace where all peoples can get along together.

But what happens to the lands?

"A big gas company will do all the work, and pay your tribe well for it." This is the most shameless imperialist politics. Facing the relatively crude crooks of the past and present (handicapped, moreover, by their primitive techniques), stands the sophisticated Great Uncle Company, which will resolve all problems equitably. The guy who comes in from the outside is not necessarily a bad'un, only if he fails to pay the "fair and proper price." The Company, by contrast, is benevolence incarnate.

This form of exploitation is not all. A Wigwam Motel and a souvenir shop opened, and excursions are arranged. The Indians are immobilized against their background and served up for tourist consumption.

The last two examples suggest certain differences from the classic politics of bared faced colonialism. The benevolent collaboration figuring in the Disney comics suggests a form of neo-colonialism which rejects the naked pillage of the past, and permits the native a minimal participation in his own exploitation.

Perhaps the clearest manifestation of this phenomenon is a comic, written at the height of the Alliance for Progress program about the Indians of Aztecland who at the time of the Conquest had hidden their treasure in the jungle.[11] Now they are saved by the Ducks from the new conquistadors, the Beagle Boys. "This is absurd! Conquistadors don't exist any more!" The pillage of the past was a crime. As the past is criminalized, and the present purified, its real traces are effaced from memory. There is no need to keep the treasure hidden: the Duckburgers (who have already demonstrated their kindness of heart by charitably caring for a stray lamb) will be able to defend the Mexicans. Geography becomes a picture postcard, and is sold as such. The days of yore cannot advance or change, because this would damage the tourist trade. "Visit Aztecland. Entrance: One Dollar." The vacations of the big city people are transformed into a modern vehicle of supremacy, and we shall see later how the natural and physical virtues of the noble savage are preserved intact. A holiday in these places is like a loan or a blank check on purification and regeneration through communion with nature.

All these examples are based upon common international stereotypes. Who can deny that the Peruvian is somnolent, sells pottery, sits on his haunches, eats hot peppers, has a thousand-year-old culture—all the dislocated prejudices proclaimed by the tourist posters themselves?[12] Disney does not invent these caricatures, he only exploits them to the utmost. By forcing all peoples of the world into a vision of the dominant (national and international) classes, he gives this vision coherency and justifies the social system on which it is based. These cliches are also used by the mass culture media to dilute the realities common to these people. The only means that the Mexican has of knowing Peru is through caricature, which also implies that Peru is incapable of being anything else, and is unable to rise above this prototypical situation, imprisoned as it is made to seem, within its own exoticism. For Mexican and Peruvian alike, these stereotypes of Latin American peoples become a channel of distorted self-knowledge, a form of self-consumption, and finally, self-mockery. By selecting the most superficial and singular traits of each people in order to differentiate them, and using folklore as a means to "divide and conquer" nations occupying the same dependent position, the comic, like all mass media, exploits the principle of sensationalism. That is, it conceals reality by means of novelty, which not incidentally, also serves to promote sales. Our Latin American countries become trash cans being constantly repainted for the voyeuristic and orgiastic pleasures of the metropolitan nations. Every day, this very minute, television, radio, magazines, newspapers, cartoons, newscasts, films, clothing, and records, from the dignified gab of history textbooks to the trivia of daily conversation, all contribute to weakening the international solidarity of the oppressed. We Latin Americans are separated from each other by the vision we have acquired of each other via the comics and the other mass culture media. This vision is nothing less than our own reduced and distorted image.

This great tacit pool overflowing with the riches of stereotype is based upon common cliches, so that no one needs to go directly to sources of information gathered from reality itself. Each of us carries within a Boy Scout Handbook packed with the commonplace wisdom of Everyman. . . .

The realm of Disney is not one of fantasy, for it does react to world events. Its vision of Tibet is not identical to its vision of Indochina. Fifteen years ago the Caribbean was a sea of pirates. Disney has had to adjust to the face of Cuba and the invasion of the Dominican Republic. The buccaneer now cries "Viva the Revolution," and has to be defeated. It will be Chile's turn yet.

Searching for a jade elephant, Scrooge and his family arrive in Unsteadystan, "where every thug wants to be ruler," and "where there is always someone shooting at someone else."[13] A state of civil war is immediately turned into an incomprehensible game of someone-or-other against someone-or-other, a stupid fratricide lacking in any ethical direction or socio-economic *raison d'etre*. The war in Vietnam becomes a mere interchange of unconnected and senseless bullets, and a truce becomes a siesta. "Wahn Beeg Rhat, yes, Duckburg, no!" cries a guerilla in support of an ambitious (communist) dictator, as he dynamites the Duckburg embassy. Noticing that his watch is not working properly, the Vietcong (no less) mutters "Shows you can't trust these watches from the 'worker's paradise.' " The struggle for power is purely personal, the eccentricity of ambition: "Hail to Wahn Beeg Rhat, dictator of all the happy people," goes the cry and sotto voce "happy or not." Defending his conquest, the dictator gives orders to kill. "Shoot him, don't let him spoil my revolution." The savior in this chaotic situation is

Figure 9.5 Walt Disney Productions.

Prince Char Ming, also known [in the Spanish version] as Yho Soy ["I am"—the English is Soy Bheen], names expressive of his magical egocentricity. He comes to reunify the country and "pacify" the people. He is destined to triumph, because the soldiers refuse to obey the orders of a leader who has lost his charisma, who is not "Char Ming." So one guerrilla wonders why they "keep these silly revolutions going forever." Another denounces them, demanding a return to the King, "like in the good old days."

In order to close the circuit and the alliance between Duckburg and Prince Char Ming, Scrooge McDuck presents to Unsteadystan the treasure and the jade elephant which once had belonged to the people of that country. One of the nephews observes: "They will be of use to the poor." And finally, Scrooge, in his haste to get out of this parody of Vietnam, promises "When I return to Duckburg, I will do even more for you. I will return the million dollar tail of the jade elephant."

But we can bet the Scrooge will forget his promises as soon as he gets back. As proof we find in another comic book the following dialogue which takes place in Duckburg:[14]

Nephew: "They got the asiatic flue as well."

Donald: "I've always said that nothing good could come out of Asia."

A similar reduction of a historical situation takes place in the Republic of San Bananador, obviously in the Caribbean or Central America.[15] Waiting in a port, Donald makes fun of the children playing at being shanghaied: These things just don't happen any more; shanghai-ing, weevly beans, walking the plank, pirate-infested seas—these are all things of the past. But it turns out that there are places where such horrors still survive, and the nephews' game is soon interrupted by a man trying to escape from a ship carrying a dangerous cargo and commanded by a captain who is a living menace. Terror reigns on board. When the man is forcibly brought back to the ship, he invokes the name of liberty ("I'm a *free* man! Let me *go!*"), while his kidnappers treat him as a *slave*. Although Donald, typically, makes light of the incident ("probably only a little rhubarb about wages," or "actors making a film"), he and his nephews are also captured. Life on board is a nightmare; the food is weevly beans, even the rats are prevented from leaving the ship. and there is forced labor, with slaves, slaves, and more slaves. All is subject to the unjust, arbitrary and crazy rule of Captain Blight and his bearded followers.

Surely these must be pirates from olden days. Absolutely not. They are revolutionaries (Cuban, no less) fighting against the government of San Bananador, and pursued by the navy for trying to supply rebels with a shipment of arms. "They'll be scouting with *planes!* Douse all lights! We'll give 'em the slip in the *dark!*" And the radio operator, fist raised on high, shouts: "Viva the Revolution!" The only hope, according to Donald, is "the good old navy, symbol of law and order." The rebel opposition is thus automatically cast in the role of tyranny, dictatorship, totalitarianism. The slave society reigning on board ship is the replica of the society which they propose to install in place of the legitimately established regime. Apparently, in modern times it is the champions of popular insurgency who will bring back human slavery.

The political drift of Disney is blatant in these few comics where he is impelled to reveal his intentions openly. It is also inescapable in the bulk of them, where he uses animal symbolism, infantilism, and "noble savagery" to cover the network

Figure 9.6 Walt Disney Productions.

133

of interests arising from a concrete and historically determined social system: U.S. imperialism.

NOTES AND REFERENCES

1. *Tio Rico* (Scrooge McDuck), No. 106; *Uncle Scrooge.* September 1964.

2. *Tio Rico* (Scrooge McDuck), No. 113; *Uncle Scrooge,* June–August 1956, "The Lost Crown of Genghis Khan."

3. For the theme of physical superdevelopment with the connotation of sexual threat, see Eldridge Cleaver, *Soul on Ice,* 1968.

4. Special Number, *Disneylandia,* No. 423.

5. *Tio Rico* (Scrooge McDuck), No. 117.

6. *Disneylandia,* No. 453.

7. *Tio Rico* (Scrooge McDuck), No. 48; *Uncle Scrooge,* December–February 1959.

8. Original: Carrote y Caritas. Caritas is an international organization under the auspices of a sector of the North American and European Catholic Church (Trans.).

9. *Tribilin* (Goofy), No. 62.

10. *Disneylandia,* No. 430; *Donald Duck,* March 1966, "Ambush at Thunder Mountain."

11. *Disneylandia,* No. 432; *Donald Duck,* September 1965, "Treasure of Aztecland."

12. In Inca-Blinca, *Tribilin* (Goofy), No. 104.

13. *Tio Rico* (Scrooge McDuck), No. 99; *Uncle Scrooge,* July 1966, "Treasure of Marco Polo."

14. *Disneylandia,* No. 445.

15. *Disneylandia,* No. 364; (Walt Disney's) *Comics and Stories,* April 1964, "Captain Blight's Mystery Ship."

Additional Readings

Carnoy, Martin. *Education as Cultural Imperialism*. New York: David McKay Co., 1974.

Johnson, H. B. "The Location of Christian Missions in Africa," *Geographical Review*, 57 (1967): 168–202.

Meggers, B. T. "Environmental Limitations on the Development of Culture," *American Anthrologist*, 56 (1954): 801–824.

Simoons, F. S. *Eat Not This Flesh: Food Avoidances in the Old World*. Madison: University of Wisconsin, 1961.

Social Science Research Council, " 'Acculturation': An Explanatory Formulation," *American Anthropologist*, 56 (1954): 973–1002.

Tawney, R. H. *Religion and The Rise of Capitalism*. New York: J. Murray, 1926.

Tochterman, Wolf. "Architecture without Architects," *Courier*, February 1975, pp. 4–13.

Weber, M. *The Protestant Ethnic and The Spirit of Capitalism*. New York: Scribners, 1930.

Wells, Alan. *Picture Tube Imperialism: The Impact of U.S. Television on Latin America*. New York: Orbis Books. 1972.

Willems, Emilio. *Followers of the New Faith: Culture Change and the Rise of Protestantism in Brazil and Chile*. Nashville, Tenn.: Vanderbilt University Press, 1967.

Young, Crawford. *The Politics of Cultural Pluralism*. Madison: University of Wisconsin Press, 1979.

IV

EUROPEAN COLONIALISM: PLANTATION AGRICULTURE

The world's largest rubber plantation at Harbel, Liberia. More than 90,000 acres, or 30 percent of the total land area of Liberia, are cultivated by Firestone. The company also has established plantations in Brazil, Ghana, Guatemala, and the Philippines. How do plantations benefit the local economy? (Source: Firestone Tire and Rubber Company)

A tapper on the Firestone plantation makes an incision in a rubber tree. The latex will flow down the incision through a spout and into the cup attached to the tree. Some of the latex is carried in pails to collecting stations. What would this person do, if he were not working for Firestone? (Source: Firestone Tire and Rubber Company)

In the fifteenth century, the geographic expansion of European influence ushered in the first stage of Western colonialism. Two critical questions must be asked about that expansion: To what extent did colonialism provide the means by which Europe was able to rise to global economic and political power? To what extent did colonialism impoverish people in the Third World? These questions have been debated by scholars of various analytical perspectives and ideological persuasions.

Conservatives maintain that the rise of European capitalism was due primarily to *internal* changes rather than to accumulation of treasure from the Third World. Climatic changes and the decline in indigenous New World populations due to the introduction of European diseases are more important to explain Third World developments since the fifteenth century than the European draining of wealth from areas like Latin America. Conservative scientists conclude that Marxists have been unable "to draw up a sufficiently accurate balance sheet of cash flows" between the Third World and Europe to persuade non-Marxists of their claim of exploitation.

The dynamics of historical core-periphery regional relations interest radicals more than the passive description of European forms of empires. From a radical perspective, colonialism, through trading centers, seizure of slaves and agricultural lands, and looting of precious minerals, allowed European countries to accumulate the necessary capital to emerge as rich, industrial powers. The principal means to achieve this result were European military force, religious orders, and legal sanctions. On the basis of the wealth seized from the Third World, European capitalism flowered.

One of the ways Europeans seized wealth from the Third World was by introducing a new kind of farming into the tropics: plantation agriculture. Plantations were organized by and for European entrepreneurs to produce luxury crops, such as cocoa, tea, coffee, bananas, tobacco, and palm oil, and industrial crops, like rubber, jute, sisal, and cotton, for European markets. The only local resources utilized by the colonizers were manual laborers, land, and tropical climates. No one denies the existence or indeed the importance of plantation agriculture, but a great deal of controversy exists as to its role in the development of tropical countries.

The liberal perspective points to both positive and negative aspects of plantations. Beckford, using marginal economics, argues that although plantation agriculture was and is beneficial for foreign investors and foreign consumers, it is mostly detrimental to national progress. The disadvantages for national development are: a strong import bias for technology, luxury consumer goods, and even for imported food; capital transfers to metropoles in Third World and industrial countries; foreign ownership of productive land and rigid resource allocation; and unequal distribution of income and exasperated social structure.

Conservatives argue not only that plantation agriculture fosters national development but also that most of the benefits accrue to the countries of production. May and Plaza present their case of the United Fruit Company in Latin America where banana production benefits the producing nations in numerous ways. It attracts foreign investment capital; provides national income through wages, taxes, and duties; contributes to higher national agricultural productivity; introduces new technology and innovations; and offers a socially desirable infrastructure of schools, hospitals, and roads. Despite the overwhelming positive economic and social contributions of the United Fruit Company, its image seems to remain blacker than the record because of political and historical events beyond its control.

Tobis provides a fundamentally different analysis of United Fruit. His radical perspective views the firm over time in its broad economic, political, social, and structural context. United Fruit and other foreign enterprises are in the business of making money; the particular crops they produce and the consequences for the producing countries are quite secondary to them. Consequently, the Company is changing its strategies at home and abroad to safeguard and enhance its investments.

Each perspective employs a different analytical framework, marshals different sets of data, and draws profoundly different conclusions. Conservatives are convinced that plantation agriculture facilitates and encourages Third World development. Liberals believe that plantations incidently (and perhaps unfortunately) distort national development. Radicals see plantation agriculture as actively exploiting tropical countries. Which perspective do you support? For what cognitive and emotive reasons?

10 Plantation Agriculture: Firm vs. National Interests

GEORGE L. BECKFORD*

CONDITIONS OF AGRICULTURAL DEVELOPMENT

A great deal has been written about the role (or contribution) of agriculture in overall economic development. The main considerations here are, first, that agriculture must provide the food supplies required to meet an expanding demand resulting from population growth and rising incomes. When this expansion of food supply is not forthcoming, food prices increase and/or supplies must be imported. In either event, development is constrained.

Agriculture must provide not just an increasing supply but one in which the pattern of supply needs to be adjusted to satisfy changing patterns of food consumption that are associated with rising incomes. That is, the supply of high income elasticity foodstuffs must increase at a faster rate than that of low income elasticity products. This demands a certain degree of flexibility of resource use and adjustment within agriculture.

Secondly, the agricultural sector acts as a source of factor supplies for expansion of other sectors of the economy. In this connection particular emphasis has been given to labour and capital transfers. Thirdly, agriculture is the basis of important market relationships which create spread-effects for development. All primary output requires processing of some form and this provides forward linkage effects. Similarly, commercial agriculture relies increasingly on purchased off-farm inputs which provide opportunities for income and employment creation in sectors producing these inputs, the backward linkage effects. The sum of forward and backward linkage effects from agriculture can be quite substantial, given the right conditions.

Fourthly, the agricultural sector is an important earner of foreign exchange in many countries. And foreign exchange is usually required to secure certain capital inputs for development. Given the present structure of the world economy, the export trade of underdeveloped countries is dominated by primary products— mainly of agriculture and mining.

Agricultural development per se involves several necessary conditions; for a

*George L. Beckford, "The Economics of Agricultural Resource Use and Development in Plantation Economies," *Social and Economic Studies*, 18 (Jamaica, 1969): 115–151. This selection has been edited to include pp. 142–149. Reprinted by permission of author and publisher.

start, adequate supplies of resources especially land and capital. Complementary human resources—skills in management and adaptable labour services—are essential as well. A developed infrastructure—roads, water supplies, electricity, etc.—provides a foundation for development. Appropriate institutional arrangements, e.g. affecting incentive for effort, land tenure, marketing, credit and adequate scope for the organization of "large-scale units of collective action" (progress-oriented values, attitudes, social structure, etc.) are pre-conditions for development.

The *dynamics* of agricultural development, however, involve much more. Technological change is crucial. The development process involves an expansion of agricultural output at the same time that labour is moving out of agriculture. The productivity of labour remaining in agriculture must therefore expand substantially. For this, research can play an important part since it serves to increase knowledge of new inputs and of possibilities for raising the productivity of old inputs. Capital accumulation is also essential to the process. And, finally, enough flexibility to facilitate resource adjustments to changing income opportunities is necessary.

UNDERDEVELOPMENT BIASES IN PLANTATION AGRICULTURE

The characteristics of plantation agriculture are such that this type of agriculture tends not to fulfil the basic conditions set out above in the brief discussion of the role of agriculture in economic development. First, this type of agriculture is not geared to supplying food demand within the plantation economy. Instead, it is geared to metropolitan consumption requirements. As such it fulfils another condition by earning foreign exchange. The question that arises is whether over time the foreign exchange-earning ability will be more than enough to provide for imported food supplies so as to leave a residual of earnings for importation of "critical capital inputs."

Plantation export output consists of primary products with relatively low income-elasticities of demand. On the other hand, the food import requirements of plantation economies normally consist of high income-elasticity products.[1] Therefore for any given increase in consumer incomes in both the metropolis and the plantation economy, the required increase in plantation output will be less than the required increase in food imports. In order to compensate, the export price for plantation output must rise relative to food import prices. In other words, over time the terms of trade must move consistently in favour of plantation export output. But in point of fact the historical pattern has generally been the reverse; so that the export earnings of plantation economies tend toward failing to meet food import requirements unless the rate of income growth in the plantation economy falls consistently behind that in the metropolis.[2] It is of considerable interest to note here that despite the deteriorating terms of trade more export agriculture output continues to be produced in the plantation economies. The reason for this is that to the private foreign-plantation owners the commodity terms of trade has no economic significance in the private accounting of the plantation. The terms of trade is really a social concept which does not have much significance in the private accounting of the plantation. To put it another way, the terms of trade of the *firm* may be altogether different from the terms of trade of the *society*.

In addition, it must be noted that the foreign exchange-earning capacity of plantation agriculture is limited by the normally high import content of plantation production and consumption. On the production side, this results partly from the fact that metropolitan capital brings with it its own technology, which usually requires inputs not available in the plantation economy; and partly from the vertically-integrated structure of plantation enterprises. On the consumption side, because plantation labour has been mobilized for export production there is relatively little production for the home market leading to a characteristic heavy reliance on imports of food and other consumer goods. The actual available foreign exchange is therefore what is left after deducting the value of imported inputs used in plantation production, factor incomes going to the metropole and the consumer expenditure on imports in the second round.[3] On the whole, then, the foreign exchange-earning capacity of plantation agriculture seems to be less than is normally assumed.

Another effect of the primary export orientation of plantation agriculture is that the benefits of productivity improvements tend to accrue mostly to metropolitan consumers. This is so primarily in those countries where plantations exist along with farmers producing for their own consumption. In looking at the Jamaican experience, for example, Arthur Lewis observed that although productivity in export agriculture increased by 27 per cent between 1890 and 1930, consumption per head increased only by 13 per cent in the same period because the terms of trade moved adversely from 137 in 1890 to 84 in 1930.[4] Lewis explains this general pattern among tropical exporting countries as follows: ". . . so long as productivity is constant in subsistence production, practically all the benefit of increases in productivity in the commercial crops accrues to the consumer and not to the producer . . . Greater productivity is offset by adverse terms of trade."[5]

The same author had outlined the position at greater length in his *Theory of Economic Growth* as follows:

> If nothing is done to raise the productivity of peasants in producing food, they constitute a reservoir of cheap labour available for work in mines or plantations or other export enterprises . . . So long as the peasant farmers have low productivity, the temperate world can get the services of tropical labour for a very low price. Moreover when productivity rises in the crops produced for export there is no need to share the increase with labour, and practically the whole benefit goes in reducing the price to industrial consumers. Sugar is an excellent case in point. Cane sugar production is an industry in which productivity is extremely high by any biological standard. It is also an industry in which output per acre has about trebled over the past seventy years, a rate of growth unparalleled by any other major agricultural industry in the world— certainly not by the wheat industry. Nevertheless, workers in the cane sugar industry continue to walk barefooted and to live in shacks, while workers in wheat enjoy among the highest living standards in the world. However vastly productive the sugar industry may become, the benefit accrues chiefly to consumers. This is one of the disadvantages to tropical countries (advantages to industrial countries) of the fact that their economic development has concentrated upon the export sector of the economy, and that foreign entrepreneurs and foreign capital have been devoted in the first place primarily to expanding exports . . .[6]

Lewis has been quoted at length here because he is describing a phenomenon that is characteristic not so much of all export agriculture but of plantation agriculture in particular. For this is perhaps the only type of agriculture that by definition always satisfies the two basic conditions that erode retention of the benefits of productivity improvements: export production and a continuous supply of cheap labour.[7]

It should be pointed out, however, that in recent times productivity improvements have brought more benefit to the plantation economies than in the past. This has resulted mainly from increasing trade-union activity which has managed to cream off some of the benefits of improved productivity in the form of higher wages for plantation labour. But against this must be balanced the consideration that improvements in productivity on plantations have invariably involved the oft-neglected cost of increased unemployment.[8]

Plantation agriculture also has a limited capacity for the two other functions mentioned in the earlier discussion of "conditions of agricultural development." As concerns transfers of factor supplies, there are two important limitations. Firstly, because of foreign ownership capital transfers are to the metropolis and not to the non-agricultural sectors of the plantation economy. And, secondly, because the skill content of plantation labour is low (by the specification of the production function), the adaptability of plantation labour to the requirements of other sectors is extremely slow.

So far as market relationships are concerned, the vertical integration of plantation enterprises stretches across national boundaries. Linkages are established within the structure of the *firm* and not within individual plantation economies. For the latter, then, potential linkage effects are dissipated and this minimizes inter-industry transactions with their potential development-spread effects.

Some other factors which further restrict development possibilities in plantation economies and which deserve elaboration are the inherent rigidities in resource adjustment, the element of foreign ownership, the unequal pattern of income distribution and the characteristic rigid social structure.

The high degree of specificity of plantation enterprise investment and the distorted structure of agricultural output prices create a built-in rigidity in the pattern of resource use in plantation agriculture. Because of this heavy commitment to the production of a particular export crop and because foreign investors have little or no interest in production for the domestic market, opportunities for agricultural development deriving from changing patterns of consumer food expenditure tend not be taken up. The normal development pattern, implicit in a model based on more perfectly competitive conditions, does not emerge.

Foreign ownership of plantations limits development in two additional ways not previously considered. Firstly, there is the leakage of income in the form of dividends which reduces the investment capacity of the economy. Secondly, when reinvestment out of the surplus occurs, there is no assurance that the economy in which the surplus was produced will benefit. This follows from the spatial distribution of the firm's operations among a number of countries. Surpluses produced in one country can be re-invested in any other country where the firm owns plantations or at home-base in the metropolis.

The low wages of plantation labourers stand in dramatic contrast to the earnings of the skilled supervisory and management staffs which operate the plantations.

This sets the stage for a generally unequal pattern of income distribution among all households in plantation economies. The adverse development consequences of this are two-fold. Aggregate effective demand is low; this limits the size of the market and rules out the establishment of consumer goods industries with significant scale economies. In addition, the low incomes of the bulk of the population restrict household savings and the scope for domestic investment, while the high-income classes engage in conspicuous consumption of luxury imports and invest heavily in non-productive assets.

Finally, the rigid class lines and weak community cohesion of plantation societies serve to restrict social mobility and to impede the development of large-scale units of collective action. Restricted social mobility adversely affects individual incentive for economic advancement and affects labour adaptability as well.

CONTRIBUTIONS OF PLANTATION AGRICULTURE TO DEVELOPMENT

Two factors which are repeatedly mentioned in the literature on plantation agriculture deserve consideration here so as to round off the discussion. The first is that plantation agriculture has served in the past to open up previously inaccessible areas. In so doing, it has developed an infrastructure of roads, ports, water supplies, electricity, etc., in underdeveloped countries much more rapidly than would otherwise have occurred. This is undoubtedly an important contribution to these economies. But the benefits of this must be weighed against the dynamic underdevelopment biases considered above. What is more, it should be noted that, like everything else, the infrastructure is geared to the specific needs of the plantations and does not necessarily benefit other producers to any significant degree. Thus, for example, we normally find villages and farming areas just outside the boundaries of plantations without water and electricity though the plantation itself is well supplied with these.

The second consideration is that unlike other types of agriculture in underdeveloped countries, plantation agriculture is "scientific." Plantations invest in research which produces a high rate of technological change. Furthermore, the implementation of research findings is quick and easy because of the centralized authority structure of plantations. This can be contrasted with the slow rate of adoption of new techniques by peasant farmers and the overwhelming problem of extension in peasant farming areas. This point is also well taken but requires qualification. Again, the research input of plantations is specific to particular crops and may not apply across the range of technical production possibilities. For example, United Fruit undertakes an elaborate programme of research on bananas, and West Indian sugar plantations maintain their own research stations for studying the problems of sugar. Neither of these invests very much in research on other crops and/or livestock which may offer better economic prospects *to the countries* involved than the particular plantation crop. This raises the problem of the allocative efficiency of research resources. But, in addition, it underscores the existing dynamic bias against high-income production opportunities in the domestic market; for in the absence of technical knowledge such opportunities cannot be readily seized.

NOTES AND REFERENCES

1. Basic starchy staples (the low income-elasticity products in the consumer food basket) are usually supplied from within plantation economies.

2. This condition itself implies limited economic progress in the plantation economy where incomes are already at much lower levels than in the metropolis.

3. There is also the question of the valuation of exports where the product leaves the plantation economy as an intra-company transfer and not through sales. For a discussion of this problem in relation to Central American banana exports and the United Fruit Company, see R. A. La Barge, "The Imputation of Values to Intra-Company Exports: the Case of Bananas," *Social and Economic Studies,* June, 1961.

4. A. Lewis, "Foreword" in G. Eisner, *Jamaica 1830–1930: A Study in Economic Growth* (Manchester University Press, 1961).

5. Ibid., pp. xviii–xix.

6. A. Lewis, *The Theory of Economic Growth* (Allen & Unwin, 1955), p. 281.

7. Other types of agriculture may satisfy one or the other conditions but seldom both. For example, the commercial farm-firms producing wheat in Canada and the peasants producing cocoa in West Africa are export producers without the cheap labour condition while the *haciendas* of Latin America base production on cheap labour but are not export-oriented.

8. I am grateful to Havelock Brewster for reminding me of this.

11 United Fruit's Contribution to National Development

STACY MAY and GALO PLAZA*

. . . The inescapable conclusions are:

1. That the world banana trade is overwhelmingly the creation of foreign private capital investment from the major importing centers.

2. That these same private investment interests have supplied the initiative and the technology upon which the present dimension of the world trade in this commodity has been built.

3. That the benefits accruing to the local economies in the producing areas are about four and one-half times larger than their proportionate contributions to the total capital investment upon which the establishment and maintenance of this significantly important segment of the world food trade depends. Upon almost any criterion of reckoning, this constitutes a remarkably good bargain for capital-poor countries faced with the problem of financing an expanding economic development. Most scholars who have worked in the development field calculate that anywhere from $2.00 to $4.00 of capital funds normally are required to increase the annual production of an area by $1.00. Because the major burden in furnishing the capital needed for the production of bananas for export has been borne by outside investors, the producing countries have been realizing $1.00 of return for a commitment of their own scarce capital amounting to only about 34¢.

4. On every measurement basis that we have been able to devise, the return realized by producing countries from banana exports is extraordinarily high compared with any other agricultural endeavor in which they engage. Acre for acre employed, banana exports yielded to the local economies at least three times the average return from croplands as a whole, and about five times as much per agricultural worker employed. Banana exports earned them from two and one-half to three times the foreign exchange realized per acre upon coffee shipments, the largest gross export for the area as a whole. When account is taken of the fact that comparatively little local capital had to be employed to realize the far higher and much more stable per acre returns from bananas, the preponderant advantages of offering hospitality to foreign private investment in this field are irrefutably evident.

*Stacy May and Galo Plaza, *United States Business Performance Abroad: The United Fruit Company in Latin America* (Washington, D.C.: National Planning Association, 1958), pp. 224–231 and 234–241. Reprinted by permission of publisher.

Figure 11.1 Foreign and Domestic Share in the Banana Business of the Six Countries in 1955.

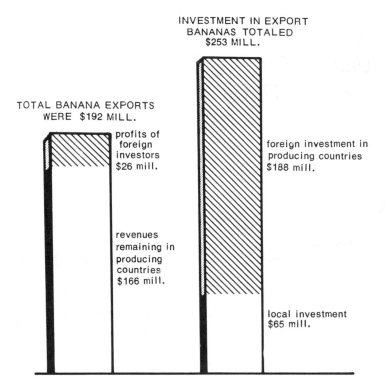

INVESTMENT IN EXPORT
BANANAS TOTALED
$253 MILL.

TOTAL BANANA EXPORTS
WERE $192 MILL.

profits of
foreign
investors
$26 mill.

foreign investment in
producing countries
$188 mill.

revenues
remaining in
producing
countries
$166 mill.

local investment
$65 mill.

UNITED FRUIT COMPANY CONTRIBUTIONS TO COUNTRIES OF PRODUCTION

With respect to the United Fruit Company as a business entity, we are able to measure with precision and in considerable detail its economic impact upon the six countries [Colombia, Dominican Republic, Ecuador, Guatemala, Honduras, and Panama] in which all but a small fraction of the bananas it handles are produced. Since . . . the company produces a variety of other crops in the six republics and none yields a profit to the company that is comparable to that realized from its banana operations, the net return to the local economies from its combined activities is higher when related to its total business than for banana operations alone.

Our accounting of the total impact of all business that United Fruit conducts in the six countries may be summarized as follows:[1]

(1) The total invested capital of the United Fruit Company in its subsidiaries operating in the six countries amounted to about $159 million.

(2) The current account receipts of these subsidiaries were slightly over $150 million ($122 million from exports and $29 million from local sales). Current

account expenditures totaled $122 million. The profit of the subsidiaries upon current account operations was thus about $28 million. Of this, something under $18 million was transferred in the form of dividends to the parent company.

(3) Upon capital account, the subsidiaries had expenditures of about $17 million. These were paid for by the $10 million of current account earnings retained by the subsidiaries, and by new company investment commitments to the area of almost $7 million.

(4) The six local economies received the direct benefit of the combined current and capital account expenditures totaling $139 million—about $103 million in the form of direct expenditures for wages, taxes and local purchases of goods and services, and $36 million of items purchased abroad that were imported and put to use in the area.

(5) Thus the total realized benefit accruing to the economies of the six countries amounted to about 92 percent of the income of the United Fruit subsidiaries operating within their borders, from exports, local sales, fees, and miscellaneous earnings combined.

(6) The dividend income drawn out by the United Fruit Company of something under $18 million amounted to about 12 percent of the subsidiaries' total sales and to about 11 percent on the depreciated book value of its investment in these subsidiaries.

(7) On the very important consideration of the effect on balance of payments, the subsidiaries' foreign exchange contributions to the local economies (that is, the total of export receipts and new capital commitments minus foreign materials and merchandise imports added to dividends transmitted) amounted to almost $76 million, or to about 62 percent of their total exports.

(8) When the United Fruit Company's contribution to local economies is compared to the overall record of U.S. direct private investments in Latin America as a whole, as developed in studies made by the U.S. Department of Commerce, its comparative showing is definitely above average. This is particularly true with respect to its foreign exchange contributions, as cited immediately above. When compared with other U.S. direct private investments in agricultural enterprises, the United Fruit record is outstanding upon every comparative count.

(9) When the realization of the combined six-country economies from United Fruit operations is compared with the return from their domestically financed and operated enterprises, the contrast is even more striking.

(9a) On the measurement of yield per acre of land put to agricultural use, the return from land owned or contracted to the United Fruit Company was more than 20 times the average for all other improved agricultural land in the area as a whole, and from United Fruit *cropland* it was three times the average from all other cropland.

(9b) On the measurement of yield per worker employed in agriculture, the returns from United Fruit operations were about five times the average for the six countries. In all cases, the wages paid by the United Fruit Company were substantially higher than the average for agricultural employees.

(9c) From its employment of one-fourth of 1 percent of all improved agricultural land in the six countries, and from 2 percent of their combined croplands, United Fruit operations have accounted for about 12 percent of total foreign exchange earnings, agricultural and non-agricultural combined, for the area as a whole.

(9d) For the five republics other than Colombia (where the United Fruit operations are of insignificant weight in the economy as a whole), the taxes paid by United Fruit amount to more than 6 percent of total central government revenues. The company's total tax payments in the six countries (to central and local governments combined) have been running in recent years to a sum that about equals its dividend withdrawals from profits earned in the area.

By every economic measure that we have been able to apply, the contribution of the United Fruit Company to the economies of the six countries is enormously advantageous when regarded from the viewpoint of their national interest. The fact that it has been leaving within the production area more than $7.00 for every dollar in profits withdrawn is an impressive but perhaps not the most important factor in determining the degree to which these host nations have gained by offering it their hospitality. Of even greater significance is the fact that the enterprise which the United Fruit Company pioneered, and for which it has played a continuing leading role in developing large temperate zone outlets, is one that is enormously productive compared to any other agricultural pursuit in which these countries engage. Because successful banana production and distribution in international trade requires far heavier investment commitments than most other agricultural products, it is doubtful that the trade would have developed to anything like its present stature if even the production end had depended upon the local financing that capital-poor countries could provide. Since the United Fruit Company furnished the major capital and technological requirements for the establishment of this type of agricultural enterprise, its operations in the six countries have yielded a return to their economies several times larger per acre of land and for each agricultural worker employed than any agricultural activity developed through local initiative and capital financing. And the growth trend in national realizations from United Fruit operations has been far more stable than those obtained from the general agricultural exports of the countries from which it operates.

From the studies of capital-output ratios that have been made in various parts of the world, it is difficult to conceive of any activity—agricultural, extractive, or industrial—organized upon the basis of capital supplied from their own resources that would have yielded these countries a comparable economic return per dollar of national investment.

The United Fruit Company has made numerous additional contributions to the progress of economic development in the six countries that are less amenable to precise measurement. Its enterprise has opened up vast areas of low, hot, humid, and heavily forested terrain that otherwise might have remained closed to settlement and productive use for many decades at best. It has supplied the basic facilities—roads, railways, port and communication facilities, electric power establishments, hospitals, and schools that have made this possible. It has introduced modern scientific agricultural methods and equipment, and has trained hundreds of thousands of the local inhabitants in their use over the span of its existence. It has pioneered in the introduction of the health and sanitation measures without which operation in the banana-producing areas is virtually untenable. It has played a leading role in the introduction to the area of new crops such as African oil palm, abaca, and a variety of timber species that have been far more profitable to the local economies than to itself. It has vastly improved the available planting stock and cultural procedures in planting and maintaining others, like cacao, and has contributed to the improvement of tropical agricultural practices in the area of its operations in literally hundreds of other ways.

Upon all *strictly economic measurements* that can be applied, the suggested test for justifying the worth of a foreign private investment to host countries—by clear demonstration that it brings them greater gains than they could have hoped to achieve without it—is answered in terms too conclusive to admit debate.

THE UNITED FRUIT COMPANY RECORD IN SOCIAL WELFARE, LABOR, AND PUBLIC RELATIONS

Obviously, the direct economic impact of a foreign investment enterprise upon the areas of its operation is only one of the ways in which its influence may be appraised. A corporate entity, whether it operates at home or abroad, is in effect an individual, created by legal fiat, subject to obligations and afforded privileges and immunities, as prescribed by the prevailing law. Its overall responsibilities include performance as a good citizen of the areas in which it operates.

We described the general scope of the company's activities in such fields as the provision of housing, health and sanitation, education, club and recreational facilities, commissaries and food purveying, and a variety of other community services for its workers. We have reviewed also its labor and public relations policies and procedures. Our general findings in this field may be summarized as follows:

(1) In the six countries of our firsthand study, the United Fruit Company in 1955 paid out approximately $53 million in direct wages and $8 million in fringe benefit payments to 59,000 employees on its payrolls. It spent a further $4.25 million on schools, hospitals, and infirmaries (on a net basis), welfare programs, and sanitation services—all of which were of direct benefit to its work force. Thus, for the six-country area, the labor cost per company employee averaged almost $1,100 without any allowance for the rental value of the living quarters provided for employees by United free of charge.

(2) In addition, the company's books show a net cost to it of about $1.2 million on staple commodities that it sold to its employees at prices below cost. Since its total commissary operations in the six countries have been run on a break-even basis with both costs and sales revenues averaging around $15.5 million per year over a five-year period, there is no reason for the loss-item portion of this business to be segregated. It is apparent, however, that the commissary privilege, through which the company's workers have spent about 30 percent of their net pay receipts for living necessities on which they have paid no distribution markups, has substantially stretched the value of their take-home pay. And this take-home pay, as already noted, is uniformly higher than the going rates in the area. There is an added bonus through the general company practice of making available garden

plots upon which its workers are encouraged to grow foodstuffs for their own tables.

(3) As our review has shown, the United Fruit Company record with respect to its furnishings of hospital, dispensary, and sanitation services has been generally excellent when measured by the objective standard of the health records of its employees. In this field, the company has pioneered in the difficult task of making traditionally disease-ridden tropical environments safer places in which to live and work, and complaints about its performance on this score are remarkably infrequent from any source.

(4) With respect to the provision of educational facilities, United Fruit usually goes well beyond what is required by law, but its performance here is less outstanding than in the fields related to health. Its schools are better equipped and manned than the average for surrounding rural areas and, in some cases, provide a longer period of instruction than the prescribed minimum. There is, however, a serious problem raised by the gap of three to six years that, under prevailing laws, exists between the normal completion of compulsory school requirements and the minimum age for the granting of work permits. There is also a largely unfilled need for vocational and domestic science instruction that applies to the United Fruit Company schools in common with the rural school system as a whole. The company recently has taken some steps to provide more of this type of instruction. It also materially assists in providing opportunities for the continuing education of its employees' children in the United States and Canada, and has invested some $6.5 million of capital in the establishment of the Escuela Agricola Panamericana in Honduras. This excellent school provides practical, hands-in-the-dirt training to about 160 pupils selected from many latin American countries. The company pays all of their expenses for a three-year course that covers horticulture, field crop production, and animal husbandry, and it strictly adheres to the rule that none of the graduates shall enter into United Fruit Company employment. By this provision, it gives assurance that the School is intended to serve the general interests of Latin American agriculture rather than forward the company's own advantage.

(5) On all of its establishments within the six republics, the company provides for its workers places of worship, clubs, recreational facilities, and athletic fields and equipment upon a scale and of a standard that are matched by few, if any, locally owned agricultural enterprises. To an important degree, its railroads, ships, radio communications, electric light and power facilities, and commissaries serve a wider community than its own employee group. In many cases, this is true of its hospitals and other amenities as well. Its general record of performing services of benefit to the communities that always tend to grow up on the fringes of company divisions is excellent. On a number of occasions, the company has even helped central governments over difficult financial emergencies by making advance payments on prospective taxes, a procedure that generally would be accepted as beyond the call of normal duty.

(6) In the important field of housing, the company record again is good to excellent if viewed in the perspective of prevailing standards. The accommodations furnished to United Fruit workers free of charge generally are far better than anything to be found on farms in the surrounding areas. But this, in itself, is less than an unqualified endorsement, since the housing of the great majority of

agricultural laborers in the six countries is deplorably substandard. The newer single-family houses that the company has been building upon a systematic replacement program would qualify as good under almost any standard. But the pace of the replacement program is necessarily limited by what the company can afford. The cost of the new single-family dwellings runs from $1,500 to $2,000 per unit, so that more than $100 million is involved in the rehousing of all of its employees in the six countries alone. This sum is equivalent to five or six years of the company's total dividend transmittals from the area at the rate that has prevailed in recent years.

Meanwhile, the major part of its agricultural laborers still are housed in barracks-type structures partitioned off into family-unit divisions. At their worst, as exemplified by some of the older buildings at Tenguel in Ecuador and Almirante in Panama, such accommodations are somewhat grim. At their best, they represent a huddled pattern of living that is in accord neither with a rural environment where space is not a luxury nor with the deeply rooted Latin American sentiment for family privacy. The multiple dwelling units are being replaced by single family units at a rate of about 5 percent each year. It is difficult to see how a faster pace than this could be provided on the current earnings record. There are, however, complementary measures through which the situation might be improved at far less cost. One of these might take the form of an intensive educational effort to encourage workers to exert their own initiative toward better standards of housekeeping and household improvements. A relatively inexpensive program of recognition and rewards for the best kept and most attractively decorated or landscaped dwelling units might serve to awaken a competitive pride that could achieve much to relieve the present somewhat drab standardization in workers' living quarters.

(7) Relations with labor in the six countries have not been uniformly happy despite United Fruit's consistent record of providing considerably higher wages, security, welfare, and other fringe benefits than those generally prevailing in the communities concerned. In the post-war period, its operations in a number of countries have, on occasion, been seriously interrupted through work stoppages incident to labor disputes.

On balance, it is probably fair to appraise United Fruit performance in the field of labor relationships over the years as generally in advance of current practices in areas to which the tradition of labor unionism is new, its leadership relatively inexperienced, worker allegiance to union principles weak, and where political overtones tend to overshadow bargaining considerations. In several of the six countries, the company is caught between a cross-fire of criticism on its labor relations. On the one hand, there are those who hold that such organizations as the Fruit Company should be taking a vigorously active position in encouraging unionism among its workers, rather than following the conventional employer role of recognizing the bargaining with such unions after they are formed. In recent years, even the U.S. government has given official support to this position through its general endorsement of ORIT, a program for affiliating free trade unions in Latin America with the AFL-CIO complex in the United States and with other noncommunist labor organizations on a world basis. On the other hand, the company often has been criticized as unduly soft in its labor terms and policies by members of the local business communities and even by government officials in several of the six countries in which traditional attitudes are profoundly suspicious of labor organization and resentful of its encouragement by foreign corporations in their midst.

Since 1954—when the United Fruit Company adopted a positive code of labor practices and took steps to see that it was generally established throughout its operating divisions—the company's position in this field clearly has moved from one of generally benevolent paternalism to one of consciously forwarding modern employer-worker relationship procedures. It freely recognizes and deals with all union agencies through which many of its workers elect to bargain. Concurrently, it is not unnaturally apprehensive about the potentially damaging effect to its peculiarly vulnerable business of concerted international labor pressure that might be exercised on purely local disputes through an affiliated international structure of labor organizations of the ORIT type. Time alone will establish whether or not such misgivings have any substantial foundation. Meanwhile, the honest attempt of the United Fruit Company, and other similarly situated corporations, to support the sound principles of independent unionism would be made easier if those responsible for shaping ORIT's policies offered assurances that its structure of union affiliation across national boundary lines would not result in expanding local disputes to international dimension, or result in the arbitrary employment of such instruments as international labor boycotts or "hot cargo" embargos.

(8) Since 1951—the United Fruit Company has been devoting an ever-increasing effort to the task of improving its public relations in the countries in which its foreign operations are centralized. The professional personnel to which this task has been entrusted operate upon the sound hypothesis that their function is to see that accurate information about the company's affairs is made available to the widest possible audience, rather than to attempt to manipulate public opinion to an attitude favorable to the company's interest.

This program has included the issuing of annual reports on subsidiary operations and a variety of educational pamphlets stressing the company's contributions to local economies through its business transactions and philanthropic activities. It has employed the publication of company newspapers to keep its workers informed, and has purchased advertising space in the local press to keep a wider public aware of what the company is doing. Increasingly, arrangements are being made to invite local journalists, public officials, and influential citizens to visit the company's divisions to gain firsthand knowledge of how its affairs are conducted. To an ever-increasing degree, the responsible local personnel of the company are being reminded of the importance of discharging the "citizenship" obligations of a corporation engaged in foreign operations through extending services to the surrounding communities in general and to their local competitors in banana production in particular.

Despite the commendable vigor of these efforts, there is a long road to be traveled before the local image of the United Fruit Company conforms to the true picture of its performance, although there are evident signs of genuine progress along this line. In our discussions of the United Fruit Company's current policy and practices with heads of state and high government officials in all six of the countries visited, recognition of its signal contributions and certification of the generally high standard of its behavior far outweighed the specific criticisms that were voiced. The same result was obtained from interviews with local business representatives, including United Fruit competitors, and with most of the company's employees, although the praise was seldom unqualified.

Yet, objective reporting compels us to register the fact that Latin American esteem for the United Fruit Company and its works is far from universal. The further one moves from those who have firsthand dealing with United Fruit, and lower is its repute. This generally holds true within the countries where it operates, and its worst reputation is in the Latin American republics with which it has no active relationships. Scarcely a week goes by in which the United Fruit Company is not denounced somewhere in the Latin American press as the epitome of arrogant foreign exploitation and greed. To the average man in the average Latin American street, the name of the United Fruit Company conjures up an image not unlike that of the Abominable Snow Man in the minds of the Sherpa guides and bearers of the high Himalayan snow slopes. Few Sherpas even claim to have seen the creature. The legend of his hostile behavior is fragmentary and shadowy. And yet the conviction of his malevolence is almost tangibly intense.

The striking disparity between the reputation and the performance of the United Fruit Company deserve further exploration. Part of the explanation lies in difficulties and complexities which are shared by many other large foreign-investment enterprises operating in economic frontier areas, to which are added special complications inherent in the banana business. Part stems from the historic setting of the United Fruit Company's incorporation and early development. And part, no doubt, must be charged to the company's own short-comings and ineptitudes.

WHY THE IMAGE IS BLACKER THAN THE RECORD

(1) From the description given in this study of the pattern of United Fruit's operations in the six countries, it is evident that it has been forced to deal with a range of human problems inordinately wider than that faced by the average corporation—whether operating at home or abroad. To establish the production end of its business, it had no other option other than to provide, at its own expense and initiative, full-scale communities with all of the physical and social utilities necessary for their support in what were essentially wilderness environments negligibly populated before it moved in.

To compound the difficulties, such operations had to be carried out in countries of less than mature political stability, and without sufficient resources to provide in such fringe areas of their terrain even a minimum complement of the services that governments normally supply in societies of more advanced economic development.

The average industrial firm builds its plant, and draws upon the surrounding community for its work force and for a host of servicing activities to support its operations. Most of its human relationship problems center on the workers in its plants during the hours of active employment. From the wages that it pays, its employees make their own arrangements for housing, food, and other purchases, and for their transport between home and job. The corporation's taxes contribute to the support of schools, health facilities, roads, and all of the public utilities that service the community life of its workers, but it has no direct responsibility for their operation.

Although such enterprises as the United Fruit Company pay the full complement of taxes with which other corporations are charged, governments provide them with relatively little in the way of community facilities in return. The terrains in which United Fruit grows its bananas fall within the do-it-yourself zones of countries in which the fabric of conventional governmental institutions is stretched unduly thin. Through necessity, not choice, the company has become enmeshed in the establishment of company towns with all of their supporting activities, and has undertaken the servicing of far broader communities with land transport, communications, port and shipping services, and a variety of other activities—from facilities primarily designed to meet the exceptionally demanding logistics of its major business.

Each of these extraneous activities stretches the normal range of corporation-community relationships. Each invites its own misunderstandings and strains. No corporation anywhere in the world has ever assumed so broad a portfolio of responsibilities and managed to maintain frictionless public relations. The United Fruit Company is no exception to this rule. When consideration is given to the fact that it has carried the extra burden of operating as a foreign-owned and foreign-managed enterprise in environments that are supersensitively nationalistic, it would be a miracle if it has been able to be the exception.

(2) Even so, the public relations path of the United Fruit Company might have been smoother if its operation had evolved in a happier historic setting. The company was incorporated in 1899, only three years after the Spanish-American War. The United States had just annexed Puerto Rico and the Philippines. In 1901, Cuba's sovereignty was gravely compromised by U.S. insistence on the terms of the Platt Amendment as a condition of terminating general occupation. In 1903, the United States intervened to assure the success of Panama's secession from Colombia, with the Canal Treaty as its concomitant reward. In 1904, it took over the management of customs services in the Dominican Republic when European intervention was threatened because of defaulted debts.

In this period, President Theodore Roosevelt was making pronouncements to the effect that "chronic wrongdoing, or an impotence which results in a general loosening of the ties of a civilized society, may in America . . . force the United States . . . to the exercise of an international police power." The terms "Manifest Destiny" and the "Big Stick Policy" were coined by the proponents of U.S. expansion, and "Dollar Diplomacy" by its adversaries. In 1909, the United States sent troops into Nicaragua; in 1915, into Haiti; and in 1916, into the Dominican Republic. Other interventions of several types and degrees occurred in Cuba and Central America over this period.

In short, the founding and early development of the United Fruit Company occurred at a time when Latin American confidence in U.S. intentions and policy toward its weaker neighbors of the Western Hemisphere was at lowest ebb. To them, the United Fruit Company was a visible symbol, and one of the largest and most conspicuous, of a potential northern dominance that they feared and resented.

NOTES AND REFERENCES

1. For this accounting, we have used the combined average of all operations of the subsidiaries in the six countries for 1954 and 1955. As explained in Chapter V, advanced tax payments made by certain of the subsidiaries in 1955, and the fact that dividends for both 1954 and 1955 were transmitted in the latter year, would make an accounting based on the 1955 operations alone something less than fairly representative.

12 United Fruit's Contribution to Underdevelopment

DAVID TOBIS*

To both North and South Americans the United Fruit Company (UFCo) is known as *the* producer of bananas (Chiquita)—the proud creator of the Banana Republics. Their early exploitation, going back to the 19th century, was typical of the first stages of U.S. imperialism. From the end of the 19th century to the middle of the 20th, U.S. capital abroad was primarily concerned with extracting raw materials (agricultural goods and minerals) from its "spheres of influence" in the underdeveloped world. Extensive transportation networks were established in each country, to help yield that country's fruits to North American capital.

As capitalism has advanced and economic contradictions have intensified at home, the imperialist countries have tried to force the underdeveloped world to assume an ever-increasing role in resolving those contradictions. But with the growing nationalism in underdeveloped countries, the Cuban Revolution and the attempt to nationalize 400,000 acres of United Fruit land in Guatemala in 1954, UFCo and other major U.S. corporations have been forced to restructure their forms of operation. This process of change has been marked by four characteristics: (1) diversification within the United States, (2) the creation and expansion of diversified markets in the underdeveloped countries, (3) the accelerated development of an indigenous bourgeoisie to promote U.S. interests and to protect U.S. companies from expropriation, and (4) the creation of multinational and multicorporate structures for better economic coordination and control.

CHARACTERISTICS OF THE NEW STRATEGY

UFCo has developed a new strategy for several reasons. First, although the Company sold 12 billion bananas throughout the world in 1972,[1] at a certain point it becomes difficult for UFCo to sell more and more bananas in those same areas. Second, dramatic competition has developed recently in the banana industry; UFCo has been replaced as the top banana salesman in North America. Shortly after World War II, UFCo controlled up to 80 percent of the North American market; today it only commands 39 percent. In U.S. sales (though not worldwide),

*David Tobis, "United Fruit is Not Chiquita," in Susanne Jonas and David Tobis (eds.), *Guatemala*. (New York: North American Congress on Latin America, 1974), pp. 122–131. Reprinted by permission of publisher.

Castle & Cooke, through its banana subsidiary Standard Fruit and Steamship Co. is top banana, with Del Monte (under the Dole label) third. Finally, the natural and political disasters, hurricanes and disease, nationalism and revolution—have made ownership of banana plantations a risky business.

Like all companies, UFCo must expand in order to survive. Since bananas sell for a penny apiece in the countries where they are grown, UFCo cannot expand its sales by marketing whole bananas there. To solve these problems, UFCo has sought new banana markets and diversified its operations in both North and South America, developing a new range of products for each region.

Diversification in North America

In the late 1960's UFCo decided to concentrate its U.S. diversification in the area it knew best: food. In addition to becoming aligned with Morrell meats, (which accounted for 33 percent of the company's income in 1973) the company acquired 2000 A&W Root Beer drive-ins, Baskin-Robbins ice cream and J. Hungerford Smith syrups, toppings and ice cream flavorings. In addition, the Company bought out Inter-Harvest lettuce to become the largest lettuce grower in the United States and a major producer of celery and cauliflower. Although seemingly inconsequential, lettuce accounts for one percent of the total grocery store sales which reach $6 billion annually, or some $60 million, and UFCo produces about 18 percent of total lettuce sales.[2]

Expansion of Markets in the Underdeveloped World

As an integral part of its overall corporate strategy, UFCo has begun to look for new markets and investments, turning eyes towards Japan and Mexico as well as towards the area of its principal overseas operations, Central America. The directors have begun to realize that in Central America alone there are 15 million people who are potential consumers of UFCo products.

With the establishment of the Central American Common Market (CACM) in the early 1960's, goods produced in any one of the five republics can be sold in the others without payment of tariffs. Companies do not have to pay import duties on machinery or raw materials brought into the country and there are no taxes on profits for five to ten years. It does not matter whether a company is U.S.-owned or owned by Central Americans because any company plant in the area is eligible for all the benefits of the Common Market if it is involved in intra-regional trade.[3]

As a producer of raw bananas, a good not traded in the Common Market, UFCo did not qualify for CACM's tax benefits. Therefore, in 1965 it bought out a Costa Rican company, NUMAR, S.A., which was the largest Central American producer of margarine, mayonnaise, salad oils and shortening. This purchase qualified UFCo for all the privileges, benefits and tax exemptions of the CACM.[4]

A majority of the new companies which UFCo has recently absorbed are in the food industry. It is obvious that one reason the company decided to expand in this area is that it had developed skills, contacts, outlets, and control from 70 years of experience in the field. There is another reason: increasingly, U.S. companies control the processing, distribution, and marketing of food destined for the Latin

American consumer sector, rather than own the land to produce the food themselves.

What is happening in the processed food industry is typical of what is happening in the entire industrial sector of Central and South America. U.S. firms in the area have begun to produce for a local market and increasingly dominate and control the industrial production of the region. As foreign investment moves from the agricultural into the industrial sector, unemployment will intensify. In Guatemala, for example, foreign companies employ twice as many people *per dollar of capital investment* in agriculture as they do in manufacturing.[5] In the last ten years, while foreign investment has doubled, the unemployment level (currently over 20 percent) has not decreased significantly.[6]

The case of United Fruit provides evidence against the theory that foreign investment creates new jobs. Although UFCo's net fixed assets (book value)[7] have increased 45 percent (or $75 million) since 1948, the number of persons employed in the Tropics where most of the Company's investments are located has actually fallen by 50 percent. While investment has been increasing, employment has been decreasing. This is what is meant by capitalist industrialization. [Table 12.1].

Table 12.1   United Fruit Company: Assets and Employees, 1948-1969

	1948	1956	1961[a]	1969
Net Fixed Assets (in thousands of dollars)	167,724	239,260	187,855	242,711
Tropical Employees	91,393	83,760	39,700	45,000
Other Employees	9,012	11,142	10,300	14,000

[a]The loss of investments in Cuba accounts for the sharp drop in assets between 1956 and 1961.

Source: Annual Reports, 1949, 1956, 1965, 1969.

The Development of a Domestic Bourgeoisie

As impoverished Latin Americans increasingly demand control over their own lives and a greater share of their national wealth, North American companies have developed new and more sophisticated methods to defend their empire. One such method entails the accelerated development of a small Latin American capitalist class whose interests and survival are directly tied to the fate of U.S. companies. These Latin American puppets perform several vital functions as junior partners of foreign capital. They administer the offices and plantations of U.S. companies, represent them before government bureaucracies, serve as their lawyers, and, of course, grow wealthy as a result of the presence of their North American benefactors.

Two examples of the above are Gonzalo Facio and Jose "Pepe" Figueres in Costa Rica. Facio has served UFCo as a lawyer, as he has also done for Allied Chemical, U.S. Steel, American Bridge and, more recently, ALCOA. In 1954,[8] when Facio was UFCo's lawyer in Costa Rica, his company signed yet another favorable contract with the Costa Rican government. On that occasion Facio said,

Operating agreements such as that which the Costa Rican government has just completed with the United Fruit Co. not only proves the falsity of the Communist charges of Yankee Imperialism, but they show how our government and peoples may profit by the cooperative attitude of American enterprise.[9]

And profit he did. As payment for his work in promoting UFCo's interests, the Company gave him a 17,300 acre estate in Costa Rica in 1964.

While he was Ambassador to Washington (appointed in 1962) the U.S. government financed and organized Cuban exile military bases in Costa Rica at Tortuguero and Saripiqui. These bases were engaged in training men for a future invasion of Cuba. Coincidentally, UFCo had large sugar plantations in pre-revolutionary Cuba, and at one time was the fifth largest producer on that island.[10]

Figueres, Costa Rica's three-time President and self-styled leader of the staunchly anti-Communist non-revolutionary left in Latin America, is also a close ally of UFCo. He and his business partner, a Cuban exile, set up a holding company called San Cristobal to administer their two coffee farms, a natural fiber (sisal) factory and a synthetic fiber (polypropylene) factory. Just before he assumed the presidency in 1970, Figueres' firms received several very lucrative contracts to produce sacks for the UFCo. Once President, Figueres repaid this generosity with tremendous government concessions and benefits to UFCo which amply remunerated UFCo for the favorable contracts the company had given him.

It is not only individuals like Gonzalo Facio and "Pepe" Figueres whose friendship and good will the UFCo cultivates to serve its interests. In addition, like other North American companies, UFCo seeks to create a small elite group of Latin American businessmen who will promote its interests. This puppet class represents one major means by which U.S. firms will protect themselves against nationization. Several means are used in this process of creating a dependent Latin American elite. Some U.S. firms have established joint ventures with Latin Americans, others have leased U.S. technology while still others have contracted Latin American companies to produce goods which the U.S. contractor then markets. These arrangements minimize and often eliminate the need for new capital investment while maintaining a relatively high rate of profit for the U.S. company involved.

An additional aspect of the drive to create a dependent capitalist class comes to light when one examines the wide range of programs and "social service" activities engaged in by U.S. and other foreign companies. These include: the technical training of local businessmen (who then manage local branch offices); financing technical schools to teach business skills, later to be used in company service; organizing and paying for trips to the United States to impress Latin Americans with North America's size and to show them the affluent side of U.S. life; and, often in conjunction with the U.S. Information Agency (USIA), sponsoring cultural events to indoctrinate local elites with North American values.

Associate Producers   UFCo's "Associate Producer" program fits neatly into the pattern of forming puppet capitalists. In the past UFCo has had difficulties with nationalizations. In 1954 the Guatemalan government caused UFCo a momentary shudder by trying to nationalize 400,000 acres of idle land owned by the company.

In 1960, when the Cuban government successfully nationalized 271,000 acres of land and two sugar mills (Preston and Boston) held by UFCo, the Company became frantic and the stockholders hysterical. At that point, UFCo put the "Associate Producer" program into full swing.

Under the program, UFCo sells or leases some of its land to middle and upper middle class locals. The leaseholders, called "Associate Producers," sell their entire production to the UFCo. To get an Associate Producer started, UFCo lends him money for an initial investment and provides technical assistance if needed. When the bananas are sold, "the difference between the final selling price and the total cost of production (the profit) is divided equally between the grower and the company."[11] Essentially, UFCo has created a risk-free means of production under which bourgeois sharecroppers pay with crops for the use of their own country's lands.

This program currently supplies the fruit for 52 percent of UFCo's total banana sales.[12] By 1963, there were a total of 1,115 Associate Producers in six South American countries, and all the banana acreage in Colombia, the Dominican Republic and Ecuador which the UFCo has developed in the last 65 years is presently under the Associate Producer program. The Associate Producer program thus serves as a deterrent to nationalization, not only by lowering the profile of the UFCo as the owner and exploiter of vast tracts of land, but also by creating a bloc of Latin Americans whose welfare is tied directly to the continued operations of the company. At the annual meeting of the UFCo in 1961, Board Chairman Thomas Sunderland clearly indicated the importance of the program in answering a stockholder's question:

> Mr. Everett Ford: I would like to ask what effect the unrest in South America will have on the business of United Fruit as a whole. I am referring particularly to nationalization.
> Chairman Sunderland: We watch areas of unrest very carefully. We have as you know large fixed investments that we cannot move. To the extent that we are successful over a period of time in changing our banana plantations over to the Associate Producer program, so that nationals operate the farms, we are better off in the kind of conditions you mention.[13]

Related to this program is the sharp drop in UFCo's land holdings. In the four Central American countries where it had investments (Costa Rica, Guatemala, Honduras, and Panama) and where its holdings in 1954 were equal to 20.4 percent of the *total* crop land, the total (not including Associate Producer lands) has fallen from 1,726,000 acres in 1954 to 672,000 acres in 1971.[14] Some of this land has been sold to banana producers no less dependent upon the company than the Associate Producers, while much of the rest has been leased under the Associate Producer program. Thus, even though the company's actual holdings have shrunk, its penetration into the economy, through indirect control and direct investment in both agricultural and industrial sectors, has grown.

Another note on the subject of nationalization should be added. If the Central American countries decided to nationalize UFCo's banana lands, they would be left with the task of marketing and distributing bananas, areas which UFCo (along with a couple of other North American companies) monopolizes. In addition, the production and distribution of bananas has become three times more capital intensive in the last ten years.[15] Without access to new capital in volume or to new capital goods and replacement parts, nationalization within a capitalist framework would prove to be costly—UFCo would turn to alternative sources of supply and, no doubt aided by its "competitors," would refuse to handle any bananas from nationalized lands.

The 1974 "banana war" illustrates the position of the exporting countries. In March 1974, seven banana exporting countries—Panama, Costa Rica, Honduras, Nicaragua, Ecuador, Colombia and Guatemala—discussed imposing an added tax on banana exports from 1 to 2½ cents per pound (or 40 cents to $1.00 per 40 pound box). The tax would provide these countries with between $160 million and $260 million a year (depending on the number of countries which imposed the tax and the amount of their tax).

The countries, which account for 60 to 70 percent of the world's banana exports, are also trying to create a Union of Banana Exporting Countries (UPEF) to strengthen their position in relation to the three multinational corporations which dominate their countries: United Fruit, Castle & Cooke and Del Monte. The banana companies were originally divided in their response. Castle & Cooke, in its attempt to dislodge UFCo from its position as industry leader, responded viciously by cutting back production, allegedly attempted to kill President Torrigos of Panama,[16] destroyed crops in Honduras, and recently threatened to sell its operations in Costa Rica at twice its stated value. Initially UFCo responded with its new-found paternalism, for several reasons. First, the Company was desperately trying to live down its image as the interventionist octopus. But more important, UFCo was able to exploit the decreased banana supply as a result of the war to increase the prices as it had wanted to. According to the Company's 1973 annual report, published in May 1974, which refers to the period right before the proposed banana tax,

> . . . sharply increased imports from Honduras have created an over-supply in the banana markets, resulting in severely depressed prices and unsatisfactory banana operations during the first quarter of 1974.

But as the situation became more polarized, UFCo also began to take a hard line, eventually being threatened by the Panamanian government for suspending banana exports.

The Central American governments have responded in two ways. Panama's response was militant: strikes of banana workers were preceded by a regional conference of representatives of the 100,000 banana workers in Central America and threats of nationalization against United Fruit. But other countries, dependent on the capitalist market, and having domestic bourgeoises whose interests are interconnected with imperialism, have given in to corporate pressure. As of August 1974, only Panama, Costa Rica and Honduras have actually imposed the tax, with Costa Rica lowering its tax from $1.00 to 25 cents per 40 pound box.

The most important setback for UPEB was the withdrawal of Ecuador, the world's largest banana exporter, accounting for 30 percent of the world's banana exports. The press has explained this withdrawal in two ways. First, the original reason for the creation of the UPEB was in response to the tremendous increase in oil prices. Ecuador, self-sufficient in oil, is not vulnerable to the increased price and therefore, does not need the increased banana tax for revenue. Second, a dubious argument at best, because Ecuador is furthest away from the major banana markets, it has higher shipping costs. An increase in the cost of bananas would price its fruit above that of other countries. But unstated and perhaps most important, the production of bananas in Ecuador (unlike the other countries) is conducted primarily through Associate Producers who sell to UFCo (which had sold all its land there in the mid-1960's) and to Castle & Cooke. The domestic bourgeoisie, more than the fruit companies, would be hurt by an increased tax on bananas. The local allies of the fruit companies and the fruit companies' control of marketing and distribution, dramatically limit the nationalistic reforms possible under capitalism.

The Creation and Expansion of Multinational/Multicorporate Structures

Multinational Structures   UFCo has always been an international corporation. In the past, however, its prime activity has been to extract raw materials from Latin America. Recently, like most large U.S. firms, UFCo is moving toward a deeper level of world penetration and integration. United Fruit is continuing to exploit the agricultural wealth from Latin America, but it has increased its banana producing base to countries outside of Latin America, has developed new markets for bananas, and has begun to use the underdeveloped nations as a base for exporting manufactured (processed) products to both developed and underdeveloped countries.

New Banana Base and Markets   Unable to expand in its traditional banana markets, and losing its historical advantages to new competitors, UFCo has tried to expand by setting up banana operations in Madagascar, Ghana and in 1973 began selling in the Persian Gulf.[17] But most important, UFCo set up plantations in the Philippines to supply the large and growing market in Japan. (In 1967, the Company sold no bananas in Japan, but by 1969 it controlled 10 percent of the banana market there, though its share of the market had not increased by 1973.[18] Aside from allowing for easier world distribution, this expansion will allow the Company to play one underdeveloped area of the world off against another, as in the recent case of UFEB which only includes Latin American countries. . . .

Export of Manufactured Products   This aspect of the UFCo's operations in not yet highly developed. Polymer, the plastics company, produces plastic bags and markets them throughout Central America. Numar will export edible oils and margarines to Czechoslovakia and Israel. UFCo has begun raising cattle in Honduras for slaughter there and consumption in the United States. Although UFCo has had less experience than other U.S. companies in using the underdeveloped nations as an export base for manufactured items, the process as a whole has had a dramatic impact on Latin America. In 1957, 11.7 percent of all Latin America's manufactured exports originated from U.S. firms based in Latin America, but by 1966 the corresponding figure was 41.2 percent.[19]

Multicorporate Structures   Contrary to popular myths, large capitalist corporations try to minimize destructive competition wherever possible. This is done legally through certain types of consortia, joint ventures, unstated agreements (regarding prices) and industry-wide organizations, and illegally through secret agreements in violation of antitrust laws. The defeat of the United States in Southeast Asia, the recent economic chaos and the decline of American hegemony, has created a period of intense capitalist rivalry, making certain alliances much more difficult. Nevertheless, corporate giants have continued to try to coordinate their efforts to preserve and promote their collective interests.

Some of UFCo's joint ventures with other companies are unimportant, such as the 77 percent joint venture with Nicaraguan interests in Aceitera Corona or the pooling of UFCo's ships with Salen Shipping Co. of Stockholm, Sweden, to improve vessel utilization.[20] But others are more important. UFCo has begun to enter into joint ventures with other major firms which at one time might have been considered its competitors, either real or potential. One specific example is the Atlantic Community Group for the Development of Latin America, the ADELA Investment Company. This is a consortium of 235 of the largest U.S. banks and industrial corporations. UFCo holds $250,000 of the $17.5 million of stock initially issued by ADELA.[21] *Business Week* has estimated that ADELA will mobilize close to $1 billion of investment in Latin America.

Similar to ADELA is the Latin American Agribusiness Development Corporation (LAAD), composed of eleven of the largest U.S. corporations plus ADELA. Among these is Standard Fruit, UFCo's major banana "competitor." Since UFCo is a member of ADELA there will be at least minor cooperations between these two companies in LAAD.

CONCLUSION

United Fruit Co. has developed the strategies discussed above as a response to difficulties which it was having during the 1950's and early 1960's: nationalizations in Guatemala (later reversed), antitrust suits in the United States, a revolution in Cuba which nationalized two sugar refineries and 271,000 acres of land, and the old stand-by, hurricanes. In part, the strategies have worked: the company continues to survive and expand. But instability, fear of nationalizations, inability to expand sufficiently, and competition from other firms continue to plague the Company.

NOTES AND REFERENCES

1. *Business Week,* July 16, 1973, p. 55. The company sold 92.7 million 40 lb. boxes of bananas in 1972.

2. *New York Times,* September 15, 1970.

3. See "Master-Minding the Mini-Market" elsewhere in this book [*Guatemala*].

4. This new company, Numar S.A., which markets under the Clover Brand, has an interesting history. A Danish technician named Tom Dundorf came to Central America in the late 1930's and hooked up with a North American, Richard C. Johnson. Johnson, a relative of J. Edgar Hoover, had access to capital. With some of Hoover's money, Johnson and Dundorf started a margarine factory. A story told in Central America is that a third partner, a man named Ramun was also involved with the margarine factory's founding. A Nazi spy who came to Costa Rica in the late 1930's as part of the extensive German pre-World War II espionage network, he had brought large supplies of espionage equipment (mostly photographic) with him. When, for one reason or another, he left the spy business, he sold the equipment and used the money as parts of the capital for the margarine plant, which was called Numar—or Ramun spelled backwards. In 1965, Numar S.A. became a

subsidiary of the UFCo and Richard Johnson became a vice-president of the company in Boston.

5. Gert Rosenthal K., *Algunos Apuntes Sobre la Inversion Extranjera Directa en el Mercado Comun Centroamericano,* Instituto para la Integracion de America Latina (Buenos Aires, Nov. 17, 1969). Material found on p. 29 and Chart III following p. 25.

6. Gert Rosenthal K., unpublished thesis in progress, Chapter III, "Magnitude and Principal Characteristics of Direct Foreign Investment in the Central American Common Market" and Valentin B. Suazo, Jr., *Job Creation in Central America and Panama* (Central American Office of the American Institute for Free Labor Development, 1971), p. 4.

7. Total investment in this case is roughly double net book value. Net book value is total investment minus a large depreciation allowance for tax purposes. In 1948 for example, total investment before depreciation allowances was $325,603,000.

8. In 1954, as U.S. Ambassador to Costa Rica, Robert C. Hill helped overthrow the Arbenz government in Guatemala. In 1960 Hill was named to the Board of Directors of United Fruit. Before serving as Ambassador in Costa Rica and later in El Salvador, he was an executive of W.R. Grace & Co., another powerful U.S. company exploiting Latin America.

9. Report sent to UFCo shareholders from the 1962 annual meeting.

10. Theodore Price & Co., Report on United Fruit Company (December 18, 1931).

11. Report sent to UFCo shareholders from the annual meeting in July 1961.

12. Paul Deutshman, "United Fruit: Partners to Campesinos," *Latin American Report,* 6 (August 1964).

13. Report sent to UFCo shareholders from the 1962 annual meeting, p. 16.

14. Stacy May and Galo Plaza, *United States Business Performance Abroad: The United Fruit Company in Latin America,* prepared for the National Planning Association (1958), p. 80, and interview with Tom McCann, Division of Public Relations, UFCo, October 1971.

15. Interview with Edward Taylor, General Manager, United Fruit Co., Guatemala, June 1971.

16. *Business Week,* June 22, 1974.

17. *Business Week,* February 22, 1969, and United Fruit, Annual Report, 1973.

18. United Fruit Proxy Report 1969 and United Fruit 10K Report 1968.

19. Herbert K. May, *The Effects of United States and Other Foreign Investment in Latin America,* prepared for the Council of the Americas (New York, January 1971), p. 29.

20. To market bananas in Japan, United Brands established a joint venture with four Japanese corporations: Mitsubishi Corp., Mitsui & Co., Fanematsu Crop. and Toshoku Ltd. They formed the Far East Fruit Co. in 1962 with United Brands currently holding 77.6 percent of the stock and each of the other four holding 5.6 percent. (In late 1972 Mitsui withdrew from the joint venture.) Though the marketing of bananas in Japan is only a small branch of UFCo's operations, a joint venture with several of Japan's leading corporations is worth watching.

21. Fred Goff, "Bank of America Has a Man on the Spot in Latin American Agribusiness," *NACLA Newsletter,* 4, no. 5 (September 1970) and Hector Melo and Israel Yost, "Funding the Empire: Part II, The Multinational Strategy," *NACLA Newsletter,* 4, no. 3 (May-June 1970).

Additional Readings

EUROPEAN COLONIALISM

Boxer, C. R. *The Dutch Seaborne Empire*. London: Hutchinson Publishing Group, 1965.

Clark, Grover, *The Balance Sheets of Imperialism: Facts and Figures on Colonies*. New York: Russell, 1936.

Cox, George. *African Empires and Civilization*. New York: African Heritage Studies Publishers, 1974.

Curtin, Philip D. *The Atlantic Slave Trade—A Census*. Madison: University of Wisconsin Press, 1969.

Fetter, Bruce, ed. *Colonial Rule in Africa: Readings from Primary Sources*. Madison: University of Wisconsin Press, 1979.

Foster, G. M. *Culture and Conquest: America's Spanish Heritage*. New York: Wenner-Gren, 1960.

Griffin, K. *Underdevelopment in Spanish America*. London: George Allen Unwin, 1969.

Jalee, Pierre. *The Pillage of the Third World*. New York: Monthly Review Press, 1969.

Lüthy, H. "Colonization and the Making of Mankind," *Economic History*, 21 (1961): 483–495.

Memmi, Albert. *The Colonizer and the Colonized*. Boston: Beacon Press, 1969.

Morgan, William B. "The Influence of European Contacts on the Landscape of Southern Nigeria," *Geographic Journal*, 125 (March 1959): 48–64.

Morel, E. D. *The Black Man's Burden: The White Man in Africa from the Fifteenth Century to World War I*. New York: Monthly Review Press, 1969.

Mukherjee, Ramkrishna. *The Rise and Fall of the East India Company*. New York: Monthly Review Press, 1974.

Murphey, Rhoads. *The Outsiders: The Western Experience in India and China*. Ann Arbor: University of Michigan Press, 1977.

Padmore, G. *Africa. How Britain Rules Africa*. Westport, Conn.: Negro University Press, 1936.

Parry, J. H. *The Spanish Seaborne Empire*. London: Hutchinson, 1966.

Parry, J. H. *The Establishment of the European Hegemony*. New York: Harper, 1961.

Price, A. G. *White Settlers in the Tropics*. New York: American Geographical Society, Special Publication No. 23, 1939.

Rai, Lajpat. *England's Debt to India*. Delhi: Publications Division of Ministry of Information, 1967.

Rodney, W. "African Slavery and other Forms of Social Oppression on the Upper Guinea Coast in the Context of the Atlantic Slave Trade," *Journal of African History*, no. 3, 1966.

Rodney, W. *How Europe Underdeveloped Africa*. Dar es Salaam: Tanazania Publishing House and Bogle-L'Overture Publications, 1972.

Sachs, Ignacy. *The Discovery of the Third World*. Cambridge, Mass.: MIT Press, 1976.

Tabb, William K. "Capitalism, Colonialism, and Racism," *Review of Radical Political Economics*, 3, no. 3 (Summer 1971): 90–106.

Waibel, L. "European Colonization in Southern Brazil," *Geographical Review*, 40 (1950): 529–547.

Wallerstein, Immanuel. *The Modern World-System, Capitalist Agriculture and the Origins of the European World-Economy in the Sixteenth Century*. New York: Academic Press, 1974.

Wolff, R. D. *The Economics of Colonialism, Britain and Kenya, 1870–1930*. New Haven: Yale University Press, 1974,

Zahar, Renate. *Frantz Fanon: Colonialism and Alienation*. New York: Monthly Review Press, 1975.

PLANTATION AGRICULTURE

Buchanan, R. O. "A Note on Labour Requirements in Plantation Agriculture," *Geography*, 23 (1938): 158–164.

Binns, Sir Bernard O. *Plantations and Other Centrally Operated Estates*. FAO Agricultural Studies, no. 28, 1955.

Church, R. J. H. "The Firestone Rubber Plantations in Liberia," *Geography*, 54 (1969): 430–438.

Courtenay, P. P. *Plantation Agriculture*. London: Bell, 1965.

Courtenay, P. P. "An Approach to the Definition of the Plantation," *Geographia Polonica*, 19 (1970): 81–90.

Fay, C. R. "Plantation Agriculture," *Economic Journal*, 46 (1936): 622–623.

Galloway, J. H. "The Sugar Industry in Barbados during the Seventeenth Century," *Journal of Tropical Geography*, 19 (1964): 35–41.

Gregor, H. F. "The Changing Plantation," *Annals of the Association of American Geographers*, 55 (1965): 221–238.

Grigg, D. B. *The Agricultural Systems of The World: An Evoluntary Approach*. London: Cambridge University Press, 1974.

Jackson, J. C. "Towards An Understanding of Plantation Agriculture," *Area*, 4 (1969): pp. 36–41.

Jackson, J. C. "Oil-Palm; Malaya's Post Independence Boom Crop," *Geography*, 52 (1967): pp. 319–321.

James, P. E. "The Coffee Lands of South East Brazil," *Geographical Review*, 22 (1932): 225–244.

Jeffreys, M. D. W. "The Banana in the Americas' " *Journal d'Agriculture tropicale et de Botanique appliqué*, 10 (1963): 196–203.

Kay, D. E. and Smith E. H. G. "A Review of the Market and World Trade in Bananas," *Tropical Science*, 2 (1960): 154–161.

Mandle, Jay R. *The Plantation Economy: Population and Economic Change in Guyana 1838–1960*. Philadelphia: Temple University Press, 1973.

McCann, Thomas P. *An American Company, The Tragedy of United Fruit*. New York: Crown Publishers, 1976.

Paige, Jeffery M. *Agrarian Revolution: Social Movements and Export Agriculture in the Underdeveloped World*. New York: The Free Press, 1975.

Pan American Union. *Plantation Systems of the New World*. Social Science Momograph, no. 7, Washington, D.C., 1959.

Schultz, T. W. *Transforming Traditional Agriculture*. New Haven: Yale University Press, 1964.

Thomas, R. P. "The Sugar Colonies of the Old Empire: Profit or Loss for Great Britain?" *Economic History Review*, 21 (1968): 30–45.

Thompson, E. T. "The Climatic Theory of the Plantation," *Agricultural History*, 15 (1941): 49–59.

Udo, R. K. "Sixty Years of Plantation Agriculture in Southern Nigeria," *Economic Geography*, 41 (1965): 356–368.

Waibel L., "The Climatic Theory of the Plantation: A Critique," *Geographical Review*, 32 (1942): 307–310.

Waibel, L. "The Political Significance of Tropical Vegetable Fats for the Industrial Countries of Europe," *Annals of the Association of American Geographers*, 33 (1943): 118–128.

V
POPULATION

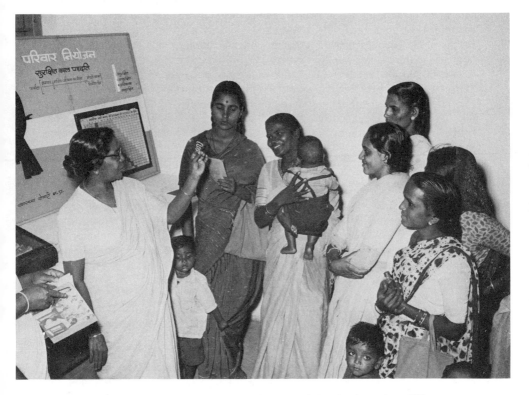

In a New Delhi birth-control clinic, a doctor explains the use of an IUD to a group of women. Who really benefits from birth-control clinics—individual women, families, local communities, national economies, and/or the world? Which classes benefit from family planning programs? (Source: P. Pittet for FAO)

Rapid population growth is often regarded as a major stumbling block to economic progress in underdeveloped countries. Various explanations of the population problem have been advanced. The conservative view is epitomized by Hardin, who argues for "lifeboat ethics." Metaphorically, each rich nation is a lifeboat full of rich people. In the ocean outside each lifeboat float the poor of the world, who would like to climb aboard. What should the lifeboat passengers do? In Hardin's view, absolutely nothing. The rich will be materially ruined if they help the poor; "complete justice is complete catastrophe."

Commoner finds Hardin's position intolerable. Although Commoner believes that in the distant future population numbers will outrun food and other necessary resources, he argues that in the short run, poverty not "overpopulation," is the problem. He believes that the demographic transition, which allowed European societies in the last two hundred years to go from high birth and high death rates to low birth and low death rates, is the solution to population growth in the Third World. The demographic transition has failed to take hold in underdeveloped countries because of the poverty imposed by colonialism. Colonialism brought death control in the form of improved medicine and sanitary conditions, but robbed the Third World of the means to achieve industrialization. The affluence produced by industrialization could lead to lower birth rates as it did in Europe. However, being impoverished, the poor have to maintain large families in order to survive.

Ritchie-Calder, a United Nations advisor, also considers the deliberate discrimination against the poor morally abhorrent. His liberal formulation, which argues that the population problem arises from the lack of birth control knowledge, contrasts sharply with the radical analysis presented by Commoner. For Western demographers and private research foundations, which support family planning programs for the poor of the world, family planning is considered an *essential* "substitute for structural and institutional change" in the world's political economy.

Harvey exposes the ideological nature of the scientific population-resource question. The use of any scientific method is "of necessity founded in ideology" and any claim to the contrary is itself ideological. Harvey examines in detail the classic works of Malthus, Ricardo, and Marx on population. Malthus' and Ricardo's theories justified and substantiated the ideological interests of European landlords and industrialists. On the other hand, Marx championed the interests of workers and the oppressed. Harvey's Marxist analysis reveals that there are numerous ways of dealing with the population-resource question:

(1) we can change our *societal goals*;
(2) we can change our *technology* and *appraisal* of natural resources;
(3) we can change our *material needs;* and
(4) we can change *population growth.*

Under capitalism, the least threatening and therefore the easiest way for most scientists to attack the population-resource question is to deal with only one option, to reduce population growth, while ignoring the other three possibilities.

13 Lifeboat Ethics: A Malthusian View

GARRETT HARDIN*

Susanne Langer has shown that it is probably impossible to approach an unsolved problem save through the door of metaphor.[1] Later, attempting to meet the demands of rigor, we may achieve some success in cleansing theory of metaphor, though our success is limited if we are unable to avoid using common language, which is shot through and through with fossil metaphors. (I count no less than five in the preceding two sentences.)

Since metaphorical thinking is inescapable it is pointless merely to weep about our human limitations. We must learn to live with them, to understand them, and to control them. "All of us," said George Eliot in Middlemarch, "get our thoughts entangled in metaphors, and act fatally on the strength of them." To avoid unconscious suicide we are well advised to pit one metaphor against another. From the interplay of competitive metaphors, thoroughly developed, we may come closer to metaphor-free solutions to our problems.

No generation has viewed the problem of the survival of the human species as seriously as we have. Inevitably, we have entered this world of concern through the door of metaphor. Environmentalists have emphasized the image of the earth as a spaceship—Spaceship Earth. Kenneth Boulding is the principal architect of this metaphor.[2] It is time, he says, that we replace the wasteful "cowboy economy" of the past with the frugal "spaceship economy" required for continued survival in the limited world we now see ours to be. The metaphor is notably useful in justifying pollution control measures.

Unfortunately, the image of a spaceship is also used to promote measures that are suicidal. One of these is a generous immigration policy, which is only a particular instance of a class of policies that are in error because they lead to the tragedy of the commons.[3] These suicidal policies are attractive because they mesh with what we unthinkingly take to be the ideals of "the best people." What is missing in the idealistic view is an insistence that rights and responsibilities must go together. The "generous" attitude of all too many people results in asserting inalienable rights while ignoring or denying matching responsibilities.

For the metaphor of a spaceship to be correct the aggregate of people on board would have to be under unitary sovereign control.[4] A true ship always has a captain. It is conceivable that a ship could be run by a committee. But it could not

*Garrett Hardin, "Living on a Lifeboat," *BioScience*, 24, no. 10 (October 1974): 561–568. Reprinted, with permission, from the October 1974 *BioScience* published by the American Institute of Biological Sciences.

possibly survive if its course were determined by bickering tribes that claimed rights without responsibilities.

What about Spaceship Earth? It certainly has no captain, and no executive committee. The United Nations is a toothless tiger, because the signatories of its charter wanted it that way. The spaceship metaphor is used only to justify spaceship demands on common resources without acknowledging corresponding spaceship responsibilities.

An understandable fear of decisive action leads people to embrace "incrementalism"—moving toward reform by tiny stages. As we shall see, this strategy is counterproductive in the area discussed here if it means accepting rights before responsibilities. Where human survival is at stake, the acceptance of responsibilities is a precondition to the acceptance of rights, if the two cannot be introduced simultaneously.

LIFEBOAT ETHICS

Before taking up certain substantive issues let us look at an alternative metaphor, that of a lifeboat. In developing some relevant examples the following numerical values are assumed. Approximately two-thirds of the world is desperately poor, and only one-third is comparatively rich. The people in poor countries have an average per capita GNP (Gross National Product) of about $200 per year; the rich, about $3,000. (For the United States it is nearly $5,000 per year.) Metaphorically, each rich nation amounts to a lifeboat full of comparatively rich people. The poor of the world are in other, much more crowded lifeboats. Continuously, so to speak, the poor fall out of their lifeboats and swim for a while in the water outside, hoping to be admitted to a rich lifeboat, or in some other way to benefit from the "goodies" on board. What should the passengers on a rich lifeboat do? This is the central problem of "the ethics of a lifeboat."

First we must acknowledge that each lifeboat is effectively limited in capacity. The land of every nation has a limited carrying capacity. The exact limit is a matter for argument, but the energy crunch is convincing more people every day that we have already exceeded the carrying capacity of the land. We have been living on "capital"—stored petroleum and coal—and soon we must live on income alone.

Let us look at only one lifeboat—ours. The ethical problem is the same for all, and is as follows. Here we sit, say 50 people in a lifeboat. To be generous, let us assume our boat has a capacity of 10 more, making 60. (This, however, is to violate the engineering principle of the "safety factor." A new plant disease or a bad change in the weather may decimate our population if we don't preserve some excess capacity as a safety factor.)

The 50 of us in the lifeboat see 100 others swimming in the water outside, asking for admission to the boat, or for handouts. How shall we respond to their calls? There are several possibilities.

One. We may be tempted to try to live by the Christian ideal of being "our brother's keeper," or by the Marxian ideal of "from each according to his abilities, to each according to his needs."[5] Since the needs of all are the same, we take all the needy into our boat, making a total of 150 in a boat with a capacity of

60. The boat is swamped, and everyone drowns. Complete justice, complete catastrophe.

Two. Since the boat has an unused excess capacity of 10, we admit just 10 more to it. This has the disadvantage of getting rid of the safety factor, for which action we will sooner or later pay dearly. Moreover, *which* 10 do we let in? "First come, first served?" The best 10? The neediest 10? How do we *discriminate?* And what do we say to the 90 who are excluded?

Three. Admit no more to the boat and preserve the small safety factor. Survival of the people in the lifeboat is then possible (though we shall have to be on our guard against boarding parties).

The last solution is abhorrent to many people. It is unjust, they say. Let us grant that it is.

"I feel guilty about my good luck," say some. The reply to this is simple: *Get out and yield your place to others*. Such a selfless action might satisfy the conscience of those who are addicted to guilt but it would not change the ethics of the lifeboat. The needy person to whom a guilt-addict yields his place will not himself feel guilty about his sudden good luck. (If he did he would not climb aboard.) The net result of conscience-stricken people relinquishing their unjustly held positions is the elimination of their kind of conscience from the lifeboat. The lifeboat, as it were, purifies itself of guilt. The ethics of the lifeboat persist, unchanged by such momentary aberrations.

This then is the basic metaphor within which we must work out our solutions. Let us enrich the image step by step with substantive additions from the real world.

REPRODUCTION

The harsh characteristics of lifeboat ethics are heightened by reproduction, particularly by reproductive differences. The people inside the lifeboats of the wealthy nations are doubling in numbers every 87 years; those outside are doubling every 35 years, on the average. And the relative difference in prosperity is becoming greater.

Let us, for a while, think primarily of the U.S. lifeboat. As of 1973 the United States had a population of 210 million people, who were increasing by 0.8% per year, that is, doubling in number every 87 years.

Although the citizens of rich nations are outnumbered two to one by the poor, let us imagine an equal number of poor people outside our lifeboat—a mere 210 million poor people reproducing at a quite different rate. If we imagine these to be the combined populations of Colombia, Venezuela, Ecuador, Morocco, Thailand, Pakistan, and the Philippines, the average rate of increase of the people "outside" is 3.3% per year. The doubling time of this population is 21 years.

Suppose that all these countries, and the United States, agreed to live by the Marxian ideal, "to each according to his needs," the ideal of most Christians as well. Needs, of course, are determined by population size, which is affected by reproduction. Every nation regards its rate of reproduction as a sovereign right. If our lifeboat were big enough in the beginning it might be possible to *live for a while* by Christian-Marxian ideals. *Might*.

Initially, in the model given, the ratio of non-Americans to Americans would be one to one. But consider what the ratio would be 87 years later. By this time Americans would have doubled to a population of 420 million. The other group (doubling every 21 years) would now have swollen to 3,540 million. Each American would have more than eight people to share with. How could the lifeboat possibly keep afloat?

All this involves extrapolation of current trends into the future, and is consequently suspect. Trends may change. Granted: but the change will not necessarily be favorable. If—as seems likely—the rate of population increases falls faster in the ethnic group presently inside the lifeboat than it does among those now outside, the future will turn out to be even worse than mathematics predicts, and sharing will be even more suicidal.

RUIN IN THE COMMONS

The fundamental error of the sharing ethics is that it leads to the tragedy of the commons. Under a system of private property the man (or group of men) who own property recognize their responsibility to care for it, for if they don't they will eventually suffer. A farmer, for instance, if he is intelligent, will allow no more cattle in a pasture than its carrying capacity justifies. If he overloads the pasture, weeds take over, erosion sets in, and the owner loses in the long run.

But if a pasture is run as a commons open to all, the right of each to use it is not matched by an operational responsibility to take care of it. It is no use asking independent herdsmen in a commons to act responsibly, for they dare not. The considerate herdsman who refrains from overloading the commons suffers more than a selfish one who says his needs are greater. As Leo Durocher says, "Nice guys finish last." Christian-Marxian idealism is counterproductive. That it *sounds* nice is no excuse. With distribution systems, as with individual morality, good intentions are no substitute for good performance.

A social system is stable only if it is insensitive to errors. To the Christian-Marxian idealist a selfish person is a sort of "error." Prosperity in the system of the commons cannot survive errors. If *everyone* would only restrain himself, all would be well, but it takes *only one less everyone* to ruin a system of voluntary restraint. In a crowded world of less than perfect human beings—and we will never know any other—mutual ruin is inevitable in the commons. This is the core of the tragedy of the commons.

One of the major tasks of education today is to create such an awareness of the dangers of the commons that people will be able to recognize its many varieties, however disguised. There is pollution of the air and water because these media are treated as commons. Further growth of population and growth in the per capita conversion of natural resources into pollutants require that the system of the commons be modified or abandoned in the disposal of "externalities."

The fish populations of the oceans are exploited as commons, and ruin lies ahead. No technological invention can prevent this fate: in fact, all improvements in the art of fishing merely hasten the day of complete ruin. Only the replacement of the system of the commons with a responsible system can save oceanic fisheries.

The management of western range lands, though nominally rational, is in fact (under the steady pressure of cattle ranchers) often merely a government-sanctioned system of the commons, drifting toward ultimate ruin for both the rangelands and the residual enterprisers.

WORLD FOOD BANKS

In the international arena we have recently heard a proposal to create a new commons, namely an international depository of food reserves to which nations will contribute according to their abilities, and from which nations may draw according to their needs. Nobel laureate Norman Borlaug has lent the prestige of his name to this proposal.

A world food bank appeals powerfully to our humanitarian impulses. We remember John Donne's celebrated line, "Any man's death diminishes me." But before we rush out to see for whom the bell tolls let us recognize where the greatest political push for international granaries comes from, lest we be disillusioned later. Our experience with Public Law 480 clearly reveals the answer. This was the law that moved billions of dollars worth of U.S. grain to food-short, population-long countries during the past two decades. When P.L. 480 first came into being, a headline in the business magazine *Forbes* revealed the power behind it: "Feeding the World's Hungry Millions: How it will mean billions for U.S. business."[6]

And indeed it did. In the years 1960 to 1970 a total of $7.9 billion was spent on the "Food for Peace" program, as P.L. 480 was called. During the years 1948 to 1970 an additional $49.9 billion were extracted from American taxpayers to pay for other economic aid programs, some of which went for food and food-producing machinery. (This figure does *not* include military aid.) That P.L. 480 was a give-away program was concealed. Recipient countries went through the motions of paying for P.L. 480 food—with IOU's. In December 1973 the charade was brought to an end as far as India was concerned when the United States "forgave" India's $3.2 billion debt.[7] Public announcement of the cancellation of the debt was delayed for two months: one wonders why.

"Famine—1974!" is one of the few publications that points out the commercial roots of this humanitarian attempt.[8] Though all U.S. taxpayers lost by P.L. 480, special interest groups gained handsomely. Farmers benefited because they were not asked to contribute the grain—it was bought from them by the taxpayers. Besides the direct benefit there was the indirect effect of increasing demand and thus raising prices of farm products generally. The manufactures of farm machinery, fertilizers, and pesticides benefited by the farmers' extra efforts to grow more food. Grain elevators profited from storing the grain for varying lengths of time. Railroads made money hauling it to port, and shipping lines by carrying it overseas. Moreover, once the machinery for P.L. 480 was established an immense bureaucracy had a vested interest in its continuance regardless of its merits.

Very little was ever heard of these selfish interests when P.L. 480 was defended in public. The emphasis was always on its humanitarian effects. The combination of multiple and relatively silent selfish interests with highly vocal humanitarian apologists constitutes a powerful lobby for extracting money from taxpayers. Foreign aid has become a habit that can apparently survive in the absence of any known justification. A news commentator in a weekly magazine, after exhaustively going over all the conventional arguments for foreign aid—self-interest, social justice, political advantage, and charity—and concluding that none of the known arguments really held water, concluded: "So the search continues for some logically compelling reasons for giving aid . . ."[9] In other words. *Act now, Justify later*—if ever. (Apparently a quarter of a century is too short a time to find the justification for expending several billion dollars yearly.)

The search for a rational justification can be short-circuited by interjecting the word "emergency." Borlaug uses this word. We need to look sharply at it. What is an "emergency?" It is surely something like an accident, which is correctly defined as *an event that is certain to happen, though with a low frequency.*[10] A well-run organization prepares for everything that is certain, including accidents and emergencies. It budgets for them. It saves for them. It expects them—and mature decision-makers do not waste time complaining about accidents when they occur.

What happens if some organizations budget for emergencies and others do not? If each organization is solely responsible for its own well-being, poorly managed ones will suffer. But they should be able to learn from experience. They have a chance to mend their ways and learn to budget for infrequent but certain emergencies. The weather, for instance, always varies and periodic crop failures are certain. A wise and competent government saves out of the production of the good years in anticipation of bad years that are sure to come. This is not a new idea. The Bible tells us that Joseph taught this policy to Pharaoh in Egypt more than 2,000 years ago. Yet it is literally true that the vast majority of the governments of the world today have no such policy. They lack either the wisdom or the competence, or both. Far more difficult than the transfer of wealth from one country to another is the transfer of wisdom between sovereign powers or between generations.

"But it isn't their fault! How can we blame the poor people who are caught in an emergency? Why must we punish them?" The concepts of blame and punishment are irrelevant. The question is, what are the operational consequences of establishing a world food bank? If it is open to every country every time a need develops, slovenly rulers will not be motivated to take Joseph's advice. Why should they? Others will bail them out whenever they are in trouble.

Some countries will make deposits in the world food bank and others will withdraw from it: there will be almost no overlap. Calling such a depository transfer unit a "bank" is stretching the metaphor of *bank* beyond its elastic limits. The proposers, of course, never call attention to the metaphorical nature of the word they use.

THE RATCHET EFFECT

An "internation food bank" is really, then, not a true bank but a disguised one-way, transfer device for moving wealth from rich countries to poor. In the absence of such a bank, in a world inhabited by individually responsible sovereign nations, the population of each nation would repeatedly go through a cycle of the sort shown in Figure 13.1. P_2 is greater than P_1, either in absolute numbers or because a deterioration of the food supply has removed the safety factor and produced a dangerously low ratio of resources to population. P_2 may be said to represent a state of overpopulation, which becomes obvious upon the appearance of an "accident," e.g., a crop failure. If the "emergency" is not met by outside help, the population drops back to the "normal" level—the "carrying capacity" of the environment—or even below. In the absence of population control by a sovereign, sooner or later the population grows to P_2 again and the cycle repeats. The long-term population curve is an irregularly fluctuating one, equilibrating more or less about the carrying capacity.[11]

Figure 13.1　The population cycle of a nation that has no effective, conscious population control, and which receives no aid from the outside. P_2 is greater than P_1.

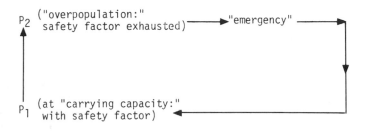

A demographic cycle of this sort obviously involves great suffering in the restrictive phase, but such a cycle is normal to any independent country with inadequate population control. The third century theologian Tertullian expressed what must have been the recognition of many wise men when he wrote: "The scourges of pestilence, famine, wars, and earthquakes, have come to be regarded as a blessing to overcrowded nations, since they serve to prune away the luxuriant growth of the human race."[12]

Only under a strong and farsighted sovereign—which theoretically could be the people themselves, democratically organized—can a population equilibrate at some set point below the carrying capacity, thus avoiding the pains normally caused by periodic and unavoidable disasters. For this happy state to be achieved it is necessary that those in power be able to contemplate with equanimity the "waste" of surplus food in times of bountiful harvest. It is essential that those in power resist the temptation to convert extra food into extra babies. On the public relations level it is necessary that the phrase "surplus food" be replaced by "safety factor."

But wise sovereigns seem not to exist in the poor world today. The most anguishing problems are created by poor countries that are governed by rulers insufficiently wise and powerful. If such countries can draw on a world food bank in times of "emergency," the population *cycle* of Figure 13.1 will be replaced by the population *escalator* of Figure 13.2. The input of food from a food bank acts as the pawl of a ratchet, preventing the population from retracing its steps to a lower level. Reproduction pushes the population upward, inputs from the world bank prevent its moving downward. Population size escalates, as does the absolute magnitude of "accidents" and "emergencies." The process is brought to an end only by the total collapse of the whole system, producing a catastrophe of scarcely

Figure 13.2 The population escalator. Note that input from a world food bank acts like the pawl of a ratchet, preventing the normal population cycle shown in Figure 13.1 from being completed. P_{n+1} is greater than P_n, and the absolute magnitude of the "emergencies" escalates. Ultimately the entire system crashes. The crash is not shown, and few can imagine it.

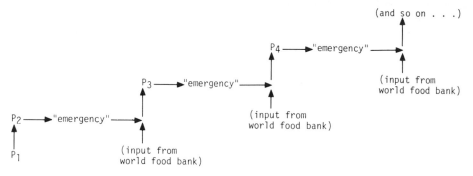

imaginable proportions. Such are the implications of the well-meant sharing of food in a world of irresponsible reproduction.

I think we need a new word for systems like this. The adjective "melioristic" is applied to systems that produce continual improvement; the English word is derived from the Latin *meliorare,* to become or make better. Parallel with this it would be useful to bring in the word *pejoristic* (from the Latin *pejorare,* to become or make worse). This word can be applied to those systems which, by their very nature, can be relied upon to make matters worse. A world food bank coupled with sovereign state irresponsibility in reproduction is an example of a pejoristic system.

This pejoristic system creates an unacknowledged commons. People have more motivation to draw from than to add to the common store. The license to make such withdrawals diminishes whatever motivation poor countries might otherwise have to control their populations. Under the guidance of this ratchet, wealth can be steadily moved in one direction only, from the slowly-breeding rich to the rapidly-breeding poor, the process finally coming to a halt only when all countries are equally and miserably poor.

All this is terribly obvious once we are acutely aware of the pervasiveness and danger of the commons. But many people still lack this awareness and the euphoria of the "benign demographic transition" interferes with the realistic appraisal of pejoristic mechanisms.[13] As concerns public policy, the deductions drawn from the benign demographic transition are these:

1) If the per capital GNP rises the birth rate will fall; hence, the rate of population increase will fall, ultimately producing ZPG (Zero Population Growth).

2) The long-term trend all over the world (including the poor countries) is of a rising per capita GNP (for which no limit is seen).

3) Therefore, all political interference in population matters is unnecessary; all we need to do is foster economic "development"—*note the metaphor*—and population problems will solve themselves.

Those who believe in the benign demographic transition dismiss the pejoristic mechanism of Figure 13.2 in the belief that each input of food from the world out-side fosters development within a poor country thus resulting in a drop in the rate of population increase. Foreign aid had proceeded on this assumption for more than two decades. Unfortunately it has produced no indubitable instance of the asserted effect. It has, however, produced a library of excuses. The air is filled with plaintive calls for more massive foreign aid appropriations so that the hypothetical melioristic process can get started.

The doctrine of demographic laissez-faire implicit in the hypothesis of the benign demographic transition is immensely attractive. Unfortunately there is more evidence against the melioristic system than there is for it.[14] On the historical side there are many counter-examples. The rise in per capita GNP in France and Ireland during the past century has been accompanied by a rise in population growth. In the 20 years following the Second World War the same positive correlation was noted almost everywhere in the world. Never in world history before 1950 did the worldwide population growth reach 1% per annum. Now the average population growth is over 2% and shows no signs of slackening.

On the theoretical side, the denial of the pejoristic scheme of Figure 13.2 probably springs from the hidden acceptance of the "cowboy economy" that Boulding castigated. Those who recognize the limitations of a spaceship, if they are unable to achieve population control at a safe and comfortable level, accept the necessity of the corrective feedback of the population cycle shown in Figure 13.1. No one who knew in his bones that he was living on a true spaceship would countenance political support of the population escalator shown in Figure 13.2.

ECO-DESTRUCTION VIA THE GREEN REVOLUTION

The demoralizing effect of charity on the recipient has long been known. "Give a man a fish and he will eat for a day: teach him how to fish and he will eat for the rest of his days." So runs an ancient Chinese proverb. Acting on this advice the Rockefeller and Ford Foundations have financed a multipronged program for improving agriculture in the hungry nations. The result, known as the "Green Revolution," has been quite remarkable. "Miracle wheat" and "miracle rice" are splendid technological achievements in the realm of plant genetics.

Whether or not the Green Revolution can increase food production is doubtful, but in any event not particularly important.[15] What is missing in this great and well-meaning humanitarian effort is a firm grasp of fundamentals. Considering the importance of the Rockefeller Foundation in this effort it is ironic that the late Alan Gregg, a much-respected vice-president of the Foundation, strongly expressed his doubts of the wisdom of all attempts to increase food production some two decades ago. (This was before Borlaug's work—supported by Rockefeller—had resulted in the development of "miracle wheat.") Gregg likened the growth and spreading of humanity over the surface of the earth to the metastasis of cancer in the human body, wryly remarking that "Cancerous growths demand food; but, as far as I know, they have never been cured by getting it."[16]

"Man does not live by bread alone"—the scriptural statement has a rich meaning even in the material realm. Every human being born constitutes a draft on all aspects of the environment—food, air, water, unspoiled scenery, occasional and optional solitude, beaches, contact with wild animals, fishing, hunting—the list is long and incompletely known. Food can, perhaps, be significantly increased: but what about clean beaches, unspoiled forests, and solitude? If we satisfy the need for food in a growing population we necessarily decrease the supply of other goods, and thereby increase the difficulty of equitably allocating scarce goods.[17]

The present population of India is 600 million, and it is increasing by 15 million per year. The environmental load of this population is already great. The forests of India are only a small fraction of what they were three centuries ago. Soil erosion, floods, and the psychological costs of crowding are serious. Every one of the net 15 million lives added each year stresses the Indian environment more severely. *Every life saved this year in a poor country diminishes the quality of life for subsequent generations.*

Observant critics have shown how much harm we wealthy nations have already done to poor nations through our well-intentioned but misguided attempts to help them.[18] Particularly reprehensible is our failure to carry out post-audits of these attempts.[19] Thus have we shielded our tender consciences from knowledge of the harm we have done. Must we Americans continue to fail to monitor the consequences of our external "do-gooding?" If, for instance, we thoughtlessly make it possible for the present 500 million Indians to swell to 1,200 millions by the year 2001—as their present growth rate promises—will posterity in India thank *us* for facilitating an even greater destruction of *their* environment? Are good intentions ever a sufficient excuse for bad consequences?

IMMIGRATION CREATES A COMMONS

I come now to the final example of a commons in action, one for which the public is least prepared for rational discussion. The topic is at present enveloped by a great silence which reminds me of a comment made by Sherlock Holmes in A. Conan Doyle's story, "Silver Blaze." Inspector Gregory had asked, "Is there any point to which you would wish to draw my attention?" To this Holmes responded:

"To the curious incident of the dog in the night-time."

"The dog did nothing in the night-time," said the Inspector.

"That was the curious incident," remarked Sherlock Holmes.

By asking himself what would repress the normal barking instinct of a watch dog Holmes realized that it must be the dog's recognition of his master as the criminal trespasser. In a similar way we should ask ourselves what repression keeps us from discussing something as important as immigration?

It cannot be that immigration is numerically of no consequence. Our government acknowledges a *net* inflow of 400,000 a year. Hard data are understandably lacking on the extent of illegal entries, but a not implausible figure is 600,000 per year.[20] The natural increase of the resident population is now about 1.7 million per year. This means that the yearly gain from immigration is at least 19%, and may be 37%, of the total increase. It is quite conceivable that educational campaigns like that of Zero Population Growth, Inc., coupled with adverse social and economic factors—inflation, housing shortage, depression, and loss of confidence in national leaders—may lower the fertility of American women to a point at which all of the yearly increase in population would be accounted for by immigration. Should we not at least ask if that is what we want? How curious it is that we so seldom discuss immigration these days!

Curious, but understandable—as one finds out the moment he publicly questions the wisdom of the status quo in immigration. He who does so is promptly charged with *isolationism, bigotry, prejudice, ethnocentrism, chauvinism,* and *selfishness.* These are hard accusations to bear. It is pleasanter to talk about other matters, leaving immigration policy to wallow in the cross-currents of special interests that take no account of the good of the whole—*or of the interests of posterity.*

We Americans have a bad conscience because of things we said in the past about immigrants. Two generations ago the popular press was rife with references to *Dagos, Wops, Pollacks, Japs, Chinks,* and *Krauts*—all pejorative terms which failed to acknowledge our indebtedness to Goya, Leonardo, Copernicus, Hiroshige, Confucius, and Bach. Because the implied inferiority of foreigners was *then* the justification for keeping them out, it is *now* thoughtlessly assumed that restrictive policies can only be based on the assumption of immigrant inferiority. *This is not so.*

Existing immigration laws exclude idiots and known criminals; future laws will almost certainly continue this policy. But should we also consider the quality of the average immigrant, as compared with the quality of the average resident? Perhaps we should, perhaps we shouldn't. (What is "quality" anyway?) But the quality issue is not our concern here.

From this point on, *it will be assumed that immigrants and native-born citizens are of exactly equal quality,* however quality may be defined. The focus is only on quantity. The conclusions reached depend on nothing else, so all charges of ethnocentrism are irrelevant.

World food banks move food to the people, thus facilitating the exhaustion of the environment of the poor. By contrast, unrestricted immigration moves people to the food, thus speeding up the destruction of the environment in rich countries. Why poor people should want to make this transfer is no mystery; but why should rich hosts encourage it? This transfer, like the reverse one, is supported by both selfish interests and humanitarian impulses.

The principal selfish interest in unimpeded immigration is easy to identify: it is the interest of the employers of cheap labor, particularly that needed for degrading jobs. We have been deceived about the forces of history by the lines of Emma Lazarus inscribed on the Statue of Liberty:

> *Give me your tired, your poor*
> *Your huddled masses yearning to breathe free,*
> *The wretched refuse of your teeming shore,*
> *Send these, the homeless, tempest-tossed, to me:*
> *I lift my lamp beside the golden door.*

The image is one of an infinitely generous earth-mother, passively opening her arms to hordes of immigrants who come here on their own initiative. Such an image may have been adequate for the early days of colonization, but by the time these lines were written (1886) the force for immigration was largely manufactured inside our own borders by factory and mine owners who sought cheap labor not to be found among laborers already here. One group of foreigners after another was thus enticed into the United States to work at wretched jobs for wretched wages.

At present, it is largely the Mexicans who are being so exploited. It is particularly to the advantage of certain employers that there be many illegal immigrants. Illegal immigrant workers dare not complain about their working conditions for fear of being repatriated. Their presence reduces the bargaining power of all Mexican-American laborers. Cesar Chavez has repeatedly pleaded with congressional committees to close the doors to more Mexicans so that those here can negotiate effectively for higher wages and decent working conditions. Chavez understands the ethics of a lifeboat.

The interests of the employers of cheap labor are well served by the silence of the intelligentsia of the country. WASPS—White Anglo-Saxon Protestants—are particularly reluctant to call for a closing of the doors to immigration for fear of being called ethnocentric bigots. It was, therefore, an occasion of pure delight for this particular WASP to be present at a meeting when the points he would like to have made were made better by a non-WASP speaking to other, non-WASPS. It was in Hawaii, and most of the people in the room were second-level Hawaiian officials of Japanese ancestry. All Hawaiians are keenly aware of the limits of their environment, and the speaker had asked how it might be practically and constitutionally possible to close the doors to more immigrants to the islands. (To Hawaiians, immigrants from the other 49 states are as much of a threat as those from other nations. There is only so much room in the islands, and the islanders know it. Sophisticated arguments that imply otherwise do not impress them.)

Yet the Japanese-Americans of Hawaii have active ties with the land of their origin. This point was raised by a Japanese-American member of the audience who asked the Japanese-American speaker: "But how can we shut the doors now? We have many friends and relations in Japan that we'd like to bring to Hawaii some day so that they can enjoy this beautiful land."

The speaker smiled sympathetically and responded slowly: "Yes, but we have children now and someday we'll have grandchildren. We can bring more people here from Japan only by giving away some of the land that we hope to pass on to our grandchildren some day. What right do we have to do that?"

To be generous with one's own possessions is one thing; to be generous with posterity's is quite another. This, I think, is the point that must be gotten across to those who would, from a commendable love of distributive justice, institute a ruinous system of the commons, either in the form of a world food bank or that of unrestricted immigration. Since every speaker is a member of some ethnic group it is always possible to charge him with ethnocentrism. But even after purging an argument of ethnocentrism the rejection of the commons is still valid and necessary if we are to save at least some parts of the world from environmental ruin. Is it not desirable that at least some of the grandchildren of people now living should have a decent place in which to live?

THE ASYMMETRY OF DOOR-SHUTTING

We must now answer this telling point: "How can you justify slamming the door once you're inside? You say that immigrants should be kept out. But aren't we all immigrants, or the descendants of immigrants? Since we refuse to leave, must we not, as a matter of justice and symmetry, admit all others?"

It is literally true that we Americans of non-Indian ancestry are the descendants of thieves. Should we not, then, "give back" the land to the Indians; that is, give it to the now-living Americans of Indian ancestry? As an exercise in pure logic I see no way to reject this proposal. Yet I am unwilling to live by it; and I know no one who is. Our reluctance to embrace pure justice may spring from pure selfishness. On the other hand, it may arise from an unspoken recognition of consequences that have not yet been clearly spelled out.

Suppose, becoming intoxicated with pure justice, we "Anglos" should decide to turn our land over to the Indians. Since all our other wealth has also been derived from the land, we would have to give that to the Indians, too. Then what would we non-Indians do? Where would we go? There is no open land in the world on which men without capital can make their living (and not much unoccupied land on which men with capital can either). Where would 209 million putatively "justice-loving, non-Indian, Americans go? Most of them—in the persons of their ancestors—came from Europe, but they wouldn't be welcomed back there. Anyway, Europeans have no better title to their land than we to ours. They also would have to give up their homes. (But to whom? And where would *they* go?)

Clearly, the concept of pure justice produces an infinite regress. The law long ago invented statutes of limitations to justify the rejection of pure justice, in the interest of preventing massive disorder. The law zealously defends property rights—but only *recent* property rights. It is as though the physical principle of exponential decay applies to property rights. Drawing a line in time may be unjust, but any other action is practically worse.

We are all the descendants of thieves, and the world's resources are inequitably distributed, but we must begin the journey to tomorrow from the point where we are today. We cannot remake the past. We cannot, without violent disorder and suffering, give land and resources back to the "original" owners—who are dead anyway.

We cannot safely divide the wealth equitably among all present peoples, so long as people reproduce at different rates, because to do so would guarantee that our grandchildren—everyone's grandchildren—would have only a ruined world to inhabit.

MUST EXCLUSION BE ABSOLUTE?

To show the logical structure of the immigration problem I have ignored many factors that would enter into real decisions made in a real world. No matter how convincing the logic may be it is probable that we would want, from time to time, to admit a few people from the outside to our lifeboat. Political refugees in particular are likely to cause us to make exceptions: We remember the Jewish refugees from Germany after 1933, and the Hungarian refugees after 1956. Moreover, the interests of national defense, broadly conceived, could justify admitting many men and women of unusual talents, whether refugees or not. (This raises the quality issue, which is not the subject of this essay.)

Such exceptions threaten to create runaway population growth inside the lifeboat, i.e., the receiving country. However, the threat can be neutralized by a population policy that includes immigration. An effective policy is one of flexible control.

Suppose, for example, that the nation has achieved a stable condition of ZPG, which (say) permits 1.5 million births yearly. We must suppose that an acceptable system of allocating birth-rights to potential parents is in effect. Now suppose that an inhumane regime in some other part of the world creates a horde of refugees, and that there is a widespread desire to admit some to our country. At the same time, we do not want to sabotage our population control system. Clearly, the rational path to pursue is the following. If we decide to admit 100,000 refugees this year we should compensate for this by reducing the allocation of birth-rights in the following year by a similar amount, that is downward to a total of 1.4 million. In that way we could achieve both humanitarian and population control goals. (And the refugees would have to accept the population controls of the society that admits them. It is not inconceivable that they might be given proportionately fewer rights than the native population.)

In a democracy, the admission of immigrants should properly be voted on. But by whom? It is not obvious. The usual rule of a democracy is votes for all. But it can be questioned whether a universal franchise is the most just one in a case of this sort. Whatever benefits there are in the admission of immigrants presumably accrue to everyone. But the costs would be seen as falling most heavily on potential parents, some of whom would have to postpone or forego having their (next) child because the influx of immigrants. The double question *Who benefits? Who pays?* suggests that a restriction of the usual democratic franchise would be appropriate and just in this case. Would our particular quasi-democratic form of government be flexible enough to institute such a novelty? If not, the majority might, out of humanitarian motives, impose an unacceptable burden (the foregoing of parenthood) on a minority, thus producing political instability.

Plainly many new problems will arise when we consciously face the immigration question and seek rational answers. No workable answers can be found if we ignore population problems. And—if the argument of this essay is correct—so long as there is no true world government to control reproduction everywhere it is impossible to survive in dignity if we are to be guided by Spaceship ethics. Without a world government that is sovereign in reproductive matters mankind lives, in fact, on a number of sovereign lifeboats. For the foreseeable future survival demands that we govern our actions by the ethics of a lifeboat. Posterity will be ill served if we do not.

NOTES AND REFERENCES

1. Susan K. Langer, *Philosophy in a New Key* (Cambridge: Harvard University Press, 1942.)

2. Kenneth Boulding, "The Economics of the Coming Spaceship Earth," in H. Jarnett, ed., *Environmental Quality in a Growing Economy* (Baltimore: John Hopkins Press, 1966).

3. G. Hardin, "The Tragedy of the Commons," *Science,* 162 (1968): 1243–1248.

4. W. Ophulus, "The Scarcity Society," *Harpers,* 248, no. 1487 (1974): 47–52.

5. K. Marx, "Critique of the Gotha Program," in R. C. Tucker, ed., *The Marx-Engles Reader.* (New York: Norton, 1972), p. 388.

6. W. C. Paddock and P. Paddock, "How Green is the Green Revolution?" *Bioscience,* 20 (1970): 897–902.

7. *Wall Street Journal,* February 19, 1974.

8. Paddock and Paddock, "How Green is the Green Revolution?"

9. K. Lansner, "Should Foreign Aid Begin at Home?" *Newsweek,* February 11, 1974, p. 32.

10. G. Hardin, in *Exploring New Ethics for Survival: The Voyage of the Spaceship "Beagle"* (New York: Viking, 1972), pp. 81–82.

11. G. Hardin, *Biology: Its Principles and Implications,* 2nd ed. (San Francisco: Freeman, 1966), Chapter 9.

12. G. Hardin, *Population, Evolution, and Birth Control,* 2nd. ed. (San Francisco: Freeman, 1969), p. 18.

13. G. Hardin, *Stalking the Wild Taboo* (Los Altos, Cal.: Kaufmann, 1973), Chapter 23.

14. K. Davis, "Population," *Scientic American,* 209, no. 3 (1963): 62–71.

15. M. Harris, "How Green the Revolution," *Natural History,* 81, no. 3 (1972): 28–30; Paddock and Paddock, "How Green the Green Revolution?" *Natural History,* 81, no. 3 (1972): and H. G. Wilkes, "The Green Revolution," *Environment,* 14, no. 8 (1972): 32–39.

16. A Gregg, "A Medical Aspect of the Population Problem," *Science,* 121 (1955): 681–682.

17. G. Hardin, "The Economics of Wilderness," *Natural History,* 78, no. 6 (1969): 20–27; and G. Hardin, "Preserving Quality on Spaceship Earth," in J. B. Trefethen, ed., *Transactions of the Thirty-Seventh North American Wildlife and Natural Resources Conference* (Wildlife Management Institute, Washington, D.C., 1972).

18. W. Paddock and E. Paddock, *We Don't Know How* (Ames, Iowa: Iowa State University Press, 1973).

19. M. T. Farvar and J. P. Milton, *The Careless Technology* (Garden City, N.Y.: Natural History Press, 1972).

20. W. Buchanan, "Immigration Statistics," *Equilibrium,* 1, no. 3 (1973): 16–19.

14 Poverty Breeds "Overpopulation"

*BARRY COMMONER**

The world population problem is a bewildering mixture of the simple and the complex, the clear and the confused.

What is relatively simple and clear is that the population of the world is getting larger, and that this process cannot go on indefinitely because there are, after all, limits to the resources, such as food, that are needed to sustain human life. Like all living things, people have an inherent tendency to multiply geometrically—that is, the more people there are the more people they tend to produce. In contrast, the supply of food rises more slowly, for unlike people it does not increase in proportion to the existing rate of food production. This is, of course, the familiar Malthusian relationship and leads to the conclusion that the population is certain eventually to outgrow the food supply (and other needed resources), leading to famine and mass death unless some other countervailing force intervenes to limit population growth. One can argue about the details, but taken as a general summary of the population problem, the foregoing statement is one which no environmentalist can successfully dispute.

When we turn from merely stating the problem to analyzing and attempting to solve it, the issue becomes much more complex. The simple statement that there is a limit to the growth of the human population, imposed on it by the inherent limits of the earth's resources, is a useful but abstract idea. In order to reduce it to the level of reality in which the problem must be solved, what is required is that we find the *cause* of the discrepancy between population growth and the available resources. Current views on this question are neither simple nor unanimous.

One view is that the cause of the population problem is uncontrolled fertility, the countervailing force—the death rate—having been weakened by medical advances. According to this view, given the freedom to do so people will inevitably produce children faster than the goods needed to support them. It follows, then, that the birthrate must be deliberately reduced to the point of "zero population growth."

The methods that have been proposed to achieve this kind of direct reduction in birthrate vary considerably. Among the ones advanced in the past are: (a) providing people with effective contraception and access to abortion facilities and with education about the value of using them (i.e., family planning); (b) enforcing legal means to prevent couples from producing more than some standard number

*Barry Commoner, "How Poverty Breeds Overpopulation (and not the other way around)," *Ramparts* (August/September 1975): 21–25, 58–59. Reprinted by permission of author.

of children ("coercion"); (c) withholding of food from the people of starving developing countries which, having failed to limit their birthrate sufficiently, are deemed to be too far gone or too unworthy to be saved (the so-called "lifeboat ethic").

It is appropriate here to illustrate these diverse approaches with examples. The family planning approach is so well known as to need no further exemplification. As to the second of these approaches, one might cite the following description of it by Kingsley Davis, a prominent demographer, which is quoted approvingly in a recent statement by "The Environmental Fund" that is directed against the family planning position: "If people want to control population, it can be done with knowledge already available . . . For instance, a nation seeking to stabilize its population could shut off immigration and permit each couple a maximum of two children, with possible license for a third. Accidental pregnancies beyond the limit would be interrupted by abortion. If a third child were born without a license, or a fourth, the mother would be sterilized."[1]

The author of the "lifeboat ethic" is Garrett Hardin who stated in a recent paper . . . that: "So long as nations multiply at different rates, survival requires that we adopt the ethic of the lifeboat. A lifeboat can hold only so many people. There are more than two billion wretched people in the world—ten times as many as in the United States. It is literally beyond our ability to save them all . . . Both international granaries and lax immigration policies must be rejected if we are to save something for our grandchildren."[2]

Actually, this recent statement only cloaks, in the rubric of an "ethic," a more frankly political position taken earlier by Hardin: "Every day we (i.e., Americans) are a smaller minority. We are increasing at only one percent a year; the rest of the world increase twice as fast. By the year 2000, one person in 24 will be an American; in one hundred years only one in 46 . . . If the world is one great commons, in which all food is shared equally, then we are lost. Those who breed faster will replace the rest . . . In the absence of breeding control a policy of "one mouth one meal" ultimately produces one totally miserable world. In a less than perfect world, the allocation of rights based on territory must be defended if a ruinous breeding race is to be avoided. It is unlikely that civilization and dignity can survive everywhere, but better in a few places than in none. Fortunate minorities must act as the trustees of a civilization that is threatened by uninformed good intentions."[3]

THE QUALITY OF LIFE

But there is another view of population which is much more complex. It is based on the evidence, amassed by demographers, that the birthrate is not affected by biological factors, such as fertility and contraception, but by equally powerful *social* factors.

Demographers have delineated a complex network of interactions among these social factors. This shows that population growth is not the consequence of a simple arithmetic relationship between birthrate and death rate. Instead, there are circular relationships in which, as in an ecological cycle, every step is connected to several others.

Thus, while a reduced death rate does, of course, increase the rate of population growth, it can also have the opposite effect—since families usually respond to a reduced rate of infant mortality by opting for fewer children. This negative feedback modulates the effect of a decreased death rate on population size. Similarly, although a rising population increases the demand on resources and thereby worsens the population problem, it also stimulates economic activity. This, in turn, improves educational levels. As a result the average age at marriage tends to increase, culminating in a reduced birthrate—which mitigates the pressure on resources.

In these processes, there is a powerful social force which, paradoxically, both reduces the death rate (and thereby stimulates population growth) and also leads people voluntarily to restrict the production of children (and thereby reduces population growth). That force, simply stated, is the quality of life—a high standard of living, a sense of well-being and of security in the future. When and how the two opposite effects of this force are felt differs with the stages in a country's economic development. In a premodern society, such as England before the industrial revolution or India before the advent of the English, both death rates and birthrates were high. But they were in balance and population size was stable. Then, as agricultural and industrial production began to increase and living conditions improved, the death rate began to fall. With the birthrate remaining high the population rapidly increased in size. However, later, as living standards continued to improve, the decline in death rate persisted but the birthrate began to decline as well, reducing the rate of population growth.

For example, at around 1800, Sweden had a high birthrate (about 33/1000), but since the death rate was equally high, the population was in balance. Then as agriculture and, later, industrial production advanced, the death rate dropped until, by the mid-nineteenth century, it stood at about 20/1000. Since the birthrate remained constant during that period of time, there was a large excess of births over deaths and the population increased rapidly. Then, however, the birthrate began to drop, gradually narrowing the gap until in the mid-twentieth century it reached about 14/1000, when the death rate was about 10/1000.[4] Thus, under the influence of a constantly rising standard of living the population moved, with time, from a position of balance *at a high death rate* to a new position of near-balance *at a low death rate*. But in between the population increased considerably.

This process, *the demographic transition*, is clearly characteristic of all western countries. In most of them, the birthrate does not begin to fall appreciably until the death rate is reduced below about 20/1000. However, then the drop in birthrate is rapid. A similar transition also appears to be under way in countries like India. Thus in the mid-nineteenth century, India had equally high birth and death rates about (50/1000) and the population was in approximate balance. Then, as living standards improved, the death rates dropped to its present level of about 15/1000 and the birthrate dropped, at first slowly and recently more rapidly, to its present level of 42/1000. India is at a critical point; now that death rate has reached the turning point of about 20/1000, we can expect the birthrate to fall rapidly—provided that the death rate is further reduced by improved living conditions.

One indicator of the quality of life—infant mortality—is especially decisive in this process. And again there is a critical point—a rate of infant mortality below which birthrate begins to drop sharply and, approaching the death rate, creates the conditions for a balanced population. The reason is that couples are interested in the number of *surviving* children and respond to a low rate of infant mortality by realizing that they no longer need to have more children to replace the ones that die. Birth control is, of course, a necessary adjunct to this process; but it can succeed—barring compulsion—only in the presence of a rising standard of living, which of itself generates the necessary motivation.

This process appears to be just as characteristic of developing countries as of developed ones. This can be seen by plotting the present birthrates against the present rates of infant mortality for all available national data. The highest rates of infant mortality are in African countries; they are in the range of 53–175/1000 live births and birthrates are about 27–52/1000. In those countries where infant mortality has improved somewhat (for example, in a number of Latin American and Asian countries) the drop in birthrate is slight (to about 45/1000) until the infant mortality reaches about 80/1000. Then, as infant mortality drops from 80/1000 to about 25/1000 (the figure characteristic of most developed countries), the birthrate drops sharply from 45 to about 15–18/1000. Thus a rate of infant mortality of 80/1000 is a critical turning point which can lead to a very rapid decline in birthrate in response to a further reduction in infant mortality. The latter, in turn, is always very responsive to improved living conditions, especially with respect to nutrition. Consequently, there is a kind of critical standard of living which, if achieved, can lead to a rapid reduction in birthrate and an approach to a balanced population.

Thus, in human societies, there is a built-in control on population size: If the standard of living, which initiates the rise in population, *continues* to increase, the population eventually begins to level off. This self-regulating process begins with a population in balance, but at a high death rate and low standard of living. It then progresses toward a population which is larger, but once more in balance, at a low death rate and a high standard of living.

DEMOGRAPHIC PARASITES

The chief reason for the rapid rise in population in developing countries is that this basic condition has not been met. The explanation is a fact about developing countries which is often forgotten—that they were recently, and in the economic sense often still remain, colonies of more developed countries. In the colonial period, western nations introduced improved living conditions (roads, communications, engineering, agricultural and medical services) as part of their campaign to increase the labor force needed to exploit the colony's natural resources. This increase in living standards initiated the first phase of the demographic transition.

But most of the resultant wealth did not remain in the colony. As a result, the second (or population-balancing) phase of the demographic transition could not take place. Instead the wealth produced in the colony was largely diverted to the advanced nation—where it helped *that* country achieve for itself the second phase of the demographic transition. Thus colonialism involves a kind of demographic parasitism: The second, population-balancing phase of the demographic transition in the advanced country is fed by the suppression of that same phase in the colony.

It has long been known that the accelerating curve of wealth and power of Western Europe, and later of the United States and Japan, has been heavily based on exploitation of resources taken from the less powerful nation: colonies, whether governed legally, or—as in the case of the U.S. control of certain Latin American countries—by extra-legal and economic means. The result has been a grossly inequitable rate of development among the nations of the world. As the wealth of the exploited nations was diverted to the more powerful ones, their power, and with it their capacity to exploit, increased. The gap between the wealth of nations grew, as the rich were fed by the poor.

What is evident from the above considerations is that this process of international exploitation has had another very powerful but unanticipated effect: rapid growth of the population in the former colonies. An analysis by the demographer, Nathan Keyfitz, leads him to conclude that the growth of industrial capitalism in the western nations in the period 1800-1950 resulted in the development of a one-billion excess in the world population, largely in the tropics. Thus the present world population crisis—the rapid growth of population in developing countries (the former colonies)—is the result not so much of policies promulgated by these countries but of a policy, colonial exploitation, forced on them by developed countries.

A VILLAGE IN INDIA

Given this background, what can be said about the various alternative methods of achieving a balanced world population? In India, there has been an interesting, if partially inadvertent, comparative test of two of the possible approaches: family planning programs and efforts (also on a family basis), to elevate the living standard. The results of this test show that while the family planning effort itself failed to reduce the birthrate, improved living standards succeeded.

In 1954, a Harvard team undertook the first major field study of birth control in India. The population of a number of test villages was provided with contraceptives and suitable educational programs; birthrates, death rates and health status in this population were compared with the comparable values in an equivalent population in control villages. The study covered the six-year period 1954–1960.

A follow-up in 1969 showed that the study was a failure. Although in the test population the crude birthrate dropped from 40 per 1,000 in 1957 to 35 per 1,000 in 1968, a similar reduction also occurred in the control population. The birth control effort had no measureable effect on birthrate.

We now know *why* the study failed, thanks to a remarkable book by Mahmood Mamdani. He investigated in detail the impact of the study on one of the test villages, Manupur. What Mamdani discovered is a total confirmation of the view that population control in a country like India depends on the economically-motivated desire to limit fertility. Talking with the Manupur villagers he discovered why, despite the study's statistics regarding ready "acceptance" of the offered contraceptives, the birthrate was not affected:

"One such 'acceptance' case was Asa Singh, a sometime land laborer who is now a watchman at the village high school. I questioned him as to whether he used the tablets or not: 'Certainly I did. You can read it in their books—From 1957 to 1960, I never failed.' Asa Singh, however, had a son who had been born sometime in 'late 1958 or 1959.' At our third meeting I pointed this out to him . . . Finally he looked at me and responded. 'Babuji, someday you'll understand. It is sometimes better to lie. It stops you from hurting people, does no harm, and might even help them.' The next day Asa Singh took me to a friend's house . . . and I saw small rectangular boxes and bottles, one piled on top of the other, all arranged as a tiny sculpture in a corner of the room. This man had made a sculpture of birth control devices. Asa Singh said: 'Most of us threw the tablets away. But my brother here, he makes use of everything.' ''[5]

Such stories have been reported before and are often taken to indicate how much "ignorance" has to be overcome before birth control can be effective in countries like India. But Mamdani takes us much further into the problem, by finding out why the villagers preferred not to use the contraceptives. In one interview after another he discovered a simple, decisive fact: that in order to advance their economic condition, to take advantage of the opportunities newly created by the development of independent India, *children were essential.* Mamdani makes this very explicit:

"To begin with, most families have either little or no savings, and they can earn too little to be able to finance the education of *any* children, even through high school. Another source of income must be found, and the only solution is, as one tailor told me, 'to have enough children so that there are at least three or four sons in the family.' Then each son can finish high school by spending part of the afternoon working . . . After high school, one son is sent on to college while the other work to save and pay the necessary fees . . . Once his education is completed, he will use his increased earnings to put his brother through college. He will not marry until the second brother has finished his college education and can carry the burden of educating the third brother . . . What is of interest is that, as the Khanna Study pointed out, it was the rise in the age of marriage—from 17.5 years in 1956 to 20 in 1969—and not the birth control program that was responsible for the decrease in the birthrate in the village from 40 per 1,000 in 1957 to 35 per 1,000 in 1968. While the birth control program was a failure, the net result of the technological and social change in Manupur was to bring down the birth rate."

Here, then, in the simple realities of the village of Manupur are the principles of the demographic transition at work. There *is* a way to control the rapid growth of populations in developing countries. It is to help them develop—and more rapidly achieve the level of welfare that everywhere in the world is the real motivation for a balanced population.

ENOUGH TO GO AROUND

Against this success, the proponents of the "lifeboat ethic" would argue that it is too slow, and they would take steps to *force* developing nations to reduce their birthrate even though the incentive for reduced fertility—the standard of living and its most meaningful index, infant mortality—is still far inferior to the levels which have motivated the demographic transition in the western countries. And where, in their view, it is too late to save a poor, overpopulated country the proponents of this so-called "ethic" would withdraw support (in the manner of the hopelessly wounded in military "triage") and allow it to perish.

This argument is based (at least in the realm of logic) on the view, to quote Hardin, that "It is literally beyond our ability to save them all." Hardin's assertion, if not the resulting "ethic," reflects a commonly held view that there is simply insufficient food and other resources in the world to support the present world population at the standard of living required to motivate the demographic transition. It is commonly pointed out, for example, that the U.S. consumes about one-third of the world's resources to support only six percent of the world's population, the inference being that there are simply not enough resources in the world to permit the rest of the world to achieve the standard of living and low birthrate characteristic of the U.S.

The fault in this reasoning is readily apparent if one examines the actual relationship between the birthrates and living standards of different countries. The only available comparative measure of standard of living is GNP per capita. Neglecting for a moment the faults inherent in GNP as a measure of the quality of life, a plot of birthrate against GNP per capita is very revealing. The poorest countries (GNP per capita less than $500 per year)[6] have the highest birthrates, 40–50 per 1,000 population per year. When GNP per capita per year exceeds $500 the birthrate drops sharply, reaching about 20/1,000 at $750–$1,000. Most of the nations in North America, Oceania, Europe and the USSR have about the same low birthrates—15–18/1,000—but their GNP's per capita per year range all the way from Greece ($941 per capita per year; birthrate 17/1,000) through Japan ($1,626 per capita per year; birthrate 18/1,000) to the richest country of all, the U.S. ($4,538 per capita per year; birthrate 18/1,000). What this means is that in order to bring the birthrates of the poor countries down to the low levels characteristic of the rich ones, the poor countries do not need to become as affluent (at least as measured, poorly, by GNP per capita) as the U.S. Achieving a per capita GNP only, let us say, one-fifth of that of the U.S.—$900 per capita per year—these countries could, according to the above relationship, reach birthrates almost as low as that of the European and North American countries.

The world average value for birthrate is 34/1,000, which is indicative of the overall rate of growth of the world population (the world average crude death rate is about 13/1,000). However, the world average per capita GNP is about $803 per year—a level of affluence which is characteristic of a number of nations with birthrates of 20/1,000. What this discrepancy tells us is that if the wealth of the world (at least as measured by GNP) were in fact evenly distributed among the people of the world, the entire world population should have a low birthrate— about 20/1,000—which would approach that characteristic of most European and North American countries (15–18/1,000).

Simply stated, the world has enough wealth to support the entire world population at a level that appears to convince most people that they need not have excessive numbers of children. The trouble is that the world's wealth is *not* evenly distributed, but sharply divided among moderately well-off and rich countries on the one hand and a much larger number of people that are very poor. The poor countries have high birthrates because they are extremely poor, and they are extremely poor because other countries are extremely rich.

THE ROOTS OF HUNGER

In a sense the demographic transition is a means of translating the availability of a decent level of resources, especially food, into a voluntary reduction in birthrate. It is a striking fact that the efficiency with which such resources can be converted into a reduced birthrate is much higher in the developing countries than in the advanced ones. Thus an improvement in GNP per capita per year from let us say $682 (as in Uruguay) to $4,538 (U.S.) reduces birthrate from 22/1,00 to 18/1,000. In contrast, according to the above relationships if the GNP per capita per year characteristic of India (about $88) were increased to only about $750, the Indian birthrate should fall from its actual value of about 42/1,000 to about 20/1,000. To put the matter more simply, the per capita cost of bringing the standard of living of poor countries with rapidly growing populations to the level which—based on the behavior of peoples all over the world—would motivate voluntary reduction of fertility is very small, compared to the per capita wealth of developed countries.

Food plays a critical role in these relationships. Hunger is widespread in the world and those who believe that the world's resources are already insufficient to support the world population cite this fact as the most powerful evidence that the world is overpopulated. Conversely, those who are concerned with relieving hunger and preventing future famines often assert that the basic solution to that problem is to control the growth of the world population.

Once more it is revealing to examine actual data regarding the incidence of malnutrition. From a detailed study of nutritional levels among various popula-tions in India by Revelle and Frisch we learn, for example, that in Madras State more than one-half the population consumes significantly less than the physiologi-cally required number of calories and of protein in their diet.[7] However, the *average* values for all residents of the state represents 99 percent of the calorie requirement and 98 percent of the protein requirement. What this means, of course, is that a significant part of the population receives *more* than the required dietary intake. About one-third of the population receives 106 percent of the required calories and 104 percent of the required protein; about 8 percent of the population receives 122 percent or more of the calorie requirement and 117 percent or more of the protein requirement. These dietary differences are deter-mined by income. The more than one-half of the population that is significantly below the physiologically required diet earn less than $21 per capita per year, as compared with the state-wide average of $33.40.

What these data indicate is that hunger in Madras State, defined simply in terms of a significantly inadequate intake of calories and protein, is not the result of a biological factor—the inadequate production of food. Rather, in the strict sense, it results from the *social* factors that govern the *distribution* of available food among the population.

In the last year, newspaper stories of actual famines in various parts of the world have also supported the view that starvation is usually not caused by the insufficient production of food in the world, but by social factors that prevent the required distribution of food. Thus, in Ethiopia many people suffered from starvation because government officials failed to mobilize readily available supplies of foreign grain. In India according to a recent *New York Times* report, inadequate food supplies were due in part from a government policy which "resulted in a booming black market, angry resentment among farmers and traders, and a breakdown in supplies." The report asserts further that "The central problem of India—rooted poverty—remains unchecked and seems to be getting worse. For the third year out of four per capita income is expected to drop. Nearly 80 percent of the children are malnourished . . . The economic torpor seems sympotomatic of deeper problems. Cynicism is rampant: the Government's socialist slogans and calls for austerity are mocked in view of bribes and corruption, luxury construction and virtually open illegal contributions by businessmen to the Congress party."[8]

Given these observations and the overall fact that the amount of food crops produced in the world at present is sufficient to provide an adequate diet to about eight billion people—more than twice the world population—it appears to me that the present, tragically widespread hunger in the world cannot be regarded as evidence that the size of the world population has outrun the world's capacity to produce food. I have already pointed out that we can regard the rapid growth of population in developing countries and the grinding poverty which engenders it as the distant outcome of colonial exploitation—a policy imposed on the antecedents of the developing countries by the more advanced ones. This policy has forcefully determined both the distribution of the world's wealth and of its different populations, accumulating most of the wealth in the western countries and most of the people in the remaining, largely tropical, ones.

Thus there is a grave imbalance between the world's wealth and the world's people. But the imbalance is not the supposed disparity between the world's *total* wealth and *total* population. Rather, it is due to the gross *distributive* imbalance among the nations of the world. What the problem calls for, I believe, is a process that now figures strongly in the thinking of the peoples of the Third World: a return of some of the world's wealth to the countries whose resources and peoples have borne so much of the burden of producing it—the developing nations.

WEALTH AMONG NATIONS

There is no denying that this proposal would involve exceedingly difficult economic, social and political problems, especially for the rich countries. But the alternative solutions thus far advanced are at least as difficult and socially stressful.

A major source of confusion is that these diverse proposed solutions to the population problem, which differ so sharply in their moral postulates and their political effects, appear to have a common base in scientific fact. It is, after all, equally true, scientifically, that the birthrate can be reduced by promulgating contraceptive practices (providing they are used), by elevating living standards, or by withholding food from starving nations.

But what I find particularly disturbing is that behind this screen of confusion between scientific fact and political intent there has developed an escalating series of what can be only regarded, in my opinion, as inhumane, abhorrent political schemes put forward in the guises of science. First we had Paddock's "triage" proposal, which would condemn whole nations to death through some species of global "benign neglect." Then we have schemes for coercing people to curtail their fertility, by physical and legal means which are ominously left unspecified. Now we are told (for example, in the statement of "The Environmental Fund") that we must curtail rather than extend our efforts to feed the hungry peoples of the world. Where will it end? Is it conceivable that the proponents of coercive population control will be guided by one of Garrett Hardin's earlier, astonishing proposals:

How can we help a foreign country to escape over-population? Clearly the worst thing we can do is send food . . . Atomic bombs would be kinder. For a few moments the misery would be acute, but it would soon come to an end for most of the people, leaving a very few survivors to suffer thereafter.[9]

There has been a long-standing alliance between psuedo-science and political repression; the Nazis' genetic theories, it will be recalled, were to be tested in the ovens at Dachau. This evil alliance feeds on confusion.

The present confusion can be removed by recognizing *all* of the current population proposals for what they are—not scientific observations but value judgments that reflect sharply differing ethical views and political intentions. The family planning approach, if applied as the exclusive solution to the problem, would put the burden of remedying a fault created by a social and political evil—colonialism—voluntarily on the individual victims of the evil. The so-called "lifeboat ethic" would compound the original evil of colonialism by forcing its victims to forego the humane course toward a balanced population, improvement of living standards, or if they refuse, to abandon them to destruction, or even to thrust them toward it.

My own purely personal conclusion is, like all of these, not scientific but political: that the world population crisis, which is the ultimate outcome of the exploitation of poor nations by rich ones, ought to be remedied by returning to the poor countries enough of the wealth taken from them to give their peoples both the reason and the resources voluntarily to limit their own fertility.

In sum, I believe that if the root cause of the world population crisis is poverty, then to end it we must abolish poverty. And if the cause of poverty is the grossly unequal distribution of world's wealth, then to end poverty, and with it the population crisis, we must redistribute that wealth, among nations and within them.

NOTES AND REFERENCES

1. Quoted from the Environmental Fund's Statement "Declaration on Population and Food," original in *Daedalus,* Fall, 1973.

2. Presented in San Francisco at the 1974 annual meeting of the American Association for the Advancement of Science.

3. *Science,* 172 (1971): 1297.

4. This and subsequent demographic information is from: Agency for International Development, *Population Program Assistance,* December, 1971.

5. *The Myth of Population Control* (New York: Monthly Review Press, 1972).

6. These and subsequent values are computed as U.S. 1969 dollars. The data relate to the 1969–70 period.

7. Vol. III, "The World Food Problem," a Report of the President's Science Advisory Committee, Washington, 1967.

8. *New York Times,* April 17, 1974.

9. "The Immorality of Being Softhearted," *Standford Alumni Almanac,* January, 1969.

15 UNICEF's Response To Population Growth: Family Planning

LORD RITCHIE-CALDER*

The "population explosion" is not due to a great orgy of procreation. Couples are not having more children than they used to have. More children are surviving the hazards of childbirth and childhood diseases to grow up, to marry and to multiply. Mothers are less frequently (but still too often) being sacrificed in giving birth. The span of life is being extended. For example, the expectation, at birth of a girl child born in India in 1946, was 27 years. Now it is 48—a long way short of the expectation in highly developed countries but covering the reproductive life-span so that the average Indian girl can go on having more children. More adults, men and women, are living longer—more mouths to be fed.

The growth-rate is highest in countries where until recently, the child mortality was worst. To have a minimal family (hands for the fields or care in old age) parents had to beget lots of children because so many of them died. Now, when the killer-diseases of infancy and childhood have, to a large extent, been curbed, the legacy of this misgiving still discourages family limitation. The unhappy consequence is that in families enlarged by survival there are more mouths to be inadequately fed and more impoverished misery to be shared. On the other hand if parents can be really convinced that the children whom they affectionately want and for whom they can better provide will stay alive, they will be more disposed to consider family planning.

A PERSONAL DECISION

The human species is the only one which can separate sex and reproduction but it is a conscious and intimate decision made by two individuals. They are not likely to be overimpressed by being told: "The demographers say that there are too many people in the world," or "The economists say that population-growth is mopping up, and defeating the purposes of national development programmes." They may be exhorted by national slogans, cajoled by fiscal inducements, encouraged to take advantage of birth-control facilities, or lectured on "responsible parenthood"; but, in the end, it depends on what having a family means to a couple.

*Lord Ritchie-Calder, "UNICEF's Grandchildren," *UNICEF News,* Issue 78 (December 1973/January 1974). Reprinted by permission of publisher.

THE FUSE IS SET

We can date the nuclear explosion to the last count-down second—five-thirty a.m. July 16th 1945. The population explosion cannot be dated so precisely but the fuse was set ten years earlier—February 1935. A young girl, Hildebrande, was dying from generalized blood infection; the doctors could offer no hope. Her desperate father gave her an injection of a red dye, the chemotherapeutic effects of which had not been tried on any human patient. She recovered. Her father was Dr. Gerhard Domagh. The dye—which had a specific action on the germ causing her disease—was prontosil, the first of the sulpha drugs.

The first extensive use of prontosil was in dealing with a "puerperal sepsis" outbreak in Britain. This infection, commonly called "child-bed fever," had been consistently fatal. Now it was under control.

The significance of the sulpha drugs was that they showed it was possible to attack a germ *within* the human body. This change in medical thinking produced by the sulphas led to Florey and Chain recognizing in Fleming's penicillin the capacity to inhibit the growth of germs within the living body. The historic success of that drug led to the search for new antibiotics with their own specificities. The discovery of DDT insecticide, with the persistence which is now considered its deplorable quality, made it possible to mount an offensive on a massive scale against the vector-borne diseases (such as malaria).

"MIRACLE" DRUGS A MILESTONE

During the war the sulphas, the antibiotics and the insecticides were given production priorities equal to those of munitions. In a real military sense they were victorious because they delivered armies from the poisoned wounds and camp diseases which had historically killed more people than weapons did. And, when the war ended, there were stockpiles and productive potential which could be extended to the broken armies, and the displaced persons of war-ravaged countries and then to the less-developed countries. Indeed it could be claimed that penicillin alone in the ten years following the war saved more people than had been lost in all the wars of all human history

With supplies available and with BCG (Bacillus Calmette Guerin) as a prophylactic against tuberculosis, the world scourge which rampaged after the First World War, international agencies moved across the world scene. UNRRA, the United Nations Relief and Rehabilitation Agency, achieved striking successes and, when it was wound up, UNICEF was given responsibility for the care of children, and is now, together with the World Health Organization, spreading supplies and services throughout the world.

The fight against disease and sickness still goes on but the immediate post-war effect was to cut off the peaks of mortality curves of the prevailing killer-diseases which had been the ruthless form of population control.

THE GHOST OF MALTHUS

In 1952, the effects of population increases in the disadvantaged countries were obvious enough to cause alarm and to raise again the ghost of Thomas Malthus who 170 years before had predicted human catastrophe because the population would increase beyond the capacity of the earth to feed it.

At the British Association for the Advancement of Science in that year, the President, Professor A. V. Hill, a Nobel Prizewinner for Medicine, said:

> Had it been possible to foresee the enormous sucess of this application (of the benefits of science) would humane people have agreed that it could better have been held back, to keep in step with other parallel progress, so that development could be planned and orderly? Some might say, yes, taking the purely biological view that if men will breed like rabbits they must be allowed to die like rabbits, until gradually improving education and a demand for a better standard of life teach them better. Most people will say, no.
>
> But suppose it were now certain that increasing population, uncontrolled by disease, would lead to wide-spread exhaustion of the soil and other capital resources, but also of increasing international tension and disorder making it hard for civilization itself to survive; would the majority of humane and reasonable people then change their minds? If ethical principles deny our right to do evil in order that good may come are we justified in doing good when the foreseeable results are evil?

This was the rhetorical question posed by a pre-eminently humane man who did not see that the answer was no less than genocide—the deliberate discrimination of advanced nations against other races. It meant also that all the international humanitarian work which has offset so much that is squalid and cynical in world politics has been "doing good when the foreseeable consequences are evil." This is an intolerable attitude.

DEATH CONTROL VERSUS BIRTH CONTROL

What was just as deplorable was the reticence about population control, and the refusal to recognize that it, by Man's intervention through science, we have death control, we must also have birth control. The reticence, whether imposed by religious objections or by the principle of "free demographic expansion", hobbled the United Nations and its agencies. The United Nations could present the demography, up-date the alarming figures, but it could not discuss what might be done about them or disseminate knowledge and means for curtailing families.

Official attitudes have changed. Religious taboos have been modified. More latitude has been allowed in official programmes. More and more governments are actively promoting birth control. Research into human reproduction and into improved methods of contraception is no longer furtive.

In the meantime, however, the graph of population has soared like a rocket from a launching pad.

A quarter of a century ago when one was trying to alert people (a dialogue with the deaf) one would say, "Every time the pendulum clock ticks, there is another mouth to be fed." Ten years later, one was saying, "Every time your wrist-watch ticks, there is another mouth to be fed." Now, one says, "Every time your pulse beats, there are three more mouths to be fed."

MULTIPLY BY FOUR

The term "mouths to be fed" is appropriate because it is the survival rate that matters. If the death-rate is lowered (i.e., if by better health measures we keep more people alive) and if the birth-rate increases (i.e., if more babies are conceived and delivered) there are that many more people for whom we have to provide. And provide we must; we have to plan to meet the needs of twice as many people in the world in the year 2,000 A.D.

That may sound a dogmatic prediction and somebody is bound to say, "Demographers have been wrong before and can be wrong again. They are always altering their figures." This is true, but nowadays they are altering them *upwards*. Today, national censuses are more painstaking and more accurate, and, invariably, countries find that they have more people than they guessed they had and the censuses are revealing not only headcounts but age-structures.

They show, for instance, that in the developing world more than half the population is under fifteen years of age (because the lethality of child-birth, infancy and childhood has been reduced). They will be reproducing and, even with the most effective birth-control propaganda, we might hope that the 2,000 A.D. figures (only 26 years away) will not be more but we would be unwise to expect them to be less. They are biologically committed. The holocaust of a nuclear war might affect them but no natural calamity will radically discount those figures.

If we continue to succeed in lowering mortality with no corresponding lowering of fertility, sixty years from now there will be four people in the world for every one living today. There is some agreement amongst experts that somewhere around that figure (fifteen to sixteen billion) a levelling out of the population graph is possible. On the other hand there are those who say that the world (with Man's ingenuity) could sustain fifty billion—twelve and half times as many as we can precariously feed today. By then we would be "eating rocks"—by that I mean that we would be *making* our food from the original elements, not as scientific sophistication but from necessity.

A RACE AGAINST TIME

It cannot be repeated often enough that it is not eventual numbers but the *rate* of growth that is the problem. Time is not on our side. If in a locality food production increases by 2½ per cent per annum and the population increases by 3 percent, the effect is chronic famine. Nor can we be deluded by global figures of available food (no longer reassuring). *Per capita* means per head but not per stomach and if by maldistribution, food is not getting to the bellies that need it, that is not much good. The Green Revolution, with its "miracle" wheat and rice, and the efforts to produce indispensable high protein, with all the amino acids essential for well-being, have to be localized. Otherwise we have the litany of malnutrition: "Better to walk than to run; better to sit than to walk; better to sleep than to sit; better to die than to wake."

And it is not just a question of food. Additional people have to be housed and clothed and presently will be demanding the artifacts of technology, with all that means in terms of natural resources, energy sources and waste-pollution. It means rapidly increasing urbanization. Kingsley Davis, the authority on population and urbanization, has pointed out that if the present trends continue all the world's population will be in cities within the lifetime of today's children.

The present migrations are producing the squalor and human indignity of shanty towns, of broken homes and juvenile deliquency, of under-employment and unemployment and of social disorder. Of course, by better municipal management we could accommodate them in World City. We could house them in tall-and-deep buildings (skyscrapers with underground storeys). We could use the techniques of factory-farming, with a flow-sheet of nutrients and removal of excrement, and put people in cubicles, like the coops of battery-fed chickens or the stalls and styes of cows and pigs. What sort of meaning life would acquire in such circumstances is another matter. One might ask how many mental hospitals are included in the present projections for cities of 60 million people.

CONCERN FOR THE WORLD'S CHILDREN

Early in the history of UNICEF (in what I called "the glass-of-milk days") the agency recognized that it must accept continuing responsibility for the children it saves. It is right, therefore, that like the other agencies of the United Nations, it should concern itself with population control so that succeeding generations should be brought up in human dignity.

It is right that it should be assisting governments to set up services which help children not only to grow and develop in health and have the right to adequate nutrition, but to acquire the skills, attitudes and knowledge required to prepare for the responsibilities of life.

This means co-operating with the World Health Organization in helping countries to build up their health services and train personnel to deliver these services, especially auxiliary workers to compensate for the shortage of fully trained doctors and nurses.

This means working with the Food and Agriculture Organization to seek ways of improving nutrition; with the United Nations Educational, Scientific and Cultural Organization to raise educational levels; and with the International Labor Organization to help young people learn a craft or trade which will prevent them from becoming drifters or deliquents.

UNICEF'S GRANDCHILDREN

Now UNICEF has grandchildren. The infants and toddlers who came to the milk-centres and were succoured through the hazardous years of childhood are now married and have children of their own.

The question is, how many? Their sexual libido will not be constrained by demographic arguments. Ascetic continence is asking too much. They must have the knowledge and the means to practice "responsible parenthood." The means must be reliable, cheap, simple to use, not irreversible (sterilization, like abortion, is a last resort) and psychologically acceptable.

"Responsible parenthood" means "to support a family in dignity and to save." How can there be any "dignity" when every successive child takes food and opportunity away from the others in increasing degradation of living conditions? And how can there be any saving, to provide investment in tools and better seeds and improved methods when a peasant with an increasing family is struggling for mere subsistence?

How can the children hope for education and better qualifications when schools are being swamped? The *rate* of literacy is improving in less developed countries but the *number* of illiterates, by addition and multiplication, is greater than it was a quarter of a century ago.

We give lip-service to "the quality of life" but that quality begins in the home. A poor family gets poorer and poorer with every unwanted child.

While recognizing the need for population control, the world community, and especially the well-to-do nations, have also to recognize the facts of life, present and foreseeable. Hundreds of millions, short of starvation, are not getting the sort of food necessary for well-being. With increasing numbers that will worsen. Human ingenuity, so often selfishly, dangerously or vaingloriously misapplied, must be addressed to human needs.

The race is between production and reproduction.

16 A Marxian Analysis of the Population-Resource Problem

DAVID HARVEY*

It would be convenient indeed if such a contentious issue as the relationship between population and resources could be discussed in some ethically neutral manner. In recent years scientific investigations into this relationship have multiplied greatly in number and sophistication. But the plethora of scientific investigation has not reduced contentiousness; rather, it has increased it. We can venture three possible explanations for this state of affairs: (1) science is not ethically neutral; (2) there are serious defects in the scientific methods used to consider the population-resources problem; or (3) some people are irrational and fail to understand and accept scientifically established results. All of these explanations may turn out to be true, but we can afford to proffer none of them without substantial qualification. The last explanation would require, for example, a careful analysis of the concept of *rationality* before it could be sustained.[1] The second explanation would require a careful investigation of the capacities and limitations of a whole battery of scientific methods, techniques, and tools, together with careful evaluation of available data, before it could be judged correct or incorrect. [Here], however, I shall focus on the first explanation and seek to show that the lack of ethical neutrality in science affects each and every attempt at "rational" scientific discussion of the population-resources relationship. I shall further endeavor to show how the adoption of certain kinds of scientific methods inevitably leads to certain kinds of substantive conclusions which, in turn, can have profound political implications.

THE ETHICAL NEUTRALITY ASSUMPTION

Scientists frequently appear to claim that scientific conclusions are immune from ideological assault. Scientific method, it is often argued, guarantees the objectivity and ethical neutrality of "factual" statements as well as the conclusions drawn therefrom. This view is common in the so-called natural sciences; it is also widespread in disciplines such as economics and sociology. The peculiarity of this view is that the claim to be ethically neutral and ideology free is itself an ideological claim. The principles of scientific method (what-

*David Harvey, "Population, Resources, and the Ideology of Science," *Economic Geography*, 50, no. 3 (July 1974): 256–277. Reprinted by permission of author and publisher.

ever they may be) are normative and not factual statements. The principles cannot, therefore, be justified and validated by appeal to science's own methods. The principles have to be validated by appeal to something external to science itself. Presumably this "something" lies in the realms of metaphysics, religion, morality, ethics, convention, or human practice. Whatever its source, it lies in realms that even scientists agree are freely penetrated by ideological considerations. I am not arguing that facts and conclusions reached by means of a particular scientific method are false, irrelevant, immoral, unjustifiable, purely subjective, or non-replicable. But I am arguing that the use of a particular scientific method is *of necessity* founded in ideology, and that any claim to be ideology free is *of necessity* an ideological claim. The results of any enquiry based on a particular version of scientific method cannot consequently claim to be immune from ideological assult, nor can they automatically be regarded as inherently different from or superior to results arrived at by other methods.

The ideological foundation of the ethical neutrality assumption can be demonstrated by a careful examination of the paradigmatic basis of enquiry throughout the history of science (both natural and social),[2] as well as by examining the history of the ethical neutrality assumption itself.[3] The ideological foundation can also be revealed by a consideration of those theories of meaning in which it is accepted that there cannot be an ethically neutral language because meaning in language cannot be divorced from the human practices through which specific meanings are learned and communicated.[4] It is not, however, [my] purpose to document the problems and defects of the ethical neutrality assumption, critical though these are. I shall, rather, start from the position that scientific enquiry cannot proceed in an ethically neutral manner, and seek to show how the inability to sustain a position of ethical neutrality inevitably implies some sort of an ideological position in any attempt to examine something as complex as a population-resources system.

Lack of ethical neutrality does not in itself prove very much. It does serve, of course, to get us beyond the rather trivial view that there is one version of some problem that is scientific and a variety of versions which are purely ideological. For example, the Malthusian terms "overpopulation" and "pressure of population on the means of subsistence" are inherently no more or less scientific than Marx's terms "industrial reserve army" and "relative surplus population," even though there is a predilection among unsophisticated analysts to regard the former phrases as adequately scientific and the latter as purely ideological. Unfortunately, it is not very informative to aver also that *all* versions of a problem are ideological, and it is downright misleading to suggest that our views on the population-resources problem depend merely upon whether we are optimists or pessimists, socialists or conservatives, determinists or possibilists, and the like. To contend the latter is not to give sufficient credit to that spirit of scientific endeavor that seeks to establish "truth" without invoking subjective personal preferences; to say that there is no such thing as ethical neutrality is not to say that we are reduced to mere personal opinion.

We are, however, forced to concede that "scientific" enquiry takes place in a social setting, expresses social ideas, and conveys social meanings. If we care to probe more deeply into these social meanings, we may observe that particular kinds of scientific method express certain kinds of ethical or ideological positions.

In something as controversial as the population-resources debate an understanding of this issue is crucial; yet it is all too frequently ignored. If, as I subsequently hope to show, the dominant method of logical empircism inevitably produces Malthusian or neo-Malthusian results, then we can more easily understand how it is that scientists raised in the tradition of logical empiricism have, when they have turned to the population-resources question, inevitably attributed a certain veracity to the Malthusian and neo-Malthusian view. When they have found such a view distasteful such scientists have rarely challenged it on "scientific" grounds; they have, rather, resorted to some version of subjective optimism as a basis for refutation. This kind of refutation has not been helpful of course, for it has perpetuated the illusion that science and ideology (understood as personal preference) are independent of each other when the real problem lies in the ideology of scientific method itself.

It is easiest to grapple with the connections between method, ideology, and substantive conclusions by examining the works of Malthus, Ricardo, and Marx, for it is relatively easy to grasp the connections in these works and thereby to discern some important and often obscured questions that lie at the heart of any analysis of the population-resources relation.

MALTHUS

It is sometimes forgotten that Malthus wrote his first *Essay on the Principle of Population* in 1798 as a political tract against the utopian socialist-anarchism of Godwin and Condorcet and as an antidote to the hopes for social progress aroused by the French Revolution. In his introduction, however, Malthus lays down certain principles of method which ought, he argues, to govern discourse concerning such an ambitious subject as the perfectibility of man:

> A writer may tell me that he thinks a man will ultimately become an ostrich. I cannot properly contradict him. But before he can expect to bring any reasonable person over to his opinion, he ought to show that the necks of mankind have been gradually elongating, that the lips have grown harder and more prominent, that the legs and feet are daily altering their shape, and that the hair is beginning to change into stubs of feathers. And till the probability of so wonderful a conversion can be shown, it is surely lost time and lost eloquence to expatiate on the happiness of man in such a state: to describe his powers, both of running and flying, to paint him in a condition where all narrow luxuries would be condemned, where he would be employed only in collecting the necessaries of life, and where, consequently, each man's share of labour would be light, and his portion of leisure ample.[5]

The method which Malthus advocates is empiricism. It is through the application of this empiricist method that the competing theories of the utopian socialists, the proponents of liberal advancement and the rights of man, and the advocates of "the existing order of things" can be tested against the realities of the world. Yet, the first edition of the *Essay* is strongly colored by a priori deduction as well as by polemics and empiricism. Malthus sets up two postulates—that food is necessary to the existence of man and that the passion between the sexes is necessary and constant. He places these two postulates in the context of certain conditions;

deduces certain consequences (including the famous law through which population inevitably places pressure on the means of subsistence); and then used the empiricist method to verify his deductions. Thus Malthus arrives at a conception of method which we may call "logical empiricism." This method broadly assumes that there are two kinds of truths which we may call "logical truths" (they are correct deductions from certain initial statements) and "empirical truths" (they are correct and verifiable factual statements which reflect observation and experiment). Logical truths may be related to empirical truths by uniting the two kinds of statements into a hypothetico-deductive system. If empirical observation indicates that certain of the derived statements are "factually true," then this is taken to mean that the system of statements as a whole is true, and we then have a "theory" of, for example, the population-resources relationship. Malthus constructs a crude version of such a theory.

Another feature of empiricism is worthy of note. Empiricism assumes that objects can be understood independently of observing subjects. Truth is therefore assumed to lie in a world external to the observer whose job is to record and faithfully reflect the attributes of objects. This logical empiricism is a pragmatic version of that scientific method which goes under the name of "logical positivism," and is founded in a particular and very strict view of language and meaning.

By the use of the logical empiricist method Malthus arrives at certain conclusions supportive of those advanced by the advocates of "the existing order of things," rejects the utopianism of Godwin and Condorcet, and rebuffs the hopes for political change. The diminution in polemics and the greater reliance on empiricism in the subsequent editions of the *Essay* may in part be regarded as a consequence of Malthus' basic discovery that scientific method of a certain sort could accomplish, with much greater credibility and power than straight polemics, a definite social purpose. The resort to empiricism was facilitated in turn by the growing body of information concerning the growth and condition of the world's population—a prime source, for example, was the work of the geographer Alexander von Humboldt.[6]

Having shown that the "power of population is indefinitely greater than the power of the earth to produce subsistence," and that it is a "natural law" that population will inevitably press against the means of subsistence, Malthus then goes on to discuss the positive and preventive checks through which population is kept in balance with the means of subsistence. The subsequent evolution in Malthus' ideas on the subject are too well-known to warrant repetition here. What is often forgotten, however, is the class character with which he invests it. Glacken, for example, who treats Malthus in the penultimate chapter of his monumental study, *Traces on the Rhodian Shore*,[7] ignores this aspect to Malthus entirely.

Malthus recognizes that "misery has to fall somewhere" and maintains that the positive checks will necessarily be the lot of the lower classes.[8] Malthus thereby explains the misery of the lower classes as the result of a natural law which functions "absolutely independent of all human regulation." The distress among the lowest classes has, therefore, to be interpreted as "an evil so deeply seated that no human ingenuity can reach it."[9] On this basis Malthus arrives, "reluctantly," at a set of policy recommendations with respect to the poor laws. By providing welfare to the lowest classes in society, aggregate human misery is only increased; freeing the lowest classes in society from positive checks only results in an expansion of their numbers, a gradual reduction in the standards of living of all members of society, and a decline in the incentive to work on which the mobilization of labor through the wage system depends. He also argues that increasing subsistence levels to "a part of society that cannot in general be considered as the most valuable part diminishes the shares that would otherwise belong to more industrious and worthy members, and thus forces more to become dependent."[10]

From this Malthus draws a moral:

> Hard as it may appear in individual instances, dependent poverty ought to be held disgraceful. Such a stimulus seems to be absolutely necessary to promote the happiness of the great mass of mankind, and every general attempt to weaken this stimulus, however benevolent its apparent intention will always defeat its own purpose. . . .
>
> I feel no doubt whatever that the parish laws of England have contributed to raise the price of provisions and to lower the real price of labour. They have therefore contributed to impoverish that class of people whose only possession is their labour. It is also difficult to suppose that they have not powerfully contributed to generate that carelessness and want of frugality observable among the poor; so contrary to the disposition to be remarked among petty tradesmen and small farmers. The labouring poor, to use a vulgar expression, seem always to live from hand to mouth. Their present wants employ their whole attention, and they seldom think of the future. Even when they have an opportunity of saving, they seldom exercise it, but all that is beyond their present necessities goes, generally speaking, to the ale-house. The poor laws of England may therefore be said to diminish both the power and the will to save among the common people, and thus to weaken one of the strongest incentives to sobriety and industry, and consequently to happiness.[11]

Thus, Malthus arrives at what we have now come to know as the "counter-intuitive solution"—namely, that the best thing to do about misery and poverty is to do nothing for anything that is done will only exacerbate the problem. The only valid policy with respect to the lowest classes in society is one of "benign neglect." This policy is further supported by a certain characterization of "typical" behaviors exhibited among the lower classes. Arguments such as these are still with us. They appear in the policy statements by Jay Forrester, Edward Banfield, Patrick Moynihan and others. In fact, welfare policy in the United States at the present time is dominated by such thinking.

Malthus' approach to the lower classes has, if it is to be judged correctly, to be set against his view of the roles of the other classes in society—principally those of the industrial and landed interests. These roles are discussed more analytically in *The Principles of Political Economy*. Here he recognizes that there is a problem to be solved in accounting for the accumulation of capital in society. The capitalist saves, invests in productive activity, sells the product at a profit, ploughs the profit back in as new investment, and commences the cycle of accumulation once more. There is a serious dilemma here, for the capitalist has to sell the product to someone if a profit is to be achieved, and the capitalist is saving rather than consuming. If the capitalist saves too much and the rate of capital accumulation increases too rapidly, then long before subsistence problems are encountered, the capitalists will find expansion checked by the lack of effective demand for the increased output. Consequently, "both capital and population may be at the same time, and for a period of great length, redundant, compared to the effective demand for produce."[12]

Malthus placed great emphasis upon the effective demand problem and sought to convince his contemporary Ricardo that in practice: "the actual check to production and population arises more from want of stimulant than want of power to produce."[13] Ricardo was not persuaded, and the idea of effective demand in relationship to capital accumulation and wage rates remained dormant until Keynes resurrected it in his *General Theory of Employment, Interest and Money.*

Malthus' solution to the problem of effective demand is to rely upon the proper exercise of the power to consume on the part of those unproductive classes—the landlords, state functionaries, etc.—who were outside of the production process. Malthus took pains to dissociate himself from any direct apologetics for conspicuous consumption on the part of the landed gentry. He was merely saying that if the capitalist, who was not giving in to what Adam Smith calls "mankind's insatiable appetite for trinkets and baubles," was to succeed in the task of capital accumulation, then someone, somewhere, had to generate an effective demand:

> It is unquestionably true that wealth produces wants; but it is a still more important truth that wants produce wealth. Each cause acts and reacts upon the other, but the order, both of precedence and importance, is with the wants which stimulate industry. . . . The greatest of all difficulties in converting uncivilized and thinly peopled countries into civilized and populous ones, is to inspire them with the wants best calculated to excite their exertions in the production of wealth. One of the greatest benefits which foreign commerce confers, and the reasons why it has always appeared an almost necessary ingredient in the progress of wealth, is its tendency to inspire new wants, to form new tastes, and to furnish fresh motives for industry. Even civilized and improved countries cannot afford to lose any of these motives.[14]

Effective demand located in the unproductive classes of society and stimulated by need creation and foreign trade, was an important and vital force in stimulating both the accumulation of capital and the expansion of employment. Labor might be unemployed, consequently, simply because of the failure of the upper classes to consume. This theory of effective demand does not sit easily with the theory of population. For one thing, it appears contradictory to assert via the theory of population that the power to consume be withheld from the lowest classes in society while asserting, through the theory of effective demand, that the upper classes should consume as much as possible. Malthus attempts to resolve this contradiction by arguing that the upper classes do not increase their numbers according to the principle of population—they consume conspicuously and regulate their numbers by the prudent habits generated out of a fear of a decline in their station in life. The lowest classes imprudently breed. The law of population is consequently disaggregated into one law for the poor and another law for the rich. But Malthus also has to explain why an effective demand cannot be generated by an increasing power to consume on the part of the laboring classes. Such a possibility Malthus quickly dismisses as illogical for: "no one will ever employ capital merely for the sake of the demand occasioned by those who work for him."[15]

He adds that the only case in which this could occur would be if the laborers "produce an excess of value above what they consume." He dismisses this possibility entirely. But even Ricardo, in annotating this passage, asks quite simply "why not?" and writes out a simple case to prove his point.[16] And, of course, it is this idea, which Malthus rejects out of hand, that forms the foundation of Marx's theory of surplus value, out of which the Marxist theory of relative surplus population stems.

Internal to Malthus' own work there is a central contradiction. On the one hand, the "natural law" of population asserts a doctrine of inevitable misery for the mass of mankind, while the theory of effective demand points to social controls to the employment of both capital and labor. Zinke suggests that Malthus did not need to reconcile these conflicting positions, for the principle of population applies in the long run, while the theory of effective demand is an explanation for short run cyclical swings.[17] Malthus does not appear to have thought this way about it. In the *Summary View of the Principle of Population,* published in 1830, Malthus attempts to reconcile these divergent views. Here he admits that "the laws of private property, which are the grand stimulants to production, do themselves so limit it as always to make the actual produce of the earth fall very considerably short of the power of production."[18]

He then goes on to point out that under a system of private property "the only effectual demand for produce must come from the owners of property," and that the control of effective demand so intervenes with respect to the principle of population that it prevents the visitation of misery on all sectors of mankind and "secures to a portion of society the leisure necessary for the progress of the arts and sciences"—a phenomena that "confers on society a most signal benefit." Claims for social reform, and particularly any challenges to the principle of private property, are misplaced. To do away with a society based on competitive individualism regulated through the institutions of private property is to permit the principle of population to operate unchecked—an eventuality that will plunge all of mankind into a state of misery. The laws of private property, insofar as they have restricted the opportunity for the laboring classes, have artificially checked the operation of the principle of population and thereby reduced the aggregate misery of mankind. Malthus thus reconciles the principle of population with the theory of effective demand:

> It makes little difference in the actual rate of increase of population, or the necessary existence of checks to it, whether the state of demand and supply which occasions an insufficiency of wages to the whole of the labouring classes be produced prematurely by a bad structure of society, and an unfavourable distribution of wealth, or necessarily by the comparative exhaustion of the soil. The labourer feels the difficulty in the same degree and it must have nearly the same results, from whatever cause it arises.[19]

Malthus was, in principle, a defender of private property arrangements, and it is this ideology that underlies his formulation of the principle of population as well as the theory of effective demand. Private property arrangements inevitably mean an uneven distribution of income, wealth, and the means of production in society. Malthus accepts some such distributional arrangement and accepts its class character. Specific distributional arrangements may be judged good or bad, but there was no way in which a rational society could be ordered which did not incorporate necessary class distinctions. Malthus bolstered his arguments with analysis and materials blended together, particularly with respect to the theory of population, by appeal to a method of logical empiricism. In his writings on political economy, however, Malthus frequently made use of a method more characteristic of Ricardo. In part the contradictory character of much of Malthus' writings on population and effective demand stems from the disjunction of method used to examine the two phenomena. At this point, therefore, we must turn to that method of investigation most clearly exhibited in the cleanly spelled-out analytics of Ricardo.

RICARDO

Ricardo accepted Malthus' principle of population without any reservations and, it must be added, quite uncritically. But the population principle plays a quite different role and is also treated according to a quite different methodology in Ricardo's work. Ricardo's method was to abstract a few basic elements and relationships out of a complex reality and to analyze and manipulate these idealized elements and relationships in order to discern the structure of the system under consideration. In this manner Ricardo built an abstract model of economic allocation through the market mechanism—a working model of capitalist society—that had little need for an empirical base. The function of such a model was to provide a tool for analysis which would both explain and predict change. Ricardo was not an empiricist in the sense that Malthus was in the *Essay on Population,* and he used facts sparingly, largely by way of illustration rather than with the intent to verify theory. The success and legitimacy of such a method depends, of course, entirely upon the reasonableness of the abstractions made. It is important to look, therefore, at the nature of the abstractions and idealizations built into Ricardo's model in order to understand both his substantive conclusions and his treatment of the population-resources problem.

At the heart of Ricardo's system we find a basic assumption concerning the nature of economic rationality: "economic man" is the model of rationality to which all human beings ought to aspire. Ricardo was, consequently, a normative rather than an empirical (positive) thinker. More deeply buried in Ricardo's work, however, is a doctrine of social harmony achieved through economically rational behavior in the market place. This doctrine of social harmony is frequently found in the political economy of the period, and its appearance in Ricardo's work is not unconnected with the use of an analytic, model-building methodology. A set of elements and relationships linked into a logical structure is bound to be internally consistent and to be internally harmonious. The model also generates equilibrium-type solutions to problems when it is subjected to manipulation and analysis. It is with respect to the social harmony concept that Ricardo's work contrasts most markedly with that of Malthus and Marx. The latter's work is expressive of the theme of class conflict throughout, whereas in Malthus' work the sense of class conflict is confused with social harmony (particularly in *The Principles of Political*

Economy) as Malthus seeks to combine results arrived at by means of logical empiricism with those arrived at by means of an abstract model of the economy. Class conflict can scarcely be found in the harmonious analytics of Ricardo's market system, although the analytical results are used for class purposes, namely, the defeat of the landed interest and the subservience of wage labor to the interests of the industrial entrepreneur.

Under these conditions it is surprising to find that Ricardo so easily accepted Malthus' principle of population. In part, the simplicity of Malthus' deductive argument must have appealed to him, but there is a much more significant reason for Ricardo's wholehearted endorsement of the principle. Only by means of it could Ricardo keep his system harmonious and in equilibrium. The analytic problem for Ricardo was to explain the equilibrium wage rate. Wages, he argued, were basically determined by two factors: scarcity and the costs of subsistence. In Ricardo's system labor was regarded abstractly as a commodity like any other, and a growing demand for it ought to elicit a supply so that wages would, in the long-run, tend to the level of a "natural wage" set by the costs of subsistence. The mechanism that Ricardo appropriated from Malthus to achieve the balance between the supply and demand for labor was, of course, the principle of population, through which the laboring population would automatically increase their numbers:

> When, however, by the encouragement which high wages give to the increase of population, the number of labourers is increased, wages again fall to their natural price, and indeed from a re-action sometimes fall below it.[20]

In the short run and under favorable circumstances, the rate of accumulation of capital could exceed that of the power of population to reproduce, and during such periods wages would be well above their "natural" price.[21] But such periods are bound to be short-lived. Also, when a population presses against the means of subsistence, "the only remedies are either a reduction of people or a more rapid accumulation of capital." Consequently, the laws determining wages and "the happiness of far the greatest part of every community" were dependent upon a balanced relationship between the supply of labor, via the principle of population, and the accumulation of capital. Population, Ricardo argued, "regulates itself by the funds which are to employ it, and therefore always increases or diminishes with the increase or diminution of capital.[22] Even Malthus, however, objected to this use of his population principle, observing that it took at least sixteen years to produce a laborer, and that the population principle was far more than just an equilibriating mechanism.[23]

Ricardo accepted that:

> The pernicious tendency of the poor laws is no longer a mystery since it has been fully developed by the able hand of Mr. Malthus and every friend of the poor must adamantly wish for their abolition.[24]

Like Malthus he argues that:

> The principle of gravitation is not more certain than the tendency of such laws to change wealth and power into misery and weakness; to call away the exertions of labour from every object, except that of providing mere subsistence; to confound all intellectual distinction; to busy the mind in supplying the

body's wants; until at last all classes should be infected with the plague of universal poverty.[25]

Further, he warns that:

if we should attain the stationary state, from which I trust we are yet far distant, then the pernicious nature of these laws become more manifest and alarming.[26]

Ricardo's evocation here of an ultimate stationary state is of interest. The analytic model-building methodology that he employed naturally suggests, as we have seen, harmony and equilibrium, and it is understandable that Ricardo should infer from his model that there must inevitably be some kind of equilibrium or stationary state. (J. S. Mill came to the same sort of conclusion using a similar methodological framework.)[27] Ricardo is here arguing also that under such an equilibrium condition, in which the demand and supply of labor are equated and the prospects for further capital accumulation eliminated, there would appear to be a choice between conditions of universal poverty (everybody receiving a mere subsistence wage) or conditions in which rational thought and civilization itself could survive, at least among an elite. Ricardo is also suggesting that social welfare provision will become particularly pernicious in non-growth situations. Again this argument is still with us and we will return to it later.

Ricardo found Malthus' arguments with respect to effective demand "quite astonishing" however, and commented that: "A body of unproductive labourers are just as necessary and useful with a view to future production as a fire which should consume in the manufacturer's warehouse, the goods which those unproductive labourers would otherwise consume."[28]

Ricardo would have no truck with Malthus' defense of the landed interest and it is clear from his remarks and policies with respect to the corn laws, rent, and the like, that Ricardo's sympathies lie entirely with the industrial entrepreneur who alone, in Ricardo's system, epitomized economic rationality. Ricardo was in fact offended by the role the landed interest played, and since he discounted the problem of effective demand entirely, Ricardo came to regard the landed interest as a mere barrier to progress and to the achievement of social harmony.

Ricardo's model building analytics permitted him to argue positively for change. He was not deterred by empirical evidence, and he had no sense of debt to history. His normative analytics allowed him to see the possibility for changing and improving reality, rather than just understanding and accepting it. Like August Lösch (another great normative thinker) Ricardo could take the view that "if my model does not conform to reality then it is reality that is wrong."[29] Ricardo would project upon the world a working model of capitalist society constructed in the image of an idealized social harmony achieved through the benificence of rational economic man. Ricardo sought to change reality to fit this image, and in the process he played an important and vital role in furthering the progress of industrialization in nineteenth century England.

MARX

Marx argues that both Ricardo and Malthus were projecting ideological assumptions without admitting or even perhaps being aware of them:

[Malthus's theory] suits his purpose remarkably well—an apologia for the existing state of affairs in England, for landlordism, 'State and Church' . . . persons and menial servants, assailed by the Ricardians as so many useless and superannuated drawbacks of bourgeois production and as nuisances. For all that, Ricardo championed bourgeois production insofar as it signified the most unrestricted development of the social productive forces. . . . He insisted upon the historical justification and necessity of this stage of development. His very lack of a historical sense of the past meant that he regarded everything from the historical standpoint of his time. Malthus also wanted to see the freest possible development of capitalist production . . . but at the same time he wants it to adapt itself to the "consumption needs" of the aristocracy and its branches in State and Church, to serve as the material basis for the antiquated claims of the representatives of interests inherited from feudalism and the absolute monarchy. Malthus wants bourgeoius production as long as it is not revolutionary, constitutes no historical factor of development, but merely creates a broader and more comfortable basis for the "old" society.[30]

The contrasts between Malthus, Ricardo, and Marx are usually portrayed in terms of their substantive views on such issues as the population-resources problem. The more fundamental contrast, however, is surely one of method. Marx's method is usually called "dialectical materialism," but this phrase conveys little and conceals a lot. Fully to understand it requires some understanding of German critical philosophy and in particular that branch of it which most fully developed a non-Aristotelian view of the world—the most eminent representatives in this tradition being Leibniz, Spinoza, and Hegel. The nature of this non-Aristotelian view requires exposition.

Marx's use of language is, as Ollman has pointed out, relational rather than absolute.[31] By this he means that a "thing" cannot be understood or even talked about independently of the relations it has with other things. For example, "resources" can be defined only in relationship to the mode of production which seeks to make use of them and which simultaneously "produces" them through both the physical and mental activity of the users. There is, therefore, no such thing as a resource in abstract or a resource which exists as a "thing in itself." This relational view of the world is fundamentally different from the usual and familiar Aristotelian view (characteristic of logical empiricism or Ricardian type model building) in which things are thought to have an essence of some sort and are, therefore, regarded as definable without reference to the relationships they have to other things.

On this basis Marx evolves certain fundamental assumptions regarding the way in which the world is structured and organized. Ollman suggests that: "The twin pillars of Marx's ontology are his conception of reality as a totality of internally related parts, and his conception of these parts as expandable relations such that each one in its fullness can represent the totality."[32] There are different ways in which we can think of such a totality. We may think of it as an aggregate of elements—a mere sum of parts—which enter into combination without being fashioned by any pre-existing relationships with the totality. The totality can alternatively be viewed as something "emergent"; it has an existence independent of its parts while it also dominates and fashions the parts contained within it. But Marx's non-Aristotelian and relational view permits him a third view of the totality in which it is neither the parts nor the whole, but the relationships within the totality which are regarded as fundamental. Through these relationships the totality shapes the parts to preserve the whole. Capitalism, for example, shapes activities and elements within itself to preserve itself as an on-going system. But conversely, the elements are also continually shaping the totality into new configurations as conflicts and contradictions within the system are of necessity resolved.

Marx rarely used the word totality to refer to everything there is. He usually focused on the "social" totality of human society, and within this totality he distinguished various structures. Structures are not "things" or "actions," and we cannot establish their existence through observation. The meaning of an observable act, such as cutting a log, is established by discovering its relation to the wider structure of which it is a part. Its interpretation will depend upon whether we view it in relation to capitalism or socialism, or whether we place it in relation to some quite different structure, such as the ecological system. To define elements relationally means to interpret them in a way external to direct observation; hence the departure from empiricism accomplished by relational modes of thought.

Within the social totality Marx distinguishes various structures.[33] The "economic basis" of society comprises two structures—the forces of production (the actual activities of making and doing) and the social relations of production (the forms of social organization set up to facilitate making and doing). Marx thus distinguished between a technical division of labor and a social division of labor. In addition, there are various superstructural features: the structures of law, of politics, of knowledge and science, of ideology, and the like. Each structure is regarded as a primary element within the social totality and each is capable of a certain degree of autonomous development. But because the structures are all interrelated, a perpetual dynamism is generated out of the conflicts and interactions among them. For example, Marx sees a major contradiction between the increasing socialization of the forces of production (through the intricacies of the division of labor) and the private-property basis of consumption and ownership in capitalist society. Within this system of interacting structures, however, Marx accorded a certain primacy of place to the economic basis. In arguing thus, Marx usually appealed to the fact that man has to eat in order to live and that production—the transformation of nature—therefore has to take precedence over the other structures in a conflict situation. There is a deeper reason for the significance which Marx attached to the economic basis; it is here that the relationship between the natural and social aspects of life become most explicit.

Marx's conception of the man-nature relation is complex.[34] At one level the human being is seen as a part of nature—an ensemble of metabolic relations involving constant sensuous interaction with a physical environment. At another level, human beings are seen as social—each as an ensemble of social relations—and capable of creating forms of social organization which can become self-regulating and self-transforming.[35] Society thereby creates its own history by transforming itself, but in the process the relationship with nature is also transformed. Under capitalism, for example:

> Nature becomes for the first time simply an object for mankind, purely a matter of utility; it ceases to be recognized as a power in its own right; and the

theoretical knowledge of its independent laws appears only as a strategem designed to subdue it to human requirements, whether as the object of consumption or as the means of production. Pursuing this tendency, capital has pushed beyond national boundaries and prejudices, beyond the deification of nature and inherited self-sufficient satisfaction of existing needs confined within well-defined bounds and [beyond] the reproduction of traditional ways of life. Capital is destructive of all this and permanently revolutionary, tearing down the obstacles that impede the development of productive forces, the expansion of need, the diversity of production and the exploitation and exchange of natural and intellectual forces.[36]

Marx saw the capitalist law of accumulation always pushing society to the limits of its potential social relations and to the limits of its natural resource base—continuously destroying the potential for "the exploitation and exchange of natural and intellectual forces." Resource limitations could be rolled back by technological change, but the tide of capitalist accumulation quickly spreads up to these new limits.

Marx also argued that capitalism had successfully brought society to the point where mankind could be free of nature in certain important material respects. Human beings are now in a position to *create* nature rather than mindlessly to alter it. Through the creation of nature—a creation that has to proceed through a knowledge and understanding of nature's own laws—human beings could be freed to discover their own essentially human nature within the system of nature. There is, for Marx, an enormous difference between this unalienated creation of nature and the mindless exploitation under capitalism which, in the haste to accumulate, is always concerned as Engels has it, "only about the first tangible success; and then surprise is expressed that the more remote effects of actions directed to this end turn out to be of a quite different, mainly of an opposite, character."[37]

In the final analysis, the conflict and contradiction between the system of nature and the social system could be resolved only by the creation of an appropriate and entirely new form of human practice. Through such a practice, human beings will "not only feel, but also know their unity with nature" and thereby render obsolete "the senseless and anti-natural idea of a contradiction between mind and matter, man and nature, soul and body."[38]

Marx's methodology allows that knowledge and the processes of gaining understanding are internal to society. Subject and object are not regarded as independent entities but as relationships one to the other. This conception is very different indeed from that of traditional empiricism in which the subject is presumed to be "instructed by what is outside of him," or from that of a priorism and innatism (clearly implied in Ricardo's method) in which the subject "possesses from the start endogenous structures which it imposes on objects."[39] Marx in fact fashions a methodology similar to the contructivism advanced by Piaget: "Whereas other animals cannot alter themselves except by changing their species, man can transform himself by transforming the world and can structure himself by constructing structures; and these structures are his own, for they are not entirely predestined either from within or without."[40] The subject is thus seen as both structuring and being structured by the object. As Marx puts it, "by thus acting on the external world and changing it, [man] at the same time changes his own nature."[41]

The thinking subject can create ideas in the imagination. But ideas have at some stage to leave the realms of abstract knowledge and to enter into human practice if they are to be validated. Once incorporated into human practice, concepts and ideas can become (via technology) a material force in production and can alter the social relations of production (through the creation of new modes of social organization). Although many ideas remain barren, some do not—'' at the end of every labour process we get a result that already existed in the imagination of the labourer at its commencement.''

Ideas are therefore regarded as social relations through which society can be structured and reconstructed. But concepts and categories are also produced under specific historical conditions which are in part internal to knowledge (the categories of thought handed down to us) and in part a reflection of the world in which knowledge is produced. The categories of thought available to us are as it were, our intellectual capital which it is open to us to improve (or destroy). If, however, ideas are social relations, then it follows that we can gain as much insight into society through a critical analysis of the relations ideas express, as we can through a study of society as object. The analysis of ideas in Marx's work is as much directed to understanding the society that produced them as it is to understanding what it is they tell us about the reality they purport to describe. Marx is, thus, adopting a methodological framework that is perpetually revolving around the question: what is it that produces ideas and what is it that these ideas serve to produce?

Marx's substantive conclusions on the ''population problem'' are in part generated out of a vigorous criticism of writers such as Malthus and Ricardo. Marx set out to transform the categories handed down to him, for he saw that to do so was necessary if the realities of life were to be transformed. Marx traced the structure of Malthus' and Ricardo's thought back to their respective theories of value. Out of a criticism of these and other theories of value, Marx arrived at the theory of surplus value. Surplus value, he argued, originated out of surplus labor, which is that part of the laborer's working time that is rendered gratis to the capitalist. In order to obtain employment, a laborer may have to work ten hours. The laborer may produce enough to cover his own subsistence needs in six hours. If the capitalist pays a subsistence wage, then the laborer works the equivalent of four hours free for the capitalist. This surplus labor can be converted through market exchange into its money equivalent—surplus value. And surplus value, under capitalism, is the source of rent, interest, and profit. On the basis of this theory of surplus value, Marx produces a distinctive theory of population.

If surplus value is to be ploughed back to produce more surplus value, then more money has to be laid out on wages and the purchase of raw materials and means of production. If the wage rate and productivity remain constant, then accumulation requires a concomitant numerical expansion in the labor force—''accumulation of capital is, therefore, increase of the proletariat.''[42] If the labor supply remains constant, then the increasing demand for labor generated by accumulation will bring about a rise in the wage rate. But a rise in the wage rate means a diminution of surplus value, falling profits, and, as a consequence, a slower rate of accumulation. But:

this diminution can never reach the point at which it would threaten the system itself. . . . Either the price of labour keeps on rising, because its rise does not interfere with the progress of accumulation. . . . Or accumulation slackens in consequence of the rise in the price of labour, because the stimulus of gain is blunted. The mechanism of the process of capitalist production removes the very obstacles that it temporarily creates.[43]

Under these conditions, the "law of capitalist production" that is at the bottom of the "pretended natural law of population" reduces itself to a relationship between the rate of capitalist accumulation and the rate of expansion in the wage-labor force. This relationship is mediated by technical change, and the increasing social productivity of labor can also be used as "a powerful lever of accumulation."[44] The use of this lever permits an expansion of surplus value through a growing substitution of capital for labor in the production process. Marx then proceeds to show how these processes combine to create a "law of population peculiar to the capitalist mode of production", adding that "in fact every special historic mode of production has its own special laws of population, historically valid within its limits along."[45] Here we can see a major departure from the thought of both Malthus and Ricardo who attributed to the law of population a "universal" and "natural" validity.

Marx largely confines attention to the law of population operative under capitalism. He points out that the laboring population produces both the surplus and the capital equipment, and thereby produces the means "by which it itself is made relatively superfluous."[46] He then goes on to say:

If a surplus labouring population is a necessary product of accumulation or of the development of wealth on a capitalist basis, this surplus population becomes, conversely, the lever of capitalist accumulation, nay a condition of existence of the capitalist mode of production. It forms a disposable industrial reserve army, that belongs to capital quite as absolutely as if the latter had bred it at its own cost. Independently of the limits of the actual increase of population, it creates for the changing needs of the self-expansion of capital, a mass of human material always ready for exploitation.[47]

This relative surplus population has, however, another vital function—it prevents wages rising and thereby cutting into profits:

The industrial reserve army, during the periods of stagnation and average prosperity, weighs down the active labour army; during the periods of over-production and paroxysm, it holds its pretensions in check. Relative surplus population is therefore the pivot around which the law of supply and demand of labour works. It confines the field of action of this law within the limits absolutely convenient to the activity of exploitation and to the domination of capital.[48]

The production of a relative surplus population and an industrial reserve army are seen in Marx's work as historically specific, as internal to the capitalist mode of production. On the basis of his analysis we can predict the occurrence of poverty no matter what the rate of population change. Marx explicitly recognizes, however, that a high rate of capital accumulation is likely to act as a general stimulus to population growth; it is likely that laborers will try to accumulate the only marketable commodity they possess, labor power itself.[49] Marx was not arguing that population growth per se was a mechanical product of the law of capitalist accumulation, nor was he saying that population growth per se did not affect the situation. But he was arguing very specifically, contra the position of both Malthus and Ricardo, that the poverty of the laboring classes was the inevitable product of the capitalist law of accumulation. Poverty was not, therefore, to be explained away by appeal to some natural law. It had to be recognized for what it really was—an endemic condition internal to the capitalist mode of production.

Marx does not talk about a population problem but a poverty and human exploitation problem. He replaces Malthus' concept of overpopulation by the concept of a relative surplus population. He replaces the inevitability of the "pressure of population on the means of subsistence" (accepted by both Malthus and Ricardo) by an historically specific and necessary pressure of labor supply on the means of employment produced internally within the capitalist mode of production. Marx's distinctive method permitted this reformulation of the population-resources problem, and put him in a position from which he could envisage a transformation of society that would eliminate poverty and misery rather than accept its inevitability.

METHODOLOGY AND THE POPULATION-RESOURCES RELATION

The contrasts between Malthus, Ricardo, and Marx are instructive for a variety of reasons. Each makes use of a distinctive method to approach the subject material. Marx utilizes a non-Aristotelian (dialectical) framework which sets him apart from Ricardo and Malthus who, in turn, are differentiated from each other by the use of abstract analytics and logical empiricism, respectively. Each method generates a distinctive kind of conclusion. Each author also expresses an ideological position, and, at times, it seems as if each utilizes that method which naturally yields the desired result. The important conclusion, however, is that the method adopted and the nature of the result are integrally related.

It is surprising, therefore, to find so little debate or discussion over the question of method for dealing with such a complex issue as the population-resources relation. Here the ethical neutrality assumption appears to be a major barrier to the advance of scientific enquiry, for if it is supposed that all scientific methods are ethically neutral, then debates over methodology scarcely matter. The materials on the population-resources relation published in recent years suggest that the Aristotelian legacy is dominant: we still usually "think Aristotle" often without knowing it. Yet the Aristotelian cast of mind seems ill-suited for dealing with the population-resources relation, and so there has been a methodological struggle internal to the Aristotelian tradition to overcome the limitations inherent in it. There has been, as it were, a convergence toward Marx without overthrowing the Aristotian trappings. Marx accepts that the appropriate method to deal with the population-resources relation has to be holistic, system-wide in its compass, capable of handling dynamics (feedbacks in particular), and most important of all, *internally dynamic* in that it has to be capable of producing new concepts and categories to deal with the system under investigation and, through the operationalization of these new concepts and categories, change the system from within. It is this last feature that gives to Marx's work its dialectical quality. Most contemporary investigations of the population-resources relation recognize all of Marx's requirements save the last, and rely upon systems theory for their methodological foundation. Systems-theoretic formulations are sophisticated enough (in principle) to do everything that Marx sought to do except to transform concepts and categories dialectically, and thereby to transform the nature of the system from within. Some examples will bear out this point.

Kneese *et al.* adopt what they call a "materials balance" approach to the population-resources relation which is, in effect, a two-stage input-output model.[50] The first stage describes the flows within the economy; the second stage describes the flows within the ecological system; and the two systems are linked by the physical principle that matter can neither be created nor destroyed. The model is descriptive in the sense that the coefficients have to be estimated from empirical data, but experimentation on the model is possible by examining the sensitivity of results to changes in the coefficients.

In the study of Meadows *et al.* methods derived from systems dynamics are used; a system of difference equations is simulated to indicate future outcomes of population growth, industrial expansion, resource use (both renewable and non-renewable), and environmental deterioration.[51] The system in this case incorporates feedbacks (both positive and negative) and is, in contrast to that of Kneese *et al.*, oriented to development through time. The Meadows model has come in for a great deal of criticism and a team from the University of Sussex has examined the model in detail.[52] They reformulated it in certain important respects; showed some of the problems inherent in the data used to estimate the equations; and concluded that some unnecessarily pessimistic assumptions were injected into the Meadows model.

The essential point to note, however, is that *all* of these formulations lead to neo-Malthusian conclusions: strongly voiced in the Meadows model; somewhat muted in the case of Kneese *et al.* (who speak of the *new* Malthusianism); and long run in the case of the Sussex team's investigation (rather like Ricardo they seem to suggest that the stationary state is inevitable but a long way off).

The neo-Malthusian results of these studies can be traced back to the Aristotelian form in which the question is posed and the answers constructed. And it is, of course, the ability to depart from the Aristotelian view that gets Marx away from both the short run and long run inevitabilities of neo-Malthusian conclusions. Marx envisages the production of new categories and concepts, of new knowledge and understanding, through which the relationships between the natural and social system will be mediated. This relational and dialectical view of things comes closest to impinging upon traditional concerns with respect to the problem of technological change. It has, of course, long been recognized that Malthus was wrong in his specific forecasts because he ignored technological change. Ricardo saw the possibilities of such change, but in the long run he saw society inevitably succumbing to the law of dimishing returns. The difference between the Meadows model and the Sussex team's refashioning of it is largely due to the pessimism of the former and the optimism of the latter. In all of these cases, technological change is seen as something external to society—an unknown that cannot be accounted for. But, for Marx technological change was both internal to and inevitable within society; it is the product of human creativity, and stems from the inevitable transformation of the concepts and categories handed down to us. Only if we let ourselves be imprisoned within the system of knowledge handed down to us will we fail to innovate. Further, it is unnecessarily restrictive to think that human-inventiveness and creativity apply only in the sphere of technology—human beings can and do create social structures as well as machines. This process Marx regards as essential and inevitable precisely because man could and would respond to the necessities of survival. The only danger lies in the tendency to place restrictions on ourselves and, thereby, to confine our own creativity. In other words, if we become the prisoners of an ideology, prisoners of the concepts and categories handed down to us, we are in danger of making the neo-Malthusian conclusions true, of making environmental determinism a condition of our existence.

It is from this standpoint that Marx's method generates quite different perspectives and conclusions from those generated by simple logical empiricism, Ricardian type normative analytics, or contemporary systems theory. Let me stress that I am not arguing that the latter methods are illegitimate or erroneous. Each is in fact perfectly appropriate for certain domains of enquiry. Logical empiricism has the capacity to inform us as to what is, given an existing set of categories. Insofar as we make use of this method, we are bound to construct what I have elsewhere called a *status quo* theory.[53] The Aristoelian manner in which normative, analytical model building proceeds yields "ought-to" prescriptive statements, but the categories and concepts are idealized, abstracted, and *stationary* tools imposed upon a changing world. Systems theory is a more sophisticated form of modelling relying upon various degrees of abstraction and a varying empirical content. Dialectical materialism, in the manner that Marx used it, is "constructivist" in that it sees change as an internally generated necessity that affects categories of thought and material reality alike. The relationships between these various methods are complex. The methods are not, obviously, mutually exclusive of each other; but different methods appear appropriate for different domains of enquiry. And it is difficult to see how anything other than a relational, constructivist, and internally dynamic method can be appropriate for looking into the future of the population-resources relation, particularly when it is so evident that knowledge and understanding are such important mediating forces in the construction of that future. Results arrived at by other means may be of interest, only if they are set within the broader interpretive power provided by Marx's method. All of this would be a mere academic problem (although one of crucial significance) were it not for the fact that ideas are social relations, and the Malthusian and neo-Malthusian results arrived at (inevitably) by means of other methods are projected into the world where they are likely to generate immediate political consequences. And it is to these consequences that we now turn.

THE POLITICAL IMPLICATIONS OF POPULATION-RESOURCES THEORY

At the Stockholm Conference on the Environment in 1972, the Chinese delegation asserted that there was no such thing as a scarcity of resources and that it was meaningless to discuss environmental problems in such terms. Western commentators were mystified and some concluded that the Chinese must possess vast reserves of minerals and fossil fuels the discovery of which they had not yet communicated to the world. The Chinese view is, however, quite consistent with Marx's method and should be considered from such a perspective. To elucidate it we need to bring into our vocabulary three categories of thought:

(1) *Subsistence*. Malthus appears to regard subsistence as something absolute, whereas Marx regards it as relative. For Marx, needs are not purely biological; they are also socially and culturally determined.[54] Also, as both Malthus and Marx agree, needs can be created, which implies that the meaning of subsistence cannot be established independent of particular historical and cultural circumstances if, as Marx insisted, definitions of social wants and needs were produced under a given mode of production rather than immutably held down by the Malthusian laws of population. Subsistence is, then, defined internally to a mode of production and changes over time.

(2) *Resources*. Resources are materials available "in nature" that are capable of being transformed into things of utility to man. It has long been recognized that resources can be defined only with respect to a particular technical, cultural, and historical stage of development, and that they are, in effect, technical and cultural appraisals of nature.[55]

(3) *Scarcity*. It is often erroneously accepted that scarcity is something inherent in nature, when its definition is inextricably social and cultural in origin. Scarcity presupposes certain social ends, and it is these that define scarcity just as much as the lack of natural means to accomplish these ends.[56] Furthermore, many of the scarcities we experience do not arise out of nature but are created by human activity and managed by social organization (the scarcity of building plots in central London is an example of the former; the scarcity of places at university is an example of the latter). Scarcity is in fact necessary to the survival of the capitalist mode of production, and it has to be carefully managed, otherwise the self-regulating aspect to the price mechanism will break down.[57]

Armed with these definitions, let us consider a simple sentence: "Overpopulation arises because of the scarcity of resources available for meeting the subsistence needs of the mass of the population." If we substitute our definitions into this sentence we get: "There are too many people in the world because the particular ends we have in view (together with the form of social organization we have) and the materials available in nature, that we have the will and the way to use, are not sufficient to provide us with those things to which we are accustomed." Out of such a sentence all kinds of possibilities can be extracted:

(1) we can change the ends we have in mind and alter the social organization of scarcity;

(2) we can change our technical and cultural appraisals of nature;

(3) we can change our views concerning the things to which we are accustomed;

(4) we can seek to alter our numbers.

A real concern with environmental issues demands that all of these options be examined in relation to each other. To say that there are too many people in the world amounts to saying that we have not the imagination, will, or ability to do anything about propositions (1), (2), and (3). In fact (1) is very difficult to do anything about because it involves the replacement of the market exchange system as a working mode of economic integration; proposition (2) has always been the great hope of resolving our difficulties; and we have never thought too coherently about (3) particularly as it relates to the maintenance of an effective demand in capitalist economies (nobody appears to have calculated what the effects of much reduced personal consumption will have on capital accumulation and employment).

I will risk the generalization that nothing of consequence can be done about (1) and (3) without dismantling and replacing the capitalist market exchange economy. If we are reluctant to contemplate such an alternative and if (2) is not performing its function too well, then we have to go to (4). Much of the debate in the western world focusses on (4), but in a society in which all four options can be integrated with each other, it must appear facile to discuss environmental problems in terms of naturally arising scarcities or overpopulation—this, presumably, is the point that the Chinese delegation to the Stockholm Conference was making.

The trouble with focusing exclusively on the control of population numbers is that it has certain political implications. Ideas about environment, population, and resources are not neutral. They are political in origin and have political effects. Historically it is depressing to look at the use made of the kind of sentence we have just analyzed. Once connotations of absolute limits come to surround the concepts of resource, scarcity, and subsistence, then an absolute limit is set for population. And what are the political implications (given these connotations) of saying there is "overpopulation" or a "scarcity of resources"? The meaning can all too quickly be established. Somebody, somewhere, is redundant, and there is not enough to go around. Am I redundant? Of course not. Are *you* redundant? Of course not. So who is redundant? Of course, it must be *them*. And if there is not enough to go around, then it is only right and proper that *they*, who contribute so little to society, ought to bear the brunt of the burden. And if we hold that there are certain of *us* who, by virtue of our skills, abilities, and attainments, are capable of "conferring a signal benefit upon mankind" through our contributions to the common good and who, besides, are the purveyors of peace, freedom, culture, and civilization, then it would appear to be our bound duty to protect and preserve ourselves for the sake of all mankind.

Let me make an assertion. Whenever a theory of overpopulation seizes hold in a society dominated by an elite, then the non-elite invariably experience some form of political, economic, and social repression. Such an assertion can be justified by an appeal to the historical evidence. Britain shortly after the Napoleonic Wars, when Malthus was so influential, provides one example. The conservation movement in the United States at the turn of this century was based on a gospel of efficiency that embraced natural resource management and labor relations alike. The combination of the Aryan ethic and the need for increased lebensraum produced particularly evil results in Hitler's Germany. The policy prescriptions that frequently attach to essays on the problems of population and environment convey a similar warning. Jacks and Whyte, writing in the twilight years of the British Empire, could see only one way out of the scarcity of land resources in Africa:

> A feudal type of society in which the native cultivators would to some extent be tied to the lands of their European overlords seems most generally suited to meet the needs of the soil in the present state of African development. . . . It would enable the people who have been the prime cause of erosion [the Europeans] and who have the means and ability to control it to assume

responsibility for the soil. At present, humanitarian considerations for the natives prevent Europeans from winning the attainable position of dominance over the soil.[58]

Such direct apologetics for colonialism sound somewhat odd today.

Vogt, whose book *The Road to Survival* appeared in 1948, saw in Russian overpopulation a serious military and political threat. He argued that the Marshall Plan of aid to Europe was the result of an unenviable choice between allowing the spread of communism and providing international welfare, which would merely encourage population increase. He also points to the expendability of much of the world's population:

> There is little hope that the world will escape the horror of extensive famines in China within the next few years. But from the world point of view, these may be not only desirable but indispensable. A Chinese population that continued to increase at a geometric rate could only be a global calamity. The mission of General Marshall to this unhappy land was called a failure. Had it succeeded, it might well have been a disaster.[59]

It is ironic indeed that this prediction was published in the very year that Mao Tse-tung came to power and sought, in true dialectical fashion, to transform China's problem into a solution through the mobilization of labor power to create resources where there had been none before. The resultant transformation of the Chinese earth (as Buchanan calls it)[60] has eliminated famine, raised living standards, and effectively eliminated hunger and material misery.

It is easier to catch the political implications of overpopulation arguments in past eras than it is in our own. The lesson which these examples suggest is simply this: if we accept a theory of overpopulation and resource scarcity but insist upon keeping the capitalist mode of production intact, then the inevitable results are policies directed toward class or ethnic repression at home and policies of imperialism and neo-imperialism abroad. Unfortunately this relation can be structured in the other direction. If, for whatever reason, an elite group requires an argument to support policies of repression, then the overpopulation argument is most beautifully tailored to fit this purpose. Malthus and Ricardo provide us with one example of such apologetics. If a poverty class is necessary to the processes of capitalist accumulation or a subsistence wage essential to economic equilibrium, then what better way to explain it away then to appeal to a universal and supposedly "natural" law of population?

Malthus indicates another kind of apologetic use for the population principle. If an existing social order, an elite group of some sort, is under threat and is fighting to preserve its dominant position in society, then the overpopulation and shortage of resources arguments can be used as powerful ideological levers to persuade people into acceptance of the status quo and of authoritarian measures to maintain it. The English landed interest used Malthus' arguments thus in the early nineteenth century. And this kind of argument is, of course, even more effective if the elite group is in a position to create a scarcity to demonstrate the point.

The overpopulation argument is easily used as part of an elaborate apologetic through which class, ethnic or (neo-) colonial repression may be justified. It is difficult to distinguish between arguments that have some real foundation and arguments fashioned for apologetic reasons. In general the two kinds of arguments get inextricably mixed up. Consequently, those who think there is a real problem of some sort may, unwittingly contribute strength to the apologists and individuals may contribute in good faith to a result which as individuals, they might find abhorrent.

And what of the contemporary ecology and environmental movement? I believe it reflects all of the currents I have identified, but under the stress of contemporary events it is difficult to sort the arguments out clearly. There are deep structural problems to the capitalist growth process (epitomized by persistent "stagflation" and international monetary uncertainties). Adjustments seem necessary. The welfare population in America is being transformed from a tool for the manipulation of effective demand (which was its economic role in the 1960s) into a tool for attacking wage rates (through the work-fare provision)—and Malthus' arguments are all being used to do it. Wage rates have been under attack, and policies for depressing real earnings are emerging in both America and in Europe to compensate for falling rates of profit and a slowdown in the rate of capital accumulation. There can be no question that the existing social order perceived itself to be under some kind of threat in the late 1960s (particularly in France and the U.S.A., and now in Britain). Was it accidental that the environmentalist argument emerged so strongly in 1968 at the crest of campus disturbances? And what was the effect of replacing Marcuse by Ehrlich as campus hero? Conditions appear to be exactly right for the emergence of overpopulation arguments as part of a popular ideology to justify what had and what has to be done to stabilize a capitalist economic system that is under severe stress.

But at the same time there is mounting evidence (which has in fact been building up since the early 1950s) of certain ecological problems that now exist on a world-wide as opposed to on a purely local scale (the DDT example being the most spectacular). Such problems are real enough. The difficulty, of course, is to identify the underlying reason for the emergence of these difficulties. There has been some recognition that consumption patterns induced under capitalism may have something to do with it, and that the nature of private enterprise, with its predilection for shifting costs onto society in order to improve the competitive position of the firm, also plays a role.[61] And there is no question that runaway rates of population growth (brought about to a large degree by the penetration of market and wage-labor relationships into traditional rural societies) have also played a role. But in their haste to lay the origin of these problems at the door of "overpopulation" (with all of its Malthusian connotations), many analysts have unwittingly invited the politics of repression that invariably seem to be attached to the Malthusian argument at a time when economic conditions are such as to make that argument extremely attractive to a ruling elite.

Ideas are social relations; they have their ultimate origin in the social concerns of mankind and have their ultimate impact upon the social life of mankind. Arguments concerning environmental degradation, population growth, resource scarcities, and the like can arise for quite disparate reasons and have quite diverse impacts. It is therefore crucial to establish the political and social origins and impacts of such arguments. The political consequences of injecting a strongly pessimistic view into a world structured hierarchically along class and ethnic lines and in which there is a ideological commitment to the preservation of the capitalist order are quite terrifying to contemplate. As Levi-Strauss warns in *Tristes Tropiques:*

> Once men begin to feel cramped in their geographical, social, and mental habitat, they are in danger of being tempted by the simple solution of denying one section of the species the right to be considered human.[62]

CONCLUSIONS

Twentieth century science in the western world is dominated by the tradition of Aristotelian materialism. Within that tradition, logical empiricism, backed by the philosophical strength of logical positivism, has provided a general paradigmatic basis for scientific enquiry. More recently the "model builders" and the "systems theorists" have come to play a larger role. All of these methods are destined to generate Malthusian or neo-Malthusian results when applied to the analysis of global problems in the population-resources relation. Individual scientists may express optimism or pessimism about the future, while the results of scientific investigation may indicate the inevitable stationary state to be far away or close at hand. But, given the nature of the methodology, all the indicators point in the same direction.

The political consequences that flow from these results can be serious. The projection of a new-Malthusian view into the politics of the time appears to invite repression at home and neo-colonial policies abroad. The neo-Malthusian view often functions to legitimate such policies and, thereby, to preserve the position of a ruling elite. Given the ethical neutrality assumption and the dominant conception of scientific method, all a ruling elite has to do to generate neo-Malthusian viewpoints is to ask the scientific community to consider the problems inherent in the population-resources relation. The scientific results are basically predetermined, although individual scientists may demur for personal "subjective" reasons.

It is, of course, [my] central argument that the only kind of method capable of dealing with the complexities of the population-resources relation in an integrated and truly dynamic way is that founded in a properly constituted version of dialectical materialism.

This conclusion will doubtless be unpalatable to many because it *sounds* ideological to a society of scholars nurtured in the belief that ideology is a dirty word. Such a belief is, as I have pointed out, ideological. Further, failure to make use of such a method in the face of a situation that all regard as problematic, and some regard as bordering on the catastrophic, is to court ignorance on a matter as serious as the survival of the human species. And if ignorance is the result of the ideological belief that science is and ought to be ideology free, then it is a hidden ideology that is the most serious barrier to enquiry. And if, out of ignorance, we participate in the politics of repression and the politics of fear, then we are doing so largely as a consequence of the ideological claim to be ideology free. But then, perhaps, it was precisely that participation that the claim to be ideology free was designed to elicit all along.

NOTES AND REFERENCES

1. M. Godelier, *Rationality and Irrationality in Economics* (London: New Left Books, 1972).

2. D. Harvey, *Social Justice and the City* (Baltimore: Johns Hopkins Press, 1973); T. S. Kuhn, *The Structure of Scientific Revolutions* (Chicago: Chicago University Press, 1962); and I. Mesjaros, "Ideology and Social Science," *Socialist Register,* 1972.

3. Mesjaros, "Ideology and Social Science" and U. J. Tarascio, *Paerto's Methodological Approach to Economics* (Chapel Hill, North Carolina: University of North Carolina Press, 1966).

4. W. D. Hudson, *Modern Moral Philosophy* (London: Macmillan, 1970) and L. Wittgenstein, *Philosophical Investigations* (Oxford: Oxford University Press, 1958).

5. T. R. Malthus, *An Essay on the Principle of Population and a Summary View of the Principle of Population* (Harmondsworth, Middlesex: Penguin Books, 1970) p. 70.

6. A von Humboldt, *Essai Politique sur le Royaume de la Nouvelle Espagne* (Paris: F. Schoell, 1811).

7. C. Glacken, *Traces on the Rhodian Shore* (Berkeley: University of California Press, 1967).

8. Malthus, *An Essay on the Principle of Population and a Summary View of the Principle of Population,* p. 82.

9. Ibid., p. 101.

10. Ibid., p. 97.

11. Ibid., p. 98.

12. T. R. Malthus, *An Essay on the Principle of Political Economy* (New York: Augustus Kelley, 1968), p. 402.

13. J. M. Keynes, *Essays in Biography* (New York: Meridian Books, 1951), p. 117.

14. Malthus, *An Essay on Principles of Political Economy,* p. 403.

15. Ibid., p. 404.

16. D. Ricardo. *The Works and Correspondence of David Ricardo.* Vol. 2 (London: Cambridge University Press, 1951), p. 429.

17. I. W. Zinke, *The Problem of Malthus: Must Progress End in Overpopulation.* (Boulder, Colorado: University of Colorado Studies, Series in Economics, No. 5, 1967).

18. Malthus, *An Essay on the Principle of Population and a Summary View of the Principle of Population,* p. 245.

19. Ibid., p. 247.

20. D. Ricardo, *Principles of Political Economy* (London: Cambridge University Press, 1951), p. 94.

21. Ibid., p. 98.

22. Ibid., p. 78.

23. Malthus, *Principles of Political Economy* (New York. Augustus Kelley, 1968), pp. 319–320.

24. Ricardo, *Principals of Political Economy,* p. 106.

25. Ibid., p. 108.

26. Ibid., p. 109.

27. J. S. Mill, *Principles of Political Economy* (Toronto: University of Toronto Press, 1965), pp. 752–757.

28. Ricardo, *The Works and Correspondence of David Ricardo,* p. 421.

29. A. Lösch, *The Economies of Location* (New Haven: Yale University Press, 1954), p. 363.

30. K. Marx, *Theories of Surplus Value.* Part 3 (Moscow: Progress Publishers, 1972), pp. 52–53.

31. B. Ollman, *Alienation: Marx's Conception of Man in Capitalist Society* (London: Cambridge University Press, 1971).

32. B. Ollman, "Marxism and Political Science: Prologomenon to a Debate on Marx's Method," *Politics and Society,* 3 (1973): 495.

33. Godelier, *Rationality and Irrationality in Economics.*

34. A. Schmidt, *The Concept of Nature in Marx* (London: New Left Books, 1971).

35. K. Marx, *The Economic and Philosophic Manuscripts of 1884* (New York: International Publishers, 1964).

36. K. Marx, *The Grundrisse* (London: Macmillan, 1971), p. 94.

37. F. Engels, *The Dialects of Nature* (New York: International Publishers, 1940), p. 296.

38. Ibid., p. 293.

39. J. Piaget, *The Principles of Genetic Epistelomology* (London: Cambridge University Press, 1951), p. 19.

40. J. Piaget, *Structuralism* (New York: Harper, 1970), p. 118.

41. K. Marx, *Capital.* 3 Vols (New York: International Publishers, 1967), Vol. 1, p. 175.

42. Ibid., Vol. 1, p. 614.

43. Ibid., Vol. 1, p. 619.

44. Ibid., Vol. 1, p. 621.

45. Ibid., Vol. 1, pp. 632–33.

46. Ibid., Vol. 1, p. 632.

47. Ibid., Vol. 1, p. 632.

48. Ibid., Vol. 1, p. 632.

49. Ibid., Vol. 3, p. 218.

50. A. V. Kneese, R. V. Ayres, and R. C. D'Arge, *Economics and the Environment* (Washington, D.C.: Resources for the Future, 1970).

51. D. H. Meadows, D. L. Meadows, J. Randers and W. W. Behrens, *The Limits to Growth* (New York: Universe Books, 1972).

52. H. S. D. Cole, C. Freeman, M. Jahoda, and K. L. R. Pavitt, *Thinking about the Future: A Critique of the Limits to Growth* (London: Chatto and Windus, 1973).

53. D. Harvey, *Social Justice and the City.*

54. M. Orans, "Surplus," *Human Organization,* 25 (1966): 24–32.

55. W. Firey, *Man, Mind and the Land* (Glencoe, Illinois: Free Press, 1960) and A. Spoehr, "Cultural Differences in the Interpretation of Natural Resources," in W. L. Thomas (ed.), *Man's Role in Changing the Face of the Earth* (Chicago: Chicago University Press, 1956).

56. H. Pearson, "The Economy Has No Surplus: A Critique of a Theory of Development," in K. Polanyi, D. M. Arensbergy, and H. W. Pearson, *Trade and Market in Early Empires* (Glencoe, Illinois: Free Press, 1957).

57. Harvey, *Social Justice and the City.*

58. G. V. Jacks and R. O. Whyte, *Vanishing Lands* (New York: Doubleday, 1939), p. 276.

59. W. Vogt, *The Road to Survival* (New York: W. Sloane Associates, 1948), p. 238.

60. K. Buchanan, *The Transformation of the Chinese Earth* (New York: Praeger, 1970).

61. K. W. Kapp, *The Social Costs of Private Enterprise* (Cambridge, Massachusetts: Harvard University Press, 1950).

62. C. Levi-Strauss, *Tristes Tropiques* (New York: Atheneum, 1973).

Additional Readings

Borgstrom, Georg. *The Ford and People Dilemma*. North Scituate, Mass.: Duxbury Press, 1973.

Cole, H. S. D., Cole, Freeman, C., Jahoda, Marie and Pavitt, K. L. R., ed., *Models of Doom*. New York: Universe Books, 1973.

Cipolla, C. M. *The Economic History of World Population*. Harmondsworth, England: Penguin Books, 1970.

Ehrlich, P. R. and Ehrlich, A. H. *Population, Resources, Environment: Issues in Human Economy*. San Francisco: W. H. Freeman and Company, 1970.

Green, Ronald Michael. *Population Growth and Justice: An Examination of Moral Issues Raised by Rapid Population Growth*. Missoula, MT: Scholars Press, 1976.

Kamerschen, D. R. "On an Operational Index of 'Overpopulation,' " *Economic Development and Cultural Change*, 13, no. 2 (1965): 169–187.

Mamdani, Mahmood. *The Myth of Population Control*. New York: Monthly Review Press, 1973.

Mass, Bonnie. *Political Economy of Population Control in Latin America*. Montreal, Quebec: Editions Latin America, 1972.

Meadows, D., H., Meadows, D. L., Randers, J., and Behhrens, W. W., III. *The Limits to Growth*. New York: The New American Library, 1972.

Mesarovic, N., and Pestal, Edward. *Mankind at the Turning Point*. New York: Signet, 1976.

Notestein, F. W. "Zero Population Growth: What is it?" *Family Planning Perspectives*, 2 (1970): 20–24.

Overbeek, J. *History of Population Theories*. The Netherlands: Universitaire Per Rotterdam Press, 1974.

Peccei, A. "Controlling the Population will be the Rule," *Development Forum*, 2, no. 7 (1974); 4.

Piotrow, P. T., ed. *Population and Family Planning in the People's Republic of China*. Washington, D.C.: The Brookings Institution, 1971.

Pohlman, E. *Population: A Clash of Prophets*. New York: Mentor, 1973.

Sauvey, A. *Fertility and Survival: Population from Malthus to Mao Tse-Tung*. New York: Chatto, 1961.

Smith, T. Lynn. *The Race between Population and Food Supply in Latin America*. Alburquerque: University of New Mexico, 1976.

Stycos, Mayone J. *Rapid Population Growth–Consequences and Policy Implications*. Baltimore: Johns Hopkins Press, 1971.

Suyin, H. "Controlling the Population is not the Cure," *Development Forum*, 2, no. 7 (1974): p. 5.

Teitelbaum, M. S. "Relevance of Demographic Transition Theory for Developing Countries," *Science*, 188 (1975): 420–425.

Weeks, John R. *Population: An Introduction to Concepts and Issues*. Belmont, Cal.: Wadsworth Publishing Co., 1978.

VI
TOURISM

White woman meets "savage." Foreign travelers seek adventure in East Africa by going on wildlife safaris and by taking excursions through native villages.

Nyali beach hotel, Mombasa, Kenya. Tourists and expatriates seek out Third World destinations for sun, sand, and sex.

What role does international tourism play in the development or underdevelopment of Third World nations? Who benefits? Multinational corporations, the travel industry, and affluent consumers in the developed countries? Or Third World elites? Or the bulk of the populations in the underdeveloped countries? Each analytical perspective answers these questions differently.

Bond and Ladman believe that tourism can transform traditional agricultural economies into modern industrial societies. Most Third World countries have a comparative advantage in tourism because they can supply "appropriate climate," surplus labor which can provide inexpensive services, and "exotic characteristics of a unique culture, history, and unusual natural scenery." North American and European consumers are demanding more foreign travel because of higher incomes, taste for exotic places, longer paid vacations, and lower travel costs. Individual decisions are determining the nature and destination of international tourist spots. As an export industry, tourism circumvents the problems associated with conventional trade. International tourism would create national development because of several kinds of backward linkages; labor-intensive technology; small-scale, locally owned and operated enterprises; and a few imports. Thus tourism would conserve on the use of foreign exchange. Tourists would also provide a demonstration effect to the "natives" who would "begin to realize the benefits of alternative and more remunerative employment."

Britton presents a critique of tourism. Although commercial interests would want to convince First World and Third World people of the advantages of tourism, Britton wonders why academics and international organizations advocate tourism as a sensible development strategy. He cites numerous negative factors which make tourism an "ineffective engine of development." Foreign airlines and hotel chains largely determine the destination sites of tourists, and frequently dictate the conditions under which recreation areas will be "developed." Government subsidies in the form of tax shelters, and duty-free importation of materials and equipment encourage international tourism to the detriment of local needs. Right-wing regimes with the support of local elites create the appropriate atmosphere for law and order for the foreign travel industry. In addition to the adverse economic consequences, tourism creates major cultural and social disruptions, and environmental degradations. In short, what Bond and Ladman see as advantages, Britton sees as major disadvantages. A conservative analysis is challenged by a progressive liberal analysis.

For Pérez, tourism is yet another way of institutionalizing the sources of underdevelopment. Despite the pious conservative conviction that international travel benefits Caribbean societies, Pérez shows that tourism drains capital from Third World economies; reinforces monoculture economies (not based on plantation crops or minerals but on hotel receipts); produces chronic balance-of-payment deficits; creates seasonal employment of menial jobs, like waiters, dishwashers, and porters; results in foreign ownership of national resources; and fails to stimulate local artisan industries. Pérez also identifies the critical role of the State with its police power, and the role of local elites that make tourism profitable in the Third World. Although Pérez and Britton raise many of the same points, their analyses differ. Pérez provides an explanatory framework which draws together the various disadvantages described by Britton. Tourism, from a radical perspective, is part of the historical process of underdevelopment inherent in the political economy of global capitalism; from a liberal perspective, the major problems associated with tourism can be overcome by national governments.

17 International Tourism: An Instrument For Third World Development

M. E. BOND and JERRY R. LADMAN*

INTRODUCTION

It is widely recognized that the key to modernization of today's less-developed countries is their internal transformation from preponderantly traditional agricultural economies to industrialized economies. Given that such countries typically have a historical base of exporting primary commodities and that such a transformation has large requirements for foreign exchange as a source of savings and capital formation, much attention has been directed to the role of international trade as a facilitator in this process.[1] It was early recognized, in view of the limited and unstable world markets, that the exporting of primary products was not sufficient to perform this facilitating role. Therefore, attention was directed to export diversification programs whereby manufactured goods would be sold abroad through schemes of regional integration and preferential trade agreements. In practice, however, such policies encountered economic and noneconomic difficulties and consequently have been very slow to become viable strategies. As a result, aspirants to development, realizing the importance of wider markets and more foreign exchange for a program of rapid development, continue to be frustrated by these obstacles.

It is not common in the literature to encounter theories dealing with the role of a specific industry in the development process. The authors believe, however, that the international tourism industry deserves such treatment. Although only under quite unusual circumstances would tourism be great enough to be the prime mover of a country's development,[2] it has many characteristics that make it an important part of a viable development strategy for a broad group of countries. The peculiar characteristics of tourism as an export product provide an escape from many of the above-mentioned dilemmas and frustrations. In addition to its possibilities as a source of foreign exchange, the industry has features that readily lend themselves to the basic transformation of the country's economy from traditional agricultural to a more modern industrial society.

The purpose of this paper is to set forth the role of international tourism as a

*M. E. Bond and Jerry R. Ladman, "Tourism: A Strategy for Development," *Nebraska Journal of Economics and Business*, 11, no. 1 (Winter 1972): 37–52. Reprinted by permission of publisher.

development strategy. To fulfill this purpose the paper attempts to: (1) establish a theoretical base with which to analyze the role of tourism in development, (2) examine the characteristics of the tourism industry when employed as a development strategy, (3) set forth its limitations, and (4) summarize the conclusions and the recognizable problems of implementation.

TOURISM: THE MODEL

This analysis of the tourism industry employs the usual three-sector growth model because this model outlines in detail the basic phenomena underlying the transformation of the economy from traditional to modern.[3] In it the fundamental growth relations are between the traditional and modern sectors with the third or foreign sector performing a facilitating role. Growth occurs as a result of capital formation in the modern sector resulting from the reinvestment of the "capitalist surplus" made possible by the transfer of low-cost redundant labor from the traditional sector through the foreign sector and ultimately to the modern sector. As labor is moved its average productivity rises, creating a marketable surplus that is then available for consumption and/or direct or indirect investment.

The foreign sector facilitates the process of transformation for two basic reasons: first, through exportation and capital flows it provides a source of foreign exchange that can be used to acquire scarce capital goods and necessary raw materials; second, through production in the export sector, there develops an opportunity for labor absorption (limited in the case of an enclave) and profits, which, through direct or indirect reinvestment (also limited in the case of an enclave), can lead to capital formation.

Tourism, within the context of the three-sector model, would be part of the foreign sector, since it is producing goods and services for consumption by foreigners.[4] In view of the limitations of raw materials and manufactured exports faced by less-developed countries, there are compelling arguments for some of these countries to consider fostering the tourism industry as a development strategy.

CHARACTERISTIC OF TOURISM

The Market

Many underdeveloped countries may have a comparative advantage in tourism. The ingredients for the "tourism package" are variable but include an appropriate climate and sufficient service outlets. Many of these countries are located in appealing climates, and because of redundant labor supplies services are inexpensive. This combination along with the exotic characteristics of a unique culture, history, and unusual natural scenery give such countries a supply-side comparative advantage in tourism. The development in Mexico and Spain as tourist meccas in recent years is illustrative of the point.

It is also important to consider the prospects of demand for the product and this too appears favorable. Davis estimates that total tourism receipts have been growing at the rate of 11 percent a year.[5] (For almost the same time period, 1955–1965, world trade in manufactures and primary products increased 9.2 percent and 4.8 percent, respectively.)[6]

The largest tourist generating countries are the United States, Canada, and those of Western Europe. In these countries it appears that the major factors accounting for the increase in demand for foreign travel are (1) higher incomes and more favorable income distribution, (2) changes in tastes and preferences, (3) longer paid vacations, and (4) declining travel costs. The nature and strength of these factors lead to the conclusion that the market for tourism should continue to be strong in the future.

(1) *Larger incomes* are possibly the most important source of the increase in demand for foreign travel. As real per capita incomes increase and income distributions become less skewed it can be expected that more persons will have the means to become international tourists.

The effect of increasing incomes as a major factor in explaining the increase in tourism expenditures can be examined. Using the United States as an example, from 1955 to 1966 the income elasticity of demand for foreign travel expenditure (not including transportation to and from destination countries) by U.S. citizens was 1.33.[7] Many less-developed countries are located some distance from the largest international tourist generating countries. An increasing demand for long-distance tourism is reflected in the higher than average income elasticity coefficients of U.S. travelers for the faraway regions: 2.21 for Japan, Hong Kong, Australia, and New Zealand; 1.66 for South America; 1.40 for the West Indies and Central America. Countries contiguous to the United States, such as Mexico and Canada, had lower than average income elasticity coefficients of 1.29 and 1.27, respectively. The coefficient for Europe and the Mediterranean was slightly lower at 1.22, possibly reflecting the fact that this long-distance market, although still healthy, is more saturated and has been affected by competition from newly developing tourist areas.

Evidence, therefore, points to a strong income elasticity of demand for foreign travel and an even stronger income elasticity of demand for long-distance tourism to regions that have recently begun to develop their tourism industry. There is no reason to expect this long-run trend to diminish in the foreseeable future.

(2) *Tastes and preferences* for tourism are impossible to measure accurately. It is plausible, however, to assume that the rapid dissemination of information regarding other countries, their culture, their history, and so on has led, and probably will continue to lead, to a change in tastes and preferences in favor of international tourism. No doubt effective advertising has reinforced this trend.

(3) *Longer paid vacations,* toward which there has been a definite trend in the developed countries, make tourism more feasible, since they permit the tourist not only to travel while on the payroll but also to lower the average daily fixed cost of his vacation. With transportation costs figuring as a large proportion of total fixed travel costs, this factor is significant.

(4) *Travel costs* have been reduced with jet aircraft and now with jumbo-jet airliner. Lower transportation costs, due to more efficient operations and group fares, have caused a significant reduction in the fixed cost of traveling, which is an important component of long-distance tourism. A recent study in Hawaii shows that tourism to that state is price elastic, which if true elsewhere would indicate that falling travel prices should cause a large increase in the number of tourists.[8] Shortening the travel time eases the discomfort of travel and allows more time at the destination.

It would appear, therefore, that several factors are working to increase the demand for tourism. Barring any unforeseeable change in tourist preferences, all of the indicators point to continued expansion of the demand for tourism.

Tourism as an Export Product

D. H. Robertson has linked the disadvantages of trade as a development catalyst for the raw material or foodstuff producing, less-developed country to four factors:[9]

(1) the long-run terms of trade turn against raw-material and foodstuff producers;

(2) the export products of these countries are concentrated in one or two products;

(3) the export markets are unstable and make foreign exchange earnings uncertain;

(4) the consumption patterns of these countries suggest a continual deterioration in the "balance of trade," that is, they have unfavorable "backwash effect."

Trade in *correct* products, however, such as tourism, does not involve all these disadvantages and therefore trade in this product can be a cayalyst to growth.

The export of tourism circumvents the problems mentioned by Robertson. The nature of the product—especially as demanded by the more developed areas—shows it to be income elastic and price elastic. These characteristics negate his first criticism. The income elasticity coefficients are high, especially when compared to those for most primary products, and there is little reason to expect this relationship to change. If the tourism income elasticity coefficients remain high and those of primary products low, then with the establishment of tourism industry a country's terms of trade would become more favorable as tourism came to comprise a larger relative portion of its exports. . . .

Since tourism is a differentiated product, the tourist-receiving country will have some degree of monopoly power in establishing prices for the tourist. With this price policy and with the product not subject to any "world market price," fewer conditions are established for a terms-of-trade problem.

Robertson's second criticism also is not applicable. The export of tourism complements other export products of the foreign sector. The consequent diversity in exports will add stability to export earnings. When compared to other exports of the foreign sector—primary products or manufactures—there are less opportunities for constructing trade barriers. Conceivably certain conceptual types of travel taxes could be assessed on international tourists (for example, the U.S. 1965 rule reducing the amount of duty-free merchandise into the United States), but there is little evidence to support the notion that travel taxes, in the amounts known, are as trade discouraging as present monetary or quantitative restrictions on many traditional export products.

Tourism does not escape Robertson's third criticism. There are two sources of instability: (1) the regular seasonal fluctuations and (2) irregular fluctuations due to world economic conditions. Tourism is certainly subject to both. A counteracting factor is that receipts from exporting tourism should tend to cycle around a stronger upward trend than exists for primary products.

With respect to the fourth criticism, the export of tourism does not suggest any more unfavorable backwash effects on the economy than those created by other exports. In fact, tourism should create strong backward linkages for domestic production rather than linkages to imports, thus reducing the backwash effects.

Developing countries in the process of modernization face the need to import capital goods and scarce raw materials and to service foreign debt. One of the major advantages of tourism compared to other exports is its ability to fill this foreign exchange gap. With an expanding world market and relatively few import requirements per dollar of foreign exchange generated, tourism can complement the modernization of the economy by generating foreign exchange.

The experience of Mexico, depicted in Table 17.1, provides evidence that a growing tourism industry has tended to offset the unfavorable balance of trade. In 1960, 1964, 1965, and 1966, the excess of imports over exports was about the same. During these same years tourism receipts were increasing to account for 33.9, 51.1, 61.7, and 74.2 percent, respectively, of the trade deficit. *Ceteris paribus,* this would have a favorable effect on the balance of payments and give more flexibility to the use of foreign exchange.

Table 17.1   Comparison between Tourism and Export Receipts: Mexico 1960–1967

Year	Tourism Income	Export Income	Tourism Income as a Percentage of Export Income	Tourism Income as a Percentage of Trade Balance Deficit
	(millions of pesos)			
1960	1,902.5	9,233.8	20.6	33.9
1961	2,050.6	10,043.3	20.4	48.9
1962	2,232.9	11,244.5	19.8	73.4
1963	2,632.1	11,699.9	22.5	69.3
1964	3,007.1	12,780.6	23.5	51.1
1965	3,435.5	13,923.7	24.7	61.7
1966	4,104.5	14,534.5	28.2	74.2
1067	4,638.8	13,797.5	02.9	50.0

Source: *Mexico 1968,* pp. 291, 296, and 332, and *Mexico 1966,* pp. 173 and 180 (Mexico City: Banco de Comerico Exterior).

A separate argument often leveled against trade as a source of growth is that export sectors of many less-developed countries are enclaves characterized by foreign ownership of the production, limited employment opportunities for domestic laborers at the unskilled and managerial levels, few backward linkages to other areas of the economy, and creation of few external economies. Historically, it is notable that the export industries in primary materials have been foreign-owned and that foreign capital and technology are important in establishing export of manufacturing products. Experience shows that in the case of tourism, although there is some foreign ownership of hotels, facilities are essentially domestically owned.[10]

The effect of tourism on employment and income would depend on the size of the market, the geographical dispersion of the industry, the backward linkages, and the external economies created. We have already suggested that the market is expanding. The geographical dispersion depends upon what parts of the country are appropriate as tourist areas. If the industry were limited to isolated regions, such as seacoast resorts, the direct employment effects would be limited compared to a situation where tourist areas were spread across the country.

There are several potential backward linkages associated with tourism. The figures in Tables 17.2, showing how the tourist spends his money in Mexico, give some indication of the nature of these linkages. The backward linkages to the agricultural and the construction industries should be strong, given the expenditures for food and hotels; demand for handicrafts will create linkages back to small factories and cottage industries. There would also be an increased demand for government services (for example, policemen, customs officials, street cleaners).

Table 17.2   Estimated Distribution of Tourist Expenditures in Mexico

Type of Expenditure	Percentage of Total
Food	34
Housing	24
Merchandise	14
Transportation	14
Entertainment and shows	13
Other expenses	1
	100

Source: Abel Garrid Ruiz, "Effectos del Tourismo en La Economia Nacional" en *Reunion Nacional de Chapala,* Diciembre 2, 1969. Mexico D.F. Departamento de Turismo.

There are three salient features of the backward linkages. First, they are readily adaptable to labor-intensive technology and are therefore employment-creating and capital-saving. Second, they lend themselves to small-scale production. That is, these backward linkages are not restricted by low levels of aggregate demand.[11] Third, most of the production resulting from the backward linkages requires few imports and serves to conserve on the use of foreign exchange.

Enclaves are also criticized since they preclude the formulation of external economies. Manufacturing, not generally considered to be an enclave, allegedly creates many external economies (for example, specialized management and production line cost reductions). The external economies resulting from tourism are confined essentially to two areas. First, the requirements for infrastructure such as an adequate transportation system, water supplies, and sanitation facilities are essential. The creation of a transportation system, which interconnects markets and reduces transport costs, constitutes an example of external economies. Most other infrastructure projects serve the tourism industry and indirectly benefit other industries indigenous to the country. Second, acquired skills resulting from tourism production readily spill over into the rest of the economy. Since workers are drawn out of the traditional sector for employment in the tourism industry, their mobility is increased and their skills transfer to other occupations.

The enclave is a distinct possibility for *any* export product. For tourism, however, with small-scale nontechnical production, local ownership, and definite backward linkages, the chances are diminished. The biggest problem might be geographical dispersion of employment opportunities.

In the view of many, the export of manufactures offers the best path to development; yet there are serious limitations to this strategy. First, unfavorable technical conditions or high initial costs of production may make it difficult to produce and to compete. Second, the sale of manufactures abroad in particularized markets requires highly-developed marketing skills. Often these are absent. Third, there are significant trade barriers that are difficult to overcome.[12] Although it is likely that all of these obstacles can be surmounted, time is required. The tourism industry faces only the second of these obstacles; therefore, a country with a comparative advantage in tourism can utilize its tourism industry as a means of laying a base for the concurrent or later development of its manufacturing sector. This base—as essential as it is for growth—consists of providing a source of foreign exchange, fostering the development of infrastructure, creating external economies, and creating conditions for employment, capital formation, and changing values.

Labor Absorption and Capital Formation

Since the tourism industry is service oriented, it has the advantage (aside from infrastructure) of being labor-intensive and capital-saving, a desirable situation in a country where capital is scarce and labor is redundantly employed. Figures from an input-output study in Mexico show that for $80,000 (dollars) invested in tourism, there are forty-one jobs created. The same investment would create sixteen jobs in petroleum, fifteen jobs in metal products, or eight jobs in electricity.[13]

In the tourism industry not only is the capital-labor ratio low, but also many of the jobs created by investment are low skill. The data in Table 17.3 show the degree of labor specialization required in the Mexican hotel industry. Using these data as a crude proxy of the tourism industry indicates that a large number of the workers can be readily absorbed from the traditional sector into tourism with little training. With some investment in human capital, others should be readily integrated into more specialized jobs such as waiters, cooks, or tour guides. There is a limited number of administrative positions; some of these are highly skilled

Table 17.3   Degree of Labor Specialization in Mexican Hotel Industry

Group	Percentage of Total
Nonspecialized	50
Specialized	42
Supervision and management	6
Top-level administration	2
	100

Source: El Club Italiano de Turismo y Automovilismo as reported in *El Estudio General de Desarollo de Turismo en Mexico*. Mexico D.F., Impulsora de Empresas Turisticas, S.A. de C.V. 1969, p. 204.

and could be a serious bottleneck if not properly filled. In the short run it may be necessary to import skilled management or to lure qualified persons away from other domestic employment until more local persons can be properly trained.

Given the low capital-labor ratio and the ease of absorbing traditional workers into the tourism industry, the conditions of the three-sector model for labor absorption and capital formation are readily filled. The transfer of labor to the tourism industry at low wages will create conditions for a capitalists' surplus in tourism as well as a marketable surplus in the traditional sector, thus leading to a dual potential for capital formation. If the tourism industry is expanding, there should be incentive for direct investment of this surplus; if not, appropriate fiscal and monetary measures could be employed to direct savings into other productive activities. . . .

Values and Mobility

The presence of a tourism industry should affect the value judgments of the domestic population. The demonstration effect (on both the demand and supply sides) is one example of how fundamental values are altered. The demand-creating aspects result as the natives, coming in contact with tourists, become aware of the differences between their way of life and that of the tourist. If the native attempts to emulate the tourist, a change in demand has occurred.

On the supply side, the native, attempting to alter his standard of living, may begin to realize the benefits of alternative and more remunerative employment and attempt to extricate himself from his present class. Moreover, profitable operations in tourist-related firms should help to keep domestic capital at home. In fact, through the demonstration effect, some capital may be channeled into productive units.

The tourism industry essentially requires emphasizing the interesting or appealing features of a country. When features such as historical sites, parks, monuments, archeological sites, and recreational and entertainment centers are developed, a stronger spirit of nationalism should emerge. Feelings of pride can go a long way, albeit in an intangible way, to encourage a society to desire better things and to work toward them.

Another intangible but important factor is that international tourism creates the environment and the social intercourse that are preconditions for developing better understanding and goodwill among nations. Understanding is an apparent key to mimimizing differences between people and maximizing the understanding of their similarities.

LIMITATIONS OF TOURISM

Although the tourism industry has definite advantages, it has some limitations, five of which merit discussion. First, the composition of a tourism package within any country will set a limit to the size of the industry. If the industry is small, there will be a strong tendency toward developing an enclave. Enclaves limit opportunities for employment and income generation, few externalities and backward linkages appear, and the contribution of tourism to development is circumscribed. Nevertheless, tourism confined to an enclave would still have positive advantages not only as a source of foreign exchange but also as a source of development in the particular region. Its effect would not be as widespread, but it would still be beneficial to the economy and in particular to the region of location.

Second, even if a country has a sizable tourism package, it must compete on the world market. This means the package should be a quality product and should be marketed effectively. Services, facilities, and accommodations meet the standards of the tourists. This will require adequate infrastructure and may require the establishment of a government tourism office to regulate and control the quality of service. In marketing the product, effective economies of scale can be achieved through government advertising rather than individual effort. This marketing approach considerably reduces the number of skilled personnel needed to put the industry in contact with its customer.

Third, there is the likelihood that tourism receipts will vary with economic conditions in other countries. With the high income elasticity of demand for tourism, the industry will be susceptible to foreign cyclical fluctuations. A token solace is the recent record of most developed countries and their improved ability to control major cyclical downturns.

A fourth disadvantage, which may be the most economically disastrous, is the hazard of excess capacity creation. Given a large number of small autonomous producers, there may be a tendency to overbuild. This, coupled with the regular seasonal fluctuations in the tourism market, may lead to an excess capacity problem. This problem may be overcome in part by offseason price reductions which, if effective in attracting budget-minded tourists, would keep the physical facilities in use.

Fifth, the tourism industry definitely requires a substantial outlay for infrastructure (transportation, water, and sanitation) if this does not already exist. It is estimated that half the investment in tourism in Mexico is in infrastructure.[14] Clearly, this creates a need for an extensive government outlay which must, in large part, precede the development of private tourism facilities. The limitation is apparent—limited government funds to finance tourism without creating inflation. Although the infrastructure would be expected to create a significant external economies, these must be considered in comparison with alternative opportunities for employment of government resources.

CONCLUSIONS

For a less-developed country that has the ingredients for an attractive tourism package—culture, climate, history, and geography—the tourism industry is potentially a leading sector (facilitator) in the development process. The world demand for tourism has grown and is expected to continue its growth. The product, when compared to traditional exports of primary products, has the advantages of: (1) a source of foreign exchange with growth potential; (2) a source of domestic savings and capital formation; (3) a means of implementing labor absorption; and (4) a means whereby conditions become propitious for changing traditional values. When compared to exports of manufactures, tourism has the advantage of easier short-term implementation. Each of these advantages is extremely important to a country in the early growth stage. Although the serious limitations of tourism must be recognized, most of these problems can be solved and, on balance, the negative factors of tourism are outweighed by the positive factors as tourism provides a base for longer-run development. . . .

NOTES AND REFERENCES

1. See, for example, John C. Fei and Gustav Ranis, *Development of the Surplus Labor Economy: Theory and Policy* (Homewood, Ill.: Richard D. Irwin, Inc., 1964), pp. 288–319.

2. A notable exception would be a country, region, state, or territory—typified by Hawaii—that would have such a comparative advantage in tourism that the tourism industry would be the prime mover.

3. This section is based on the type of model set forth by Fei and Ranis, op. cit.

4. In treating tourism the discussion is confined to the industry in the homeland excluding ownership of airlines. It is assumed that the tourist travels to the country via foreign carriers.

5. H. David Davis, "Potentials for Tourism in Developing Countries," *Finance and Development*, 4 (December, 1968): 36.

6. United Nations Conference on Trade and Development Secretariat, *Review of Trade in Manufactures and Semi-Manufactures*, TD/10/Supp. 1, October 31, 1967.

7. H. David Davis, op. cit.

8. "The Visitor Industry and Hawaii's Economy: A Cost-Benefit Analysis," *Mathematica* (1970), pp. 100–101. This report shows that the number of visitors is highly responsive to the cost of air fare between Hawaii and the Mainland.

9. Reported in Benjamin Higgins, *Economic Development* (New York: W. W. Norton and Company, 1968), p. 268.

10. Frank Brandenberg, *The Making of Modern Mexico* (Englewood Cliffs, N.J.: Prentice-Hall, Inc., 1964), p. 309. Brandenberg reports that at the time of his writing 95 percent of the Mexican hotel industry was Mexican-owned. He attributes this ownership not only to Mexican nationalism but also to Mexican entrepreneurs seizing the opportunity to develop a quality tourism industry beginning in the late 1930s.

11. For a discussion of the alleged limitations of aggregate demand to backward linkages see Albert O. Hirschman, "The Political Economy of Import-Substitution Industrialization in Latin America," *The Quarterly Journal of Economics*, 82, no. 1 (February 1968): 13–17.

12. Gerald Meier, "The Prospects for Export of Manufactures—Note," *Leading Issues in Economic Development* (New York: Oxford University Press, 1970), pp. 552–556.

13. Abel Garrido Ruiz, "Effectos del Turismo en La Economia Nacional," *Reunion Nacional de Chapala*, Diciembre 2, 1969. Mexico, D.F., Departamento de Turismo.

14. Antonio Enriquez Scvignac, "Financiamiento Inversion Publica," *Reunion Nacional de Chapala*, Diciembre 2, 1969. Mexico, D.F., Departamento de Turismo.

18 Shortcomings Of Third World Tourism

ROBERT BRITTON*

Viewed from an air-conditioned hotel, tourism in the tropical Third World seems to work. The airliners regularly bring vacationers from North America and Europe, metropolitans eager for sun, sand, sea, sex, and perhaps a small dose of local culture. Hotels appear to function normally: rum punches are served with a smile, guest rooms are clean, the swimming pool holds water, and the air-conditioning works, though it is seldom as efficiently frigid as visitors would like.

Yet it is clear that those who look more deeply find substantial problems with the tourism industries of many poor nations, problems quite separate from the smooth processing of visitors. The essential concern is that tourism does not contribute much to development efforts. Not only did the proponents of tourism exaggerate the economic benefits, but they also gave almost no warning about adverse social, political, cultural, and environmental impacts. My hypothesis is that certain institutional and operational characteristics of the industry constrain its contribution to *indigenously defined* economic and social development. In this paper I will briefly review the rise of international tourism in the Third World: who has advocated it as a viable development strategy, and most important, why the industry is not an effective engine of development.

THE IMPORTANCE OF TOURISM

Tourism is an economically significant and nearly ubiquitous industry.[1] Revenue from international tourism is among the largest single items in world trade.[2] In 1976 there were about 220 million international tourist arrivals, and receipts exceeded $40 billion.[3] While slowing somewhat in the mid-seventies, since 1960 the growth rate has been about ten percent per year.[4] The underdeveloped world's share of this revenue, however, is less than twenty percent; Europe receives almost three-fourths of all transborder visitors.[5] Nevertheless, many underdeveloped economies have become dependent on tourism. The Caribbean offers outstanding examples. The industry accounts for about three-fourths of the Bahamas' GNP.[6] Yearly tourist arrivals exceed the local population in Antigua, Aruba, the Bahamas, St. Maarten, and the U.S. Virgin Islands.[7] Elsewhere, the industry is the major export earner in Kenya, Tunisia, Morocco, Greece, and other countries.[8] Despite this concentration, international travelers continue to

*Robert Britton, "Third World Tourism: Ineffective Engine for Development," an invited paper for this book.

disperse throughout the Third World. Cohen and others observed the phenomenon of "youth tourism," the throngs of Europeans and Americans that venture across Asia, Africa, and Latin America.[9] Even the durable mass marketer Thomas Cook ran a 1972 trip to visit, among others, the cannibalistic Biami people of Papua New Guinea![10]

The rise of mass tourism from rich to poor countries after World War II can be explained by combining factors in the origin and destination. In the former, five reasons are most important: (1) technological advances in transport and the export of hotel innovation; (2) sustained growth in real disposable incomes and amount of leisure time; (3) the emergence of mass marketing; (4) an increase in foreign consciousness, the result of the war and the pre-war journeys of leisure-class Americans; and (5) legitimation of travel as a leisure form and an acceptable mode of middle-class consumption.

PROPONENTS OF TOURISM

Academic observers, development "experts," industry officials, and others cite the significant economic benefits of tourism and the absence of marketable resources or industrial possibilities as the principal reasons for establishment of a tourism industry.[11] Proponents note three major benefits: (1) accumulation of foreign exchange, (2) the effect of an expenditure multiplier on domestic economic growth (dollars recycling through the local economy), and (3) employment. Other alleged advantages include (4) promotion of regional development in lagging areas, (5) greater stability in revenues and a shorter gestation period (between investment and return) compared to other activities, (6) tourism as an equilibrating mechanism for global income, and (7) it ensures a fairer distribution of wealth within host societies.[12] In varying degrees these benefits have been advanced by advocates of centrally planned and of market economies, and have been accepted across the same spectrum. Indeed, international tourism is remarkable in that its appeal is universal. In late 1978, for example, the People's Republic of China and Pan Am's Inter-Continental Hotels signed an agreement for the construction and operation of five hotels in major Chinese cities.[13]

Although it is hardly surprising that transnational firms would attempt to convince receiving countries of some mutuality of interest, a wide range of academics and international organizations have also purveyed tourism as a sensible part of development strategy. The United Nations has grown somewhat more cautious since its 1963 Conference on International Travel and Tourism,[14] but the Conference on Trade and Development, the Economic and Social Council, and lately the Center for Building, Housing, and Planning have actively promoted the industry, as have affiliated groups like the International Labor Organization and the World Tourism Organization (a group dominated by a booster mentality). The OECD and agencies of governments in the wealthy countries support Third World tourism because it is a proven customer of exports, capital, and management expertise.[15] European and American consulting firms and academics—organized in groups like The Travel Research Association and the International Association of Scientific Experts in Tourism—are another source of promotion. Levitt and Gulati observed "a powerful metropolitan tourist lobby which operates at the national and international governmental level through the agency of professional consulting firms. The purpose of this lobby appears to be the dissemination of misleading information concerning the economic benefits of tourism to poorer regions and countries.''[16]

Initial activity and continued growth in tourism could not have taken place without the approval of politicians and administrators in receiving countries. Especially in the Caribbean, this elite might argue with some justification that the present state of the industry is more the product of colonial decision-making than the policy of independent states, and that they are attempting to improve a suboptimal situation—to move the economy away from single crop export agriculture and to relieve unemployment. On the other hand, many of these officials have legislated fiscal incentives and special concessions that engender further dependence on foreign capital and imported provisions. Typical "Hotels Aid Acts" in the Commonwealth Caribbean provide for: (1) duty-free importation of materials and equipment, without regard for local substitutes; (2) a tax holiday of ten to fifteen years (after which the property may be sold so that the new owner will reap another tax break); and (3) a specified minimum percentage of local manpower without reference to structure, which means that expatriates claim the better jobs.[17] Ad hoc concessions may include free land, favorable interest rates, free access roads, and others.[18] Often these incentives are only available to foreign investors, and tax policy or capital requirements frequently discourages local participation. Many critical observers believe that a considerable amount of investment would have taken place without incentives or with less generous provisions, and that governments have been indiscriminate in their efforts to attract capital.[19]

Elite self-interest has been amply documented elsewhere; in tourism, too, it is undoubtedly a powerful force. An extreme example comes from Manila, where fourteen international hotels with a total capacity of about 13,000 rooms were built to meet a predicted shortage during the 1976 World Bank conference. Construction firms with ties to the Marcos family harvested large profits, and other friends and relatives of Marcos own the properties. Financing came from various state sources, and it was reported that twelve percent of the Philippines Development Bank's funds were committed to the projects.[20]

DISADVANTAGES OF TOURISM

The strength and pervasiveness of metropolitan influence and the numerous economic and noneconomic maleffects are the fundamental weaknesses of international tourism in the Third World. Although most casual observers of tourism recognize dependence on overseas groups, they fail to recognize the extent of this dependency.

Some Third World destinations are served by national airlines; in 1975, however, carriers based in the industrial nations flew about three-fourths of all passenger kilometers.[21] Vulnerability to suspension of service is a serious problem, as Pan Am demonstrated when it withdrew from Antigua just before the 1974–75 high season.[22] With the rise in pre-assembly of vacation services (transport, hotel rooms, ground transfer, sightseeing, and the like), the travel wholesaler and tour operator have emerged as powerful influences. Hansen noted that "several of the Caribbean island countries' major tourist facilities are heavily price-influenced and even controlled by the tourist-supplier end of the industry abroad."[23] Turner and Ash found that wholesalers' and tour operators' lobbies routinely visit destinations to protest—and get action on—taxes, service standards, currency restrictions, and other policies.[24] Since these packagers follow *and direct* travel tastes, receiving places can easily fall from grace ("tourists are notoriously fickle") or be passed up for places that offer the mass marketer the most attractive terms.

International hotel companies are another source of control. Increasingly, chain hotels opt for management contracts, leasing, or franchising instead of equity participation; profits are greater and the risks can be shifted, usually to the state.[25] These firms can thus appear to encourage local ownership while doing better than if they were the proprietors. Regulatory bodies like the Civil Aeronautics Board and its British counterpart affect receiving places through route awards, pricing, and other controls. U.S. and European advertising and public relations firms handle marketing problems for government and private organizations; Jamaica's 1977 advertisement budget, for example, was over $2 million.[26] Metropolitan travel writers, hotel representatives, and trade associations are other sources of dependence; together with the specialized "experts" mentioned earlier, these groups hold the power of success or failure of many Third World destinations.

There are also six general influences of the metropolitan industry, traits shared by more than one type of firm or agency. First, overseas interests invoke the rhetoric of internationalism ("world peace through world travel," and other hype) to rationalize the global scale of firms like Holiday Inn and to justify the unfettered movement of capital, manpower, and technology. Second, overseas firms and "experts" believe that tourism belongs to and is an appropriate extension of the industrial world regardless of where it happens. They advocate the appropriation of entire regions of poor countries for the exclusive use of tourism, plan facilities without local consultation, support foreign ownership or management of all facilities as well as the unrestricted importation of goods and manpower, and they vigorously resist regulation. The increasing concentration of tourists at a limited number of destinations and of the industry itself is a third trait, which tends to exclude smaller distinations and smaller entrepreneurs within destinations from participation. Increasing scale ensures dependence on external decision-making.

A fourth characteristic is an inauthentic attitude toward place and placemaking, manifest in contempt for local design solutions, reliance on "international" styles of architecture, furnishings, and cuisine, false or misleading representation of place in promotion, and the growing homogenization of tourism landscapes. Fifth, metropolitan tourism embraces its own view of development, one that sees colonialism as beneficial, inflates tourism's role in the economy (a Hilton official in the Caribbean remarked "without the large hotels, most of the islands would dry up and blow away . . ."),[27] finds selective, tourism-induced "modernization" as appropriate, and congratulates itself for its philanthropy (another Hilton executive claimed that "heads of government and their advisers have compared the contribution of a new hotel with those of international government-aid programs"[28]). Lastly, the metropolitan industry demands suppression of domestic and international political expression, as Mexico discovered after its vote on the U.N. Zionism-racism resolution.[29] The industry supports those right-wing regimes which permit freer operation; a prominent U.S. travel trade paper, for example, wrote that Manila's streets were safe, "thanks to martial law."[30] Conversely, some interests have challenged socialist governments—such as the hotel and gambling firms, many of which were Mafia-controlled, that were among Castro's most threatening opponents after the Cuban revolution.[31]

Three external influences are similar to those felt in other export industries. One is the group of problems associated with strong involvement with foreign currency—fluctuating values, black marketing, and impact on domestic prices. Another is susceptibility to swings in Western economic cycles. The third is that just as European and American manufacturers turn to substitutes or synthetics when tropical agricultural commodity prices rise, tourism organizers find that demand for destinations is quite elastic: one warm place with beaches and plenty of rum is as good as another.

The plethora of negative impacts on receiving places is perhaps more important than metropolitan influence. The economic benefits of the industry, always the strong point of advocates, have been vigorously challenged recently.[32] Eight adverse economic effects are important. First, revenue leakage to purchase imported inputs of food and drink, manpower, and overseas marketing; leakage, which often exceeds fifty percent, obviously reduces the revenues that are to multiply through the domestic economy. Second, government expenditure for infrastructure (airports, road, water supplies, sewers, electricity, and promotional costs) is substantial. Bryden found that public outlays often matched private investment in West Indian tourism, and that the burden fell unjustly on local citizens rather than tourists or the industry.[33] Third, the high capital demands when hotels and other facilities are built by government counters the contention that tourism is labor-intensive, and more importantly, government participation often diverts funds from other development efforts, particularly domestic agriculture. Fourth, by increasing the reserve price of labor, tourism draws workers from other sectors (this is not a universal problem, but has been observed in many places). Fifth, tourism has often deprived agriculture of better quality land (notably on smaller islands where narrow coastal plains are well suited for domestic food crop raising). In nearly all receiving countries inflation in land prices has been dramatic. The combined effect of manpower and land competition produces a decline in local food self-sufficiency, a drop in export crop production, or both. Sixth, the balance of payments suffers from the previously mentioned import demands and black marketing, as well as by the increased demand for imported goods spurred by increased incomes and the ubiquity of tourists as a reference group. Seventh, excess capacity in hotels, caused by overbuilding and seasonality, exacerbates the overall stability of the industry, which in turn can reverberate through the local economy. Eight, instead of alleviating regional and socioeconomic inequalities as proponents maintain, tourism heightens the differences. The major criticism of the regional development argument of Christaller and others,[34] is that regardless of where tourism facilities are located, most inputs are processed through the urban economy. The hotel is an economic as well as a social enclave.

The neglect of non-economic effects in tourism has been striking. Proponents cheerfully believe that only good can come from contact between locals and visitors. Although critics are skeptical, the neglect of non-economic effects has been surprisingly widespread, perhaps because such impacts are difficult to measure (that they cannot be included in a dollar-based matrix is hardly reason not to consider them). Shivji wrote that "the justification for tourism in terms of being 'economically good' though it may have adverse social, cultural, and political effects, completely fails to appreciate the integrated nature of the system of underdevelopment."[35] In the conclusion of his rigorous economic cost-benefit study of Caribbean tourism, Bryden acknowledged that "in fact most of the case 'against' tourist development appears to rest on its non-pecuniary or 'transcendental' impact on society. . . ."[36] The danger in an exposition of social and cultural changes wrought by tourism is the failure to recognize that cultures do change. There seems to be a need for some middle position, however, one critical of the industry's sanguine belief that contact is only salubrious and of the romantic notion that non-Western cultures ought to remain just as they are. Tourism is obviously not the first change agent; even in recent times imported forces such as Western education for the national elite, imported instructional materials and methods, foreign broadcast and print media, family members employed overseas, missionaries, and other factors have influenced culture and society. Two points are important: the rate of change and the absorptive capacity of the receiving country, and the distinction between beneficial effects and detrimental ones. White defined beneficial effects as those "conducive to the survival of the local social system," while detrimental ones were those "that lead to greater homogenization between societies . . . since in time they lead to the break-up of the host society."[37] Negative effects also include those that increase tensions between individuals, families, and larger groups. Ten major groups can be listed: (1) the displacement of indigenous lifeways and simultaneous importation of inappropriate elements of Western cultures; (2) resentment of visitors' leisure and affluence; (3) emergence of dual standards for personal interaction, one set for tourists and one for local people; (4) role and identity problems, including the demand for obsequious, neo-colonial behavior and the possibility that locals will modify their demeanor to fit the advertised image; (5) rise in class and ethnic tensions; (6) the distraction of citizens from the development effort or the quest for legitimate social change; (7) migration to tourism centers and the consequent problems of urbanization; (8) pressures on family life; (9) prostitution; and (10) changes in annual and diurnal rhythms.

In other industries, some environmental degradation may be a necessary trade-off for expansion. For tourism, however, environmental quality must be protected because it is precisely what attracts visitors. Protection is obviously more difficult where residents derive few benefits from tourism, and those that do profit from it have shown little concern. The absence of effective land use controls and the insensitivity of many builders has produced land speculation, higher installation costs for infrastructure, and offense to local residents. Undesirable aesthetic effects such as the destruction of sight lines by injudicious location of large buildings, removal of vegetation, theft or degradation of historical or archaeological sites, and litter and large-scale refuse dumping are also problematic. Damage to eco-systems, however, is the most threatening to the long-term viability of receiving countries. Beach erosion, destruction of reefs and mangroves, depletion of groundwater, soil erosion, and threats to plant and animal species from the injudicious use of pesticides are examples. Finally, negative political impact assumes several forms: the previously noted tendency to stifle political expression in order not to jeopardize the confidence of tourists or the industry; the inhibition of worker organization because of dispersed hotels and the difficulty of maintaining adversary relationships in personal service industries; and the threat to national or territorial unity posed by the success of tourism in one part of the state.

NOTES AND REFERENCES

1. Barry Floyd, "International Tourism: A Case Study from Jamaica," unpublished research paper, Department of Geography, University of Durham, 1974, p. 1; cf. David Mercer, "The Geography of Leisure—A Contemporary Growth Point," *Geography,* 55 (1970): 261–62.

2. G. Donald Jud, "Tourism and Economic Growth in Mexico Since 1950," *Inter-American Economic Affairs,* 28, no. 1 (1974): p. 22.

3. ASTA Travel News, *Travel '77/'78: The Big Picture* (New York: ASTA Travel News, 1977), p. 5.

4. World Tourism Organization, *Economic Review of World Tourism, 1976* (Madrid: World Tourism Organization, 1977), p. 12.

5. H. Robinson, *A Geography of Tourism* (London: MacDonald and Evans, 1976), p. 66.

6. Ralph Blumenthal, "The Caribbean," *Signature,* November 1976, p. 34.

7. Caribbean Tourism Association, *Visitors Statistics, 1976* (New York: Caribbean Tourism Association, 1977), p. 2.

8. Louis Turner, "The International Division of Leisure: Tourism and the Third World," *World Development,* 4 (1976): 253.

9. Erik Cohen, "Nomads from Affluence: Notes on the Phenomenon of Drifter Tourism," *International Journal of Comparative Sociology,* 14 (1973): 89–103.

10. Louis Turner and John Ash, *The Golden Hordes: International Tourism and the Pleasure Periphery* (London: Constable, 1975), p. 170.

11. H. Peter Gray, *International Travel–International Trade* (Lexington, Massachusetts: Heath-Lexington, 1970); Walter Krause, G. Donald Jud, and Hyman Joseph, *Tourism and Latin American Development* (Austin: Bureau of Business Research, University of Texas, 1973); Donald Lundberg, *The Tourist Business,* 2nd ed (Boston: Cahners, 1974); Robert McIntosh, *Tourism: Principles, Practices, Philosophy* (Columbus, Ohio: Grid, 1972); and Michael Peters, *International Tourism* (London: Hutchinson, 1969).

12. Walter Christaller, "Some Considerations of Tourism Location in Europe: The Peripheral Regions—Underdeveloped Countries—Recreation Areas," *Papers, Regional Science Association,* 12 (1964): 96; Jeffrey Harrop, "The Economics of the Tourist Boom," *Journal of World Trade Law,* 7 (1973): p. 214; and James J. Eyster, "Economic Development and Public Policy: Tourism As An Alternative," *Cornell Hotel and Restaurant Administration Quarterly,* 17, no. 3 (1976): p. 23.

13. *New York Times,* 10 November 1978, p. 1.

14. United Nations, Conference on International Travel and Tourism, *Recommendations on International Travel and Tourism.* E. CONF. 47/18, 1964.

15. Organization for Economic Cooperation and Development, *Tourism Development and Economic Growth: Report of the Conference at Estoril, Portugal, May 1966* (Paris: Organization for Economic Cooperation and Development, 1966), p. 37; cf. World Bank, *Tourism: Sector Working Paper* (Washington: World Bank, 1972); and U. S. Department of Commerce, "World Trade Outlook for Latin America and the Caribbean," *Overseas Business Reports,* December 1970, p. 5.

16. Kari Levitt and Iqbal Gulati, "Income Effect of Tourist Spending: Mystification Multiplied," *Social and Economic Studies,* 19 (1970): 326.

17. John Bryden, *Tourism and Development: A Case Study of the Commonwealth Caribbean* (Cambridge: Cambridge University Press, 1973), p. 135.

18. Ibid., pp. 138–39.

19. Shankland-Cox Partnership, *Tourism Supply in the Caribbean Region* (Washington: World Bank, 1974), p. 83.

20. *New York Times,* 29 September 1976, p. 61.

21. United Nations, Department of Economic and Social Affairs, *Statistical Yearbook 1976* (E/F.77.XVII.1), 1977, pp. 539–53.

22. *Travel Weekly,* 14 November 1974, p. 46.

23. Kenneth R. Hansen, *Latin America Tourism: Prospects, Problems, and Alternative Approaches* (Washington: Inter-American Development Bank, 1974), p. 55.

24. Turner and Ash, p. 221.

25. Irving Tragen, *Tourism: Resource for Development* (Washington: Foreign Service Institute, U.S. Department of State, 1969), p. 8 and Andrew Harris, First National Bank of Chicago, personal letter.

26. *New York Times,* 8 March 1977, p. 51.

27. *Travel Weekly,* 6 October 1972, p. 2.

28. Curt Strand, "Breakthrough in World Travel," *Cornell Hotel and Restaurant Administration Quarterly,* 10, no. 4 (1970): 39.

29. "National Report No. 33: Mexico," *International Tourism Quarterly,* no. 3 (1976): pp. 25–38.

30. *Travel Weekly,* 27 September 1976, p. 48.

31. *New York Times,* 14 August 1976, p. 20.

32. Anthony Bottomley, Michael Hartnett, and Vaughan Evans, "Is Tourist Residential Development Worthwhile?—The Anegada Project," *Social and Economic Studies,* 25 (1976): 1–33; Bryden, *Tourism and Development;* John Bryden and Mike Faber, "Multiplying the Tourist Miltiplier," *Social and Economic Studies,* 20 (1971): 61–82; J. Diamond, "Tourism's Role in Economic Development: The Case Reexamined," *Economic Development and Cultural Change,* 25 (1977): 539–53; Walter Elkan, "The Relation Between Tourism and Employment in Kenya and Tanzania," *Journal of Development Studies,* 11 (1975): pp. 123–30; Levitt and Gulati, "Income Effect of Tourist Spending"; and Norman Myers, "The Tourist as an Agent for Development and Wildlife Conservation: The Case of Kenya," *International Journal of Social Economics,* 2 (1975): 26–42.

33. Bryden, pp. 146–47.

34. Christaller, p. 96; Peters, *International Tourism.*

35. I. G. Shivji, ed., *Tourism and Socialist Development* (Dar es Salaam: Tanzania Publishing House, 1973), p. x.

36. Bryden, p. 215.

37. P. E. White, *The Social Impact of Tourism on Host Communities: A Study of Language Change in Switzerland,* Research paper No. 9, School of Geography, University of Oxford, 1974, p. 4.

19 Tourism Underdevelops Tropical Islands

LOUIS A. PÉREZ, JR.*

Travel from metropolitan centers to the West Indies has served historically to underwrite colonialism in the Caribbean. Descriptions of the Antilles circulated throughout expanding Europe, arousing widespread interest in the region. Columbus devoted pages of his journal to the "very beautiful" islands "distinguished by a diversity of scenery," a region that surpassed "anything that would be believed by anyone who had not seen it."[1] Accounts such as these permitted the state, with some facility, to encourage travel to the area as an instrument of expansionist policies. Migration was designed to substantiate *de jure* claims in the Antilles through effective occupation; once jurisdictional disputes had passed, imperial centers required the presence of a metropolitan population to defend the islands against the occasional foreign interloper. More important, a metropolitan population abroad in the service of colonial authorities and mercantile agencies served to underwrite the emergent imperial economic system.

Metropolitan centers have continued to invoke the imagery reminiscent of 16th-century imperialism to encourage 20th-century travel. The Caribbean fauna and flora remain key attractions; the ideological construct, however, now confers on 20th-century travel the virtue of possessing the capacity to promote West Indian economic development.

In the past 25 years, international agencies, metropolitan authorities, and West Indian politicians have joined to promote tourism in the Caribbean. Immediately after World War II an Anglo-American Caribbean Commission convened to study the efficacy of an "area appeal" in the Caribbean for tourism.[2] In January 1972, the Caribbean Travel Association sponsored a tourism seminar in Puerto Rico under the motto, "Towards a lasting tourism."[3] The Organization of American States recently committed itself to tourism in the Western Hempisphere; the OAS effort resulted in a Special Inter-American Travel Congress in Rio de Janeiro in August 1972 in recognition that "tourism is considered one of the world's leading income-yielding industries."[4]

Travel expenditures in the Western Hemisphere support the OAS appraisal. The receipts from one million North American tourists to Latin America in 1970 totaled $500 million. Foreign travel receipts in Jamaica in 1970 surpassed $111

*Louis A. Pérez, Jr., "Aspects of Underdevelopment: Tourism in the West Indies," *Science and Society*, 37, no. 4 (Winter 1973–1974): 473–480. Reprinted by permission of publisher.

million.[5] Visitors' spending in the Virgin Islands reached $125 million in 1969.[6] In the same year, tourist expenditures in the Bahama Islands passed $235 million.[7]

Travel receipts, however, failed singularly to generate economic development, but instead further institutionalized the sources of underdevelopment: inaccessibility to capital and the concomitant flow of capital abroad and reinforcement of monoculture economies. The nature of tourism further substantiates André Gunder Frank's observation that "underdevelopment was and still is generated by the very same historical process which also generated economic development: the development of capitalism itself."[8]

As an industry that seems directed toward the appropriation of the West Indies for the pleasure and enjoyment of foreigners, tourism seeks exoneration by invoking the rhetoric of development. Popular indignation is assuaged, West Indian political careers are redeemed, and tourist guilt is mollified—indeed, replaced with a pious conviction that tourism benefits Caribbean societies. The industry finds a convenient rationale in the proposition that tourism contributes to West Indian treasuries through indirect taxation and duties. Increased travel to the area, it is suggested, creates job opportunities and results in widespread employment of local labor; labor contractors and workers, local materials, and local economies in general are said to benefit. The Anglo-American Caribbean Commission contended in 1945:

> Local agriculture would gain through the creation of a much larger body of consumers. Standard food products of the West Indies would find a larger domestic market, and a demand on the part of hotels, restaurants and other places of entertainment for products not normally produced to any great extent in the area would stimulate new production. Vegetable gardeners, fruit growers, fishermen, dairymen, and cattlemen would be encouraged to increase their production and improve standards of quality.

Tourism, in addition, presumably promotes local industries and "native handicraft." "Tourist visitors," the Commission suggested, "are inclined to buy souvenirs and products of all kinds manufactured in the countries they visit."[9]

The West Indies lack the resources to support the volume of tourists and the concomitant vacation life-style metropolitan agencies impose on the region. Tourism produces immediately, in yet another sphere, dependent economies—the structural basis of underdevelopment. The large import component necessary to support tourism in the West Indies serves at once to sustain metropolitan economic growth and foreign imports while reinforcing underdevelopment; imported materials, foods prepared abroad, and expatriate staffs make up the "invisible" support system accompanying the traveler to the region. Nowhere has the Ango-American Caribbean Commission prediction that tourism stimulates local economies materialized. Indeed, local agricultural economies have had little access to the tourist market; on the contrary, increased foreign imports serve the foreign traveler. Expanded United States exports to service the growing number of North American travelers has been the dominant feature of tourism in the West Indies. United States exports to the Caribbean in 1970 reached $968 million—about 15 percent of total North American exports to Latin America.[10] In 1969 the British Leeward and Windward Islands imported from the United States goods valued at nearly $21 million, including such tourist-related commodities as food, boats, furniture, heating and cooling equipment, telecommunication apparatus, and finished aluminum structures.[11] The United States supplied the Netherlands Antilles with more than 50 percent ($67 million) of non-oil imports, of which "prepared food and tourist-related goods (e.g., clothing, cameras, jewelry, china, etc.) were the major items."[12] The Bahama Islands tourist economy in 1970 depended entirely on foreign imports—the United States held 55 percent of the Bahamian market.[13] Assessing tourist prospects for 1972 in Trinidad and Tobago, the U.S. Department of Commerce suggested the direction tourist-generated income flowed:

> Tourism and the hotel industry are certain growth areas. Construction plans for several hotels are presently underway and room capacity is expected to double by 1972. The tourist activity will create a further demand for hotel and restaurant equipment that offer an opportunity for American suppliers of hotel furnishings, electrical and air-conditioning installations, refrigeration equipment, and swimming pools. In addition, American food product lines will be necessary to supply the North American tourists expected to fill these new hotels.[14]

The immediate impact of tourist-related imports is twofold. The expansion of tourism with this high import coefficient, in the first place, exacerbates the chronic balance-of-payments deficit. Barbadian exports, for example, have increased by about $4.2 million since 1967; in the same period, imports have more than doubled, increasing from $50 million to $117 million in 1970.[15] The five-fold increase in the numbers of tourists to the Bahama Islands (from 250,000 in 1959 to 1,300,000 in 1970) was accompanied by a rise of imports from $71 million to $302 million and an increase in trade deficit from $64 million to $248 million.[16]

Tourist-generated employment is reminiscent of the colonial monoculture systems which produced cyclical employment patterns. Employment and income tend to be concentrated in the winter months (December to April), followed frequently by months of precarious marginality.

The parallel between monoculture systems and tourist employment does not end with seasonal cycles. Tourist employment casts West Indians in the capacity of waiters, maids, bartenders, dishwashers, chauffeurs, and porters, receiving low wages in inflationary economies. An entire sector of West Indian society survives by gratifying the wants and needs of vacationing white foreigners.

Outside small national elites, West Indians have not been able to secure access to the multimillion-dollar industry. Indeed, West Indian measures designed to promote tourism frequently frustrate national ownership. Legislation to encourage hotel and resort construction, for example, refunds all import duties paid on construction material needs for the building, extension, and furnishing of new facilities; taxes levied normally on property, hotel earnings, and corporate dividends are waived for a period of 10 to 20 years. Legislation of this type favors foreign ownership. In the Bahama Islands, for example, the benefits provided under the Hotel Encouragement Act apply only to enterprises having a minimum of 200 bedrooms.[17] In St. Kitts and Montserrat the project is required to have a minimum of 30 bedrooms to receive full benefits.[18] The Jamaican government very early opted in favor of larger hotel operations:

> From the island's point of view and the quicker attainment of our Tourist Industry expansion we believe the encouragement of the large-size hotel

would be advisable. Large hotels, either individual or operated as a "chain," mean the investment of large capital, and large capital means that the interests concerned must protect it by up-to-date and efficient management and operation. Part of their effort and a good deal of capital must be devoted to advertising and selling abroad from which the island in general benefits largely. On the other hand, many small hotels are too often operated on little or no capital, their small capacity is not capable of supporting experienced management or the highest class service, and they are able to participate only to a very limited extent, if at all, in either individual or collective advertising or publicity measures from which the island would generally benefit.[19]

International and regional aid agencies, furthermore, discriminate against the small hotel, considered to be too unreliable an investment.[20]

Soaring land values, moreover, have made ownership of land on many islands prohibitive for all but small national elites and foreigners. In the Bahama Islands, for example, land values have doubled and trebled in the past decade.[21] Tourism has resulted in the alienation of national property by and/or for foreigners; beaches and coasts have become the patrimony of tourists. The local population, in search of cheaper land, is pushed further into the mountainous interior away from the coast. Increasingly beaches are withdrawn from public use by hotels and resorts; underdeveloped ones are held for speculation or with plans for future hotel and resort sites. The best beach frontage in St. Vincent, Antigua, Montserrat, and Barbados is owned privately and denied to the public.

Nor has tourism stimulated to any significant extent the local artisan economy. Expectations that tourism would promote "native handicraft" have not materialized. In-bond shops in the West Indies offer more attractive luxury merchandise to the tourist, free of duty and other imports. Foreign imports are sold to foreign visitors in shops largely expatriate-owned. As one member of the Jamaican Parliament complained, "Most tourist spending in Montego Bay was in the In-bond shops, and of little benefit to the ordinary people of the town."[22] Japanese photographic and electronic equipment, French perfumes, Swiss watches, English dinnerware, and Scotch whiskies account for a preponderance of tourist expenditures in the West Indies; the token purchase of "native handicraft" is often a coincidental afterthought.

In the final analysis tourism is operative only through the collaboration of West Indian governments with metropolitan agencies. Caribbean politicians underwrite underdevelopment; increasing portions of national expenditures are committed to sustain the conditions demanded by the tourist industry. Political stability, the safety of the traveler, and a national climate hospitable to the foreigners are provided by West Indian governments at significant cost. Concern for tourist safety inspired the Jamaican government to augment police patrols to "stamp out," as the Minister of Industry and Tourism indicated, crime "menacing . . . the source of livelihood of a large number of people."[23] Growing Caribbean criticism of tourism is met by government campaigns to "revise certain dubious attitudes."[24] When the mass of Jamaicans "fail to give appropriate support to the industry," when Jamaicans "abuse and curse visitors," the industry is placed in jeopardy.[25] One North American public relations firm reminded the Jamaica Tourist Board that this situation was "working in counterpoint to our promotion efforts and expenditures," resulting in few "returnees" and decreasing numbers of "first-time visitors."[26] To counteract growing criticism of tourism, one Jamaican official urged: "Massive efforts must be made to sell the Industry to our people, starting with children in the schools; a public relations firm should provide the expertise."[27] The morale of the service sector is propped up with government expenditures. In Jamaica, for example, a growing demoralization within this sector led to the establishment of the Jamaica Training School in 1969 for receptionists, waiters, cooks, room maids, bell boys and bar waiters to supply "trained personnel to meet the demand by new hotels . . . [and] improve standards and morale in the service sector."[28]

Government expenditures are committed to tourism at the expense of vital services. Millions of dollars are allocated to Caribbean tourist boards. The United States, as the major source of tourists, receives a preponderance of West Indian tourist-related expenditures.[29] The Jamaica Tourist Board, for example, received $3.2 million for 1968–69.[30] Much of this allocation covered expenses incurred by the service of North American public relations agencies, United States television and radio time, newspaper and magazine space, and special promotional projects in the United States.[31] Jamaica Tourist Board literature, travel brochures, and tourist pamphlets are printed in the United States; Price Waterhouse and Company audits the Jamaican Tourist Board books.

Infrastructure support of tourism makes additional claims on West Indian budgets. Road construction, airports, communication systems, utility services, and deep-water dock facilities provide additional opportunities for North American investment and United States exports. And while the ultimate desirability of these facilities is apparent, at present expenditures on such projects accommodate the needs imposed upon the area by tourism instead of meeting national priorities. One of the finest highway sections in Jamaica connects Negril on the western tip to Montego Bay on the north coast, while highway construction elsewhere languishes. Airport facilities are already inadequate to serve the growing volume of air traffic and the large jumbo jets. The government of Trinidad and Tobago has alloted $11.5 million for the modernization of the airports at Pearco and Crown Point.[32] In Curaçao and Aruba airport improvement projects will cost an estimated $25 million.[33] The fresh water reserves of many islands, barely adequate for local consumption, are already strained beyond present resources; expanded tourism has necessitated expenditures and capital outlay for desalination plants. The large number of tourists arriving by cruise ships require new dock and pier facilities to accommodate the increase in sea traffic. The recently completed deep-water pier in St. Martin, for example, is already considered inadequate.[34]

The expansion of tourist-generated infrastructure support compels, in yet another area, expenditure of West Indian capital to support the industry. When the Dominican Republic launched its tourist drive in 1970, it began to direct an increasing share of national expenditure to providing the infrastructure support required to accommodate tourism. Construction contracts, foreign materials, and expatriate technicians further contribute to the flow of capital abroad. United Dutch aid to the Netherlands Antilles frequently finds its way to the United States. North American firms received the contract for the water plant on Aruba and the UHF Omni Range Distance Measuring equipment recently installed at the airports in Curaçao and Aruba. Assistance from the Agency for International Development, tied-aid and allocated to finance infrastructure projects, further increases

North American exports. The deep-water harbor at St. John's, Antigua, was partly financed through a loan from the Export-Import Bank in Washington.

Tourism has contributed little to economic development in the West Indies. The industry is foreign-owned and controlled from abroad; air and sea carriers, hotels, entertainment and restaurant facilities, and local automobile agencies are dominated by foreigners. Tourist expenditures, in short, do not remain within the region but are repatriated to metropolitan centers. For every dollar spent in the Commonwealth Caribbean, 77 cents returns in some form to the metropolis.[35] Tourism adds still one more industry that demands immediate and short-range gratification at the expense of sustained and long-range economic development. In converting former agricultural monoculture economies to travel monoculture, tourism renews and reinforces the historical process of underdevelopment.

NOTES AND REFERENCES

1. Christopher Columbus, *Four Voyages to the New World,* ed. R. H. Major (New York, 1961), pp. 5–6.

2. Anglo-American Caribbean Commission, *Caribbean Tourist Trade. A Regional Approach* (Port-of-Spain, 1945), p. 17.

3. Irene Hawkins, "Turning Point for Caribbean Tourist Industry," *The Daily Gleaner* (Kingston), August 26, 1972, p. 20.

4. "OAS Plans to Expand Tourist Industry," *The Daily Gleaner* (Kingston), August 24, 1972, p. 11.

5. Jamaica Tourist Board, *Travel Statistics—Jamaica, 1971.* Kingston, 1972, p. 3.

6. U.S. Department of Agriculture, *Agriculture and Trade of the Caribbean Region.* Washington, D.C., 1971, p. 47.

7. U.S. Department of Commerce, "World Trade Outlook for Latin America & Caribbean," *Overseas Business Report,* December, 1970, p. 5.

8. André Gunder Frank, *Latin America: Underdevelopment or Revolution?* (New York, 1969), p. 9.

9. *Caribbean Tourist Trade,* pp. 15–23.

10. U.S. Dept. of Com., "World Trade Outlook . . . Caribbean," p. 2.

11. U.S. Dept. of Com., "Basic Data on the British Leeward Islands," *Overseas Business Report,* August 1970, p. 6.

12. U.S. Dept. of Com., "World Trade Outlook . . . Caribbean," p. 5.

13. U.S. Dept. of Com., "Basic Data on the Economy of the Bahama Islands," *Overseas Business Report,* August 1971, p. 8.

14. U.S. Dept. of Com., "World Trade Outlook . . . Caribbean," p. 5. For full breakdown of exports to the region see U.S. Department of Commerce, Bureau of the Census, *U.S. Foreign Trade: Exports Commodity by Country. Schedule B Commodity Quantity and Value. Current and Cumulative. January 1972.* Washington, D.C., 1972.

15. U.S. Dept. of Com., *Foreign Economic Trends.* February 1972, p. 6.

16. U.S. Dept. of Com., *Foreign Economic Trends.* June 1971, p. 4.

17. U.S. Dept. of Com., "Basic Data on the Economy of the Bahama Islands." p. 4.

18. U.S. Dept. of Com., "Basic Data on the British Leeward Islands," p. 5.

19. Jamaica Tourist Trade Development Board and the Tourist Trade Convention Committee, *Survey and Report on the Potentialities of the Tourist Industry of Jamaica.* Kingston, 1945, p. 8.

20. Irene Hawkins, "Regional Approach to the Caribbean Tourist Industry," *The Daily Gleaner* (Kingston), August 29, 1972, p. 9.

21. U.S. Dept. of Com., "Basic Data on the Economy of the Bahama Islands," p. 4.

22. "Crafts Market," *The Daily Gleaner* (Kingston), August 25, 1972, p. 15.

23. P.J. Patterson, "Tourism Problems," *The Daily Gleaner* (Kingston), August 26, 1972, p. 18.

24. Ibid.

25. K. R. Abrahams, "The Socio-Economic Factors in Tourism," *The Daily Gleaner.* (Kingston), August 26, 1972.

26. Sontheimer and Company, Inc. "Master Plan of Public Relations for Jamaica Tourist Board for Fiscal 1972–73." Unpublished Report, copy in author's possession, pp. 12–12a.

27. K. R. Abrahams, *loc. cit.*

28. *Jamaica Tourist Board Annual Report,* 1968/69. Kingston, 1970, p. 1.

29. In the Bahama Islands, Americans account for 85 to 90 percent of total visitors. In 1968, Americans made up over 78 percent of all travelers to Jamaica. A survey of tourism in the British Virgin Islands in 1968 indicated that 57 percent of the visitors came from the United States.

30. *Jamaica Tourist Board Annual Report,* 1968/69, p. 10.

31. Ibid., pp. 2–5.

32. U.S. Dept. of Com., "Basic Data on the Economy of Trinidad and Tobago," *Overseas Business Report,* December 1970, p. 8.

33. U.S. Dept. of Com., *Foreign Economic Trends,* February 1971, pp. 4–5.

34. U.S. Dept of Agr., *Notes on the Agricultural Economies of Dependent Territories in the Western Hemisphere and Puerto Rico.* Washington, 1971, p. 21.

35. Frank McDonald, "The Commonwealth Caribbean," in *The United States and the Caribbean,* Tad Szulc, ed. (Englewood Cliffs, N.J., 1971), p. 40.

Additional Readings

Bugnicourt, Jacques. "Tourism with no Return." *Development Forum, 5., no. 5 (June-July 1977): 1–2.*

Bugnicourt, Jacques. "The Other Face," *Development Forum,* 5, no. 6 (August-September 1977): 8.

"Boola-Boola: A Fable of Modern Tourism Development," *Cornell Hotel and Restaurant Administration Quarterly,* 7, no. 4 (1967): 61–64.

"Tourism Travels to the Third World," *Dollars and Sense,* no. 36 (April 1978): 14–15.

Grynbaum, Gail. "Tourism and Underdevelopment," *NACLA Newsletter,* 5, no. 2 (April 1971): 1–18.

Jud, Donald G. "Tourism and Economic Growth in Mexico Since 1950," *Inter-American Economic Affairs,* 28, no. 1 (1974): 19–43.

Matley, Ian M. *The Geography of International Tourism.* Washington D.C.: Association of American Geographers, 1976.

Matthews, H. G. "Radicals and Third World Tourism," *Annals of Tourism Research,* 5, Special Number (October/December 1977): 20–29.

Mings, Robert C. *The Tourist Industry in Latin America: A Bibliography for Planning and Research.* Monticello, Ill.: Council of Planning Librarians, Exchange Bibliography No. 614, 1974.

Mitchell, Frank. "Evaluating the Roles of Tourism in Tanzanian Development," in I. G. Shijui (ed.), *Tourism and Socialist Development.* Dar es Salaam: Tanzania Publishing House 1973.

Mitchell, Frank. "The Value of Tourism in East Africa," *Eastern Africa Economic Review,* 2, no. 1 (1970): 1–21.

Ouma, Joseph P. B. *Evolution of Tourism in East Africa (1900–2000).* Nairobi, Dar es Salaam, Kampala: East African Literature Bureau, 1970.

Peppelenbosch, P. G. N. and Tempelman, G. J., "Tourism and the Developing Countries," *Tijdschrift voor Economische en Social Geografie,* 64 (1973): 52–58.

Strand, Curt. "Breakthrough in World Travel," *Cornell Hotel and Restaurant Administration Quarterly,* 10, no. 4 (1970): 39.

Turner, Louis and Ash, John. *The Golden Hordes: International Tourism and the Pleasure Periphery.* London: Constable, 1975.

Williams, Anthony V. and Zelinsky, Wilbur. "On Some Patterns in International Tourist Flows," *Economic Geography,* 46, no. 4 (Oct. 1970): 549–567.

Young, George. *Tourism: Blessing or Blight?* Harmondsworth: Penguin Books, 1973.

VII

IMPERIALISM

Center-Periphery Relations. (Source: Paul Cavadino, *Get Off Their Backs*)

Foreign Aid: free assistance, loans, or rip-offs? (Source: Paul Cavadino, *Get Off Their Backs*)

The periphery in the Center is illustrated by these shacks occupied by recent North African migrant workers in Paris, France. (Source: ILO, 1-France-Migration: 26)

Transnationals and World Trade. Third World protein for First World tables. Tuna caught in the Gulf of Guinea is frozen with dry ice in Tema, Ghana. The unprocessed fish is then exported to Puerto Rico, where the fish is canned by Starkist, and sold in the continental United States. Puerto Rico offers some of the lowest wages and greatest tax advantages to corporations and lies within U.S. tariff barriers. What are the effects of these transactions on the people of Ghana and Puerto Rico?

For radicals, imperialism is a profoundly important and complex ingredient of world capitalism. The concept of imperialism links the emergence of European and North American global power to the impoverishment of the Third World. Indeed, many of the previous radical selections in this book are integrated by the discussion of imperialism here. Radical scholars of many persuasions have written on the topic, but only a sample of this vast literature is presented in this section.

According to Galtung, traditional Marxism "conceives of imperialism as an economic relationship under private capitalism, motivated by the need for expanding markets," and when capitalism vanishes, so will economic imperialism and dominance. Galtung rejects the reductionist approach of traditional Marxist-Leninist theory of imperialism. Instead he presents a radical structuralist theory of imperialism, based on center-periphery relations. The Center is represented by wealthy industrial nations and the Periphery corresponds to underdeveloped nations. Both the Center and the Periphery have a center, mainly urban elites and some rural elites, and a periphery, essentially the rural poor and also the urban powerless. The dominant economic and political power lies with the center in the Center, i.e. the elites in the industrialized countries; the dominant numerical strength lies with the periphery in the Periphery, i.e. the majority of Third World people. Galtung embellishes his Center-Periphery theory by identifying two mechanisms, five types, and three phases of imperialism. The validity of economic imperialism, the one type of imperialism for which data are readily accessible, is empirically and statistically tested. Since his hypothesis is strongly confirmed, he suggests that the Center-Periphery theory provides ample basis for further empirical research both "within liberal and marxist schools of thought."

Dependency theory, which was developed to reflect Latin American circumstances, is another way of examining imperialistic relationships. Dependency theory views the consequences of market exchange economies from the perspective of the periphery. Chilcote synthesizes this literature and finds two distinctive formulations. Non-Marxists conceive of dependency in terms of a diffusion model. In a dualistic society, progress comes through the spread of modern institutions to backward areas. Outside technology and capital are the principle vectors of modernization. The developed urban centers may produce a progressive middle class, who might support anti-imperialistic and nationalistic interests. The Marxist formulation of dependency relates "the underdevelopment of parts of Latin America to the development of industrial countries." Neo-Marxists, such as Dos Santos, Cardoso, Faletto, Frank, and Baran, discuss imperialism from the perspective of the Third World. On the other hand, some traditional Marxists, such as Harvey, reject the dependency model because it obscures the analysis of imperialism.

Harvey argues that "Marx's general theory of capitalist accumulation on an expanding and intensifying geographical scale" provides the basis for an all-embracing discussion of imperialism in its proper theoretical and historical context. In fact, locational analysis is the crucial missing link between the theory of accumulation and the theory of imperialism. Harvey presents his case based on the original works of Marx. Under capitalism, periodic crises shift "the accumulation process onto a new and higher plane." One way of temporarily eliminating a crisis is by expanding effective demand, to take but one of the four characteristics mentioned by Harvey. Greater effective demand is achieved through "*intensification* of social activity" and through "geographical expansion," i.e. commonly referred to as imperialism. Marx's comments on transportation relations, location theory, and foreign trade indicate for Harvey the general direction of Marx's unfinished theory of imperialism. Most analyses of imperialism, developed since Marx, however, start with an actual historical situation. Classical Marxists, like Luxemburg and Lenin, and neo-Marxists, like Baran, Frank, and Amin, develop Marx's general theory of accumulation in a one-sided manner. For example, Luxemburg stresses only one aspect of Marx's theory, the violent penetration of capitalism into non-capitalist societies. Harvey concludes that "the problem with the Marxist theory of imperialism in general is that it has been a theory 'unto itself,' divorced from Marx's theory of capital accumulation."

20 A Structual Theory of Imperialism

JOHAN GALTUNG*

INTRODUCTION

This theory takes as its point of departure two of the most glaring facts about this world: the tremendous inequality, within and between nations, in almost all aspects of human living conditions, including the power to decide over those living conditions; *and* the resistance of this inequality to change. The world consists of Center and Periphery nations; and each nation, in turn, has its centers and periphery. Hence, our concern is with the mechanism underlying this discrepancy, particularly between the center in the Center, and the periphery in the Periphery. In other words, how to conceive of, how to explain, and how to counteract inequality as one of the major forms of *structural violence*.[1] Any theory of liberation from structural violence presupposes theoretically and practically adequate ideas of the dominance system against which the liberation is directed; and the special type of dominance system to be discussed here is *imperialism*.

Imperialism will be conceived of as a dominance relation between collectivities, particularly between nations. It is a sophisticated type of dominance relation which cuts across nations, basing itself on a bridgehead which the center in the Center nation establishes in the center of the Periphery nation, for the joint benefit of both. It should not be confused with other ways in which one collectivity can dominate another in the sense of exercising power over it. Thus, a military occupation of B by A may seriously curtail B's freedom of action, but is not for that reason an imperialist relationship unless it is set up in a special way. The same applies to the *threat* of conquest and possible occupation, as in a balance of power relationship. Moreover, *subversive* activities may also be brought to a stage where a nation is dominated by the pin-pricks exercised against it from below, but this is clearly different from imperialism.

Thus, imperialism is a species in a genus of dominance and power relationships. It is a subtype of something, and has itself subtypes to be explored later. Dominance relations between nations and other collectivities will not disappear with the disappearance of imperialism; nor will the end to one type of imperialism (e.g. political, or economic) guarantee the end to another type of imperialism (e.g. economic or cultural). Our view is not reductionist in the traditional sense pursued

*Johan Galtung, "A Structural Theory of Imperialism," *Journal of Peace Research*, no. 2 (1971): 81–116. This selection has been edited to include pp. 81–107 and 110–116. Reprinted by permission of author and publisher.

in marxist-leninist theory, which conceives of imperialism as an economic relationship under private capitalism, motivated by the need for expanding markets, and which bases the theory of dominance on a theory of imperialism. According to this view, imperialism and dominance will fall like dominoes when the capitalistic conditions for economic imperialism no longer obtain. According to the view we develop here, imperialism is a more general structural relationship between two collectivities, and has to be understood at a general level in order to understand and counteracted in its more specific manifestations—just like smallpox is better understood in a context of a theory of epidemic diseases, and these diseases better understood in a context of general pathology.

Briefly stated, imperialism is a system that splits up collectivities and relates some of the parts to each other in relations of *harmony of interest,* and other parts in relations of *disharmony of interest,* or *conflict of interest.*

DEFINING "CONFLICT OF INTEREST"

"Conflict of interest" is a special case of conflict in general, defined as a situation where parties are pursuing incompatible goals. In our special case, these goals are stipulated by an outsider as the "true" interests of the parties, disregarding wholly or completely what the parties themselves say explicitly are the values they pursue. One reason for this is the rejection of the dogma of unlimited rationality: actors do *not* necessarily know, or they are unable to express, what their interest is. Another, more important, reason is that rationality is unevenly distributed, that some may dominate the minds of others, and that this may lead to "false consciousness." Thus, learning to suppress one's own true interests may be a major part of socialization in general and education in particular.

Let us refer to this true interest as LC, *living condition.* It may perhaps be measured by using such indicators as income, standard of living in the usual materialistic sense—but notions of *quality of life* would certainly also enter, not to mention notions of *autonomy.* But the precise content of LC is less important for our purpose than the definition of conflict of interest: There is *conflict,* or *disharmony of interest* if the two parties are coupled together in such a way that the LC *gap* between them is *increasing;* There is *no conflict,* or *harmony of interest,* if the two parties are coupled together in such a way that the LC *gap* between them is *decreasing down to zero.*

Some points in this definition should be spelled out.

First, the parties have to be coupled together, in other words *interact.* A difference between mutually isolated parties does not in itself give rise to problems of interest. There was neither harmony, nor disharmony of interest between the peoples in Africa, Asia, and America before the white Europeans came—there was *nothing.*

Second, the reference is to *parties,* not to actors. In the theory of conflict of *interests,* as opposed to the theory of conflict of *goals,* there is no assumption that the parties (better: categories) have crystallized into actors. This is what they may have to do after they see their own situation more clearly, or in other words: the conflict of interest may have to be transformed into a conflict of *goals.* Thus, if in a nation the center, here defined as the "government" (in the wide sense, not the "cabinet") uses its power to increase its own LC much more than does the rest of the nation, then there is disharmony of interest between government and people according to this definition. This may then be used as a basis for defining the government as illegitimate—as opposed to the usual conception where illegitimacy is a matter of opinion, expressed in the legislature or in the population. The trouble with the latter idea is that it presupposes a level of rationality, an ability of expression and political consciousness and party formation that can only be presupposed at the center of the more or less vertical societies in which human beings live. It is a model highly protective of the center as a whole, however much it may lead to rotation of groups within the center, and hence protective of vertical society.

Third, there is a problem of what to do with the case of a *constant gap*. The parties grow together, at the same rate, but the gap between them is constant. Is that harmony or disharmony of interest? We would refer to it as disharmony, for the parties are coupled such that they will not be brought together. Even if they *grow* parallel to each other it is impossible to put it down as a case of harmony, when the distribution of value is so unequal. On the contrary, this is the case of disharmony that has reached a state of equilibrium.

Fourth, this definition has the advantage of enabling us to talk about degrees of *harmony and disharmony* by measuring the angle between two trajectories, perhaps also taking speed into account. Thus we avoid the difficulty of talking simplistically in terms of polar opposites, harmony vs. disharmony, and can start talking in terms of weak and strong harmony and disharmony.

Fifth, there is an implicit reference to *time* in the two terms "increasing" and "decreasing." We have not been satisfied with a time-free way of operationalizing the concept in terms of static LC gaps. It is much more easy with conflict of *goals*, as we would then be dealing with clearly demarcated actors whose values can be ascertained, and their compatibility or incompatibility likewise: there is no need to study the system over time. To understand conflict of *interest* it looks as if at least a bivariate, diachronic analysis should be carried out to get some feel of how the system operates.

But we should obviously make a distinction between the *size* of the gap, and what happens to the gap over time. If we only had access to static, synchronic data, then we would of course focus on the magnitude of the gap and talk about *disharmony of interest if it is wide, harmony of interest if it is narrow or zero*.

As a first approximation this may not be too bad, but it does lead us into some difficulties. Thus, how do we rank these combinations in terms of increasing disharmony of interest (Table 20.1)? As we see from the Table, the only doubt would be between combinations B and C. We would favor the alphabetical order for two reasons: first, becoming is more important than being (at least if the time-perspective is reasonably short), and second, the diachronic relationship probably reveals more about the coupling between them. For example, the gap in living condition between Norway and Nepal in 1970 is not significant as an indicator of any imperialism. If it keeps on increasing there may be a bit more basis for the suspicion, but more evidence is needed to state the diagnosis of imperialism. The crucial word here is "coupling" in the definition. The word has been put there to indicate some type of social causation in interaction relation and interaction structure which will have to be demonstrated, over and above a simple correlation.

Table 20.1   Four Types of Harmony/Disharmony of Interest

Gap		Decreasing	Increasing
Gap	Narrow	A	C
	Wide	B	D

Let us conclude this discussion by pointing out that a gap in living condition, of at least one important kind, is a necessary, if not sufficient, condition for conflict or disharmony of interest. If in addition the gap can be observed over time, a more satisfactory basis for a diagnosis in terms of imperialism may emerge.

And then, in conclusion: it is clear that the concept of interest used here is based on an ideology, or a *value premise of equality*.[2] An interaction relation and interaction structure set up such that inequality is the result is seen as a coupling not in the interest of the weaker party. This is a value premise like so many other value premises in social science explorations, such as "direct violence is bad," "economic growth is good," "conflict should be resolved," etc. As in all other types of social science, the goal should not be an "objective" social science freed from all such value premises, but a more honest social science where the value premises are made explicit.

DEFINING "IMPERIALISM"

We shall now define imperialism by using the building blocks presented in the preceding two sections. In our two-nation world, imperialism can be defined as one way in which the Center nation has power over the Periphery nation, so as to bring about a condition of disharmony of interest between them. Concretely, *Imperialism* is a relation between a Center and a Periphery nation so that:

(1) there is *harmony of interest* between the *center in the Center* nation and the *center in the Periphery* nation.

(2) there is more *disharmony of interest* within the Periphery nation than within the Center nations.

(3) there is *disharmony of interest* between the *periphery in the Center* nation and the *periphery in the Periphery* nation.[3]

Diagrammatically it looks something like Fig. 20.1. This complex definition, borrowing largely from Lenin, needs spelling out.[4] The basic idea is, as mentioned, that the center in the Center nation has a bridgehead in the Periphery nation, and a well-chosen one: the center in the Periphery nation. This is established such that the Periphery center is tied to the Center center with the best possible tie: the tie of harmony of interest. They are linked so that they go up together and down, even under, together. How this is done in concrete terms will be explored in the subsequent sections.

Inside the two nations there is disharmony of interest. They are both in one way or another vertical societies with LC gaps—otherwise there is no possibility of locating a center and a periphery. Moreover, the gap is not decreasing, but is at

Figure 20.1   The structure of imperialism.

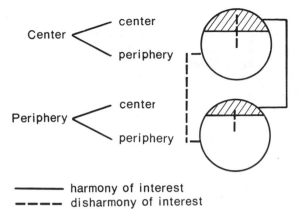

harmony of interest

disharmony of interest

best constant. But the basic idea, absolutely fundamental for the whole theory to be developed, is that *there is more disharmony in the Periphery nation than in the Center nation.* At the simplest static level of description this means there is more inequality in the Periphery than in the Center. At the more complex level we might talk in terms of the gap opening more quickly in the Periphery than in the Center, where it might even remain constant. Through welfare state activities, redistribution takes place and disharmony is reduced for a least some LC dimensions, including income, but usually excluding power.

If we now would capture in a few sentences what imperialism is about, we might perhaps say something like this:

In the Periphery nation, the center grows more than the periphery, due partly to how interaction between center and periphery is organized. Without necessarily thinking of economic interaction, the center is more enriched than the periphery—in ways to be explored below. However, for part of this enrichment, the center in the Periphery only serves as a transmission belt (e.g. as commercial firms, trading companies) for value (e.g. raw materials) forwarded to the Center nation. This value enters the Center in the center, with some of it drizzling down to the periphery in the Center. Importantly, there is less disharmony of interest in the Center than in the Periphery, so that *the total arrangement is largely in the interest of the periphery in the Center.* Within the Center the two parties may be opposed to each other. But in the total game, the periphery see themselves more as the partners of the center in the Center than as the partners of the periphery in the Periphery—and this is the essential trick of that game. Alliance-formation between the two peripheries is avoided, while the Center nation becomes more and the Periphery nation less cohesive—and hence less able to develop long-term strategies.

Actually, concerning the three criteria in the definition of imperialism as given above, it is clear that no. (3) is implied by nos. (1) and (2). The two centers are tied together and the Center periphery is tied to its center: that is the whole essence of the situation. If we now presuppose that the center in the Periphery is a smaller proportion of that nation than the center in the Center, we can also draw one more implication: *there is disharmony of interest between the Center nation as a whole and the Periphery nation as a whole.* But that type of finding, frequently referred to, is highly misleading because it blurs the harmony of interest between the two centers, and leads to the belief that imperialism is merely an international relationship, *not a combination of intra- and inter-national relations.*[5]

However, even if the definition given above purports to define the pure case of imperialism, we may nevertheless fruitfully think in terms of degenerate cases. Thus, the first point in the definition about harmony between the two centers is obviously the most important one. If the second point does not hold, and consequently not the third point either, it may still be fruitful to talk about imperialism. But in this degenerate case the two peripheries may more easily find each other, since they are now only kept apart by geographical distance (assuming that the two nations are nation states, often even located far apart), not in addition by disharmony of interest. Thus, if the relationship between the two peripheries and their centers should become more similar, periphery alliance formation might easily be the result, and the two centers would have to resort to more direct means of violence rather than, or in addition to, the delicate type of structural violence that characterizes the pure type of imperialistic relationship.

But what if there is no distinction between center and periphery in the two nations, what if they are completely horizontal societies? In that case, we should not talk about the dominance relationship whereby the Center nation extracts something from the Periphery nation as an imperialistic one, but rather as something else—looting, stealing, etc. Where there is no bridgehead for the Center nation in the center of the Periphery nation, there cannot be any imperialism by this definition.

From this an important methodological remark may follow. Imagine we now start from the other end and discover that over time some nations increase their living conditions more than other nations—the "increasing gap" so often referred to today—and that there seems to be some kind of structure to this, some kind of invariance. As mentioned, this does not in itself constitute proof of any diagnosis in terms of imperialism, but should prompt the researcher to look for data in that direction. More particularly, we should try to study the precise nature of the interaction between the nations or groups of nations, and see whether the nations can be differentiated in terms of centers and peripheries that relate to each other in the way indicated. But to do this is at all a concrete manner, we must make our definition of imperialism much less abstract. To this we now turn, in successive stages, exploring two *mechanisms,* five *types,* and three *phases* of imperialism.

THE MECHANISMS OF IMPERIALISM

The two basic mechanisms of imperialism both concern the *relation* between the parties concerned, particularly between the nations. The first mechanism concerns the *interaction relation* itself, the second how these relations are put together in a larger interaction structure:

(1) the principle of *vertical interaction relation*
(2) the principle of *feudal interaction structure.*

The basic point about interaction is, of course, that people and nations have different values that complement each other, and then engage in exchange. Some nations produce oil, other nations produce tractors, and they then carry out an exchange according to the principles of comparative advantages. Imagine that our two-nation system has a prehistory of no interaction at all, and then starts with this type of interaction. Obviously, both will be changed by it, and more particularly: a gap between them is likely to open and widen if the interaction is cumulatively asymmetric in terms of what the two parties get out of it.

To study whether the interaction is symmetric or asymmetric, on equal or unequal terms, *two* factors arising from the interaction have to be examined:

(1) *the value-exchange between the actors—inter-*actor effects
(2) *the effects inside the actors—intra-*actor effects

In *economic* relations the first is most commonly analyzed, not only by liberal but also by Marxist economists. The inter-actor flow can be observed as flows of raw material, capital, and financial goods and services in either direction, and can literally be measured at the main points of entry: the customs houses and the national banks. The flow both ways can then be compared in various ways. Most important is the comparison in terms of *who benefits most,* and for this purpose intra-actor effects also have to be taken into consideration.

In order to explore this, the interaction budget indicated in Table 20.2 may be useful. In the Table the usual exchange pattern between a "developed" nation A and a "developing" nation B, where manufactured goods are exchanged for raw materials, is indicated. Whether it takes place in a barter economy or a money economy is not essential in a study of exchange between completely unprocessed goods like crude oil and highly processed goods like tractors. There are negative intra-actor effects that accrue to both parties, indicated by the terms "pollution" for A and "depletion" for B, and "exploitation" for either. So far these negative spin-off effects are usually not taken systematically into account, nor the positive spin-off effects for A that will be a corner-stone in the present analysis.

It is certainly meaningful and important to talk in terms of unequal exchange or symmetric interaction, but not quite unproblematic what its precise meaning should be. For that reason, it may be helpful to think in terms of three stages of types of exploitation, partly reflecting historical *processes* in chronological order, and partly reflecting types of *thinking* about exploitation.

In the first stage of exploitation, A simply engages in looting and takes away the raw materials without offering anything in return. If he steals out of pure nature

Table 20.2 An Interaction Budget

	A ("developed")		B ("developing")	
	Inter-actor Effects	Intra-actor Effects	Inter-actor Effects	Intra-actor Effects
Positive (in)	raw materials	spin-offs	manufactured goods	little or nothing
Negative (out)	manufactured goods	pollution, exploitation	raw materials	depletion, exploitation

there is no human interaction involved, but we assume that he forces "natives" to work for him and do the extraction work. It is like the slave-owner who lives on the work produced by slaves—which is quantitatively not too different from the land-owner who has land-workers working for him five out of seven days a week.

In the second stage, A starts offering something "in return." Oil, pitch, land, etc. is "bought" for a couple of beads—it is no longer simply taken away without asking any questions about ownership. The price paid is ridiculous. However, as power relations in the international systems change, perhaps mainly by bringing the power level of the weaker party up from zero to some low positive value, A has to contribute more: for instance, pay more for the oil. The question is now whether there is a cut-off point after which the exchange becomes equal, and what the criterion for that cut-off point would be. Absence of subjective dissatisfaction—B says that he is now content? Objective market values or the number of man-hours that have gone into the production on either side?

There are difficulties with all these conceptions. But instead of elaborating on this, we shall rather direct our attention to the shared failure of all these attempts to look at *intra* actor effects. Does the interaction have enriching or impoverishing effects *inside* the actor, or does it just lead to a stand-still? This type of question leads us to the third stage of exploitation, where there may be some balance in the flow between the actors, but great differences in the effect the interaction has within them.[6]

As an example let us use nations exchanging oil for tractors. The basic point is that this involves different levels of processing, where we define "processing" as an activity imposing Culture on Nature. In the case of crude oil the product is (almost) pure Nature; in the case of tractors it would be wrong to say that it is a case of pure Culture, pure *form* (like mathematics, music). A transistor radio, an integrated circuit, these would be better examples because Nature has been brought down to a minimum. The tractor is still too much iron and rubber to be a pure case.

The major point now is the *gap in processing level* between oil and tractors and the differential effect this gap will have on the two nations. In one nation the oil deposit may be at the water-front, and all that is needed is a derrick and some simple mooring facilities to pump the oil straight into a ship—e.g. a Norwegian tanker—that can bring the oil to the country where it will provide energy to run, among other things, the tractor factories. In the other nation the effects may be extremely far-reaching due to the complexity of the product and the connectedness of the society.

There may be ring effects in all directions, and in Table 20.3 we have made an effort to show some types of spin-off effects. A number of comments are appropriate in connection with this list, which, needless to say, is very tentative indeed.

First, the effects are rather deep-reaching if this is at all a correct image of the situation. And the picture is hardly exaggerated. It is possible to set up international interaction in such a way that the positive intra-actor effects are practically nil in the raw material delivering nation, and extremely far-reaching in the processing nation.[7] This is not in any sense strange either: if processing is the imprint of Culture on Nature, the effects should be far-reaching indeed, and strongly related to development itself.

Table 20.3 Intra-actor Effects of Interaction Across Gaps in Processing Levels

Dimension	Effect on Center Nation	Effect on Periphery Nation	Analyzed by
1. Subsidiary economic effects	New *means of production* developed	Nothing developed, just a hole in the ground	Economist
2. Political position in world structure	Central position reinforced	Periphery position reinforced	International relationists
3. Military benefits	*Means of destruction* can easily be pro-duced	No benefits, wars cannot be fought by means of raw materials	
4. Communication benefits	*Means of communi-cation* easily developed	No benefits, trans-portation not by means of raw materials	Communica-tion special-ists
5. Knowledge and research	Much needed for higher levels of processing	Nothing needed, extraction based on being, not on becoming	Scientists, Technicians
6. Specialist needed	Specialists in *making,* scientists, engineers	Specialist in *having,* lawyers	Sociologists of knowledge
7. Skill and education	Much needed to carry out processing	Nothing needed, just a hole in the ground	Education specialists
8. Social structure	Change needed for ability to convert into mobility	No change needed, extraction based on ownership, not on ability	Sociologists
9. Psychological affects	A basic psychology of self-reliance and autonomy	A basic psychology of dependence	Psychologists

Second, these effects reinforce each other. In the nine effects listed in Table 20.3, there are economic, political, military, communications, and cultural as-pects, mixed together. Thus, the nation that in the international division of labor has the task of providing the most refined, processed products—like Japan with its emphasis on integrated circuits, transistors, miniaturization, etc. (or Eastern Europe's Japan: the DDR, with a similar emphasis)—will obviously have to engage in research. Research needs an infra-structure, a wide cultural basis in universities, etc., and it has obvious spill-over effects in the social, political, and military domains. And so on: the list may be examined and all kinds of obvious types of cross-fertilization be explored.

Third, in the example chosen, and also in the formulations in the Table, we have actually referred to a very special type of gap in processing level: the case when one of the nations concerned delivers raw materials. But the general point here is the *gap,* which would also exist if one nation delivers semi-finished products and the other finished products. There may be as much of a gap in a trade relations based on exchange between textiles and transistors as one based on exchange between oil and tractors. However, and this seems to be basic: we have looked in vain for a theory of economic trade where this gap is meaningfully operationalized so that the theory could be based on it. In fact, *degree of processing,* which is the basic variable behind the spin-off effects, seems absent from most thinking about international exchange.

This, and that is observation number *four,* is not merely a question of analyzing differences in processing level in terms of what happens inside the factory or the extraction plant. It has to be seen in its social totality. A glance at the right-hand column of Table 20.3 immediately gives us some clues as to why this has not been done: academic research has been so divided that nowhere in a traditional university set-up would one come to grips with the totality of the effects of an interaction process. Not even in the most sophisticated inter-, cross- or trans-disciplinary research institute has that type of research been carried so far that a meaningful operationalization has been offered. Yet this is indispensible for a new program of trade on equal terms to be formulated: *trade, or interaction in general, is symmetric, or on equal terms, if and only if the total inter- and intra-actor effects that accrue to the parties are equal.*[8]

But, and this is observation number *five:* why has the idea of comparing the effects of interaction only at the points of exit and entry been so successful? Probably basically because it has always been natural and in the interest of the two centers to view the world in this way, not necessarily consciously to reinforce their position in the center, but basically because interaction looks more like "*inter*-action only" to the center. If the center in the Periphery has based its existence on being rather than becoming, on ownership rather than processing, then the inter-action has been very advantageous to them. What was formerly Nature is through the "beneficial inter-action" with another nation converted into Money, which in turn can be converted into many things. *Very little effort was needed:* and that this was precisely what made the exchange so disadvantageous, only became clear after some time. Japan is, possibly, the only nation that has really converted the absence of raw materials into a blessing for the economy.

Some implications of the general principle of viewing intra-actor in addition to inter-actor effects can now be spelled out.

One is obvious: *asymmetry cannot be rectified by stabilizing or increasing the prices for raw materials.* Of course, prices exist that could, on the surface compensate for the gap in intra-actor effects, convertible into a corresponding development of subsidiary industries, education industry, knowledge industry, and so on (although it is hard to see how the psychology of self-reliance can be bought for money). Much of this is what raw material producing countries can do with the money they earn. But this is not the same. One thing is to be *forced* into a certain pattern of intra-actor development *in order to* be able to participate in the inter-actor interaction, quite another thing to be free to make the decision without having to do it, without being forced by the entire social machinery.

The second implication is also obvious, but should still be put as a question to economists. Imagine that a nation A gives nation B a loan L, to be repaid after n years at an interest rate of p % p.a. There is only one condition in addition to the conditions of the loan: that the money be used to procure goods at a high level of processing in A. Each order will then have deep repercussions in A, along the eight dimensions indicated, in addition to the direct effect of the order itself. The value of these effects is certainly not easily calculated, but in addition A also gets back from B, if B has not gone bankrupt through this process in the meantime, $L(1 + p)^n$ after n years. If procurement is in terms of capital goods rather than consumer goods (usually for consumption by the center in the Periphery mainly) there will also have been intra-actor effects in B. In all likelihood the intra-actor effects of the deal in A are more far-reaching, however, for two reasons: the effects of the interaction process enter A at a higher level of processing than B, and A has already a socio-economic-political structure enabling it to absorb and convert and redirect such pressures for maximum beneficial impact.

Imagine now that n is high and p is low; the loan is said to be "on generous terms." The question is whether this generosity is not deceptive, *whether it would not have paid for A to give L for eternity, at no interest,* i.e. as a grant. Or even better: it might even have paid for A to persuade B to take on L with negative interest, i.e. to pay B for accepting the loan, because of all the intra-actor effects. The situation may be likened to a man who pays some people a certain sum on the condition that they use the money to pay him for an article on, say, imperialism. By having to produce, by having obligations to fulfill, the man is forced to create and thereby expand, and consequently forced to enrich himself.[9]

In short, we see vertical interaction as the major source of the inequality of this world, whether it takes the form of looting, of highly unequal exchange, or highly differential spin-off effects due to processing gaps. But we can also imagine a fourth phase of exploitation, where the modern King Midas becomes a victim of his own greed and turns his environment into muck rather than gold, by polluting it so strongly and so thoroughly that the negative spin-off effects from processing may outstrip all the positive effects. This may, in fact, place the less developed countries in a more favorable position: the lower the GNP, the lower the Gross National Pollution.

But this phase is still for the (near?) future. At present what we observe is an inequality between the world's nations of a magnitude that can only be explained in terms of the cumulative effect of *strong* structural phenomena over time, like the phenomena described here under the heading of imperialism. This is not to deny that other factors may also be important, even decisive, but no analysis can be valid without studying the problem of development in a context of vertical interaction.

If the first mechanism, the *vertical interaction relation,* is the major factor behind inequality, then the second mechanism, the *feudal interaction structure,* is the factor that maintains and reinforces this inequality by protecting it. There are four rules defining this particular interaction structure:

(1) interaction between Center and Periphery is *vertical*
(2) interaction between Periphery and Periphery is *missing*
(3) multilateral interaction involving all three is *missing*
(4) interaction with the outside world is *monopolized* by the Center, with two implications:
(a) Periphery interaction with other Center nations is *missing*
(b) Center as well as Periphery interaction with Periphery nations belonging to other Center nations is *missing.*[10]

Figure 20.2   A feudal center-periphery structure.

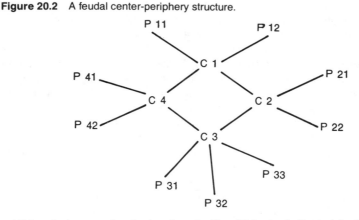

This relation can be depicted as in Fig. 20.2. As indicated in the Figure, the number of Periphery nations attached to any given Center nation can, of course, vary. In this Figure we have also depicted the rule "if you stay off my satellites. I will stay off yours."

Some important *economic* consequences of this structure should be spelled out.

First and most obvious: the *concentration on trade partners.* A Periphery nation should, as a result of these two mechanisms, have most of its trade with "its" Center nation. In other words, empirically we would expect high levels of *import concentration* as well as *export concentration* in the Periphery, as opposed to the Center, which is more free to extend its trade relations in almost any direction—except in the pure case, with the Periphery of other Center nations.

Second, and not so obvious, is the *commodity concentration:* the tendency for Periphery nations to have only one or very few primary products to export. This would be a trivial matter if it could be explained entirely in terms of geography, if e.g. oil countries were systematically poor as to ore, ore countries poor as to bananas and coffee, etc. But this can hardly be assumed to be the general case: Nature does not distribute its riches that way. There is a historical rather than a geographical explanation to this. A territory may have been exploited for the raw materials most easily available and/or most needed in the Center, and this, in turn, leads to a certain social structure, to communication lines to the deposits, to trade structures, to the emergence of certain center groups (often based on ownership of that particular raw material), and so on. To start exploiting a new kind of raw material in the same territory might upset carefully designed local balances; hence, it might be easier to have a fresh start for that new raw material in virgin territory with no bridgehead already prepared for imperialist exploits. In order to substantiate this hypothesis we would have to demonstrate that there are particularly underutilized and systematically underexplored deposits precisely in countries where one type of raw material has already been exploited.

The combined effect of these two consequences is a *dependency* of the Periphery on the Center. Since the Periphery usually has a much smaller GNP, the trade between them is a much higher percentage of the GNP for the Periphery, and with both partner and commodity concentration, the Periphery becomes particularly vulnerable to fluctuations in demands and prices. At the same time the center in the Periphery depends on the Center for its supply of consumer goods. Import substitution industries will usually lead to consumer goods that look homespun and unchic, particularly if there is planned obsolescence in the production of these goods in the Center, plus a demand for equality between the two centers maintained by demonstration effects and frequent visits to the Center.[11]

However, the most important consequence is political and has to do with the systematic utilization of feudal interaction structures as a way of protecting the Center against the Periphery. The feudal interaction structure is in social science language nothing but an expression of the old political maxim *divide et impera*, divide and rule, as a strategy used systematically by the Center relative to the Periphery nations. How could—for example—a small foggy island in the North Sea rule over one quarter of the world? By isolating the Periphery parts from each other, by having them geographically at sufficient distance from each other to impede any real alliance formation, by having separate deals with them so as to tie them to the Center in particularistic ways, by reducing multilateralism to a minimum with all kinds of graded membership, *and* by having the Mother country assume the role of window to the world.

However, this point can be much more clearly seen if we combine the two mechanisms and extend what has been said so far for relations between Center and Periphery *nations* to relations between center and periphery groups within nations. Under an imperialist structure the two mechanisms are used not only between nations but also within nations, but less so in the Center nation than in the Periphery nation. In other words, there is vertical division of labor within as well as between nations. And these two levels of organization are intimately linked to each other (as A. G. Frank always has emphasized) in the sense that the center in the Periphery interaction structure is also that group with which the Center nation has its harmony of interest, the group used as a bridgehead.

Thus, the combined operation of the two mechanisms at the two levels builds into the structure a subtle grid of protection measures against the major potential source of "trouble," the periphery in the Periphery. To summarize the major items in this grid:

(1) the general impoverishment of pP brought about by vertical division of labor within the Periphery nation, and particularly by the high level of inequality (e.g. differential access to means of communication) and disharmony of interest in the Periphery nation;

(2) the way in which interaction, mobilization, and organization of pP are impeded by the feudal structure *within* Periphery nations;

(3) the general impoverishment of the Periphery nation brought about by vertical division of labor, particularly in terms of means of destruction and communication;

(4) the way in which interaction, mobilization, and organization of the Periphery nations are impeded by the feudal interaction structure *between* nations

(a) making it difficult to interact with other Periphery nations "belonging" to the same Center nations,

(b) making it even more difficult to interact with Periphery nations "belonging" to other Center nations;

(5) the way in which it is a fortiori difficult for the peripheries in Periphery nations to interact, mobilize, and organize

(a) intra-nationally because of (1) and (2),

(b) inter-nationally because of (3) and (4),

(c) in addition: because the center in the Periphery has the monopoly on international interaction in all directions and cannot be counted on to interact in the interest of its own periphery;

(6) the way in which pP cannot appeal to pC or cC either because of the disharmony of interest.

Obviously, the more perfectly the mechanisms of imperialism within and between nations are put to work, the less overt machinery of oppression is needed and the smaller can the center groups be, relative to the total population involved. *Only imperfect, amateurish imperialism needs weapons; professional imperialism is based on structural rather than direct violence.*

THE TYPES OF IMPERIALISM

We shall now make this more concrete by distinguishing between five types of imperialism depending on the *type* of exchange between Center and Periphery nations: (1) *economic;* (2) *political;* (3) *military;* (4) *communication;* (5) *cultural.*

The order of presentation is rather random: we have no theory that one is more basic than the others, or precedes the others. Rather, this is like a Pentagon or a Soviet Star: imperialism can start from any corner.[12] They should all be examined regarding the extent to which they generate interaction patterns that utilize the two *mechanisms* of imperialism so as to fulfill the three *criteria* of imperialism, or at least the first of them.

The most basic of the two mechanisms is *vertical* interaction, which in its modern form is conceived of as interaction across a gap in processing level. In other words, what is exchanged between the two nations is not only not the same things (which would have been stupid) but things of a quite different kind, the difference being in terms of where the most complex and stimulating operations take place. One tentative list, might look like Table 20.4. The order of presentation parallels that of Table 20.3, but in that Table cultural imperialism was spelled out in more detail as spin-off effects from economic imperialism.

The vertical nature of this type of *economic* interaction has been spelled out in detail above since we have used that type of imperialism to exemplify definition and mechanisms. Let us look more at the other types of vertical interaction.

Table 20.4   The Five Types of Imperialism

Type	Economic	Political	Military	Communication	Cultural
Center nation provides	processing, means of production	decisions, models	protection, means of destruction	news, means of communication	teaching, means of creation—autonomy
Periphery nation provides	raw materials, markets	obedience, imitators	discipline, traditional hardware	events, passengers, goods	learning, validation—dependence

The *political* one is clear: the concept of a "mother" country, the Center nation, is also an indication of how the decision-making center is dislocated, away from the nation itself and towards the Center nation. These decisions may then affect economic, military, communication, and cultural patterns. Important here is the division of labor involved: some nations produce decisions, others supply obedience. The decisions may be made upon application, as in "bilateral technical assistance," or in consultation—or they may simply emerge by virtue of the model-imitator distinction. Nothing serves that distinction quite so well as uni-linear concepts of "development" and "modernization," according to which Center nations possess some superior kind of structure for others to imitate (as long as the Center's central position is not seriously challenged), and which gives a special aura of legitimacy to any idea emanating from the Center. Thus, structures and decisions developed in the "motherland of liberalism" or in the "fatherland of socialism" serve as models by virtue of their place of origin, not by virtue of their substance.

The *military* implications or parallels are also rather obvious. It cannot be emphasized enough that the economic division of labor is also one which ensures that the Center nations economically speaking also become the Center nations in a military sense: only they have the industrial capacity to develop the technological hardware—and also are often the only ones with the social structure compatible with a modern army. He who produces tractors can easily produce tanks, but he who delivers oil cannot defend himself by throwing it in the face of the aggressors. He has to depend on the tank-producer, either for protection or for acquisition (on terms dictated by the Center). And just as there is a division of labor with the Center nation producing manufactured goods on the basis of raw materials extracted in the Periphery nations, there is also a division of labor with the *Center nations processing the obedience provided by the Periphery nations into decisions that can be implemented.* Moreover, there is also a division of labor with the Center providing the protection (and often also the officers or at least the instructors in "counter-insurgency") and the Periphery the discipline and the soldiers needed—not to mention the apprentices of "military advisors" from the Center.

As to the fourth type, *communication* imperialism, the emphasis in the analysis is usually turned towards the second mechanism of imperialism: the feudal interaction structure. That this largely holds for most world communication and transportation patterns has been amply demonstrated.[13] But perhaps more important is the vertical nature of the division of labor in the field of communication/transportation. It is trivial that a high level of industrial capacity is necessary to develop the latest in transportation and communication technology. The preceding generation of *means of communication/transportation* can always be sold, sometimes second-hand, to the Periphery as part of the general vertical trade/aid structure alongside the *means of production* (economic sector), the *means of destruction* (military sector), and the *means of creation* (cultural sector). The Center's planes and ships are faster, more direct, look more reliable, attract more passengers, more goods. And when the Periphery finally catches up, the Center will already for along time have dominated the field of communication satellites.

One special version of this principle is a combination of cultural and communication exchange: *news communication*. We all know that the major agencies are in the hands of the Center countries, relying on Center-dominated, feudal networks of communication.[14] What is not so well analyzed is how Center news takes up a much larger proportion of Periphery news media than vice versa, just as trade with the Center is a larger proportion of Periphery total trade than vice versa. In other words, the pattern of partner concentration as something found more in the Periphery than in the Center is very pronounced. The Periphery nations do not write or read much about each other, especially not across bloc borders, and they read more about "their" Center than about other Centers—because the press is written and read by the center in the Periphery, who want to know more about that most "relevant" part of the world—for them.

Another aspect of vertical division of labor in the news business should also be pointed out. Just as the Periphery produces raw material that the Center turns into processed goods, *the Periphery also produces events that the Center turns into news*.[15] This is done by training journalists to see events with Center eyes, and by setting up a chain of communication that filters and processes events so that they fit the general pattern.

The latter concept brings us straight into *cultural* imperialism, a subtype of which is scientific imperialism. The division of labor between teachers and learners is clear: it is not the division of labor as such (found in most situations of transmission of knowledge) that constitutes imperialism, but the location of the teachers, and of the learners, in a broader setting. If the Center always provides the teachers and the definition of that worthy of being taught (from the gospels of Christianity to the gospels of Technology), and the Periphery always provides the learners, then there is a pattern which smacks of imperialism. The satellite nation in the Periphery will also know that nothing flatters the Center quite so much as being encouraged to teach, and being seen as a model, and that the Periphery can get much in return from a humble, culture-seeking strategy (just as it will get little but aggression if it starts teaching the Center anything—like Czechoslovakia, who started lecturing the Soviet Union on socialism). For in accepting cultural transmission the Periphery also, implicitly, validates for the Center the culture developed in the center, whether that center is intra- or inter-national. This serves to reinforce the Center as a center for it will then continue to develop culture along with transmitting it, thus creating lasting demand for the latest innovations. Theories, like cars and fashions, have their life-cycle, and whether the obsolescence is planned or not there will always be a time-lag in a structure with a pronounced difference between center and periphery. Thus, the tram workers in Rio de Janeiro may carry banners supporting Auguste Comte one hundred years after the center of the Center forgot who he was.

In science we find a particular version of vertical division of labor, very similar to economic division of labor: the pattern of scientific teams from the Center who go to Periphery nations to collect data (raw material) in the form of deposits, sediments, flora, fauna, archeological findings, attitudes, behavioral patterns, and so on for data processing, data analysis, and theory formation (processing, in general) in the Center universities (factories), so as to be able to send the finished product, a journal, a book (manufactured goods) back for consumption in the center of the Periphery—after first having created a demand for it through demonstration effect, training in the Center country, and some degree of low level participation in the data collection team.[16] This parallel is not a joke, it is a *structure*. If in addition the precise nature of the research is to provide the Center with information that can be used economically, politically, or militarily to maintain an imperialist structure, the cultural imperialism becomes even more clear. And if to this we add the *brain drain* (and body drain) whereby "raw" brains (students) and "raw" bodies (unskilled workers) are moved from the Periphery to the Center and "processed" (trained) with ample benefits to the Center, the picture becomes complete.

THE PHASES OF IMPERIALISM

We have mentioned repeatedly that imperialism is *one* way in which one nation may dominate another. Moreover, it is a way that provides a relatively stable pattern: the nations are linked to each other in a pattern that may last for some time because of the many stabilizing factors built into it through the mechanism of a feudal interaction structure.

The basic idea is that the center in the Center establishes a bridgehead in the Periphery nation, and more particularly, in the center of the Periphery nation. Obviously, this bridgehead does not come about just like that: there is a phase preceding it. The precise nature of that preceding phase can best be seen by distinguishing between three phases of imperialism in history, depending on what type of concrete method the center in the Center has used to establish the harmony of interest between itself and the center in the Periphery. This is enumerated in Table 20.5.

Table 20.5   Three Phases of Imperialism in History

Phase	Period	Form	Term
I	Past	*Occupation,* cP physically consists of cC people who engage in *occupation*	Colonialism
II	Present	*Organization,* cC interacts with cP via medium of international *organizations*	Neo-colonialism
III	Future	*Communication,* cC interacts with cP via international communication	Neo-neo-colonialism

From the Table we see that in all three cases, the Center nation has a hold over the center of the Periphery nation. But the precise nature of this grip differs, and should be seen relative to the means of transportation and communication. No analysis of imperialism can be made without a reference to these means that perhaps are as basic as the means of production in producing social dynamics.

Throughout the overwhelming part of human history, transportation (of human beings, of goods) did not proceed at a higher speed than that provided by pony expresses and quick sailing ships; and communication (of signals, of meaning) not at higher speed than that provided by fires and smoke signals which could be spotted from one hilltop to another. Precise control over another nation would have to be exercised by physically transplanting one's own center and grafting onto the top of the foreign body—in other words, colonialism in all its forms, best known in connection with "white settlers." According to this vision, colonialism was not a discovery of the Europeans subsequent to the Great Discoveries: it could just as well be used to describe great parts of the Roman Empire that through textbooks and traditions of history-writing so successfully has dominated our image of racial and ethnical identity and national pride.[17]

Obviously, the quicker the means of transportation could become, the less necessary would this pattern of permanent settlement be. The break in the historical pattern came when the steam engine was not only put into the factory to provide new *means of production* (leading to conditions that prompted Marx to write *Das Kapital*) but also into a vessel (Fulton) and a locomotive (Stephenson): in other words *means of transportation* (the book about that is not yet written). This gave Europeans a decisive edge over peoples in other regions and colonialism became more firmly entrenched. Control could be accurate and quick.

But decolonialization also came, partly due to the weakening of cC, partly due to the strengthening of cP that might not challenge what cC did, but want to do so itself. Neo-colonialism came; and in this present phase of imperialism control is not of the direct, concrete type found in the past. It is mediated through the means of transportation (and, of course, also communication) linking the two centers to each other. The control is less concrete: it is not physical presence, but a link; and this link takes the shape of international organizations. The international organization has a certain permanence, often with physical headquarters and a lasting general secretary in the mother country. But above all it is a medium in which influence can flow, with *both* centers joining as members and finding each other. Their harmony of interest can be translated into complete equality within the international organization, and vice versa. Their identity is defined relative to the organization, not to race, ethnicity, or nationality. But with differential disharmony *within* nations, this actually becomes an instrument of disharmony *between* nations.

These organizations are well-known for all five types of imperialism. For the economic type, the private or governmental multinational corporations (BINGOs) may serve;[18] for the political type, many of the international governmental organizations (IGOs); for the military type, the various systems of military alliances and treaties and organizations (MIGOs?);[19] for communication the shipping and air companies (CONGOs?), not to mention the international press agencies, offer ample illustration; and for cultural imperialism, some of the international nongovernmental organizations (INGOs) may serve as the conveyor mechanisms. But this is of course not to say that international organizations will necessarily serve such purposes. According to the theory developed here, this is an empirical question, depending on the degree of division of labor inside the organization and the extent to which it is feudally organized.

Next, the third phase. If we now proceed even further along the same line of decreasingly concrete (but increasingly effective?) ties between the two centers, we can envisage a phase where even the international organizations will not only go into disrepute, but dissolve. What will come in their place? *Instant communication,* whereby parties who want to communicate with each other set up ad hoc communication networks (telesatellites, etc.) that form and dissolve in rapid succession, changing scope and domain, highly adjustable to external circumstance, guided by enormous data-banks and idea-banks that permit partici-pants to find their "opposite numbers" without having them frozen together in a more permanent institutional network that develops its own rigidities.[20]

In other words, we envisage a future where very many international organiza-tions will be threatened in two ways. First, they will be exposed to increasing criticism as to their function as a tie between two centers, communicating and coordinating far above the masses in either country, which will in itself lead to a certain disintegration. Second, this does not mean that the centers, if they are free to do so, will cease to coordinate their action, only that they will do so by other means. Instead of going to ad hoc or annual conventions, or in other ways instruction a general secretary and his staff, they may simply pick up their videophone and have a long distance conference organized, where the small group of participants can all see and talk to each other—not like in a conference, but in the more important adjoining lobbies, in the coffee-houses, in private quarters—or wherever they prefer to carry out communication and coordination.[21]

To penetrate more deeply into the role of international organization as an instrument of imperialistic dominance, let us now distinguish between five phases in the development of an international organization. As example we take one economic organization, General Motors Corporation (GMC) and one political organization, the International Communist Movement (ICM)—at present not organized formally as an international. The stages are indicated in Table 20.6. Needless to say, these two are taken as *illustrations* of economic and political imperialism—this is not a *study* of GMC and ICM respectively.

In the beginning, the organization exists only within national boundaries. Then comes a second phase when it sends representatives, at that stage usually called "agents," abroad. This is a critical stage: it is a question of gaining a foothold in

Table 20.6 Stages in the Development of an International Organization

	General Motors Corporation (GMC)	International Communist Movement (ICM)
Phase 1 National only	in one country only ("mother country")	in one country only ("father-land")
Phase 2 National goes abroad	subsidiary, or branch office established by "agents"	subversive organization, established by "agents"
Phase 3 Multi-national, asymmetric	other national companies started, with "mother country" dominating	other national parties estab-lished, with "fatherland" party dominating
Phase 4 Multinational, symmetric	total network becomes symmetric	total network becomes symmetric
Phase 5 Global, or trans-national organization	national identities dissolve	national dissolve

another nation, and usually subversive, from below. If the other nation is completely new to this economic or political pattern, the "agents" often have to come from the "mother country" or the "fatherland" upon the invitation of dissatisfied individuals who find their own mobility within the system blocked *and* who think that the present system does not satisfy the needs of the population. But this phase is not imperialist, for the center in the mother country has not established any bridgehead in the *center* of the offspring country—yet.

The agents may be highly instrumental of social change. They may set into motion patterns in economic life that may reduce significantly the power of feudal landlords and introduce capitalist patterns of production; or they may set into motion patterns in political life that may reduce equally significantly the power of industrialists and introduce socialist patterns of production. Both activities are subversive of the social order, but not imperialist, and are, consequently, examples of other ways in which one nation may exercise influence over another.[22]

But in Phase 3 this development has gone a significant step further. The agents have now been successful, so to speak: national companies/parties have been established. Elites have emerged in the Periphery nations, strongly identified with and well harmonizing with the Center elites. The whole setting is highly asymmetric; what we have identified as mechanisms and types of imperialism are now discernible.

There is *division of labor:* the "daughter" company in the Periphery nation is particularly concerned with making raw materials available and with securing markets for the mother company in the Center nation. If it enters into processing, then it is often with a technology already by-passed by "development" in the Center country, or only leading to semi-finished products. Correspondingly, the company/party in the mother country makes more decisions and the parties in the Periphery provide obedience and secure markets for the implementation of orders. Thus, in both cases the implicit assumption is always that the top leadership of the international organization shall be the top leadership of the company/party in the Center country. Headquarters are located there and not elsewhere; this location is not but rotation of random choice.[23]

Further, the *general interaction structure is clearly feudal:* there is interaction along the spokes, from the Periphery to the Center hub; but not along the rim, from one Periphery nation to another. These may be multilateral meetings, but they are usually very heavily dominated by the Center, which takes it for granted that it will be in the interest of the Periphery to emulate the Center. And this then spans across all five types of interaction, one way or the other—in ways that are usually fairly obvious.

We have pointed to what seem to be basic similarities between the two international organizations (GMC and ICM). Precisely because they are similar, they can do much to impede each other's activities. This similarity is not strange: they both reflect the state of affairs in a world that consists of (1) nation-states, of (2) highly unequal power and level of development along various axes, and is (3) too small for many nation-states to stay within their bonds—so they spill over with their gospels, and patterns are established that are imperialist in nature. *For phase 3 is clearly the imperialist phase;* and because so many international organizations are in this third phase, they at present stand out as vehicles of asymmetric forms of center-center cooperation.[24]

This is the present state of most international organizations. Most are extensions of patterns developed first in one nation, and on assumptions that may have been valid in that country. They are usually the implementation in our days of the old missionary command: "Go ye all forth and make all peoples my disciples." This applies not only to economic and political organizations, but to the other three types as well. Typical examples are the ways in which cultural patterns are disseminated. In its most clear form, they are even handled by official or semi-official institutions more or less attached to the diplomatic work (such as USIS, and the various cultural activities of the Soviet and Chinese embassies in many countries; and to a lesser extent, the British Council and Alliance Française). But international organizations are also used for this purpose by Center nations who firmly believe that their patterns are good for everybody else because they are good for themselves.

However, the Periphery does not necessarily rest content with this state of affairs. There will be a dynamism leading to changes towards Phase 4, so far only brought about in very few organizations. It will probably have its roots in the division of labor, and the stamp as second-class members given to the Periphery in general, and to heads of Periphery companies and parties in particular. Why should there be any written or unwritten law that GMC and ICM heads are located in the United States and the Soviet Union, respectively?[25] Why not break up the division of labor completely, distribute the research contracts and the strategic planning evenly, why not rotate the headquarters, why not build up interaction along the rim and build down the interaction along the spokes so that the hub slowly fades out and the resulting organization is truely symmetric? This is where the Norwegian GMC president and the Rumanian ICM general secretary have, in a sense, common interests—and we predict that this movement will soon start in all major international organizations following some of the very useful models set by the UN and her Specialized Agencies. It should be noted, however, that it is not too difficult to obtain equality in an international organization where only the elites participate, since they already to a large extent harmonize with each other.

But this is not the final stage of development, nothing is. The multi-national, symmetric form will always be artificial for at least two reasons: the nations are not symmetric in and by themselves—some contribute more than others—and they form artificial pockets relative to many of the concerns of the organizations. Any multi-national organization, however symmetric, is a way of reinforcing and perpetuating the nation-state. If nation-states are fading out in significance, much like municipalities in many parts of the world, multi-national organizations will also fade out because they are built over a pattern that is becoming less and less salient. What will come in its place? The answer will probably be what has here been called a hypothetical Phase 5—*the global* or *world organization,* but we shall not try to spell this out here.

FROM SPIN-OFF TO SPILL-OVER: CONVERTIBILITY OF IMPERIALISM

We have now presented a theory of imperialism based on *three* criteria, *two* mechanisms, *five* types, and *three* phases. In the presentation, as is usually done in any presentation of imperialism, economic imperialism was used for the purpose of illustration. However, we tried to carry the analysis further: for economic imperialism, exploitation was not only defined in terms of unequal exchange because A gives less to B than he gets from B, but also in terms of differential intra-actor or spin-off effects. Moreover, it is quite clear from Tables 20.3 and 20.4 that these spin-off effects are located in other areas in which imperialism can also be defined. Vertical economic interaction has political spin-offs, military spin-offs, communication spin-offs, and cultural spin-offs; and vice-versa, as we shall indicate.

For that reason we shall now make a distinction between *spin-off* effects and *spill-over* effects. When a nation exchanges tractors for oil it develops a tractor-producing capacity. One possible spin-off effect is a tank-producing capacity, and this becomes a spill-over effect the moment that capacity is converted into military imperialism, for instance in the form of *Tank-Kommunismus* or *Tank-Kapitalismus*. Of course, this does not become military imperialism unless exercised in cooperation with the ruling elite in the Periphery nation. If it is exercised against that elite, it is a simple *invasion*—as distinct from an *intervention* that is the product of cC-cP cooperation.

Table 20.7 Convertibility of Types of Imperialism

	Economic	Political	Military	Communication	Cultural
Economic	1	2	3	4	5 –9
Political					
Military					
Communication					
Cultural					

A glance at Tables 20.3 and 20.4 indicates that the road from spin-off to spill-over is a short one, provided that there are cooperating or even generalized elites available both in the Center and the Periphery nations. It is not necessary for the same person in Center and Periphery to be on top on both the economic, political, military, communication, and cultural organizations—that would be rather super-human! Many would cover two or three such positions, few would command four or five. But if the five elites defined through these five types of exchange are *coordinated* into generalized upper classes based on a rich network of kinship, friendship, and association (not to mention effective cooperation), then the basis is laid for an extremely solid type of *generalized imperialism*. In the extreme case there would be rank concordance in both Center and Periphery, which means that there would not even be some little disequilibrium present in either case to give some leverage for a revolutionary movement. All groups would have learned, in fact been forced, to play generalized roles as dominant and dependent, respectively.

For this rank concordance to take place, gains made from one type of imperialism should be readily convertible into the other types. The analytical instrument here could be what we might call the *convertibility matrix,* given in Table 20.7.

The numbers in the first row correspond to the spin-off effects for vertical division of labor in economic transactions, as indicated in Table 20.3. A more complete theory of imperialism would now try to give corresponding spin-off effects, convertible into spill-over effects, for the other four types with regard to all five types. We shall certainly not engage fully in this taxonomic exercise but only pick one example from each row.

Thus, it is rather obvious how political imperialism can be converted into economic imperialism by dictating terms of trade, where the latter are not seen so much in terms of volume as trade composition.[26]

Correspondingly, military imperialism can easily be converted into communication imperialism by invoking the need for centralized command over communication and transportation facilities. It is no coincidence that the capital in so many Center countries is located inland and well protected, whereas the capital in most Periphery countries is a port, easily accessible from the Center country, and with a feudal interaction network inland facilitating the flow of raw materials to the capital port and a trickling of consumer goods in the other direction (most of it being absorbed in the capital port itself). Precise command of territory may be necessary to establish a communication network of this type, but once established, it is self-reinforcing.

Similarly, to take another example: communication imperialism may be converted into cultural imperialism by regulating the flow of information, not only in the form of news, but also in the form of cheaply available books, etc. from the Center country.

Finally, cultural imperialism is convertible into economic imperialism in ways very commonly found today: by means of technical assistance processes. A technical assistance expert is not only a person from a rich country who goes to a poor country and stimulates a demand in the poor country for the products of the rich country.[27] He is also a man who goes to the poor country, reserving for himself all the benefits of the challenges of this entrepreneurial activity. He *writes* the SOP (Standard Operating Procedure); it is for his "counterpart" to *follow* the SOP. That this challenge is convertible into more knowledge (more culture) and eventually also into economic benefits upon the return of the technical assistance expert is hardly to be doubted in principle, but it is another question whether the Center country understands this and fully utilizes the resource.

Convertibility could now be studied at two levels: the extent to which the nation as such can use such spin-offs from one type and direct them towards consolidation of another type, and the extent to which an individual may do so. If an individual can, the result is some type of rank concordance; if the nation can, we might perhaps talk of imperialism concordance.

But the only point we want to make here is that the convertibility matrix seems to be complete. It is hard to imagine any cell in Table 20.7 that would be empty in the sense that there could be no spill-over effects, no possibility of conversion. If everything can be bought for money, obtained by political control, or ordered by military imposition, then that alone would take care of the first three horizontal rows. Correspondingly, most authors would talk about economic, political, and military imperialism, but we have added the other two since they seem also to be primordial. Perhaps the first three will build up more slowly along the lines established by division of labor in communication and cultural organizations, but it is very easy to imagine scenarios as well as concrete historical examples.

The completeness of the convertibility matrix, more than anything else, would lead us to reject the assumption of one type of imperialism as more basic than the others. It is the mutual reinforcement, the positive feedback between these types rather than any simple reductionist causal chain, that seems the dominant characteristic. If economic, political, and military imperialism seem so dominant today, this may be an artifact due to our training that emphasizes these factors rather than communication and cultural factors. Belief in a simple causal chain is dangerous because it is accompanied by the belief that imperialism can be dispensed with forever if the primary element in the chain is abolished, e.g. private capitalism. The more general definition of imperialism presented here directs our search towards the two mechanisms as well as the particular criteria of exploitation within and between nations.

In order to talk about imperialism, not only economic inequality but also political, military, communication, and cultural inequality should be distributed in an inegalitarian way, with the periphery at the disadvantage. Are they? We think yes. The not-so-blatantly-unequal access to acquisite power, to some *political* power through voting, to some control over the *use of violence* (through political power, through civilian control of the military and through equality of opportunity as to access to ranking positions in the military), to *communication* (usually via access to acquisitive power, but also via denser, less feudal communication networks linking periphery outposts more directly together in Center nations), and to *cultural* goods (through widespread literacy and equality in access to education institutions)—all these are trademarks of what is referred to as a liberal democracy. And that form of socio-political life is found in the Center rather than the Periphery of the world.[28]

This leads to an important point in the theory of imperialism. *Instead of seeing democracy as a consequence or a condition for economic development within certain nations, it can (also) be seen as the condition for exercising effective control over Periphery nations.* Precisely because the Center is more egalitarian and democratic than the Periphery, there will be more people in the Center who feel they have a stake in the present state of affairs, since the fruits of imperialist structures are more equally shared on the top than on the bottom. And this will make it even less likely that the periphery in the Center will really join with the periphery in the Periphery against the two centers. Rather, like Dutch workers they will oppose the independence of Indonesia, and like US workers they will tend to become hardhats over the Indo-China issue.

It is now relatively clear what would be the perfect type of imperialism. In perfect imperialism, regardless of phase, we would assume all three criteria, both mechanisms, and all five types to be completely operative. This would mean complete harmony between the centers, with the elites in the Periphery nations almost undistinguishable from the elites in the Center nations where living conditions are concerned; much better distribution in the Center nations than in the Periphery nations; a perfectly vertical division of labor along all five types of exchange, and a perfectly feudal interaction network.

Where in the world, in space and/or in time, does one find this type of relation? The answer is perhaps not only in the colonial empires of the past, but also in the neo-colonial empires of the present using international organizations as their medium. To what extent it is true is an empirical question, and all the factors mentioned above can be operationalized. In other words, what is often called "positivist" methodology can be brought to bear on problems of structuralist or even marxist analyses. A crude and limited exercise in this direction will be given in the following section.

Suffice it here only to say that no system is perfect, and no system is a perfect copy of some ideal-type model. It may be that the neo-colonial empire United States had in Latin America in the 1950's and into the 1960's was a relatively perfect case,[29] and that this also applies to the relation between the EEC countries and the Associated States.[30] But it does not apply to the United States in Western Europe, nor to the Soviet Union in Eastern Europe to the Soviet Union in the Arab World or to Japan in Southeast Asia. This is not to deny that United States in Western Europe and Soviet Union in Eastern Europe are at the summit of military organizations that seem to satisfy all conditions, although the parallel is not entirely complete. But both of the super-powers are peripheral to the communication networks, their cultures are largely rejected in Western and Eastern Europe respectively, and where economic penetration is concerned there is a vertical division of labor in favor of the United States relative to Western Europe, but in favor of Eastern Europe (in general) relative to the Soviet Union—with Soviet Union as a provider of raw materials for, for instance, high level processing in the DDR. But it may then be argued that what the Soviet Union loses in economic ascendancy it compensates for in a political organization with strong feudal components.[31]

Similar arguments may be advanced in connection with the Soviet Union in the Arab World, and with Japan in Southeast Asia. Where the latter is concerned there is no doubt as to the economic imperialism, but there is neither political, nor military, no communication, nor cultural ascendancy.[32]

And this, then, leads to the final conclusion in this section. Imperialism is a question of degree, and if it is perfect it is a perfect instrument of structural violence. When it is less than perfect something must be substituted for what is lost in structural violence: direct violence, or at least the threat of direct violence. This is where the military type of imperialism becomes so important, since it can be seen as a potential to be activated when the other types of imperialism, particularly the economic and political types, show important cracks in the structure. This does not, incidentally, necessarily mean that direct violence only has to be applied in Periphery nations; it may also be directed against the periphery in Center nations if there is a danger of their siding with the periphery in the Periphery. The structural conditions for this would be that criterion no. 2 in the definition does not hold, in other words that there is not less, but possibly even more, inequality in the Center than in the Periphery.[33]

SOME EMPIRICAL EXPLORATIONS

The theory developed above is too complex in its empirical implications to be tested in its entirety. But some data can at least be given for economic imperialism, not because we view this as the basic type of imperialism, but because it is the type for which data are most readily available.

Everybody knows that there is the gap in GNP per capita, that there are rich nations and poor nations. From one point of view this gap poses a problem, the answer to which is in terms of *redistribution*. But from the structuralist point of view taken here the gap poses a problem that can only be answered in terms of *structural change*. It may be that redistribution can contribute to this change; but it may also be that it only serves to postpone the solution because symptoms rather than the disease itself is cured.

The claim, therefore, is that when some nations are rich and some nations are poor, when some nations are developed and some nations are under-developed, this is intimately related to the structure within and between nations. To explore this in line with the theory developed above we shall use the following seven variables:[34]

Development variables:	1. GNP/cap
	2. Percentage employed in non-primary sectors
Inequality variables:	3. Gini index, income distribution
	4. Gini index, land distribution
Vertical trade variable:	5. Trade composition index
Feudal trade variables:	6. Partner concentration index
	7. Commodity concentration index

The first two variables place the nation in the international ranking system using two types of development variables that are, of course, highly but not completely correlated. The next two variables, the Gini indices, say something about the internal structure of the nation, whereas the last three variables say something about the structure of the relations between them. Of these three, the first one relates to the first mechanism of imperialism and the other two to the second mechanism of imperialism. More precisely, the trade composition index is based on the following formula:

Trade composition index

$$\frac{(a + d) - (b + c)}{(a + d) + (b + c)}$$

where

a is value of raw materials imported
b is value of raw materials exported
c is value of processed goods imported
d is value of processed goods exported

There is no doubt that this index is a crude measure, among other reasons because the variable *degree of processing,* so crucial to the whole analysis, has here been dichotomized in "raw materials" vs. "processed goods" neglecting completely the problem of degree, *and* because the basis for dichotomization is the division made use of in UN trade statistics. However, despite its shortcomings it serves to sort nations apart. The highest ranking nation on this variable is Japan with an import consisting almost entirely of raw materials and an export consisting almost entirely of processed goods. Correspondingly, at the bottom according to this index are the nations that export raw materials, and import processed goods only; but the relative position of several countries in between may certainly be disputed.

As to the last two variables, they are simply the ratios between the proportion of the export going to the *one* most important partner, or consisting of the *three* most important commodities relative to the total export, respectively.[35]

According to our general theory we should now expect some countries to be developed and to be on top of the vertical trade index but low in terms of inequality and position on the feudal trade index—whereas other countries would be undeveloped and low on the vertical trade index but on the other hand high in terms of inequality and position of the feudal trade index. The correlation structure should be something like Fig. 20.3 where the solid lines indicate positive relations and the broken lines negative relations, and the numbers in parentheses are the numbers of indicators for each dimension.

Figure 20.3 The correlation pattern according to the imperialism hypothesis.

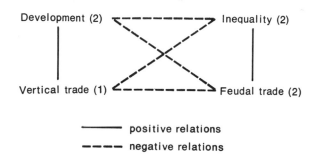

Thus, of the twenty-one bivariate correlations we predict six positive and twelve negative correlations. In addition there are the three correlations between indicators of the same dimension: we expect them to be positive, but not too positive since that would reduce the usefulness for independent testing of the hypotheses.

Because of the grave doubts as to the validity and reliability of all variables we decided to dichotomize them, either at the point where there is a "natural" cut (a large interval between one country and the next) or at the median cut. The correlation coefficient used was Yule's Q, and the results were as shown in Table 20.8. All correlations are in the expected direction, most of them rather substantial. There are only three low correlations, and two of them are between indicators of the same dimension. Hence we regard the hypothesis as very well confirmed.

Of course, this is only a test of a theory along the edges of that theory; it does not in itself prove that the system is in fact working as described above. But if these findings had not come out so strongly as they do, we would have been forced to conclude that the imperialist model cannot possibly be a good model of the world system today. Hence, as a test of the hypotheses the findings provide

Table 20.8   A Test of the Hypothesis of Economic Imperialism (Yule's Q)

	1	2	3	4	5	6	7
1. GNP/cap		0.79	−0.90	−0.80	0.89	−0.52	−0.89
2. Percent non-primary			−1.00	−0.83	0.77	−0.72	−0.87
3. Gini income				0.20	−0.83	0.80	0.86
4. Gini land					−0.95	0.21	0.85
5. Trade composition						−0.69	−0.97
6. Partner concentration							0.35
7. Commodity concentration							

positive confirmation, but as a test of a theory only the negative support that a theory would have to be rejected if the findings had been in the opposite direction.[36]

We should also add that the theory in itself is so rich in implications that it provides ample basis for empirical research, within liberal and marxist schools of thought, and employing synchronic statistical methods as well as diachronic case studies. It would be sad if ideological and other types of conflicts between adherents of different schools should lead to any systematic neglect as to mobilizing general social science for a deeper understanding of how this system works.

FURTHER THEORETICAL EXPLORATIONS

Let us then make use of the results of the theoretical and empirical explorations to go somewhat more deeply into four problems.

Defining "Center" and "Periphery"

We are now in a better position to define our basic terms, "center" and "periphery," whether they refer to relations between or within nations.[37] Actually, implicit in what has been said above are three approaches when it comes to defining these terms:

(1) in terms of *absolute properties* (e.g. development variables): center is high on rank dimensions, periphery is low

(2) in terms of *interaction relation* (e.g. trade composition index): center enriches itself more than the periphery

(3) in terms of *interaction structure* (e.g. partner and commodity concentration index): center is more centrally located in the interaction network than the periphery—the periphery being higher on the concentration indexes.

Empirically it may not matter that much which of these three dimensions is used to define center and periphery, since Table 20.8 shows them highly correlated—at least today. According to one type of theory this is because (1) above is primordial, basic: the richer, more educated, stronger nation (individual) is able to place itself in the world structure (social structure) so that it can be on top of a vertical interaction relation and in the center of a feudal interaction structure.

According to another type of theory (2) and (3) are basic: if an individual or nation is able to place itself on top of a vertical relation, and possibly, in addition, in the center of a feudal interaction structure, it will also be able to climb higher on the dimensions on which nations (individuals) climb—whatever they might be.

We find it difficult to be dogmatic about these two theories. Rather, they seem to complement each other. One nation (individual) may have gotten an edge over another in one way or another, and been able to convert that into an advantageous interaction position, as the Europeans did after the Great Discoveries. Or—it may have come into an advantageous interaction position by some lucky circumstance, e.g. in a communication network—and been able to convert this into some absolute value for itself, and so on.

In general, we think there are reasons to say that the relative significance of the three *aspects* of the center-periphery distinction varies with time and space, with historical and geographical circumstances. For that reason we would prefer to view them precisely as three different *aspects* of that distinction. Thus, we define center vs. periphery as nations (individuals) that satisfy (1) *or* (2) *or* (3); "or" taken in the usual sense of and/or. This may lead to confusion, but since both theories above would lead to the same conclusion we do not worry so much about that. Rather, the definition should be accompanied with a warning to the analyst: he should always be sensitive to possible cases of divergence, that a nation (individual) may be in the center relative to one aspect and in the periphery relative to another, and so on. That this in itself would provide rich sources for theories about dynamism, about how a center position of one kind can be converted into a center position of the other kind, is obvious. And in that connection the second aspect, the relation itself, may perhaps be more basic, since it provides, through accumulation, a constant flow of resources towards the center. The advantage of this aspect is that it is so *concrete*. According to this aspect the sorting into center and periphery is not only an operation carried out by the analyst, it takes place, *in concreto*, in the interaction process itself. The two actors "sort" themselves away from each other by participating in vertical interaction, and become increasingly unequal in the process.[38]

Generalization to Three Nations and Three Classes

So far we have operated with a simple scheme involving two nations and two classes; time has now come to break out of that limitation. Here we shall only offer some remarks in that connection, not carry the analysis through in detail.

Thus, the introduction of a middle class between the center and the periphery would be entirely consistent with thinking in most social science schools. Whether the center is defined in terms of economic, political, military, communication, or cultural interaction, a strict dichotomy between center and periphery will often be too crude. The alternative to a dichotomy may be a continuum, but on the way towards that type of thinking a trichotomy may also be useful. Strict social dichotomies are usually difficult to obtain unless hedged around by means of highly visible and consensual racial, ethnic, or geographical distinctions. A country composed of three races may therefore provide a stable three-class structure; if there is only one race, the continuous model may be more useful.

However, it is difficult to see that this should significantly affect our theory.

Whether there are two or three classes or a continuum from extreme center to extreme periphery does not invalidate descriptions of the nation in terms of averages (such as GNP/capita) and dispersions (such as Gini indices). Nor will it invalidate the comparisons between the nations in such terms. In fact, there is nothing in this theory that presupposes a dichotomous class structure since the theory is not based on a dichotomy like owner vs. non-owner of means of production.

More interesting results can be obtained by interspersing a third nation between the Center and Periphery nations. Such a nations could, in fact, serve as a go-between. Concretely, it would exchange semi-processed goods with highly processed goods upwards and semi-processed goods with raw materials downwards. It would simply be located in between Center and Periphery where the degree of processing of its export products is concerned. Moreover, such go-between nations would serve as an intermediate layer between the extreme Center and the extreme Periphery in a feudal interaction structure. And needless to say: the intra-national centers of all three nations would be tied together in the same international network, establishing firm ties of harmony of interest between them.

Table 20.9   Some Hypotheses about Go-between Relations

Center	Go-Between	Periphery
USA	Western Europe	Eastern Europe
USA	Canada	Anglo-America (Trinidad, etc.)
USA	Mexico Argentina Brazil	Central America
USA	Japan	Southeast Asia
Japan	South Korea Taiwan	Southeast Asia (and North America)
Western Europe	Eastern Europe	Soviet Union

In another version of the same conception the go-between nation would be one cycle behind the Center as to technology but one cycle ahead of the Periphery; in line with its position as to degree of processing.[39] This would also apply to the means of destruction and the means of communication.

If the United States is seen as *the* Center nation in the world (with Japan as an extremely dangerous competitor precisely in terms of degree of processing), then several such chains of nations suggest themselves, as shown in Table 20.9.

Just as for the generalization to three classes this could also be generalized to a continuous chain which would then serve to make for considerable distance between the extreme Center and the extreme Periphery.

Generalizations to More Than One Empire

So far all our thinking has been within one empire, except for passing references to countries outside the empire that the Periphery is prevented from interacting with. But the world consists of more than one empire, and any realistic theory should see an empire in its context—especially since direct violence is to relations between empires what structural violence is within empires.

Clearly, relations between empires are above all relations between the centers of the Centers; these relations can be negative, neutral, or positive. Two capitalistic empires may be in competition, but they may also sub-divide the world between them into spheres of interest so perfectly that the relations become more neutral. In this first phase one empire may fight to protect itself in the competition with another capitalist empire, but in a second phase they may join forces and more or less merge to protect not this or that particular capitalist empire, but the system of capitalism as such. And we could also easily imagine a third phase where non-capitalist empires join with capitalist empires in the pattern of "united imperialism," for the protection of imperialism as such.

All this is extremely important from the viewpoint of the Periphery nations. A world with more empires, which above all means a world with more Center nations, is at least potentially a world with more possibilities. To explore this in more detail, let us assume that we have Center and Periphery nations, vertically related to each other. For each type of nation there are three cases: one nation alone, two nations either very low on interaction or hostile to each other, and two nations in so friendly cooperation as to constitute one actor. The result is shown in Fig. 20.4, which permits us to recognize many and politically very important situations (the arrows in Fig. 20.4 stand for relations of vertical interaction).

Here, situation *a, b,* and *c* take place within one empire and lead to a situation

Figure 20.4 Possible relations in a multi-empire world.

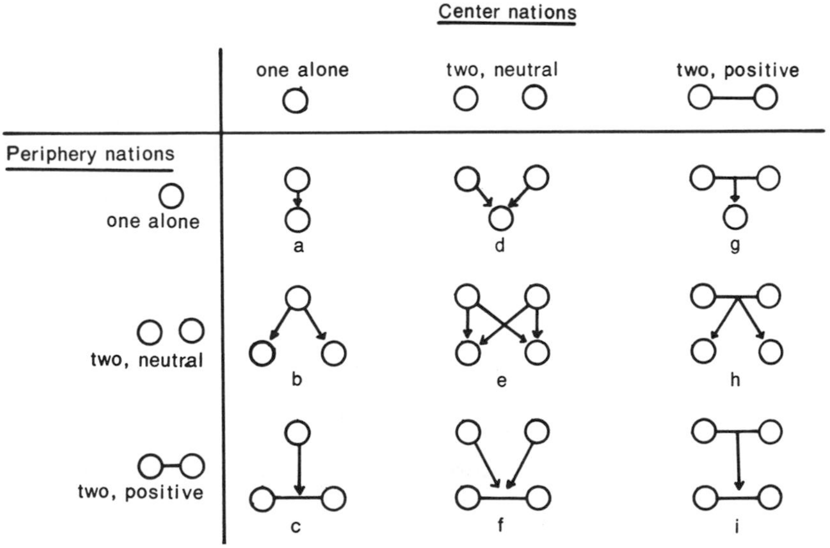

with a certain element of defeudalization: horizontal interaction has been established between the two Periphery nations.

In situations *d, e,* and *f* Periphery nations are able to interact with more than one Center nation, possibly even play one against the other because of their hostile relationship. In this situation the Periphery will have a vested interest in protracting the Center conflict, and may even join forces (model *f*) to make optimum gains from the conflict.

In situations *g, h,* and *i* it is the Center side that cooperates, for instance by establishing a "consortium" whereby several rich nations join together to help one or more poor nations, singly or combined.[40]

Importantly, none of these strategies will lead to any changes in the vertical interaction *relation,* only to some changes in the feudal interaction *structure.* As such they attack only one aspect of imperialism, not the other, possibly more important aspect. And if we look more closely at model *i,* this is nothing but model *a* writ large, as when EEC rather than France alone stands in a relationship of vertical interaction with 18 Associated States rather than with one of them alone. It is difficult to see that imperialistic relationships become less imperialistic by being established between super-Center and a super-Periphery rather than between the original Center and Periphery nations (we should add that *h* rather than *i* is a more correct model of the relationship between EEC and the Associated States).

This factor notwithstanding, there is no reason to deny that a multi-empire world not only creates more bargaining possibilities, but also is a more realistic model of the world in which mankind lives—at present.

Generalization to Non-Territorial Actors

We have defined non-territorial actors above, in Table 20.5, phases 3, 4, and 5—where phases 3 and 4 refer to multi-national or inter-national non-territorial actors and phase 5 to transnational actors. These are collectivities, they consist of human beings, they have more often than not a vertical division of labor within, and there is little reason why they should not also often have vertical division of labor between and be chained together in imperialistic relationships. Thus, there may be a division of labor between governmental and non-governmental international organizations, with the more far-reaching decisions taken by the former and some of the implementations carried out by the latter. For this system to function well, the governmental organizations will have to harmonize the policy-making centers of the non-governmental organizations with themselves, and one concrete way of doing this would be to have a member on the Council or Executive Committee. This article is not the occasion to spell this point out in any detail or with empirical examples, but we should point out that imperialism as a structure is not at all tied to territorial actors alone.[41]

CONCLUSION: SOME STRATEGIC IMPLICATIONS

From a general scheme, we cannot arrive at more than general policy implications that can serve as guide-lines, as strategies. More concreteness is needed to arrive at the first tactical steps. But theory developed in peace research should lead to such guide-lines; if it merely reflects what is empirical, not what is potential, then it is not good theory.

Our point of departure is once more that the world is divided into have's and have-not's, in have and have-not nations. To decrease the gap, one aspect of the fight against structural violence, redistribution by taking from the have's and giving to the have-not's is not enough: the structure has to be changed.[42] The imperialist structure has inter-national as well as intra-national aspects and will consequently have to be changed at both levels. . . .

NOTES AND REFERENCES

1. For an exploration of this concept, see J. Galtung: Violence, Peace and Peace Research, *Journal of Peace Research*, 6 (1969): 167–91.

2. This equality premise may be formulated in terms of distribution, or redistribution, of values generated by the society in liberal theory, or as absence of exploitation in marxist theory. The two approaches have in common the idea that a party may have an interest even if it does not proclaim that it has this interest, but whereas the liberal approach will keep the social structure but carry out some redistribution along the road, the marxist approach will change the social structure itself. In both cases one may actually also make a further distinction as to whether harmony is to be obtained by equalization of what the society produces of material and spiritual value, or equalization when it comes to the power to decide over what the society produces. But imperialism as a structure cuts across these distinctions and is, in our view, based on a more general concept of harmony and disharmony of interests.

3. No attempt will be made here to explore similarities and dissimilarities between this definition of imperialism and that given by such authors as Hobson, Luxemburg, Lenin, Hilferding and very many others. This definition has grown out of a certain research tradition, partly inductively from a long set of findings about international interaction structures, and partly deductively from speculations relating to structural violence in general and the theory of inequality in particular.

4. Particularly one aspect of Lenin's conception of imperialism has been picked up in our definition: the general idea of a labor aristocracy. Lenin quotes Engels when he says that "—quand aux ouvriers, ils jouissent en toute tranquillité avec eux de monopole colonial, de l'Angleterre et de son monopole sur le marché mondial". (*L'imperialisme: Stade supreme de Capitalisme* (Moscow, 1969), p. 139.)—The same idea is expressed by L. S. Senghor: "les prolétaires d'Europe ont bénéficié du régime colonial; partant, ils ne s'y sont jamais réellement, je veux dire efficacement, opposés". (*Nation et voie africaine du socialisme,* p. 51.) And T. Hopkins in Third World Modernization in Transnational Perspective (*The Annals,* 1969, pp. 126–36) picks up the other angle of this: ". . . there are strong indications that in most Third World Countries, internal inequality in increasing. The educated are markedly more advantaged; urban workers are relatively well-off; unemployment is high and increasing; rural population are poor".

5. Thus, international statistics should not be given only for national aggregates since this conceals the true nature of the relations in the world. It would be much more useful if statistics were given for the four groups defined in our definition. In general we would assume such statistics over time to show that cC and cP grow most quickly and more or less together, then follows pC and at the bottom is pP that is not only located much below the other two, but also shows very little growth or none at all. The more numerous the group, the lower the growth: it is the accumulated work from these vast masses that permits the growth of the dominating minorities. One highly stimulating analysis in this direction is given by Th. E. Weisskopf who tries to disaggregate the growth rates and is led to the conclusion that the growth in the developing countries has taken place in the upper and middle strata of the population, in the secondary sector of economic production, and in the urban areas. The growth rates in these parts of the developing nations are not too different from growth rates in corresponding parts in developed nations, but due to the absence of mechanisms for redistribution this leaves the vast periphery of the developing nations with close to zero or

even negative growth. T. E. Weisskopf: Underdevelopment, Capitalistic Growth and the Future of the Poor Countries, World Order Models Project, 1970.

6. This argument is carried much further for the case of interindividual rather than international interaction in J. Galtung: Structural Pluralism and the Future of Human Interaction, paper presented at the Second International Future Research Conference, Kyoto, April 1970, and J. Galtung: Perspectives on Development: Past, Present and Future, paper presented at the International Sociological Association Conference, Varna, September 1970.

7. The basic point here is that a demand generates a chain of demands. Economists have made some estimates in this connection. For instance, H. B. Chenery and T. Watanabe conclude, "In the four industrial countries studied here (United States, Japan, Norway, and Italy), between 40% and 50% of total domestic demands for goods and services comes from other productive sectors rather than from final users" (International Comparisons of the Structure of Production, *Econometrica,* 1958, p. 504). The more connected the economy of a country, the more will demand proliferate. Other social scientists should have tools corresponding to the input-output analyses of the economists in order to study the degree of connectedness of a society. Characteristic of a traditional society is precisely the low level of connectedness: the spread effect into other branches of economic activity and into other districts is much lower.—Also see F. Stirton-Weaver: Backwash, Spread and the Chilean State, *Studies in Comparative International Development,* 5, no. 12, and A. O. Hirschman: *The Strategy of Economic Development* (New Haven: Yale University Press, 1958), especially his discussion of backward and forward linkages (pp. 100–119).

8. It is this equality that we stipulate to be in the interest of both parties, both for the exploiter and the exploited. Obviously, there are two approaches: the interaction structure can be changed so that the inter- and intra-actor effects are equal and/or redistribution can take place. But if this interaction structure has been in operation for a long time and has already generated considerable differences in living conditions then both methods may have to be used, a point to be further elaborated in section 10 below. For highly stimulating discussions of unequal exchange, see P. G. Casanova: *Sociologia de la Explotación* (Mexico: Siglo Veintiuno, 1969); and Arghiri Emmanuel: *L'exchange inégal* (Paris: Maspero, 1969).

9. What we have in mind here, concretely, is of course all the various forms of development assistance based on the idea that grants are given to poor countries on the condition that they use them to procure capital goods in developed countries. In an excellent article, "Prospectives for the Third World", S. Sideri summarizes much of the literature showing how well development assistance pays. However, these analyses are by no means complete since only some aspects of the economic spin-off effects are considered, not all the others that may also, incidentally, be convertible into economic effects, at least in the long run.

10. For an analysis of social status systems using feudal interaction as the basic concept, see J. Galtung: Feudal Systems, Structural Violence and the Structural Theory of Revolutions, *in Proceedings of the IPRA Third General Conference,* pp. 110–188 (Van Gorcum, Assen, 1970).

11. For a penetrating analysis of the relation between dependency and development, see F. H. Cardoso & E. Faletto: *Dependencia y desarrollo en America Latina* (Mexico: Siglo Veinnuno, 1969). One important difference between that book and the present analysis lies in the warning the authors give against generalization beyond the concrete case. While sympathetic to this, we nevertheless feel there is considerable virtue in general theory, as a baseline for understanding the concrete case.

Another basic analysis of this type of relationship is, of course, A. G. Frank: *Capitalism and Underdevelopment in Latin America* (N.Y.: Monthly Review Press, 1967). The basic key to Frank's analysis is the structure that "extends from the macrometropolitan system center of the world capitalist system 'down' to the most supposedly isolated agricultural workers, who, through this chain of interlinked metropolitan-satellite relationships, are tied to the central world metropolis and thereby incorporated into the world capitalist system as a whole" (p. 16), and he goes on (p. 17) to talk about "the exploitation of the satellite by the metropolis or—the tendency of the metropolis to expropriate and appropriate the economic surplus of the satellite". All this is valid as general formulas, but too little emphasis is given to the type of exploitation referred to here as "asymmetric distribution of spin-offs" and the special organization referred to as "feudal interaction structure". And economists with no

Marxist inclination at all are certainly not helpful when it comes to reflecting imperialistic types of relations. Thus, in Jan Tinbergen, *The Design of Development* (Baltimore: Johns Hopkins, 1966), development is discussed throughout the book as if the government in a developing country is free to make its decisions. And in T. Haavelmo, *A Study in the Theory of Economic Evolution* (Amsterdam: North-Holland Publishing Company, 1954) it is difficult to see that any theory at all based on *relations* between nations is offered to explain the tremendous disparities in this world; just to mention two examples. And even Myrdal's *Asian Drama* has little to say on international relations, as pointed out by Lars Rudebeck in an excellent review article (*Cooperation and Conflict* 1969, pp. 267–81).

12. One book that gives a fairly balanced account of Soviet dominance patterns is *The New Imperialism* by Hugh Seton-Watson (N.Y.: Capricorn Books, 1961). Andre Amalrik's analysis *Will the Soviet Union Survive Until 1984* (N.Y.: Harper & Row, 1970) also deserves reading, not so much for its apocalyptic scenario as for its penetrating analysis of the internal dominance system. The question of whether the total Soviet system should be referred to as imperialism remains open, however, among other reasons because the Soviet Union does not enjoy spin-offs from processing of raw materials and because the internal inequality is hardly lower than in dependent countries. But the elite harmonization criterion will probably hold to a large extent mediated through the cooperation between party elites.—Comparative studies of imperialistic structures, in the tradition of Helio Jaguaribe, comparing different types of empires in this century as well as long-time historical comparisons bringing in, for instance, the Roman Empire, would be highly useful to shed more light over this particular international structure. At present this type of exercise is hampered by the tendency to use "imperialism" as an abusive term, as a category to describe the other camp. We have preferred to see it as a technical term, which does not mean that he who struggles for peace will not have to struggle against imperialism regardless of what shape it takes.

13. For an analysis of international air communication, see N. P. Gleditsch: "Trends in World Airline Patterns," *Journal of Peace Research* (1967): 366–408.

14. For an analysis of the role of the international press agencies, see E. Østgaard; Factors Influencing the Flow of News, *Journal of Peace Research,* 2: 39–63.

15. For an analysis of this, see J. Galtung & M. H. Ruge: The Structure of Foreign News: The Presentation of the Congo, Cuba and Cyprus Crises in Four Norwegian Newspapers, *Journal of Peace Research,* 2: 64–91.

16. For an analysis of this, see J. Galtung: After Camelot, in Horowitz, I. L. (ed.): *The Rise and Fall of Project Camelot* (Cambridge, Mass.: M. I. T. Press, 1967).

17. As one example, and a very explicit one, may serve the following quotation: . . . "can we discharge our responsibility in God and to man for so magnificent, so populous a proportion of the world?—Our answer is off hand ready and simple. We are adequate. We do discharge our responsibilities. We are a conquering and imperial race. All over the world we have displayed our mettle. We have discovered and annexed and governed vast territories. We have encircled the globe with our commerce. We have penetrated the pagan races with our missionaries. We have innoculated the Universe (sic!) with our institutions. We are apt indeed to believe that our soldiers are braver, our sailors hardier, our captains, naval and military skilfuller, our statesmen wiser than those of other nations. As for our constitution, there is no Briton at any hour of the day or night who will suffer it to be said that any approaches it." From Lord Boseberry; Questors of Empire 1900, *in Miscellanies, Literary and Historical, vol. II* (London: Hodder & Stoughton, 1921). I am indebted to Fiona Rudd for this remarkable reference.

18. This is extremely clearly expressed in Report of a US Presidential Mission to the Western Hemisphere (The Rockefeller report): . . . "Just as the other American republics depend upon the United States for their capital equipment requirements, so the United States depends on them to provide a vast market for our manufactured goods. And as these countries look to the United States for a market for their primary products whose sale enables them to buy equipment for their development at home, so the United States looks to them for raw materials for our industries, on which depend the jobs of many of our citizens. . . ." (Quality of Life in the Americas, Agency for International Development, August 1969, pp. 5–113.)—The paragraph is as if taken out of a textbook on imperialism, emphasizing how the Center countries provide capital equipment and manufactured goods, and the Periphery countries raw materials and markets. The only interesting thing about the quotation is that it is still possible to write like this in 1969.

19. One example is the Brezhnev Doctrine: "Speaking in Warsaw on November 12, 1968 to the V Congress of the Polish United Workers Party Brezhnev emphasized the need for 'strict respect' for sovereignty of other socialist countries, and added: 'But when internal and external forces that are hostile to Socialism try to turn the development of some socialist country towards the restoration of a capitalist regime, when socialism in that country and the socialist community as a whole is threatened, it becomes not only a problem of the people of the country concerned, but a common problem and concern of all Socialist countries. Naturally an action such as military assistance to a fraternal country designed to avert the threat to the social system is an extraordinary step, dictated by necessity.' Such a step, he added, 'may be taken only in case of direct actions of the enemies of Socialism within a country and outside it, actions threatening the common interests of the Socialist camp.' " (*Keesing's Contemporary Archives*, 1968, p. 23027.) Its similarity to the Monroe doctrine has often been pointed out, but there is the difference that the US sometimes seems to be acting as if they had a Monroe doctrine for the whole world.

Without implying that the following is official Soviet policy, it has nevertheless appeared in *International Affairs* (April, 1970): "The socialist countries, united in the Warsaw Treaty Organization, are profoundly aware that the most reliable guarantee that their security will be preserved and strengthened is all round cooperation with the Soviet Union, including military cooperation. They firmly reject any type of anti-Soviet slander and resist attempts by imperialism and the remnants of domestic reaction to inject into the minds of their people any elements of anti-Sovietism, whether open or veiled.

With the two worlds—socialist and capitalist—in global confrontation, any breach of internationalist principles, any sign of nationalism, and especially any toleration, not to say use, of anti-Sovietism in policy turns those who pursue such policies into an instrument of imperialist strategy and policy, regardless of whether their revisionist slogan is given a Right or ultra-Left twist, regardless of the subjective intentions of the advocates and initiators of the course. And whether it is very big or very small, it remains nothing but an instrument in the hands of imperialism and in either case retains its ignominious essence, which is incompatible with truly revolutionary socialist consciousness". (V. Razmerov: Loyalty of Proletarian Internationalism—Fundamental Condition for Success of All Revolutionary Forces).—What this quotation says is in fact that not only hostile deeds, but also all hostile worlds are to be ruled out. It is also interesting to note that the types of attitudes that are not to be expressed are referred to as "anti-Soviet." In other words, the reference is to the Center country in the system not even to the masses of that country, nor to anti-socialism.

20. In general, international contacts between ministries seem to become increasingly transnational. Where the minister of defense in country A some time ago would have to use a channel of communication involving at least one embassy and one ministry of foreign affairs to reach his opposite number in country B direct telecommunication would now be the adequate channel. What this means in terms of cutting our filtering effects and red tape is obvious. It also means that trans-national ties may be strengthened and some times be posted against the nation state. Obviously, this system will be expanding, for instance with a system of telesatellites available for telecommunication between Center and Periphery countries with a bloc. For the Francophone countries the projected satellite Symphonie may perhaps, be seen as a step in this direction. Although it is targeted on audiences rather than concrete, specific persons. The NATO satellite communication system is another example.

21. Very important in this connection is, of course, the quick development of the telephone concept from essentially bilateral (one person talks with one other person, possibly with some others listening in at either end, or in the middle!) towards the telephone as a multilateral means of communications. Bell Telephone Company can now organize conferences over the telephone by connecting a number of subscribers. Obviously, if combined with a video-screen the conversation may be more orderly because participants may also react on non-verbal, visual cues such as facial expressions, etc. More particularly, they may raise a finger and ask for the "floor."

22. The battle between the two types of imperialism is perhaps more important in the imagination of those who try to uphold one of the types than in social reality. Thus, what happened in the Dominican Republic in 1965 was interpreted by those who are upholding a pattern of economic imperialism as an attempt by "the other bloc" to establish political imperialism; just as the events in Czechoslovakia in 1968 were interpreted by the servants of

political military imperialism as an effort by "the other bloc" to introduce economic imperialism. Whatever history's judgement may be in terms of these two hypotheses it is obvious that two types of imperialism, directed from antagonistic blocs, cannot at the same time be in the same phase. One pattern would be that the dominant type is in phase 3 and the competitive type is in phase 1—and that is what was claimed by the Center countries in the two cases.

23. The best analysis we have read of division of labor in multinational corporations is by Stephen Hymer. (The Multi-national Corporation and the Law of Uneven Development—to appear in J. N. Bhagwati, (ed.): *Economics and World Order* (N.Y.: World Law Fund, 1970.)

24. This is not a random event: international organizations are in that phase because they reflect the relationships between national actors, that in the present stage of development are the major carriers of these relations.

25. Thus, when Stalin died in 1953 there must have been great expectation in China that Mao Tsetung would be the next head of the international Communist movement. His revolution was more recent, the country in which the revolution had taken place was by far the biggest, and he was also older as a revolutionary fighter in a leading position than possible competitors. Nevertheless, it was quite clear that the Soviet conception was that the leader of the international Communist movement would have to be the leader of what they interpreted as the leading Communist nation: the Soviet Union herself.

26. This is a major difference between liberal and structuralist peace theory. It is hardly unfair to interpret liberal peace theory as somehow stating that "peace" is roughly proportionate to the volume of trade, possibly interpreted as an indicator of the level of interdependence, whereas structural peace theory would bring in the factor of equality and ask for the composition as well as the volume of trade. If structural theory is more correct and if the present world trade structure is such that only the Center nations can enjoy both high level of interdependence and high level in equality in exchange, then "peace" is one extra benefit that will accrue to the Center layer of the world.

27. Another concept would be the frequently quoted saying that "technical assistance is taken from the poor man in the rich country and given to the rich man in the poor country". The model of the world implied by the dominance theory would certainly not contradict this quite elegant statement: technical assistance is to a large extent paid for by tax-payers' money, not to mention by the surplus produced by the masses working in the rich countries, and given via public channels for investment in infrastructures in poor countries, often for the benefit of the layers in the poor countries that have a consumption structure compatible with a production structure that the rich countries can offer.

28. J. Galtung: International Relations and International Conflicts: A Sociological Approach, *Transactions of the Sixth World Congress of Sociology* (International Sociological Association, 1966), pp. 121–61.

29. Eg. H. Magdoff: *The Age of Imperialism* (N.Y.: Monthly Review, 1969).

30. Research on this is currently in progress at the International Peace Research Institute, Oslo.

31. But it is still an open question whether this should really be referred to as imperialism, since so many of the criteria do not seem to be fulfilled. Once more this seems to bring up the importance of seeing imperialism as a special case of a wider set of social relationships, conveniently lumped together under the heading "domination".

32. Relations between Soviet Union and the Arab World and Japan and Southeast Asia are being explored at the International Peace Research Institute, Oslo by Tormod Nyberg and Johan Galtung respectively.

33. This type of structural reasoning seems particularly important in the Soviet case. It can hardly be claimed that the Soviet periphery participates more in the decision-making made by the Soviet center than the Czech periphery participated in the decision-making made by the Czech center in the months prior to the invasion in August 1968. On the contrary, the opposite hypothesis seems more tenable. And if this is the case the Soviet center could no longer necessarily count on the allegiance of its own periphery, particularly not on the Ukrainian periphery, bordering Czechoslovakia not only geographically, but also linguistically and culturally (and apparently listening attentively to broadcasts). This means that what happened in Czechoslovakia became a threat to the Soviet center, perhaps more than to the Soviet Union as a Center nation.

34. See Appendix [found in the original article] for data for 60 nations on these seven variables (but missing for most of the nations for Gini i, and for many of the nations for Gini 1). The trade composition index was developed by Knut Hongrø after some suggestions by the present author. It may, however, be that the index $\dfrac{(a + d) - (b - c)}{(a + d) + (b + c)}$ would be better, since values of trade are usually added, not multiplied, and since this would attain the value 1 not when b *or* c equals 0, but when b *and* c equals 0. (J. Galtung: Vertical and Horizontal Trade Relation: A Note on Operationalization, WOMP 1970).

35. References are given in the Appendix [found in the original article].

36. In this connection it should be pointed out that the theory of imperialism would not be disconfirmed if these correlation coefficients had been much lower. It is only the theory as a model for the concrete empirical world here and now that would have been disconfirmed, not imperialism as one factor in systems of collectivities, and particularly as a factor that together with other factors may rise to the constellation known in the present world. What Table 20.8 seems to indicate is that the theory of imperialism as presented here is not a bad map for orientation in the contemporary world.

37. For one exposition of the center-periphery theory for individuals see J. Galtung: Foreign Policy Opinion as a Function of Social Position, *Journal of Peace Research,* 1 (1964): 206–31.

38. This, of course, would also be true inter-individually: division of labor may be organized in such a way that it is personality expanding for some actors and personality contracting for others so that they "sort" themselves away from each other by participating in this type of vertical interaction.

39. See the article by Stephen Hymer referred to in footnote 23 above.

40. We are thinking particularly of the Pakistan consortium and the India consortium.

41. Thus, center-periphery theory in connection with nonterritorial actors should perhaps not be stated so much in terms of size or age of organizations, as in terms of whether they are able to establish bridgeheads in other non-territorial actors, and whether they are able to organize systematically some vertical type of division of labor. Thus, the system of "consultative status" clearly indicates who to be consulted.

42. It should be pointed out that no strategy seems to exist for reducing the gap. There is not even any strategy for reducing the increase of the gap, the only strategy that perhaps may be said to exist is a strategy for improving the level of poor nations. A strategy for reducing the gap does not necessarily imply a basic change of the structure of the relations between rich and poor nations, however. It might also come about by reducing significantly the growth in the rich nations.

21 Theories of Dependency: The View from the Periphery

RONALD H. CHILCOTE *

THEORETICAL DIRECTIONS

The literature on dependency moves in many directions and criticisms emerge from a variety of ideological positions. Clearly dependency theory is eclectic in nature. Some dependency theorists focus on assumptions about a progressive bourgeoisie whose nationalist inclinations serve as a foundation for opposing outside influence. Some critics oppose dependency theory on the grounds that it focuses on external dependency and thereby avoids consideration of internal class struggle. Others argue that the theory obscures analysis of imperialism.

In all the writings of dependency only two offer a synthesis of the many directions and positions. Fernando Henrique Cardoso provides the most recent of these.[1] He finds the foundation for the concept in the writings of Lenin and Trotsky, then attempts to relate these classical formulations to the literature of the past decade. He notes three tendencies in the recent literature. One concentrates on analysis which critiques the obstacles to national development, a good example being the publications of the Instituto Superior de Estudos Brasileiros (ISEB), established in the middle fifties to study and introduce to Brazilian society a new conception of nationalism and development. Helio Jaguaribe, a founder of ISEB, has carried this tradition forward in his view that Latin America faces three alternatives: dependency, autonomy or revolution.[2] Dependency will be overcome, he argues, through autonomous national development and non-revolutionary change. This view of development falls into the diffusion model; it has been criticized by Frank,[3] Theotônio dos Santos,[4] and Cardoso.[5] A second tendency incorporates analysis on international capitalism in its monopolistic phase. The thrust of this tendency springs from Marx and Lenin, especially the latter. Refinements and elaboration of the early ideas were offered by Paul Baran and Paul Sweezy;[6] and Harry Magdoff[7] effectively ties theory to fact in contemporary world affairs. A raging debate from differing perspectives is found in recent issues of *Socialist Revolution;* particularly noteworthy are the views of Robert Fitch who is critical of Baran and Sweezy's corporate model. The

*Ronald H. Chilcote, "Dependency: A Critical Synthesis of the Literature," *Latin American Perspectives*, I, no. 1 (Spring 1974): 4–29. This selection has been edited to about half its length. For case studies and an extensive bibliography, see the original source. Reprinted by permission of author and publisher.

third tendency identified by Cardoso attempts to describe "a historical structural process of dependency in terms of class relations, tying the economy and International politics to corresponding local factors which in turn generate internal contradictions and political struggle . . ." Cardoso's own contributions fall into this tendency.

Claire Savit Bacha has contributed the other synthesis of the literature ın a study that embraces theory and relates to the Brazilian experience.[8] She examines five conceptions of dependency as elaborated in the writings of Vasconi, Lenin, Frank, Dos Santos, and Cardoso. Let us briefly examine each conceptualization.

Bacha describes the effort by Tomás Vasconi[9] as oriented to a "systematization of the concept of dependency." Vasconi's conceptualization of dependency relates to distinctions between underdevelopment and development, on the one hand, and between the center and the periphery, on the other. Dependency, he argues, permits one to see the center and the periphery as parts of a capitalist structure, this structure being a system of relations of international interdependence. Accordingly, a central economy expands as it reaches the peripheral economy, incorporating it within that system. Vasconi then suggests a number of propositions. First, dependent nations may or may not develop, but the process of development can lead to a rupture in the ties of dependence. Second, dependency is determined historically. Third, dependency includes all internal and external forces that historically affect a nation, forming its structures relation to its historical and international position. Vasconi elaborates. During the development of capitalism, he says, dependent nations are isolated from the center. These peripheral nations remain dependent until they break their dependent relations, but in either case they may or may not experience development. Changes in dependent relationships, however, are tied to historical forces.

Another major conceptualization of dependency is closely tied to imperialism. Both concepts deal with relations between the center and the periphery and both explain underdevelopment. Drawing upon Hobson and others, Lenin refined the concept of imperialism as the consequence of capitalism itself. Monopoly capital, he argued, needed to export its surplus of capital, to search for new external markets, and to expand profit-making opportunities. Lenin identified two types of nations: imperialist and dominated nations and he referred in his work to the concept of dependency:

> Since we are speaking of colonial policy in the epoch of capitalist imperialism, it must be observed that finance capital and its foreign policy, which is the struggle of the great powers for the economic and political division of the world, give rise to a number of *transitional* forms of state dependence. Not only are there two main groups of countries, those owning colonies, and the colonies themselves, but also the diverse forms of dependent countries which, politically, are formally independent, but in fact, are enmeshed in the net of financial and diplomatic dependency . . .[10]

Thus, dependentistas can turn to Lenin for the theoretical underpinnings of their argument. Lenin makes clear the external imposition that imperialist nations force upon many nations, and by also focusing on dependency, he is able to combine internal with external forces in interpreting the national reality of a dependent nation.

Economist André Gunder Frank offers a third conceptionalization of dependency. In his early work, Frank affirms that "it is capitalism, both world and national, which produced underdevelopment in the past and which still generates underdevelopment in the present."[11] His analysis centers on the metropolis-satellite structure of the capitalist system as he traces throughout the history of certain countries the development of underdevelopment. He identifies the internal contradictions of capitalism as "the expropriation of economic surplus from the many and its appropriation by the few, the polarization of the capitalist system into metropolitan center and peripheral satellites, and the continuity of the fundamental structure of the capitalist system throughout the history of its expansion and transformation. . . ." His central thesis focuses on these contradictions; capitalism, he argues, has "generated underdevelopment in the peripheral satellites whose economic surplus was expropriated, while generating economic development in the metropolitan centers which appropriate that surplus." With this thesis, Frank suggests a series of hypotheses which contend with some literature which explains backwardness through a dualist model of society and advocates change through a progressive national bourgeoisie. His critique of these ideas set in motion new thinking and provoked a multitude of criticisms. Further, Frank concentrates attention on exploitation, thereby turning attention to the internal consequences of nations caught up in industrial dependence.

A fourth conceptualization offers a further refinement. Known as the "New Dependency" and elaborated by Brazilian sociologist Theotonio dos Santos,[12] this conceptualization differs from colonial dependency, based on trade export, and from financial-industrial dependency, characterized by the domination of big capital in the hegemonic centers at the end of the nineteenth century. The new dependency is a recent phenomenon, based on multinational corporations which after the Second World War invested in industries geared to the internal market of underdeveloped countries. Dos Santos characterizes it as a "technological-industrial dependence."

Finally, Bacha turns to the early work of Cardoso and Faletto on dependency.[13] They stress internal structure. For example, classes or groups are analyzed in relation to the structure of outside domination. Dependency, therefore, is viewed not only as an external variable but within "a system of relations among different social classes in an environment characteristic of dependent nations." Like Frank and Dos Santos, they trace dependency through history. They also criticize the economic emphasis of these writers, and attempt to elaborate on theory by suggesting that politics and the internal forces are more decisive than economics and external forces in determining forms of dependency. Their own approach embraces these four levels of analysis: internal and external, political and economic.

Bacha observes that there are as many conceptions of dependency as there are authors, that the proponents of the theory work at various levels of analysis, and that there are limitations to the formulation of a workable conceptualization. No single author is able to apply the theory to all levels of analysis which pervade the literature. Most authors fail to define external components of their theory tending instead to rely upon a national perspective. Relations among structural elements are not explicitly identified. Bacha believes that such inconsistencies account for the varying conclusions reached by different writers of dependency. While none of the writers affirms the possibility of autonomous capitalist development, Lenin admits the existence of capitalist development within the dominant countries. Dos Santos looks for autonomous development in some countries after industrialization, and Cardoso, Faletto, and Vasconi acknowledge that some development can occur in a state of dependency. Frank, in contrast, sees persistent underdevelopment as the outcome of the dominated countries.

My own synthesis of the dependency theory builds upon the earlier efforts of Cardoso and Bacha. I shall recast the categories to reflect the evolution of the literature from the early conceptualization until the present time. Rather than focus on particular writers, I concern myself with two thrusts and six formulations which seem to stand out in the literature. The thrusts revolve around distinctions between the diffusionist and dependency models . . . while the formulations relate to one or the other model. These formulations are not necessarily mutually exclusive. Indeed they overlap, but they are representative of particular theoretical directions. I now turn to a discussion of each in an effort to identify major theoretical works, attempts to implement the theory, and critical assessment.

THE DIFFUSION MODEL AND THE ECLA AND INTERNAL COLONY FORMULATIONS

The diffusion model embraces a number of fundamental premises. Progress comes about through the spread of modernism to backward areas. Inescapably these areas evolve from a traditional toward a modern state as technology and capital are introduced. Underdevelopment is a condition which all nations have experienced at one time. Some nations have managed to develop, while others have not. In some underdeveloped nations, modern cities have arisen through contact with the developed world, while the countryside maintains a system of unproductive agriculture of large feudal estates.

These premises lead to two controversial propositions. One is that developing nations are structured into dual societies, one advanced and modern and the other backward and feudal. The other proposition suggests that in the advanced society there will emerge a new bourgeoisie, commercial and industrial in character. This bourgeoisie may become progressive and a supporter of national interests as capitalist development diffuses itself into rural areas and as economic and political policies restrict the domination and penetration of foreign interests. Both propositions are embraced, at least partially, by two formulations which sometimes are linked to the foundations of dependency theory. These formulations were proposed, on the one hand, by the United Nations' Economic Commission for Latin America (ECLA) and, on the other by advocates of internal colonialism.

The ECLA school of thought evolved after the Second World War. It was nationalist and sometimes anti-imperialist but non-Marxist in orientation. Its analysis sprang from Latin American economists grouped around the Argentine, Raúl Prebisch. Their philosophy was shaped by beliefs and principles set forth in a manifesto on development.[14] The history of the ECLA movement dates from its manifesto and breaks into three phases: from 1950 to 1953 when its ideology was formed, elaborated, and tested; from 1953 until 1958 when intensive studies were made of individual Latin American countries with the objective of proposing plans for their future development; and since 1958 when attention shifted to the study and promotion of regional integration through formation of a common market. The

ECLA thesis divides the world into an industrial center and a primary producing periphery, both of which should benefit from the maximizing of production, income, and consumption. However, unrestrained competition tends to result in appropriation to the center of most of the increment in world income. In short, the thesis correctly links Latin American underdevelopment to the international economic system, and thus affirms an underlying assumption of dependency theory. But analysis also is limited. For example, the thesis neglects an adequate examination of the conscious policies and specific needs of the nations of the center; it mistakenly attributes Latin American backwardness to traditional or feudal oligarchies; it inappropriately assumes that development would be promoted by a progressive, nationalist bourgeoisie, an assumption thus far negated by historical experience; and its stress on import substitution as a solution to consumptive dependence on the outside world has resulted in even greater dependence on the international system and in economic stagnation.

Theories of internal colonialism relate to dependency. The early work of the Mexican sociologist, Pablo González Casanova, proposed a framework for analysis of internal colonialism.[15] With the elimination of traditional forms of colonialism, characterized by foreign domination over nations, he suggests that the same conditions of the past colonialism may be found internally: "With the disappearance of the direct domination of foreigners over natives, the notion of domination and exploitation of natives by natives emerges." He describes the forms of internal colonialism, focusing on monopoly and dependence (the metropolis dominates the isolated communities, creating deformation of the native economy and decapitalization); relations of production and social control (exploitation plunders lands and discriminates everywhere); and culture and living standards (subsistence economies accentuate poverty, backward techniques, low productivity, lack of services, and traditionalism).

González Casanova stresses internal conditions of colonialism and suggests that external conditions no longer have great impact in Mexico. His formulation is similar in this respect to the culture of poverty thesis of Oscar Lewis.[16] Lewis attempts to demonstrate through his experience in poor Mexican and Puerto Rican communities that the culture of poverty applies to those people at the bottom of the socio-economic scale, the poorest workers, the poorest peasants and plantation laborers, and others. These people are marginal, have low levels of education and literacy, suffer from unemployment and underemployment as well as the absence of food supplies in the home. They experience a sense of resignation and fatalism based on the reality of their life situation. These traits are precisely those recognized by González Casanova. They are very similar to the conditions of colonized peoples described, in the case of French Algeria by Frantz Fanon and of French Tunisia by Albert Memmi. At one point Fanon writes about the "so-called dependency complex of colonized peoples" and asserts that this form of dependency emerges as a psychological response to a colonial situation, not a phenomenon that antedates colonization, as some observers believe.[17] Memmi draws a portrait of the colonizer and the colonized; he clarifies the differences between the two: "One is disfigured into an oppressor, a partial, unpatriotic and treacherous being, worrying only about his privileges and their defense; and the other, into an oppressed creature, whose development is broken and who compromises by his defeat."[18]

These writers emphasize the forms or conditions of colonialism. Our selection of examples of colonialism and internal colonialism suggest that González Casanova's stress on internal aspects alone may be misleading. He believes that marginal peoples will be absorbed into a collective society through the formation of a national bourgeoisie. Lewis speaks of the defense mechanisms without which the poor could not carry on, for the culture of poverty, he feels, is "a way of life, remarkably stable and persistent, passed down from generation to generation along family lines." Memmi provides two answers for the colonized: assimilation and revolt, but he offers no strategy for revolution. In a preface to Memmi's work, Jean-Paul Sartre describes the struggle against colonialism: "And when a people has no choice but how it will die; when a people has received from its oppressors only the gift of despair, what does it have to lose? A people's misfortune will become its courage; it will make, of its endless rejection by colonialism, the absolute rejection of colonialization."[19] Fanon is perhaps most instructive in this respect for his insights and understandings of colonial oppression are based on a struggle for national liberation. He is able to combine an identification of forms and conditions with an understanding and interpretation of the violent phenomenon of decolonialization.[20]

THE DEPENDENCY MODEL: FOUR FORMULATIONS

The dependency model distinguishes underdeveloped Latin America from precapitalist Europe. It does not view underdevelopment as an original condition, but instead assumes that nations may once have been undeveloped but never underdeveloped and that the contemporary underdevelopment of many parts of Latin America was created by the same process of capitalism that brought development to the industrialized nations. Latin America is underdeveloped because it has supported the development of Western Europe and the United States. When the center of the expanding world economic system needed raw materials, it was supplied by Latin America. This relationship has not basically changed, even though the United States has replaced Great Britain as the metropolis which dominates over the area, resulting in a strengthening of dependency through foreign corporate and government penetration of banking, manufacturing, retailing, communications, advertising, and education. Within each country the pattern of metropolis-periphery relations is replicated as the economic surplus of the countryside drains into urban areas.

These premises lead dependentistas to a number of propositions. First, they argue that while feudalistic conditions and relationships exist, the backwardness of the countryside cannot be explained by the image of a dual society. Rural areas are poor not because of feudalism but because they have been reponsive to urban and international market influences. The consequence has been the enrichment of the cities and the dominant nations. Second, dependentistas assert that the capitalist link between the city and the countryside is characterized by commerce between landowners and merchants who form an agro-commercial bourgeoisie which is subject to the market forces of a national and international capitalist economy. Empirical evidence verifies that agriculture, financial, and industrial interests are often found in the same economic groups, the same firms, and even in the same families. Thus, the capital of archaic latifundia may be invested by their owners in lucrative enterprise in the cities; or the grand families of the city, associated with foreign capital, may also be the owners of the backward latifundias. Thus, the landowning aristocracy and the urban commercial bourgeoisie often align with the manufacturing bourgeoisie. Third, dependentistas believe that dominant class interests are dependent on world imperialism for the manufacture of some goods, for foreign currency, and for foreign capital. Even if a segment of this class manifests nationalist xenophobia or resentment against imperialism, it has no other choice than to accept its condition as a dependent bourgeoisie. (The clearest case for these prepositions is in Quijano's analysis of contemporary Peru.[21]) Let us now examine four formulations of dependency theory which relate to the above propositions. These formulations relate to directions in the literature which we might label (1) the development of underdevelopment; (2) the new dependency; (3) dependency and development; and (4) dependency and imperialism.

THE DEVELOPMENT OF UNDERDEVELOPMENT

The bulk of writing during the past decade has focused on the development of underdevelopment. The thesis was most explicitly set forth in the early writing of André Gunder Frank.[22] He emphasized commercial monopoly rather than feudalism and pre-capitalist forms as the economic means whereby national and regional metropolises exploit and appropriate the economic satellites. Thus, capitalism on a world scale produces a developing metropolis and an underdeveloped periphery. This same process can also be found within nations between a domestic metropolis (a capital city, for example) and the surrounding satellite cities and regions.

Frank's theoretical perspective has been neatly summed up and critiqued by Emesto Laclau.[23] The summary includes the following theses: First, development does not occur through a succession of stages, and today's developed countries were never underdeveloped, although they were once undeveloped. Second, underdevelopment is part of the historical product of relations between the underdeveloped satellites and the present developed metropolises. Third, the dualist interpretation must be rejected because capitalism has effectively and completely penetrated the undeveloped world. Fourth, metropolitan-satellite relations are found within countries as well as in the imperialist world order. Fifth, Frank hypothesizes that development of satellites is limited by their dependent status; satellites experience their greatest growth only when their links to the metropolis are weakened, say during depression or world war; the most underdeveloped regions are those which were closely linked to the metropolis, originally latifundia were capitalist enterprises responsive to the growing demand in the national and international market. These ideas emerged in his earlier works cited above and were refined in a series of essays, reprinted as an anthology.[24] . . .

The New Dependency

Much of the thrust of dependency theory emanates from the notion of the new dependency. Types of dependence are identifiable through periods of history, according to Dos Santos.[25] Colonial dependency characterized the relations between Europeans and the colonies whereby a monopoly of trade complemented a monopoly of land, mines, and manpower in the colonized countries. Financial-industrial dependency consolidated itself at the end of the nineteenth century with, on the one hand, domination of capital in hegemonic centers and, on the other, investment of capital in the peripheral colonies for raw materials and agricultural products which in turn would be consumed by the centers. A new dependency based on investments by multinational corporations emerged after the Second World War. Dos Santos labels this a technological-industrial dependency. An elaboration of theory on the new dependency is found in several of his writings.[26] The thrust of his argument is directed against prevailing bourgeois assumptions about development in Latin America;[27] and it attempts to relate traditional notions of imperialism to the internal situation of the Latin American countries. Let us explore this latter concern.

The new dependency places limits on the development of Latin American economics. Industrial development is dependent on exports which generate foreign currency to buy imported capital goods. Exports in turn are usually tied to traditional sectors of the economy which are controlled by oligarchies. Often the oligarchies are tied to foreign capital; and they remit their high profits abroad. Thus, it is not surprising that foreign capital controls the marketing of exported products, even though dependent countries have attempted to impose policies of exchange restrictions and taxes on foreign exports and have leaned toward the nationalization of production. Industrial development then is conditioned by fluctuations in the balance of payments which in dependent countries often leads to deficits caused by trade relations in a highly monopolized international market, the repatriation of foreign profits, and the need to reply on foreign capital and aid.

Dependency and Development

The notion that capitalist development takes place within dependent situations has evolved primarily in the writings of Fernado Henrique Cardoso. Let us trace his line of argument.[28] Cardoso begins with the assumption that modern capitalism and imperialism differs from Lenin's earlier conceptions. Capital accumulation, for example, is more the consequence of corporate rather than financial control. Investment by multinational corporations in Latin America is moving away from raw materials and agriculture to industry. More often than not these corporations comprise "local and state capital, private national capital, and monopoly international investment (but in the last analysis under foreign control)."[29] Thus monopoly capitalism and development are not contradictory terms; and dependent capitalist development has become a new form of monopolistic expansion in the Third World. This development is oriented to a restricted, limited, and upper class-oriented type of market and society. At the same time, the amount of net foreign capital in dependent economies is decreasing. New foreign capital is not needed in some areas where there are local savings and reinvestment of profits in local markets, further, dependent economies during times of monopolistic imperialistic expansion are exporting capital to the dominant economies.

This analysis leads Cardoso to a critique of other dependentistas. First, analysis "based on the naive assumption that imperialism unifies the interests and reactions of dominated nations is a clear oversimplification of what is really occurring.''[30] Second, the notion of development of underdevelopment and the assumption of a lack of dynamism in dependent economies because of imperialism are misleading.[31] On the one hand, new trends in international capitalism have resulted in increased interdependence in production activities at the international level and in a modification in the patterns of dependence that limit developmental policy in the peripheral countries of the international capitalist system.[32] On the other hand, international capitalism has gained disproportional influence in industry. Whether or not industrial firms are owned by foreigners or nationals, in either case "they are linked to market investment, and decision-making structures located outside the dependent country.''[33]

Dependency and Imperialism

As mentioned above, Lenin related imperialism to dependency. A recent synthesis elaborates on this relationship. According to Benjamin Cohen, imperialism refers to "any relationship of effective domination or control, political or economic, direct or indirect, of one nation over another. . . .''[34] This relationship involves dominance and dependence among nations which are large and small, rich and poor. Three principal forms of imperialism are evident through history. First, during the sixteenth and seventeenth centuries European mercantilism characterized the "old imperialism." Second, the European empire building of 1870 and thereafter represented a shift from informal to formal mechanisms of control and influence in the colonies during a period known as the "new imperialism" (see Fieldhouse,[35] for a useful review of ideas on the literature on the old and new imperialisms.) Third, the breakup of empires was accomplished by analysis of neo-colonialism and what today might be called "modern imperialism." Analytically, the theory of modern imperialism moves in two directions. One emphasizes the view from the metropolis and argues that imperialism is necessary for the advancement of capitalist economies. The other stresses the view from the periphery and focuses on the detrimental consequences of capitalist trade and investment in the poorer economies of the world.

Both these theoretical directions incorporate analysis of dependency, although the view from the periphery has provoked a variety of perspectives, some being non-Marxist and others Marxist. Some of these perspectives have attempted to relate imperialism to dependency, while others have refuted dependency altogether in favor of an interpretation based solely on imperialism. Recent events in the Middle East and the Arab oil embargo have prompted speculation about U.S. dependency on such raw materials as petroleum. While Henry Kissinger places policy emphasis on building an "interdependence" among nations, the U.S. press talks of the need for self-sufficiency and freedom from the Arab oil barons. Other views have begun to reflect on the question of dependency between the Soviet Union and other socialist nations.

While theories of imperialism assume an inequality between nations, some nations dominate over dependent nations which erodes autonomy and perpetuates exploitation. Non-Marxist theories differ from Marxist theories of imperialism on two levels. First, non-Marxist theory tends to associate imperialism with expansionism, thereby obscuring the subtle mechanisms through which imperialism has been internalized. Second, non-Marxist theory addresses itself to political and military explanations rather than to economic explanations in a context of capitalist global expansion. . . .

In summary, we can suggest several assumptions which most proponents of dependency theory support, even though their work may not yet have proven their validity. We draw these assumptions from the literature in the hope that they might guide the reader to further understanding, constructive critique, and refinement of dependency theory. First, it is generally believed that dependency theory provides a framework for explanation of underdevelopment and development. Second, dependency theory offers a foundation for analysis of class struggle and strategies to promote class struggle in the interest of resolving societal contradictions and problems. Finally, an understanding of dependency and the adoption of certain strategies to break dependency leads to the restructuring of societies, a restructuring which limits capitalism and promotes socialism in the seeking of a new and better society.

NOTES AND REFERENCES

1. Fernando Henrique Cardoso, "Notas sobre estado e dependencia" (São Paulo: Centro Brasileiro de Analise e Planejamento, Caderno 11, 1973).

2. Helio Jaguaribe, Aldo Fener, Miguel S. Wionczek, and Theotonio dos Santos, *La dependencia politico-economica de America Latina*, 2nd. ed. (Mexico City: Siglo Veintiuno Editores, 1970).

3. André Gunder Frank, *Capitalism and Underdevelopment in Latin America: Historical Studies of Chile and Brazil* (New York: Monthly Review Press, 1967).

4. Theotonio dos Santos, "La crisis de la teoria del desarrollo y las relaciones de dependencia en America Latina," in Helio Jaguaribe et al., *La dependencia politicio-economica de America Latina* (Mexico City: Siglo Veintuina Editors, 1970), pp. 147–187.

5. Fernando Henrique Cardoso, "Analises sociologicas del desarrollo economico," *Revista Latinoamericana de Sociologia,* 1 (July 1965): 178–198.

6. Paul Baran, *The Political Economy of Growth* (New York: Monthly Review Press, 1957); and Paul Baran and Paul Sweezy, *Monopoly Capital: An Essay on the American Economic and Social Order* (New York: Monthly Review Press, 1966).

7. Harry Magdoff, *The Age of Imperialism: The Economics of U. S. Foreign Policy* (New York: Monthly Review Press, 1969).

8. Claire Savit Bacha, "A dependencia nas relacoes internacionais: uma introducao a enperrenca brasileira." (Rio de Janiero: Master's Thesis, Instituto Universitario De Pesqusas Do Rio de Janeiro, n.d.).

9. Tomás Vasconi, "De la dependencia como una categoria basico para el analisis de desarrollo Latinamericano," in Carlo Lessa and Tomas Vasconi, *Hacia una critica de las interpretaciones del desarrollo Latinoamericana.* (Caracas: Universidad Central de Venezula, 1969), pp. 34–51.

10. V. I. Lenin, *Selected Works in Three Volumes,* Vol. 1 (Moscow: Progress Publishers, 1967) pp. 742–743.

11. Frank, *Capitalism and Underdevelopment in Latin America.*

12. Theotonio dos Santos, *El nuevo carácter de la dependencia* (Santiago: Cuadernos de Estudios Socio-Economicos (10), Centro De Estudios Socio-Economicos (CESO), Universidad de Chile, 1968).

13. Fernando Henrique Cardoso and Enzo Faletto, *Dependencia y desarrollo en America Latina* (Mexico: Siglo Veintuino Editors, 1969). Published in Portuguese a year later by Editora Zahar.

14. United Nations, Economic Commission for Latin America, *The Economic Development of Latin Americ͏ and its Principal Problems* (New York: United Nations, 1950).

15. Pablo González Casanova, *Sociologia de la explotacion,* 2nd ed. (Mexico City: Siglo Veintuino Editors, 1970).

16. Oscar Lewis, "The Culture of Poverty," in John J. Tepaske and Sydney Mettleton

Fisher, eds., *Explosive Forces in Latin America* (Columbus: Ohio State University Press, 1964), pp. 149–173.

17. Frantz Fanon, *Black Skin, White Masks* (New York: Grove Press, 1967), pp. 83–108.

18. Albert Memmi, *The Colonizer and the Colonized.* Introduced by Jean-Paul Sartre (New York: Orion Press, 1965), p. 89.

19. Ibid., p. xxix.

20. Frantz Fanon, *The Wretched of the Earth* (New York: Grove Press, 1963), and *A Dying Colonialism* (New York: Monthly Review Press, 1965).

21. Anibal Quijano, *Nationalism and Colonialism in Peru: A Study in Neo-Imperialism* (New York: Monthly Review Press, 1971).

22. André Gunder Frank, "The Development of Underdevelopment," *Monthly Review,* 18 (September 1966): 17–31, and *Capitalism and Underdevelopment in Latin America.*

23. Ernesto Laclau, "Feudalism and Capitalism in Latin America," *New Left Review,* 67 (May-June 1971): 19–38.

24. André Gunder Frank, *Latin America: Underdevelopment or Revolution. Essays in the Development of Underdevelopment and the Immediate Enemy* (New York: Modern Reader/Monthly Review Press, 1969).

25. Dos Santos, "The Structure of Dependency," p. 232.

26. Dos Santos, El neu carácter de la dependencia; *Dependencia y. cambio social;* and "El nucvo carácter de la independencia, *Pensamiento Critico,* 43 (August 1970): 60–106.

27. Theotonio dos Santos, "La crisis de la teoria del desarrollo y las relaciones de dependencia en America Latina," and "Dependencia economica y alternativas de cambio en America Latina," *Revista Mexicana de Sociologia,* 32 (March-April 1970): pp. 417–463.

28. Ferrado Henrique Cardoso, "Dependency and Development in Latin America," *New Left Review,* 74 (July-August 1972): 83–95.

29. Fernando Henrique Cardoso, "Imperialism and Dependency in Latin America," pp. 7–16 in *Structures of Dependency,* edited by Frank Bornilla and Robert Girling (Nairobi, (E. Palo Alto) California, 1973), p. 11.

30. Fernando Henrique Cardoso, "Dependency and Development in Latin America," p. 94.

31. Ibid.

32. Fernando Henrique Cardoso, "Associated Dependent Development: Theoretical and Practical Implications," pp. 142–76 in *Authoritarian Brazil: Origins, Policies and Future,* ed. Alfred Stepan (New Haven, Conn.: Yale University Press, 1973), p. 146.

33. Ibid.

34. Benjamin J. Cohen, *The Question of Imperialism: The Political Economy of Dominance and Dependence* (New York: Basic Books, 1973), p. 15.

35. D. K. Fieldhouse, " 'Imperialism': An Historiographical Revision," *Economic History,* 14, no. 2 (1961): 187–209.

22 Imperialism as Capital Accumulation: The View from the Metropolis

DAVID HARVEY*

The spatial dimension to Marx's theory of accumulation under the capitalist mode of production has for too long been ignored. This is, in part, Marx's fault since his writings on the matter are fragmentary and often only sketchily developed. But careful scrutiny of his works reveals that Marx recognized that capital accumulation took place in a geographical context and that it in turn created specific kinds of geographical structures. Marx further develops a novel approach to location theory (in which dynamics are at the center of things) and shows that it is possible to connect, theoretically, the general processes of economic growth with an explicit understanding of an emergent structure of spatial relationships. And it further transpires that this locational analysis provides, in albeit a limited form, a crucial link between Marx's theory of accumulation and the Marxian theory of imperialism—a link which many have sought but none have so far found with any certainty, in part, I shall argue, because the mediating factor of Marx's location theory has been overlooked.

In this paper I shall try to demonstrate how the theory of accumulation relates to an understanding of spatial structure and how the particular form of locational analysis which Marx creates provides the missing link between the theory of accumulation and the theory of imperialism.

THE THEORY OF ACCUMULATION

Marx's theory of growth under capitalism places accumulation of capital at the center of things. Accumulation is the engine which powers growth under the capitalist mode of production. The capitalist system is therefore highly dynamic and inevitably expansionary; it forms a permanently revolutionary force which continuously and constantly reshapes the world we live in. A stationary state of simple reproduction is, for Marx, logically incompatible with the perpetuation of the capitalist mode of production. "The historical mission of the bourgeoisie," is expressed in the formula "accumulation for accumulation's sake, production for production's sake."[1] Yet this historical mission does not stem from the inherent

*David Harvey, "The Geography of Capitalist Accumulation: A Reconstruction of the Marxian Theory," *Antipode: A Radical Journal of Geography,* 7, No. 2 (September 1975): 9–21. Reprinted by permission of author and publisher.

greed of the capitalist; it arises, rather, out of forces entirely independent of the capitalist's individual will:

> Only as personified capital is the capitalist respectable. As such, he shares with the miser the passion for wealth as wealth. But that which in the miser is mere idiosyncrasy, is, in the capitalist, the effect of the social mechanism, of which he is but one of the wheels. Moreover, the development of capitalist production makes it constantly necessary to keep increasing the amount of capital laid out in a given industrial undertaking, and competition makes the immanent laws of capitalist production to be felt by each individual capitalist, as external coercive laws. It compels him to keep constantly extending his capital, in order to preserve it, but extend it he cannot, except by means of progressive accumulation.[2]

Economic growth under capitalism is, as Marx usually dubs it, a process of internal contradictions which frequently erupt as crises. Harmonious or balanced growth under capitalism is, in Marx's view, purely accidental because of the spontaneous and chaotic nature of commodity production under competitive capitalism.[3] Marx's analyses of this system of commodity production led him to the view that there were innumerable possibilities for crises to occur as well as certain tendencies inherent within capitalism which were bound to produce serious stresses within the accumulation process. We can understand these stresses more easily if we recognize that the progress of accumulation depends upon and presupposes:

(1) The existence of a surplus of labor—an industrial reserve army which can feed the expansion of production. Mechanisms must therefore exist to increase the supply of labor power by, for example, stimulating population growth, generating migration streams, drawing "latent elements"—labor power employed in non-capitalist situations, women and children, and the like—into the workforce, or by creating unemployment by the application of labor-saving innovations.

(2) The existence in the market place of requisite quantities of, or opportunities to obtain, means of production—machines, raw materials, physical infrastructures, and the like—to permit the expansion of production as capital is reinvested.

(3) The existence of a market to absorb the increasing quantities of commodities produced. If uses cannot be found for goods or if an effective demand (need backed by ability to pay) does not exist, then the conditions for capitalist accumulation disappear.

In each of these respects the progress of accumulation may encounter a serious barrier which, once reached, will likely precipitate a crisis of some sort. Since, in well-developed capitalist economies, the supply of labor power, the supply of means of production and of necessary infrastructures, and the structure of demand are all "produced" under the capitalist mode of production, Marx concludes that capitalism tends actively to produce some of the barriers to its own development. This means that crises are endemic to the capitalist accumulation process.

Crises can be manifest in a variety of ways, however, depending on the conditions of circulation and production at the time. We can see more clearly how this can be so by examining, briefly, how Marx looks at production, distribution, consumption and reinvestment as separate phases (or "moments") within the totality of the capitalist production process. He argues, for example, that:

> not only is production immediately consumption and consumption immediately production, not only is production a means for consumption and consumption the aim of production . . . but also, each of them . . . creates the other in completing itself and creates itself as the other.[4]

If production and consumption are necessarily dialectically integrated with each other within production as a totality, then it follows that the crises which arise from structural barriers to accumulation can be manifest in each and any of the phases in the circulation and production of value.

Consider, for example, a typical realization crisis which arises because accumulation for accumulation's sake means, inevitably, the "tendency to produce without regard to the limits of the market."[5] Capitalists constantly tend to expand the mass and total value of commodities on the market at the same time as they try to maximize their profits by keeping wages down which restricts the purchasing power of the masses.[6] There is a contradiction here which periodically produces a realization crisis—a mass of commodities on the market with no purchasers in sight. This overproduction is relative only, of course, and it has nothing to do with absolute human needs—"it is only concerned with demand backed by ability to pay."[7] Absolute overproduction in relation to all human wants and needs is, in Marx's view, impossible under capitalism.

But such relative overproduction may appear also as underconsumption or as an overproduction of capital (a capital surplus). Marx regards these forms as manifestations of the same basic overaccumulation problem.[8] The fact that there is a surfeit of capital relative to opportunities to employ that capital means that there has been an overproduction of capital (in the form of an overproduction of commodities) at a preceeding stage and that capitalists are over-investing and underconsuming the surplus at the present stage. In all of these cases, overproduction:

> is specifically conditioned by the general law of the production of capital: to produce to the limit set by the productive forces, that is to say, to exploit the maximum amount of labour with a given amount of capital, without any consideration for the actual limits of the market or the needs backed by ability to pay.[9]

This same general law produces, periodically, a:

> plethora of capital [which] arises from the same causes as those which call forth a relative overpopulation, and is, therefore, a phenomenon supplementing the latter, although they stand at opposite poles—unemployed capital at one pole, and unemployed worker population at the other.[10]

The various manifestations of crisis in the capitalist system—chronic unemployment and underemployment, capital surpluses and lack of investment opportunities, falling rates of profit, lack of effective demand in the market, and so on, can therefore be traced back to the basic tendency to overaccumulate. Since there are no other equilibrating forces at work within the competitive anarchy of the capitalist economic system, crises have an important function—they enforce some kind of order and rationality onto capitalist economic development. This is not to say that crises are themselves orderly or logical—they merely create the conditions which force some kind of arbitrary rationalization of the capitalist production system. This rationalization extracts a social cost and has its tragic human consequences in the form of bankruptcies, financial collapse, forced devaluation of capital assets and personal savings, inflation, increasing concentration of economic and political power in a few hands, falling real wages, and unemployment. Forced periodic corrections to the course of capital accumulation can all too easily get out of hand, however, and spawn class struggles, revolutionary movements and the chaos which typically provides the breeding ground for fascism. The social reaction to crises can affect the way in which the crisis is resolved so that there is no necessary unique outcome to this forced rationalization process. All that has to happen is that appropriate conditions for renewed accumulation have to be created if the capitalist system is to be sustained.

Periodic crises must in general have the effect of expanding the productive capacity and renewing the conditions of further accumulation. We can conceive of each crisis as shifting the accumulation process onto a new and higher plane. This "new plane" will likely exhibit certain combined characteristics of the following sorts:

(1) The productivity of labor will be much enhanced by the employment of more sophisticated machinery and equipment while older fixed capital equipment will, during the course of the crisis, have become much cheaper through a forced devaluation.

(2) The cost of labor will be much reduced because of the widespread unemployment during the crisis and, consequently, a larger surplus can be gained for further accumulation.

(3) The surplus capital which lacked opportunities for investment in the crisis will be drawn into new and high profit lines of production.

(4) An expanding effective demand for product—at first in the capital goods industry but subsequently in final consumption—will easily clear the market of all goods produced.

It is, perhaps, useful to pick up on the last element and consider how a new plane of effective demand, which can increase the capacity to absorb products, can be constructed. Analysis suggests that it can be constructed out of a complex mix of four overlapping elements:

(1) The penetration of capital into new spheres of activity by (i) organizing preexisting forms of activity along capitalist lines (e.g., the transformation of peasant subsistence agriculture into corporate farming), or by (ii) expanding the points of interchange within the system of production and diversifying the division of labor (new specialist businesses emerge to take care of some aspect of production which was once all carried on within the same factory or firm).

(2) Creating new social wants and needs, developing entirely new product-lines (automobiles and electronic goods are excellent twentieth century examples) and organizing consumption so that it becomes "rational" with respect to the accumulation process (working class demands for good housing may, for example, be coopted into a public housing program which serves to stabilize the economy and expand the demand for construction products of a certain sort).

(3) Facilitating and encouraging the expansion of population at a rate consistent with long-run accumulation (this obviously is not a short-run solution but there appears to be a strong justification for Marx's comment that "an increasing population appears as the basis of accumulation as a continuous process" from the standpoint of expanding the labor supply and the market for products).[11]

(4) Expanding geographically into new regions, increasing foreign trade, exporting capital and in general expanding towards the creation of what Marx called "the world market."

In each of these respects, or by some combination of them, capitalism can create fresh room for accumulation. The first three items can be viewed really as a matter of *intensification* of social activity, of markets, of people within a particular spatial structure. The last item brings us, of course, to the question of spatial organization and geographical expansion as a necessary product of the accumulation process. In what follows we shall consider this last aspect in isolation from the others. But it is crucial to realize that in practice various trade-offs exist between intensification and spatial extension—a rapid rate of population growth and the easy creation of new social wants and needs within a country may render capital export and an expansion of foreign trade unnecessary for the expansion of accumulation. The more difficult intensification becomes, the more important geographical extension is for sustaining capital accumulation. Bearing this in mind, we will proceed to examine the way in which the theory of accumulation relates to the production of spatial structures.

TRANSPORTATION RELATIONS, SPATIAL INTEGRATION AND THE "ANNIHILATION OF SPACE BY TIME"

We will start from the proposition that the "circulation of capital realizes value while living labour creates value."[12] Circulation has two aspects; the actual physical movement of commodities from point of production to point of consumption and the actual or implicit costs that attach to the time taken up and to the social mediations (the chain of wholesalers, retailers, banking operations, and the like) which are necessary in order for the produced commodity to find its ultimate user. Marx regards the former as integral to the production process and therefore productive of value.[13] The latter are regarded as necessary costs of circulation which are not, however, productive of value—they are to be regarded, therefore, as necessary deductions out of surplus, because the capitalist has to pay for them.

The transportation and communications industry which "sells change in location"[14] is directly productive of value because "economically considered, the spatial condition, the bringing of the product to market, belongs to the production process itself. The product is really finished only when it is on the market."[15] However, the means of transportation and communication, because they are made up almost entirely of fixed capital, have their own peculiar laws of realization—laws which stem from the fact that transportation is simultaneously produced and consumed at the moment of its use.[16] Although the transport industry is *potentially* a source of surplus value, there are good reasons for capital not to engage in its production except under certain favorable circumstances. The state is often, therefore, very active in this sphere of production.[17]

The cost of transportation "is important insofar as the expansion of the market and the exchangeability of the product are connected with it."[18] Prices, both of raw materials and finished goods, are sensitive to the costs of transportation and the ability to draw in raw materials over long distances and to dispatch the finished product to a distant market is obviously affected by these costs. The costs of circulation "can be reduced by improved, cheaper and more rapid transportation."[19] One by-product of this is a cheapening of many elements of constant capital (raw material inputs) and the extension of the geographical market. Viewed from the standpoint of production as a totality, "the reduction of the costs of real circulation [in space] belongs to the development of the forces of production by capital."[20]

Placed in the context of accumulation in general, improvements in transportation and communication are seen to be inevitable and necessary. "The revolution in the modes of production of industry and agriculture made necessary a revolution . . . in the means of communication and transport" so that they "became gradually adapted to the modes of production of mechanical industry, by the creation of a system of river steamers, railways, ocean steamers and telegraphs."[21] The imperative to accumulate consequently implies the imperative to overcome spatial barriers:

> The more production comes to rest on exchange value, hence on exchange, the more important do the physical conditions of exchange—the means of communication and transport—become for the costs of circulation. Capital by its nature drives beyond every spatial barrier. Thus the creation of the physical conditions of exchange . . . becomes an extraordinary necessity for it.[22]

The capitalist mode of production promotes the production of cheap and rapid forms of communication and transportation in order that "the direct product can be realized in distant markets in mass quantities" at the same time as new "spheres of realization for labour, driven by capital" can be opened up.[23] The reduction in realization and circulation costs helps to create, therefore, fresh room for capital accumulation. Put the other way around, capital accumulation is bound to be geographically expansionary and to be so by progressive reductions in the costs of communication and transportation.

The opening up of more distant markets, new sources of raw materials and of new opportunities for the employment of labor under the social relations of capitalism, has the effect, however, of increasing the turnover time of capital unless there are compensating improvements in the speed of circulation. The turnover time of a given capital is equal to the production time plus the circulation time.[24] The longer the turnover time of a given capital, the smaller is its annual yield of surplus value. More distant markets tie capital up in the circulation process for longer time periods and therefore have the effect of *reducing* the realization of surplus value for a particular capital. By the same token, any reduction in circulation time increases surplus production and enhances the accumulation process. Speeding up "the velocity of circulation of capital" contributes to the accumulation process. Under these conditions "even spatial distance reduces itself to time: the important thing is not the market's distance in space, but the speed . . . with which it can be reached."[25] There is thus a strong incentive to reduce the circulation time to a minimum for to do so is to minimize "the wandering period" of commodities.[26] A dual need, both to reduce the cost and the time involved in movement, thus emanates from the imperative to accumulate:

> while capital must on one side strive to tear down every spatial barrier to intercourse, i.e., to exchange, and conquer the whole earth for its market, it strives on the other side to annihilate this space with time . . . The more developed the capital . . . the more does it strive simultaneously for an even greater extension of the market and for greater annihilation of space by time.[27]

Long distance trade, because it separates production and realization by a long time interval, may still be characterized by a long turnover period and a lack of continuity in the employment of capital. This kind of trade, and "overseas commerce in general" thus forms "one of the material bases, . . . one of the sources of the credit system."[28] In the *Grundrisse* Marx develops this argument at greater length:

> It is clear . . . that circulation appears as an essential process of capital. The production process cannot be begun anew before the transformation of the commodity into money. The *constant continuity* of this process, the un-obstructed and fluid transition of value from one form into the other, or from one phase of the process into the next, appears as a fundamental condition for production based on capital to a much greater degree than for all earlier forms of production. [But] while the necessity of this continuity is given, its phases are separate in time and space . . . It thus appears as a matter of chance . . . whether or not its essential condition, the continuity of the different processes which constitute its process as a whole, is actually brought about. The suspension of this chance element by capital itself is *credit*.[29]

The credit system allows of a geographical extension of the market by establishing continuity where there was none before. The necessity to annihilate space by time can in part be compensated for by an emerging system of credit.

The need to minimize circulation costs as well as turnover times promotes agglomeration of production within a few large urban centres which become, in effect, the workshops of capitalist production.[30] The "annihilation of space by time" is here accomplished by a "rational" location of activities with respect to each other so as to minimize the costs of movement of intermediate products in particular. "Along with this concentration of masses of men and capital thus accelerated at certain points, there is the concentration of these masses of capital in the hands of the few."[31] The ability to economize on circulation costs depends, however, on the nature of the transportation relations established and here there appears to be a dynamic tendency towards concentration. Improvements in the means of transportation tend:

> in the direction of the already existing market, this is to say, towards the great centres of production and population, towards ports of export, etc. . . . These particularly great traffic facilities and the resultant acceleration of the capital turnover . . . give rise to quicker concentration of both the centres of produc-tion and the markets.[32]

This tendency towards agglomeration in large urban centers may be diminished or enhanced by special circumstances. On the one hand we find that "the territorial division of labour . . . confines special branches of production to special districts of a country."[33] On the other hand, "all branches of production which by the nature of their product are dependent mainly on local consumption, such as breweries, are . . . developed to the greatest extent in the principle centres of population."[34]

The geographical rationalization of the processes of production is in part dependent upon the changing structure of transport facilities, the raw material and marketing demands of the industry and the inherent tendency towards agglomeration and concentration on the part of capital itself. The latter required a technological innovation to sustain it, however. Hence the importance of the steam engine which "permitted production to be concentrated in towns" and which "was of universal application, and, relatively speaking, little affected in its choice of residence by local circumstances."[35]

Innovations of this sort, which relatively speaking free production from local power sources and which permit the concentration of production in large urban agglomerations accomplish the same purpose as those transport innovations which serve to annihilate space with time. Geographical expansion and geographical concentration are both to be regarded as the product of the same striving to create new opportunities for capital accumulation. In general, it appears that the imperative to accumulate produces concentration of production and of capital at the same time as it creates an expansion of the market for realization. As a consequence, "flows in space" increase remarkably, while the "market expands spatially, and the periphery in relation to the centre . . . is circumscribed by a constantly expanding radius."[36] Some sort of centre-periphery relation is bound to arise out of the tension between concentration and geographical expansion. We will examine certain aspects of this relation further in the section on foreign trade.

Since the structure of transport facilities does not remain constant, we find "a shifting and relocation of places of production and of markets as a result of the changes in their relative positions caused by the transformation in transport facilities."[37] These transformations alter "the relative distances of places of production from the larger markets" and consequently bring about "the deterioration of old and the rise of new centres of production."[38]

The emergence of a distinct spatial structure with the rise of capitalism is not a contradiction-free process. In order to overcome spatial barriers and to "annihilate space with time," spatial structures are created which themselves ultimately act as a barrier to further accumulation. These spatial structures are expressed, of course, in the fixed and immovable form of transport facilities, plant, and other means of production and consumption which cannot be moved without being destroyed. Once the mode of production of capital is brought into being, it "establishes its residence on the land itself and the seemingly solid presuppositions given by nature themselves [appear] in landed property as merely posited by industry."[39] Capital thus comes to represent itself in the form of a physical landscape created in its own image, created as use values to enhance the progressive accumulation of capital on an expanding scale. The geographical landscape which fixed and immobile capital comprises is both a crowning glory of past capital development and a prison which inhibits the further progress of accumulation because the very building of this landscape is antithetical to the "tearing down of spatial barriers" and ultimately even to the "annihilation of space by time."[40]

This contradiction is characteristic of the growing dependency of capitalism on fixed capital of all kinds. With "fixed capital the value is imprisoned within a specific use value"[41] while the degree of fixity increases with durability, other things being equal.[42] The necessary increase in the use of fixed capital of the immobile sort which the imperative to accumulate implies imposes a further imperative:

> The value of fixed capital is reproduced only insofar as it is used up in the production process. Through disuse it loses its value without its value passing on to the product. Hence the greater the scale on which fixed capital develops . . . the more does the continuity of the production process or the constant flow of reproduction become an externally compelling condition for the mode of production founded on capital.[43]

Capitalist development has to negotiate a knife-edge path between preserving the values of past capital investments in the built environment and destroying these investments in order to open up fresh room for accumulation.[44] As a consequence we can expect to witness a perpetual struggle in which capitalism builds a physical landscape appropriate to its own condition at a particular moment in time, only to have to destroy it, usually in the course of a crisis, at a subsequent point in time. Temporal crises in fixed capital investment, often expressed as "long-waves" in economic development are therefore usually expressed as periodic re-shapings of the geographic environment to adapt it to the needs of further accumulation.[45]

This contradiction has a further dimension. In part the drive to overcome spatial barriers and to annihilate space with time is designed to counteract what Marx saw as a pervasive tendency under capitalism for the profit rate to fall. The creation of built environments in the service of capitalism means "a growth of that portion of social wealth which, instead of serving as direct means of production, is invested in means of transportation and communication and in the fixed and circulating capital required for their operation."[46] Investment in the means of transportation is bound to increase the organic composition of social capital which tends to generate a fall in the rate of profit at the same time as its effects are supposed to increase the rate of profit. Again, capitalist development has to negotiate a knife-edge between these two contradictory tendencies.

The location theory in Marx is not much more specific that this (although there is much in the analysis of fixed and immovable capital investment which is of interest but which space precludes from considering here). The virtue of these fragmentary analyses lies not in their sophistication. It lies, rather, in the way in which they can be tightly integrated into the fundamental insights into the production of value and the dynamics of accumulation. In this the Marxian approach is fundamentally different to that typical of bourgeois economic analysis of locational phenomena. The latter typically specifies an optimal configuration under a specific set of conditions and presents a partial static equilibrium analysis. Dynamics are considered at the end of the analysis—usually as an afterthought—and the dynamics never get much beyond comparative statics. Consequently, it is generally acknowledged that bourgeois location theory has failed to develop a satisfactory dynamic representation of itself. The Marxian theory, on the other hand, commences with the dynamics of accumulation and seeks to derive out of this analysis certain necessities with respect to geographical structures. The landscape which capitalism creates is also seen as the locus of contradiction and tension, rather than as an expression of harmonious equilibrium. And crises in fixed capital investments are seen as synonymous in many respects with the dialectical transformation of geographical space. The contrast between the two theoretical stances is important. It suggests that the two theories are really concerned with quite different things. Bourgeois locational analysis is only adequate as an expression of optimal configurations under set conditions. The Marxian theory teaches us how to relate, theoretically, accumulation and the transformation of spatial structures and ultimately, of course, it provides us with the kinds of theoretical and material understanding which will allow us to understand the reciprocal relationships between geography and history.

FOREIGN TRADE

Marx considers foreign trade from two rather different standpoints; first, as an attribute of the capitalist mode of production and second, as an historical phenomenon relating an evolving capitalist social formation with pre-capitalist societies and generating various intermediate social forms (such as colonies, plantation economies, dependent economies, and the like).

Marx invariably abstracts from questions of foreign trade in his analysis of the capitalist mode of production.[47] He concedes, of course, that "capitalist production does not exist at all without foreign commerce" but suggests that consideration of the latter merely serves to "confuse without contributing any new element of the problem [of accumulation], or of its solution."[48] He also accepts that foreign trade may counteract the tendency to a falling rate of profit because it cheapens the elements of constant capital as well as necessities and so permits a rising surplus value to be appropriated. But since this raises the rate of accumulation, it merely hastens the fall in the rate of profit in the long run.[49] The increase in foreign trade, which inevitably arises with the expansion of accumulation, merely "transfers the contradictions to a wider sphere and gives them greater latitude."[50]

Most of Marx's comments on foreign trade relate to it as an historical phenomenon and are therefore peripheral to his main purpose in *Capital*. Foreign trade is treated as a pre-condition for capitalist accumulation as well as a consequence of the expansion of the market. Since consequences at one stage become pre-conditions at the next, the development of foreign trade and capitalist social formations are seen as integrally related. "Special factors" also arise in relation to foreign trade which can confuse, conceal and distort matters. The significance of such factors to actual historical situations is not denied—they are just not regarded as crucial for understanding the inner logic of the capitalist mode of production.

The theoretical and historical analyses intersect at certain points, however. Some of Marx's statements on foreign trade can be interpreted as logical extensions of his theoretical views on how the accumulation process generates transportation relations and locational structures. These views are usually projected into a pre-existing structure of nation states, territories with different natural productive capacities and non-capitalist production systems.

Marx recognizes, for example, that "the productiveness of labour is fettered by physical conditions."[51] In agriculture he expects unequal returns on capital advanced to result from differences in both fertility and relative location.[52] Natural differences form, therefore, a "physical basis for the social division of labour,"[53] although they present possibilities only (and not unmodifiable ones at that) because in the last instance the productiveness of labour "is a gift, not of Nature, but of a history embracing thousands of centuries."[54]

Capitalist production and circulation tends to transform these possibilities into an integrated geographical system of production and exchange which serves the purposes of capitalist accumulation. In the process certain countries may establish a monopoly over the production of particular commodities,[55] while center-periphery relations will be produced on a global scale:

> A new and international division of labour, a division suited to the requirements of the chief centres of modern industry springs up, and converts one part of the globe into a chiefly agricultural field of production, for supplying the other part which remains a chiefly industrial field.[56]

Capitalists in the advanced countries may also gain a higher rate of profit by selling their goods above their value in competition with "commodities produced in other countries with inferior production facilities . . . in the same way that a manufacturer exploits a new invention before it has become general.[57] Relative productive advantages yield excess profits and if they are perpetuated in the form of a permanent "technology-gap" it follows (although Marx did not apparently make the point) that technology-rich regions always have the capacity to earn higher profits within a given line of production compared to technology-poor regions.

The international credit system also has a vital role to play in creating the world market and fashioning its structure:

> The entire credit system . . . rests on the necessity of expanding and leaping over the barrier to circulation and the sphere of exchange. This appears more colossally, classically, in the relations between people than in the relations between individuals. Thus, e.g., the English [are] forced to lend to foreign nations in order to have them as customers.[58]

Capital export—a theme which Lenin elaborates on as crucial to the theory of imperialism as the highest stage of capitalism[59]—can, in Marx's view, provide temporary opportunities for surplus capital. But capital export can take different forms as we will shortly see and be engaged in for quite different reasons.

The general drive to overcome all spatial barriers produces a variety of results in relation to non-capitalist forms of production and social organization:

> When an industrial people, producing on the foundation of capital, such as the English, e.g., exchange with the Chinese, and absorb value . . . by drawing the latter within the sphere of circulation of capital, then one sees right away that the Chinese do not therefore need to produce as capitalists.[60]

The interaction of capitalist and non-capitalist modes of production within the sphere of circulation creates strong interdependencies. The circulation of value within the capitalist system becomes dependent on the continued contribution of products and money from non-capitalist societies—"to this extent the capitalist mode of production is conditional on modes of production lying outside of its own stage of development."[61] This is a theme which Luxemburg develops at great length in her *The Accumulation of Capital*—she argues, in effect, that the fresh room for accumulation which capitalism must define can exist only in the form of pre-capitalist societies which provide untapped markets to absorb what is a perpetual tendency for the overproduction of commodities under capitalism.[62] Once these societies are all brought into the capitalist network then, in her view, accumulation must cease.

Marx also argued that the historic tendency of capitalism is to destroy and absorb non-capitalist modes of production at the same time as it uses them to create fresh room for capital accumulation. Initially, the mere penetration of the money form has a disrupting influence—"where money is not the community, it must dissolve the community" and "draw new continents into the metabolism of circulation."[63] In the early stages capital is accumulated out of this "metabolism of circulation"—indeed, such accumulation is an historical premise for the development of capitalist production. The towns accumulate use values and hence values from the countryside while merchant's capital, as an historically prior form of organization to producer's capital:

> appropriates an overwhelming portion of the surplus product partly as a mediator between commodities which still substantially produce for use value . . . and partly because under those earlier modes of production the principle owners of the surplus product with whom the merchant dealt, namely, the slave-owner, the feudal lord, and the state (for instance, the oriental despot) represent the consuming wealth and luxury which the merchant seeks to trap. . . . Merchant's capital, when it holds a position of dominance, stands everywhere for a system of robbery, so that its development among the trading nations of old and modern times is always directly connected with plundering, piracy, kidnapping, slavery and colonial conquest. . . . The development of merchant's capital gives rise everywhere to the tendency towards production of exchange values. . . . Commerce, therefore, has a more or less dissolving influence everywhere on the producing organization which it finds at hand and whose different forms are mainly carried on with a view to use value.[64]

The resultant forms which emerge from such disruptions depend, however, upon the form of the pre-existing society and the extent of capitalist penetration. One effect, for example, is to create scarcities in the non-capitalist society where there were none before. Necessaries are thereby transformed into luxuries and this:

> determines the whole social pattern of backward nations . . . which are associated with a world market based on capitalist production. No matter how large the surplus product, they (the non-capitalist producers) extract from the surplus labour of their slaves in the simple form of cotton or corn, they can adhere to this simple undifferentiated labour because foreign trade enables them to convert these simple products into any kind of use value.[65]

The creation of "underdevelopment" by means of a capitalist penetration which transforms non-capitalist societies from relatively self-sufficient organizations for the production of use-values to specialized and dependent units producing exchange values, is a theme which has been explored by contemporary writers such as Baran and Frank.[66] The latter, for example, coins the phrase "the development of underdevelopment" to call attention to the kinds of processes that Marx had in mind.

These forms of dependency are possible only *after* capitalist production had come to dominate merchant's capital so that the latter now basically serves the purposes of the former. We then find:

> the cheapness of the articles produced by machinery, and the improved means of transport and communication furnish the weapons for conquering foreign markets. By ruining handicraft production in other countries, machinery forcibly converts them into fields for the supply of its raw material. In this way, East India was compelled to produce cotton, wool, hemp, jute and indigo for Great Britain.[67]

The manner of such a transformation is of interest and India provides a good example. Originally a field for "direct exploitation"—the direct appropriation of use values—India was transformed after 1815 into a market for British textile products:

> But the more the industrial interest became dependent on the Indian market, the more it felt the necessity of creating fresh productive powers in India, after having ruined her native industry. You cannot continue to inundate a country with your manufactures, unless you enable it to give you some produce in return.[68]

Capital export in this case served a different purpose from the mere loan of money to finance imports of manufactures. Capital was exported to India to promote commodity production which could, via foreign trade, provide the wherewithal to pay for the goods which were being imported from Britain. Britain had to build up commodity production for exchanges in India if it was to maintain India as an important market.

The same sort of logic, operating under rather different conditions, applies to the development of colonies through settlement. Marx insists here on drawing a distinction:

> There are the colonies proper, such as the United States, Australia, etc. Here the mass of the farming colonists, although they bring with them a larger or smaller amount of capital from the motherland, are not *capitalists* nor do they carry on *capitalist* production. They are more or less peasants who work themselves and whose main object, in the first place, is to produce their own livelihood. . . . In the second type of colonies—plantations—where commercial speculations figure from the start and production is intended for the world market, the capitalist mode of production exists, although only in a formal sense, since the slavery of Negroes precludes free wage labour, which is the basis of capitalist production. But the business in which slaves are used is conducted by capitalists.[69]

Colonies of the latter sort hold out the prospect for high profits because of the higher rates of exploitation, the lower price of necessaries and, usually, higher natural productivity. Capital may move into such colonies and in the process reduce the excess profit there, but in the process the average rate of profit will rise.[70] There exists here a positive inducement to the export of capital:

> If capital is sent abroad, this is not done because it absolutely could not be applied at home, but because it can be employed at a higher rate of profit in a foreign country.[71]

With complete mobility, of course, the profit rate will ultimately be equalized although at a higher average rate than before. But colonies of this second sort are still advantageous because they permit the importation of cheap raw materials on the basis of a higher rate of exploitation (which presumes, by the way, certain immobilities to labour power, such as that imposed by slavery).

Colonies of the first sort exist in a very different relation to the capitalist mode of production, however:

> There the capitalist regime everywhere comes into collision with the resistance of the producer, who, as owner of his own conditions of labour, employs that labour to enrich himself, instead of the capitalist. The contradiction of these two diametrically opposed economic systems, manifests itself here practically in a struggle between them. Where the capitalist has at his back the power of the mother-country, he tries to clear out of his way by force, the modes of production and appropriation, based on the independent labour of the producer.[72]

Colonies made up of small independent producers, trading some surplus into the market, are typically characterised by labor shortages and a high wage rate which is not attractive to the capitalist form of exploitation (this is particularly the case where there is an abundance of free land for settlement). Commodity production does not exist in the complete capitalist sense. Colonial forms of this sort may be, therefore, just as resistant to the penetration of the capitalist mode of production as traditional more long-established non-capitalist societies. But since such non-capitalist colonies are created by spin-offs of surplus population and small quantities of capital from the centres of accumulation, and since they also form markets for capitalist production, they are to be viewed as both the result of past accumulation and a precondition for further capital accumulation. The United States prior to the Civil War, for example, provided an important, largely non-capitalist market for the realization of commodities produced under capitalist social relations in Britain.

The final stage of capitalist penetration is that which comes with the organization of production along capitalist lines. In 1867 Marx noted how the United States was being transformed from an independent, largely non-capitalist, production system into a new centre for capital accumulation. "Capitalistic production advances there with giant strides, even though the lowering of wages and the dependence of the wage worker are yet far from being down to the European level."[73] Marx expected a similar transformation in India:

> when you have once introduced machinery into the locomotion of a country, which possesses iron and coals, you are unable to withhold it from its

fabrication. You cannot maintain a net of railways over an immense country without introducing all those industrial processes necessary to meet the immediate and current wants of railway locomotion, and out of which there must grow the application of machinery to those branches of industry not immediately connected with railways. The railways system will therefore become, in India, truly the forerunner of modern industry . . . (which) will dissolve the hereditary divisions of labour, upon which rest the Indian castes, those decisive impediments to Indian progress and Indian power. . . . The bourgeois period of history has to create the material basis of the new world . . . Bourgeois industry and commerce create these material conditions of a new world in the same way that geological revolutions have created the surface of the earth.[74]

Such a transformation did not occur in India but it did in the United States. The failure to predict correctly in the Indian case has no bearing whatsoever on the validity of the Marxian theory of accumulation under the capitalist mode of production. All the theory says is that capitalism is bound to expand through both an intensification of relationships in the centres of capitalist production and a geographical extension of those relationships in space. The theory does not pretend to predict where, when and exactly how these intensifications and geographical extensions will occur—the latter are a matter for concrete historical analyses. Marx's failure to predict correctly in the case of India was a failure of historical analysis, not of theory.

But it so happens that there are also good *theoretical* reasons for believing that the capitalist *production* system could not and cannot become universal in its scope. For this to be the case would require the equalization of profits, through competition, on a global scale. To begin with, of course, there are all kinds of barriers to be overcome before such an equalization in profit rates could occur. We would have to presume the complete mobility of capital and labour and adequate institutional arrangements (free trade, universal money and credit system, "the abolition of all laws preventing the labourers from transferring from one sphere of production to another and from one locality to another," and so on).[75] Under capitalism, there are always tendencies pushing in these directions. For example:

it is only foreign trade, the development of the market to a world market, which causes money to develop into world money and abstract labour into social labour. Abstract wealth, value, money, hence abstract labour, develop in the measure that concrete labour becomes a totality of different modes of labour embracing the world market. Capitalist production rests on the value or the transformation of the labour embodied in the product into social labour. But this is only possible on the basis of foreign trade and the world market. This is at once the pre-condition and the result of capitalist production.[76]

The tendency of capitalism, therefore, is to establish a universal set of values, founded on "abstract social labour" as defined on a global scale. There is, in like manner, a tendency for capital export to equalize the rate of profit on a global scale. An accumulation process implies a tendency for the penetration of capitalist social relations into all aspects of production and exchange throughout the world.

But different organic compositions of capital between countries, different productivities of labour according to natural differences, the different definition of "necessities" according to natural and cultural situation, mean that these equalizations will not be accompanied by an equalization in the rate of exploitation between countries.[77] It follows that "the favoured country recovers more labour in exchange for less labour, although this difference, this excess is pocketed, as in any exchange between capital and labour, by a certain class."[78] Marx then notes that:

> Here the law of value undergoes essential modification. The relationship between labour days of different countries may be similar to that existing between skilled, complex labour and unskilled, simple labour within a country. In this case the richer country exploits the poorer one, even where the latter gains by the exchange.[79]

There are the kinds of "special factors" which make of foreign trade a very complex issue, which generate certain peculiarities in the terms of trade between developed and undeveloped societies[80] and which prevent any direct "levelling out of values by labour time and even the levelling out of cost prices by a general rate of profit" between different countries.[81] These kinds of factors are picked up on by Emmanuel in his analysis of imperialism as "unequal exchange."[82]

These complexities do not derive from the failure of capitalist development to overcome the social and cultural barriers to its penetration (although these barriers can be exceedingly resistant). They stem, rather, from the inherent contradictory and hence imperfect character of the capitalist mode of production itself. They are to be interpreted, therefore, as global manifestations of the internal contradictions of capitalism. And underlying all of these manifestations is the fact that capitalism ultimately becomes the greatest barrier to its own development. Let us consider how this is manifest on the world stage.

Capitalism can escape its own contradiction only through expanding. Expansion is simultaneously *intensification* (of social wants and needs, of population totals and the like) and *geographical extension*. Fresh room for accumulation must exist or be created if capitalism is to survive. If the capitalist mode of production dominated in every respect, in every sphere and in all parts of the world, there would be little or no room left for further accumulation (population growth and the creation of new social wants and needs would be the only options). Long before such a situation was reached the accumulation process would slow. Stagnation would set in attended by a whole gamut of economic and social problems. Internal checks within the capitalist mode of production would begin to be felt particularly in the sphere of competition:

> As long as capital is weak, it still itself relies on the crutches of past modes of production, or of those which will pass with its rise. As soon as it feels strong, it throws away the crutches and moves in accordance with its own laws. As soon as it begins to sense itself and becomes conscious of itself as a barrier to development, it seeks refuge in forms which, by restricting free competition, seem to make the rule of capital more perfect, but are at the same time the heralds of its dissolution and of the dissolution of the mode of production resting on it.[83]

SOME COMMENTS ON THE THEORY OF IMPERIALISM

Marx himself never proposed a theory of imperialism. In his comments on transportation relations, location theory and foreign trade he clearly indicates, however, that he has in mind some sort of general theory of capital accumulation on an expanding and intensifying geographical scale. We have, in the preceeding two sections, already sketched in some of the main features of that general theory, to the extent that Marx articulated it.

The theory of imperialism which has emerged post-Marx obviously has something to contribute towards an understanding of that general theory and therefore to an understanding of the ways in which capitalism creates fresh room for accumulation. The trouble is, however, that there is not one theory of imperialism, but a whole host of representations of the matter—Marxist, neo-Marxist, Keynesian, neo-classical and so on. And there are innumerable divergences and differences within each school.[84] I shall confine myself to some general comments.

The problem for the Marxists and neo-Marxists, it is generally argued, is to derive a theory of imperialism out of Marx. And it is generally agreed that no one has yet succeeded in doing so although many have tried. There is a fairly simple explanation for this state of affairs. Marx constructed a theory of accumulation for a capitalist mode of production in a "pure" state without reference to any particular historical situation. On this basis, as we have seen, he demonstrates the necessity for intensification and expansion as a concomitant of accumulation. The theory of imperialism, as it is usually conceived of in the literature is, by way of contrast, a theory of history. It is to be used to explain the historical development of capitalist social formations on the world stage. It has to address the way in which conflicting forces and class interests relate to each other in specific historical situations, determine outcomes through their interactions and thereby set the preconditions for the next stage in the evolution of capitalist social formation. Marx never constructed such an historical theory, although there is some evidence that he intended to do so in unwritten books on the State, Foreign Trade and the World Market.[85]

Marx's theory of the capitalist mode of production plainly cannot be used as the basis for deriving an historically specific theory of imperialism in any direct manner. Yet, as we have seen in the preceeding section on foreign trade, Marx's theoretical insights intersect with historical analyses at certain points. And the crucial mediating influence, which most of the writers on imperialism ignore, is the necessary tendency to overcome spatial barriers and to annihilate space with time—tendencies which Marx derives directly from the theory of accumulation. Marx's theories of transportation relations, location and geographical concentration, expanding spheres of realization—in short the general theory of accumulation on an expanding and intensifying geographical scale—in fact comprise Marx's own theory of imperialism (although he did not call it that). Since most writers ignore this general theory embedded in Marx it would appear that this provides us with the missing link between Marx's theory of accumulation and the various theories of imperialism that have been put forward since.

But even here we cannot make direct derivations. Marx's general theory tells us of the necessity to expand and intensify geographically. But it does not tell us exactly how, when or where. Looking at the intersection of these general arguments with concrete historical analyses, we will usually be able to identify the underlying logic dictated by capital accumulation at work. But the underlying logic does not, and indeed cannot uniquely determine outcomes. The latter have to be understood in terms of the balance of forces—economic, social, political, ideological, competitive, legal, military, and the like—through which interest groups and classes become conscious of the contradictory underlying logic and seek by their actions to "fight it out" to some sort of resolution.[86] To specify the relationships between the Marxian theory of accumulation and the theory of imperialism as it is usually construed poses, therefore, a double difficulty. We have to specify how the "inner logic" of the capitalist mode of production, abstractly conceived, relates to the concrete realities, the phenomenal forms, of the historical process. And we also have to take account of the mediating influence of political, ideological, military and other structures which, although they must be generally organized so as to be coherent with the course of capital accumulation, are not uniquely determined by it.

Most analyses of imperialism usually start in fact from the analysis of actual historical situations. This is particularly true in the work of Third World writers, such as Fanon, Amin and Frank, whose starting point is the experience of domination and exploitation by the advanced capitalist countries.[87] This experience is then projected into the Marxian framework for understanding exploitation in general. The consequence of this is a variety of representations of the Marxian theory of imperialism. Each representation may be accurate for its own place and time, but each ends up drawing upon just one or two factors of Marx's own theory of capital accumulation for support. By implication, and sometimes quite explicitly, it is suggested that other facets of Marx's theory of accumulation are either irrelevant or wrong.

Luxemburg is an excellent case in point.[88] She begins her analysis with a concentrated criticism of Marx's reproduction schemes in Volume 2 of *Capital* and, reacting very strongly to the idea implied there that capitalist accumulation can continue in perpetuity, she seeks to show that Marx had failed to demonstrate where the effective demand for commodities was to come from if accumulation was to be sustained. Luxemburg's own solution is that the effective demand has to be found outside of the capitalist system in pre-capitalist economic formations. Imperialism is to be explained as "the political expression of the accumulation of capital in its competitive struggle for what still remains open of the non-capitalist environment."[89] As evidence, Luxemburg assembles descriptions of the violent penetration of non-capitalist societies, such as China, by capitalists in search of markets as well as descriptions of the various imperialist rivalries amongst the capitalist powers throughout the world.

Luxemburg's argument is, in many respects, both compelling and brilliant. But her analysis amounts to a one-sided development out of Marx. The objection is not that she is wrong—indeed we have already seen that capitalist development may become contingent upon other modes of production, that the penetration and disruption of non-capitalist societies are implied by the imperative to "tear down spatial barriers," and that violence, making use of state power, can easily be resorted to. The objection is that Luxemburg sees the consequences of the imperative to accumulate *solely* in these terms. The other means whereby capitalism can create fresh room for accumulation are ignored.

Read as a theoretical treatise on what must happen if all other means for creating fresh room for accumulation are sealed off, Luxemburg's work is a brilliant exposition. Read as a documentation of how the logic of capitalist accumulation underlies the penetration and disruption of non-capitalist societies, the work is compelling. But read as a derivation of the necessity for imperialism out of a correction of Marx's errors in his specification of capitalist reproduction, Luxemburg's work is both erroneous and misconceived. To put the criticism this way is not to say, however, that the processes to which Luxemburg draws attention may not become, at a certain stage in capitalist history, vital to the perpetuation of the capitalist order. Whether or not this turns out to be the case depends, however, upon the capacity of the capitalist system to create fresh room for accumulation by other means.

The representation of imperialism in the works of Baran and Frank can be considered in a similar way.[90] Clearly implied in Marx's location theory is the emergence of a general structure of center-periphery relations in production and exchange, while the tearing down of spatial barriers to exchange may create dependency and "transform necessaries into luxuries" for the economy newly brought into the metabolism of exchange. These kinds of relationships are examined in detail in the work of Baran and Frank and they can relatively easily be integrated into the Marxian frame when the logic of accumulation is projected into an actual historical situation. Baran and Frank are therefore on strong theoretical grounds when they claim that backwardness and underdevelopment can and must be produced and perpetuated by the penetration of capitalist social relations into non-capitalist economies. They may also be on strong factual grounds when they claim that this is the general relationship which exists between the Third World and the metropolitan centres of accumulation. But, as with the work of Luxemburg, the analysis has to be regarded as a single-faceted development out of Marx's theory of accumulation. It would be both erroneous and misconceived to regard this development either as a correction to or a unique derivation out of Marx. Fresh room for accumulation can be created by a variety of strategems in actual historical situations. Whether or not a different structure of relations to that explored by Baran and Frank is possible depends *not* on the theory but on the possibilities contained in actual historical situations.

Lenin's contribution to the Marxist theory of imperialism is, of course, fundamental. And in some respects it is the most interesting both with respect to its content and its method. Lenin did not attempt to derive the theory out of Marx. He regarded the phenomena of imperialism as something to be revealed by materialist historical analysis. Specifically, he was concerned to explain the 1914-18 war as an imperialist war "for the division of the world, for the partition and repartition of colonies and spheres of influences of finance capital, etc."[91] The method is therefore historical and Lenin uses the term "imperialism" to describe the general characteristics of the phenomenal form assumed by capitalism during a particular stage of its development—specifically, during the late nineteenth and early twentieth centuries. In this he relies very heavily on the work of a non-Marxist, Hobson.[92] Yet Lenin also seeks to uncover "the economic essence of imperialism'' and to relate the understanding of the phenomenal appearance of imperialism to Marx's theoretical insights into the nature of the capitalist mode of production.

The phenomenal appearance of capitalism in the imperialist stage of its development is summarized in terms of five basic features:

> (1) the concentration of production and capital has developed to such a high stage that it has created monopolies which play a decisive role in economic life; (2) the merging of bank capital with industrial capital, and the creation, on the basis of this "finance capital," of a financial oligarchy; (3) the export of capital as distinguished from the export of commodities acquires exceptional importance; (4) the formation of international monopolist associations which share the world among themselves, and (5) the territorial division of the whole world among the big capitalist powers is completed.[93]

The tendency towards concentration and centralization of capital is, in Marx's analysis, integral to the general process of accumulation.[94] The physical concentration of production to achieve economies of scale in a locational sense is also, in Marx's theory, paralleled by a growing centralization of capital. Lenin also grounds the logic of capital export in Marx's theory. He rebuts the argument that capitalism could ever achieve an equal development in all spheres of production or alleviate the misery of the mass of workers:

> If capitalism did these things it would not be capitalism; for both uneven development and a semi-starvation level of existence of the masses are fundamental and inevitable conditions and constitute the premises of this mode of production. As long as capitalism remains what it is, surplus capital will be utilized not for the purpose of raising the standard of living of the masses in a given country, for this would mean a decline in profits for the capitalists, but for the purpose of increasing profits by exporting capital abroad to the backward countries. In these backward countries profits are usually high, for capital is scarce, the price of land is relatively low, wages are low, raw materials are cheap. . . . The export of capital influences and greatly accelerates the development of capitalism in those countries to which it is exported. While, therefore, the export of capital may tend to a certain extent to arrest development in the capital-exporting countries, it can only do so by expanding and deepening the further development of capitalism throughout the world.[95]

Lenin is here emphasizing certain of the possibilities contained in the Marxian theory of capitalist accumulation when projected into an actual historical situation. Plainly, he is not excluding the development of capitalist production in new centres, although the carving up of the world into spheres of influence with centres of accumulation and spheres of realization is regarded as a "managed" rationalization, accomplished by finance capitalism through political manipulations, of the inevitable uneven development of capitalism. But Lenin also argues that imperialism "can and must be defined differently if we bear in mind not only the basic, purely economic concepts . . . but also the historical place of this stage of capitalism in relation to capitalism in general, or the relation between imperialism and the two main trends in the working class movement."[96] Imperialism thus has the effect of "exporting" some of the tensions created by the class struggle within the centres of accumulation to peripheral areas. The "superprofits" of imperialist exploitation make it "possible to bribe the labour leaders and the upper stratum of the labour aristocracy. And that is just what the capitalists of the "advanced" countries are doing."[97] This last aspect of imperialism has to be regarded as the joint outcome of the inevitable uneven development of capitalism on a world scale and a corresponding uneven development of the class struggle. Capital becomes mobile in order to escape the consequences of a class struggle waged at a particular place and time or else it repatriates superprofits to buy off home labour force with material advancement. In either case a geographical expansion of development must occur.

Lenin blends concrete historical analysis, based on the principles of historical materialism, with some fundamental insights from Marx's theory. An evaluation of Lenin's theory must rest, therefore, on an assessment of his historical accuracy and a critical evaluation of the way in which the Marxian theory intersects with the historical materials. On the former score there are grounds for thinking that Lenin's reliance on Hobson and Hilferding led him into some factual errors. In the latter respect, Lenin, like most other writers on imperialism, develops Marx's general theory in a one-sided rather than an all-embracing manner. As a consequence the connection to the theory of capitalist accumulation is partially obscured from view.

The problem with the Marxist theory of imperialism in general, is that it has become a theory "unto itself," divorced from Marx's theory of capital accumulation. As a consequence, the argument over what imperialism is, has degenerated into an argument over which of several competing principles should be used to define it. The development of overseas markets? The attainment of cheaper raw materials? The searching out of a more easily exploited and a more docile labour force? Is it primitive accumulation at the expense of non-capitalist societies? Does it involve cheating through exchange? Is it the necessary export of capital to set up new centres of industrial accumulation? Is it the concentration of relative surplus value on a localized basis? Is it the manifestation of monopoly power, expressed through the political organization of a system of nation states? Is it finance capital operating through multinational corporations and government cooptation? It is simply the international division of labour? Is it a particular combination of any of the above? Under Marx's general theory all of the above are possible and none are to be excluded. It is, therefore, the task of careful historical analysis to discover which of these manifestations is dominant at a particular stage of development of capitalist social formations. Marx's general theory does not pretend to predict particular forms and manifestations. All it does is to indicate the underlying imperative, contained within the capitalist system, to accumulate capital and to do it, of necessity, on an expanding and intensifying geographical scale.

This is not to say that a theoretical analysis of these various manifestations in relation to capital accumulation is impossible. Indeed, a great deal can be done here. And we can also place one bet. The survival of capitalism is predicted on the continued ability to accumulate, *by whatever means is easiest*. The path of capitalist accumulation will move *to wherever the resistance is weakest*. It is the task of historical and theoretical analyses to identify these points of least resistance, of greatest weakness. Lenin once advised all revolutionary movements to look for the weakest link in capitalism. Ironically, capitalism manages, by trial and error and persistant pressure, to discover the weakest links in the forces opposed to continued accumulation and by exploiting those links to open up fresh pasture for the bourgeoisie to accomplish its historical mission—the accumulation of capital.

MARX'S THEORY OF CAPITAL ACCUMULATION ON AN EXPANDING GEOGRAPHICAL SCALE AS A WHOLE

Marx's theory of capital accumulation on an expanding geographical scale is quite complex. We have delved into Marx to try to discover in his writings some of its basic components. But to be appreciated properly these components have to be seen in relation both one to each other and to the various models which Marx devised to understand capitalist production, exchange and realization as a totality. In a rather splendid passage in the *Grundrisse*,[98] Marx provides a kind of "overview sketch" of his general theory:

> The creation by capital of *absolute surplus value* . . . is conditional upon an expansion, specifically a constant expansion, of the sphere of circulation. . . . A precondition of production based on capital is therefore *the production of a constantly widening sphere of circulation*. Hence, just as capital has the tendency on one side to create ever more surplus labour, so it has the complementary tendency to create more points of exchange.

From this, of course, we can derive "the tendency to create the world market [which] is directly given in the concept of capital itself" and the need, initially at least, "to subjugate every moment of production itself to exchange and to suspend the production of direct use values not entering into exchange." Marx then goes on to say that:

> the production of *relative surplus value* . . . requires the production of new consumption; requires that the consuming circle within circulation expands as did the productive circle previously. Firstly quantitative expansion of existing consumption; secondly, creation of new needs by propagating existing ones in a wide circle; thirdly, production of *new* needs and discovery and creation of new use values. As a result of these expansionary tendencies, capitalism creates: a system of general exploitation of the natural and human qualities. . . . Hence the great civilizing influence of capital; its production of a stage of society in comparison to which all earlier ones appear as mere *local developments* of humanity and as *nature idolatory*. For the first time, nature becomes purely an object for humankind, purely a matter of utility. . . . In accord with this tendency, capital drives beyond national barriers and prejudices as much as beyond nature worship, as well as all traditional, confined, encrusted satisfactions of present needs, and reproductions of old ways of life. It is destructive towards all of this, and constantly revolutionizes it, tearing down all the barriers which hem in the development of the forces of production, the expansion of needs, the all-sided development of production, and the exploitation and exchange of natural and mental forces. . . .
>
> But . . . since every such barrier contradicts its character, its production

moves in contradictions which are constantly overcome but just as constantly posited. Furthermore, the universality towards which it irresistably strives encounters barriers in its own nature, which will, at a certain stage of its development, allow it to be recognized as being itself the greatest barrier to this tendency, and hence will drive towards its own suspension.

Marx's sketch does not incorporate all of the elements which we have identified in this paper but it does convey a feeling for what he had in mind in constructing a theory of accumulation on an expanding geographical scale. Plainly, the drive to accumulate lies at the center of the theory. This drive is expressed primarily in the production process through the creation of absolute and relative surplus value. But the creation of value is contingent upon the ability to realize it through circulation. Failure to realize value means, quite simply, the negation of the value created potentially in production. Thus, if the sphere of circulation does not expand then accumulation comes to a halt. Capital, Marx never tires of emphasizing, is not a thing or a set of institutions; it is a process of circulation between production and realization. This process, which must expand, must accumulate, constantly re-shapes the work process and the social relationships within production as it constantly changes the dimensions and forms of circulation. Marx helps us to understand these processes theoretically. But ultimately we have to bring this theory to bear on existing situations within the structure of capitalist social relations at this point in history. We have to force an intersection between the theoretical abstractions, on the one hand, and the materialist investigations of actual historical configurations on the other. To construct and reconstruct Marx's theory of accumulation on an expanding geographical scale as a totality requires such an intersection. We have indeed to derive the theory of imperialism out of the Marxian theory of accumulation. But to do so we have to move carefully through the intermediate steps. In Marx's own thought it appears that the crucial intermediate steps encompass a theory of location and an analysis of fixed and immobile investment; the necessary creation of a geographical landscape to facilitate accumulation through production and circulation. But the steps from the theory of accumulation to the theory of imperialism, or more generally to a theory of history, are not simple mechanical derivations because down this path we have to accomplish also that transformation from the general to the concrete which comprised the central thrust of Marx's unfinished work. We have to learn, in short, to complete the project which Marx underscores at the beginning of Volume 3 of *Capital*—we have to bring a synthetic understanding of the processes of production and circulation under capitalism to bear on capitalist history and "thus approach step by step the form which they assume on the surface of society."

NOTES AND REFERENCES

1. K. Marx, *Capital,* Vol. 1. (New York: International Publishers, 1967), p. 595.
2. Ibid., p. 592.
3. Marx, *Capital,* Vol. 2, p. 495.
4. K. Marx, *Grundrisse*. (Harmondsworth, Middlesex: Penguin Books, 1973), p. 93.
5. K. Marx, *Theories of Surplus Value,* Part 2. (Moscow: Progress Publishers, 1967, 1968, and 1972), p. 552.

6. Ibid., p. 492; and Marx, *Capital,* Vol. 3, p. 484.
7. Marx. *Theories of Surplus Value,* Part 2, p. 506.
8. Ibid., pp. 497–499.
9. Ibid., pp. 534–535.
10. K. Marx, *Capital,* Vol. 3, p. 251.
11. Marx, *Theories of Surplus Value,* Part 2, p. 42; cf. *Grundrisse,* p. 474 and p. 771.
12. Marx, *Grundrisse,* p. 543.
13. Marx, *Capital,* Vol. 2, p. 150; and *Grundrisse,* pp. 533–534.
14. Marx, *Capital,* Vol. 2, p. 52.
15. Marx, *Grundrisse,* pp. 533–534.
16. Ibid., p. 253.
17. Ibid., pp. 531–533.
18. Ibid., p. 534.
19. Marx, *Capital,* Vol. 2, p. 142.
20. Marx, *Grundrisse,* pp. 533–534.
21. Marx, *Capital,* Vol. 1, p. 384.
22. Marx, *Grundrisse,* p. 524.
23. Loc. cit.
24. Marx, *Capital,* Vol. 2, p. 248.
25. Marx, *Grundrisse,* p. 538.
26. Marx, *Capital,* Vol. 2, p. 249.
27. Marx, *Grundrisse,* p. 539.
28. Marx, *Capital,* Vol. 2, pp. 251–252.
29. Marx, *Grundrisse,* p. 535.
30. Marx, *Capital,* Vol. 1, p. 352; and *Grundrisse,* p. 587.
31. Marx, *Capital,* Vol. 2, p. 250.
32. Marx, *Capital,* Vol. 2, p. 250.
33. Marx, *Capital,* Vol. 1, p. 535.
34. Marx, *Capital,* Vol. 2, p. 251.
35. Marx, *Capital,* Vol. 1, p. 378.
36. Marx, *Theories of Surplus Value,* Part 3, p. 288.
37. Marx, *Capital,* Vol. 2, p. 250.
38. Ibid., p. 249.
39. Marx, *Grundrisse,* p. 740.
40. Ibid., p. 539.
41. Marx, *Grundrisse,* p. 728.
42. Marx, *Capital,* Vol. 2, p. 160.
43. Marx, *Grundrisse,* p. 703.
44. For a special example of this issue see D. Harvey, "The Political Economy of Urbanization in Advanced Capitalist Countries—the Case of the United States" in G. Gappert and H. Rose, eds., *Urban Affairs Annual No. 9—The Social Economy of Cities* (Beverly Hills, Calif: Sage Publications, 1975).
45. See, e.g. S. Kuznets, *Capital in the American Economy, Its Formation and Financing* (National Bureau of Economic Research, Princeton University Press, 1961); and B. Thomas, *Migration and Urban Development.* (London: Methuen, 1972).
46. Marx, *Capital,* Vol. 2, p. 251.
47. Marx, *Capital,* Vol. 1, p. 581.
48. Marx, *Capital,* Vol. 2, p. 470.
49. Marx, *Capital,* Vol. 3, p. 237.
50. Marx, *Capital,* Vol. 2, p. 408.
51. Marx, *Capital,* Vol. 1, p. 512.
52. Marx, *Capital,* Vol. 3, p. 650.
53. Marx, *Capital,* Vol. 1, p. 514.
54. Ibid., p. 512.
55. Marx, *Capital,* Vol. 3, p. 119.
56. Marx, *Capital,* Vol. 1, p. 451.
57. Marx, *Capital,* Vol. 3, p. 238.
58. Marx, *Grundrisse,* p. 416; cf., *Theories of Surplus Value,* Vol. 3, p. 122.

59. V. Lenin, "Imperialism, The Highest Stage of Capitalism," in *Selected Works,* Vol. 1. (Moscow: Progress Publishers, 1963).

60. Marx, *Grundrisse,* p. 720.

61. Marx, *Capital,* Vol. 2, p. 110.

62. R. Luxemburg, *The Accumulation of Capital* (London: Routledge and Kegan Paul, 1951).

63. Marx, *Grundrisse,* pp. 224–225.

64. Marx, *Capital,* Vol. 3, pp. 331–332.

65. Marx, *Theories of Surplus Value,* Part 3, p. 243.

66. P. Baran, *The Political Economy of Growth* (New York: Monthly Review Press, 1957), and A. G. Frank. *Capitalism and Underdevelopment in Latin America* (New York: Monthly Review Press, 1969).

67. Marx, *Capital,* Vol. 1, p. 451.

68. K. Marx, *On Colonialism* (New York: International Publishers, 1971), p. 52.

69. Marx, *Theories of Surplus Value,* Part 2, pp. 302–303.

70. Ibid., 436–437.

71. Marx, *Capital,* Vol. 3, p. 256.

72. Marx, *Capital,* Vol. 1, p. 765.

73. Marx, *Capital,* Vol. 1, p. 773.

74. Marx, *On Colonialism,* pp. 85–87.

75. Marx, *Capital,* Vol. 3, p. 196.

76. Marx, *Theories of Surplus Value,* Part 3, p. 253.

77. Marx, *Capital,* Vol. 3, pp. 150–151.

78. Ibid., p. 238.

79. Marx, *Theories of Surplus Value,* Vol. 3, pp. 105–106.

80. Marx, *Theories of Surplus Value,* Vol. 2, pp. 474–475.

81. Ibid., p. 238.

79. Marx, *Theories of Surplus Value,* Vol. 3, pp. 105–106.

80. Marx, *Theories of Surplus Value,* Vol. 2, pp. 474–475.

81. Ibid., p. 201.

82. A. Emmanuel, *Unequal Exchange* (London: New Left Books, 1972).

83. Marx, *Grundrisse,* p. 651.

84. M. Barratt Brown, *The Economics of Imperialism* (Baltimore: Penguin Books, 1974).

85. K. Marx and F. Engels, *Selected Correspondence* (Moscow: Progress Publishers, 1955), pp. 112–113.

86. Cf. K. Marx, *A Contribution to the Critique of Political Economy* (New York: International Publishers, 1970), p. 21.

87. F. Fanon, *The Wretched of the Earth* (Harmondsworth, Middlesex: Penguin Books, 1967); S. Amin, *Accumulation on a World Scale* (New York: Monthly Review Press, 1973); and Frank, *Capitalism and Underdevelopment in Latin America.*

88. Luxemburg, *The Accumulation of Capital.*

89. Luxemburg, *The Accumulation of Capital,* p. 446.

90. Baran, *The Political Economy of Growth;* and Frank, *Capitalism and Underdevelopment in Latin America.*

91. Lenin, "Imperialism, the Highest Stage of Capitalism," p. 673.

92. J. A. Hobson, *Imperialism* (London: Allen and Unwin, 1938).

93. Lenin, "Imperialism, the Highest Stage of Capitalism," p. 737.

94. Marx, *Capitalism,* Vol. 1, Chapter 25.

95. Lenin, "Imperialism, the Highest Stage of Capitalism," pp. 716–718.

96. Ibid., p. 737.

97. Ibid., p. 677.

98. Marx, *Grundrisse,* pp. 407–410.

Additional Readings

Amin, Samir. *Neo-Colonialism in West Africa.* New York: Monthly Review Press, 1973.

Baird, A. [et al.] *Towards an Explanation and Reduction of Disaster Proneness.* University of Bradford, Disaster Research Unit, Occasional Paper No. 11, 1975.

Bauer, P. T. "The Economic Development of Nigeria," *Journal of Political Economy,* 63, no. 5 (October 1955): 398–411.

Baruch, Kimmerling and Lissak, Moshe. *Inner Dualism: An Outcome of the Center-Periphery Relationship during Modernization Processes in Uganda.* Beverly Hills, California: Sage Publications, 1973.

Blaut, J. M. "Geographic Models of Imperialism," *Antipode,* 2, no. 1 (1970): 65–85.

Blaut, J. M. "The Theory of Development," *Antipode,* 5, no. 2, (May 1973): 22–26.

Blaut, J. M. "Imperialism: The Marxist Theory and its Evolution," *Antipode,* 7, no. 1 (February 1975): pp. 1–19.

Brown, Michael Barratt. *The Economics of Imperialism.* Harmondsworth, England: Penguin Books, 1974.

Galeano, Eduardo. *Open Veins of Latin America, Five Centuries of the Pillage of a Continent.* New York: Monthly Review Press, 1973.

Darwent, D. F. "Growth Poles and Growth Centers in Regional Planning—a Review," *Environment and Planning,* 1 (1969): 5–32.

Gonzalez, Gilbert G. "A Critique of the Internal Colonial Model," *Latin American Perspectives,* 1 (Spring 1974): 154–161.

Harding, Timothy F. "Dependency, Nationalism, and the State in Latin America," *Latin American Perspectives,* Issue 11, 3, no. 4 (Fall 1976): 3–16.

Hensman, C. R. *Rich Against Poor.* Harmondsworth, Penguin Books Ltd., 1975.

Horowitz, Irwing. *Three Worlds of Development, The Theory and Practice of International Stratification.* London: Oxford University Press, 1972.

Jalée, Pierre. *Imperialism in the 70's.* New York: Third Press, 1973.

Lea, David, ed. *Geographical Research: Applications and Relevance.* Vancouver: Pacific Science Association, 13th Congress Proceedings, 1975.

Lerner, Daniel. "Some Comments on Center-Periphery Relations," in Richard L. Merritt and Stein Rokkan, eds., *Comparing Nations.* New Haven: Yale University Press, 1966.

Magdoff, Harry. *The Age of Imperialism.* New York: Monthly Review, 1969.

Magdoff, H. "The American Empire and the U.S. Economy," in Robert I. Rhodes, ed. *Imperialism and Underdevelopment.* New York: Monthly Review Press, 1970.

McColl, Robert W. "Vietnam, Cuba, and the Ghetto," in David A. Lanegran and Risa Palm, eds. *An Invitation to Geography.* New York: McGraw Hill, 1973, pp. 112–116.

McColl, R. W. "Geopolitical Themes in Contemporary Asian Revolutions," *Geographical Review,* 65, no. 3 (July 1975): 301–310.

Myrdal, G. M. *Economic Theory and Underdeveloped Regions.* London: Duckworth, 1957.

Roder, Wolf. "Effects of Guerilla War in Angola and Mozambique," *Antipode,* 5, no. 2 (May 1973): 14–21.

Santos, M. "Spatial Dialectics: The Two Circuits of Urban Economy in Underdeveloped Countries," *Antipode,* 9 (1977): 49–60.

Sherman, Howard. *Radical Political Economy.* New York: Basic Books, 1972. Chapter 10: *Imperialism,* pp. 148–175.

Smith, Stewart. *U.S. Neo-Colonialism in Africa.* New York: International Publishers, 1974.

Thomas, Clive Y. *Dependençe and Transformation. The Economics of the Transition to Socialism.* New York: Monthly Review Press, 1976.

Williamson, J. C. "Regional Inequality and the Process of National Development: A Description of the Patterns," *Economic Development and Cultural Change,* 13, Part 2 (1965).

Appendix: Awareness Exercises

EXERCISE 1
DESCRIPTION AND EXPLANATION OF THE THIRD WORLD

A good way to start a discussion on Third World countries is to pose two problems: (1) List about five words or phrases that describe conditions in the Third World. (2) List about five explanations to account for the conditions found in the Third World.

A national survey may be used as a norm to determine how your views on Third World conditions compare with the views of others. You will find that others frequently share your answers, and sometimes other people have contradictory answers. The readings in this book will help you sort out conflicting descriptions and explanations. A 1972 national public opinion survey by the Overseas Development Council asked students to describe conditions in the Third World (Appendix Table 1).[1] Students, like other Americans, described the Third World in negative terms. Social problems of overpopulation, hunger, primitive culture, political instability, and corruption dominate the image of the Third World. Positive characteristics—rich cultures, old civilizations, diversity of arts, strong kinship ties, and low energy consumption—are absent, yet these conditions also characterize Third World countries. Negative environmental and resource conditions are also stressed. Tropical climates, soils, and diseases are often cited. The

---

Appendix Table 1 Description of Third World Conditions[a]

	Total (percent)
Poor educational facilities, undereducated, illiterate	40
Not enough technology, manufacturing, industry; no exports for trade	24
Poor economy, low standard of living, poverty stricken	20
Can't feed their own people, hunger	19
Limited natural resources, poor land, no tools	12
Bad housing	12
Poor government, unstable governments that exploit	12
Do not use their resources to the fullest, do not work up to their potential	11
Poor medical facilities, much illness, disease, high mortality	10
Overpopulation, too many people, families too large	9
Bad living conditions, sub-standard conditions	7
The people are unaware, do not have the know-how	7
A country that is not developed	4

[a]Totals do not add up to 100 percent because respondents could give several answers.

Appendix Table 2   Explanations of Third World Conditions[a]

	Total (percent)
Lack of education, ignorance, illiteracy	43
Lazy, no ambition, no drive, don't get out and work, want to be poor, prefer welfare	40
Lack of opportunity, never had a chance, can't get decent jobs, don't have equal opportunity	25
They are born into it, the only life they know, it's environmental, they inherit it	19
Handicapped, poor health, illness	6
Don't know how to manage, take care of money, what they have	6
They are victims of the system, the social structure; government	6
Not enough job training, no skills	4
Some are just less fortunate, in the wrong place at the wrong time	3

[a]Totals do not add up to 100 percent because respondents could give several answers.

absence of natural resources and/or the lack of utilization of resources are also mentioned. These conditions are different from social ones because people cannot profoundly change the physical environment. Environmental explanations encourage a passive acceptance of human conditions, whereas socio-political explanations foster active social change.

The survey also asked students to explain why poor countries are poor (Appendix Table 2). First, elements of the culture of poverty, such as poor health and "the only life they know," are the dominant responses. These are followed by traits of individuals including laziness and lack of ambition. Finally, societal institutions, such as the economic system and the role of government, are mentioned by a few students.

Your answers to the initial questions reflect your world view which is based on your information about the Third World and your personal values. Consequently, your descriptions and explanations of Third World conditions will influence your choice of solutions.

EXERCISE 2
THIRD WORLD QUIZ

This exercise is a test of your factual knowledge about the Third World. After completing the quiz, check your responses with the answers found in the *NOTES AND REFERENCES*.[2] Also answer the questions at the end of the quiz.
(1) The average per capita wealth (Gross National Product)
    A) in the U. S. is about:
        a. $3000 b. $4000 c. $5000 d. $6000 e. $7000
    B) in the rest of the developed countries is about:
        a. $1000 b. $2000 c. $3000 d. $4000 e. $5000 f. $6000
    C) in the thirty poorest nations of the world is about:
        a. $100 b. $150 c. $200 d. $250 e. $300 f. $500
    D) in the rest of the underdeveloped nations is about:
        a. $200 b. $300 c. $400 d. $500 e. $600 f. $700

(2) The percentage of world population that lives in the "fourth world" (those nations with per capita wealth of less than $200) is about:
    a. 2% b. 5% c. 10% d. 15% e. 25%

(3) How much more will a person in the rich industrialized countries consume in food and services during his/her lifetime than will a person of a developing country?
    a. three times as much b. 50 times as much c. ten times as much

(4) In the developed nations of the world, the average per capita
  A) daily caloric intake is about:
    a. 1500 b. 2000 c. 2500 d. 3000
  B) annual consumption (direct and indirect) of grain is:
    a. 230 kilograms b. 320 kilograms c. 410 kilograms d. 455 kilograms
    e. 590 kilograms
  C) daily consumption of meat protein is about:
    a. 10 grams b. 20 grams c. 30 grams d. 40 grams

(5) How many people suffer from hunger and malnutrition?
    a. one billion b. 300 million c. 50 million

(6) In the underdeveloped nations of the world, the average per capita
  A) daily caloric intake is about:
    a. 2000 b. 2500 c. 3000 d. 3500 e. 4000
  B) annual consumption (cereals and meats) of grain is:
    a. 180 kilograms b. 270 kilograms c. 360 kilograms d. 455 kilograms
  C) daily consumption of meat protein is about:
    a. 10 grams b. 20 grams c. 30 grams d. 40 grams e. 50 grams

(7) Americans consume 90 per cent of their grain indirectly as meat, milk, and eggs. If Americans were to reduce beef consumption alone by one-third, it has been estimated that enough grain would be saved to feed how many people?
    a. 1 million b. 10 million c. 50 million d. 100 million e. 250 million

(8) How many countries produce significant overall food surpluses for export?
    a. 1 b. 3 c. 10 d. 25 e. 40 f. 60

(9) In 1960, world reserve stocks of grain were sufficient to feed the world's people for 90 days. Today, those stocks are sufficient for about:
    a. 10 days b. 30 days c. 60 days d. 90 days e. 120 days

(10) Underdeveloped nations presently import about 28 million tons of grain annually. At present rates of population growth, how many tons will these nations have to import in 1985 to maintain present marginal levels of consumption?
    a. 45 million b. 55 million c. 65 million d. 75 million e. 85 million

(11) A U. S. female has a life-expectancy of 76 years. For a Bolivian female it is:
    a. 70 years b. 37 years c. 45 years

(12) At present rates of growth, the world's population will double in about:
    a. 15 years b. 25 years c. 35 years d. 45 years e. 55 years

(13) The proportion of the world's population presently living in the underdeveloped nations is about:
    a. 50% b. 60% c. 70% d. 80% e. 90%

(14) At present rates of growth, in the year 2000, the proportion of the world's population living in the underdeveloped countries will be about:
    a. 50% b. 60% c. 70% d. 80% e. 90%

(15) How many school-age children in poor countries do *not* attend school?

   a. 10 million b. 25 million c. 100 million

(16) What percentage of their Gross National Products (GNP) has the United Nations asked rich nations to give as official development assistance to poor countries?

   a. 0.7 per cent b. 5 per cent c. 15 per cent

(17) How many of the rich nations have met this target?

   a. 20 b. 8 c. 2

(18) Which country, on a percentage of GNP basis, gives the most foreign aid funds?

   a. Canada b. Sweden c. United States

(19) Poor countries finance development projects mainly by:

   a. bilateral contributions from donor nations.

   b. multilateral assistance from various international agencies.

   c. through their own efforts.

(20) How much money do poor countries owe to rich nations and how much do they pay each year in interest charges?

   a. $100 million debt and interest charges of $5 million.

   b. $one billion debt and interest charges of $150 million.

   c. $100 billion debt and $15 billion a year in interest charges.

(21) In 1960 an underdeveloped country could export four tons of rubber to pay for one imported tractor. By 1975 one imported tractor cost:

   a. 3 tons of rubber b. 12 tons c. the same as before

Questions

How many questions did you answer correctly?

How many times did you underestimate the magnitude of the problem?

Do you generally have an optimistic or pessimistic view of problems in the Third World?

What is the basis of your hope or despair concerning major global problems?

EXERCISE 3

IDEOLOGICAL STATEMENTS[3]

Scientists make statements about the Third World which initially seem reasonable and objective, but on closer examination require clarification and further discussion. Scientists try to persuade other scholars, politicians, and the general public of their arguments. They persuade through logical and consistent statements, and more importantly they employ hidden assumptions, of which they are usually unaware. The recognition of assumptions is crucial because they may not be valid and/or acceptable by others.

   This exercise is designed to make you reflect on some common statements made in general and about the Third World. After asking clarifying questions about these statements, you will be able to understand the articles in this reader, both for their apparent content and for the ideological assumptions hidden within them. You will then be better able to make your own conclusions on the merits of the various viewpoints and arguments presented.

DIRECTIONS: Circle the word or phrase, if any, that bothers you in each sentence. Make your selections quickly; your first impressions are most important.

(1) Science is objective analysis.

(2) The United States is destined for greatness.

(3) My goal is freedom for all men and women.

(4) Every human being has a right to life.

(5) Tropical climates and soils cause malnutrition.

(6) Lack of natural resources, such as coal and iron ore, retards national economic development.

(7) Women play a relatively minor role in Third World development.

(8) Europeans brought civilization to the Third World.

(9) The advantages of colonialism at one time outweighed the disadvantages.

(10) The shortage of free labor in the Americas necessitated the enslavement of Negroes.

(11) Plantations introduced modern efficient agricultural production techniques to many countries in the tropics.

(12) Small-scale farms are less efficient than large-scale farms.

(13) United States agriculture feeds the world.

(14) Foreign aid helps Third World countries.

(15) If only the Indian people would eat their cattle, they would not go hungry.

(16) Black people have darker skin than we do.

(17) One answer to national problems in the Third World is to elect good men to public office.

(18) Multinational companies bring prosperity to the Third World.

(19) Multinational companies provide employment for people who would otherwise have no jobs.

(20) Overpopulation is the world's single most important problem.

(21) There are too many people on earth.

(22) Unfortunately, about ten million people die of starvation each year in the Third World.

(23) Family planning techniques and clinics are the best way of reducing world population growth.

(24) Some families can afford more children than others.

(25) International tourism helps Third World countries develop their economies.

(26) "Each according to one's needs" is an unrealistic goal.

After completing the above exercise, compare the words you underlined and the reasons for doing so with our choices. We have by no means indicated all the words that could be questioned.

(1) Science is *objective* analysis.
Objective: How do we know? Do all scientists agree with this statement? Do logical positivists, phenomologists, existentialists, and Marxists employ the same kind of analysis and/or achieve the same results?

(2) The United States is *destined* for *greatness*.
Destined: Does it imply inevitability, an act of God? How do countries know what their destiny is?

Greatness: How is it defined? By which countries? By which groups within the U.S.? Is this statement used to justify national actions which would otherwise be disputed more?

(3) *My goal* is *freedom* for *all* men and women.

My goal: Is this a belief only or are you actually working to achieve this goal?

Freedom: What do you mean: freedom *of* speech, assembly, and/or freedom *from* hunger, discrimination, unemployment?

All: Meaning Caucasians or Third World people too? Even for people whose country may be at war with the U. S.?

(4) *Every* human being has a *right to life*.

Every: Including criminals, revolutionaries, children in the Sahel and India?

Right to life: How is life defined? Would you be against war, against abortion, against capital punishment?

(5) Tropical climates and soils *cause* malnutrition.

Cause: Are there more relevant variables, like poverty or shortage of capital due to foreign exploitation, that might cause malnutrition? Have people in tropical environments throughout time suffered from malnutrition?

(6) Lack of natural resources, such as coal and iron ore, *retards* national economic development.

Retards: Are all Third World countries resource poor? Do prosperous European countries lack natural resources?

(7) Women play a relatively *minor* role in Third World development.

Minor: Is development defined as it relates to men only? What work do women perform? What contribution do they make towards the well-being of the community and society?

(8) Europeans *brought civilization* to the Third World.

Brought: Did indigenous civilizations exist before European conquest of the Third World?

Civilization: Is this an ethnocentric concept? Are European notions of civilization, such as the nation-state, Christianity, and political organization, used to define all other cultures?

(9) The *advantages* of colonialism at one time *outweighed* the *disadvantages*.

Advantages, disadvantages: Who defines which is which?

Outweighed: Is this a European perspective? Would all Africans, Latin Americans and Asians, now and then, agree?

(10) The *shortage* of wage labor in the Americas *necessitated* the enslavement of Negroes.

Shortage: Was the shortage real, or were plantation owners unable or unwilling to pay wages sufficiently high to attract workers?

Necessitated: Did cotton and other crops have to be grown on plantations? What alternatives existed?

(11) Plantations *introduced modern efficient* agricultural production techniques to many countries in the tropics.

Introduced: Did efficient means of food production exist in the Third World before the Europeans arrived?

Modern: What does this mean? Does the word really mean capital intensive or high natural resource utilization? Are not all techniques used today, even the most ancient in origin, modern?

Efficient: How is efficiency defined? Yields per worker, per acre, or per units of energy inputs? In which way is plantation agriculture efficient?

(12) Small-scale farms are *less efficient* than large-scale farms.

Less efficient: Same as number (11).

(13) United States agriculture *feeds the world.*

Feeds the world: Does every nation and every person on earth receive food from the U. S.? Are there no starving people? How is U. S. food distributed, sold for money, or given away to the needy of the world?

(14) *Foreign aid* helps *Third World countries.*

Foreign aid: What kind of foreign aid: unilateral or multilateral? What form does this aid take: food, loans which must be used to buy American products, or military equipment?

Third World countries: Who within the Third World is helped? How does foreign aid help the donor countries?

(15) *If only* the Indian people would eat their cattle, they would not go hungry.

If only: Does every society have religious or social taboos? How can we decide the "rational" use of resources? Is one society's rationality another's irrationality?

(16) Black people have *darker* skin than we do.

Darker: Why is Caucasian skin used as an implicit standard against which Black skin color is judged? Would you think it unusual to read the sentence the other way around? Why?

(17) One answer to national problems of the Third World is to elect *good men* to public office.

Good men: Why can individual politicians, as distinct from social movements, solve national and international problems? Are there no good women to elect? Could we agree on which "good" traits would be required?

(18) and (19) Multinational companies *bring prosperity* to the Third World and provide employment for people who would *otherwise have no jobs.*

Bring prosperity: Whose perspective is being expressed here?

Otherwise have no jobs: Would people be without work if there were no multinationals? What did Africans, Asians, and Indians do before European and American companies arrived on their shores?

((20) *Overpopulation* is the world's *single most* important problem.

Overpopulation: Too many people for what? Space on earth, food, energy? Where are too many people—in which particular countries or everywhere on earth?

Single most: How can we decide this? Why not unemployment or poverty?

(21) There are *too many people* on earth.

Too many people: Measured against what? Because the wealthy countries do not want to share their wealth? Because only people with money can receive goods in the "Free World?"

(22) *Unfortunately,* about ten million people *die* of starvation each year in the Third World.

Unfortunately: What does "unfortunately" imply? Can humans do anything about starvation? Have any Third World countries eliminated hunger?

Die: Do people die of natural or human causes? Would "killed" be a more appropriate word? If not, why not?

(23) Family planning techniques and clinics are the *best way* of reducing world population growth.

Best way: What country or group of people makes this decision? Is this a fact or a hope? Do all scientists and governments agree on this approach?

(24) *Some* families can *afford* more children than others.

Some: Who? Rich families in the Third World? Most families in the industrial countries?

Afford: How do people have the high income to "afford" large families? Why should income be related to large families? Does this word imply that poor people do not have the right to have large families?

(25) International tourism helps Third World countries *develop* their economies.

Develop: For whom? Who benefits and pays? At what expense to the local economy and culture?

(26) "Each according to one's *needs*" is an *unrealistic* goal.

Needs: What are needs? What are wants?

Unrealistic: For whom? How is reality defined? Do all people agree on the goals of living? Have any previously "unrealistic" goals ever been achieved?

Scientists and other people who make statements like those in this exercise are making ideological statements. Karl Mannheim provides one definition of ideology, consisting of four components:

(1) a belief system, a way of looking at the world;

(2) systematic distortion of reality reflected in those ideas;

(3) distortion must *not* be a conscious, intentional process; and

(4) the ideas must serve a specific function—maintaining the status quo in the interest of a specific group.[4]

Mullins' alternative and broader definition of ideology is "a logically coherent system which, within a more or less sophisticated conception of history, links the cognitive and evaluative perception of one's social condition—especially its prospects for the future—to a program of collective action for maintenance, alteration or transformation of society."[5] Ideological statements, whether explicit or implicit, are not necessarily undesirable. However, it is important that readers be able to recognize ideology in order to evaluate the writers' positions.

EXERCISE 4
CONSUMPTION[6]

In this exercise we would like you to consider two countries with very different patterns of consumption: Canada, a rich industrial country in North America, and Nigeria, a poor agricultural country in West Africa. The word "consume," by dictionary definition, means: to make away with, destroy, evaporate, to use up. About 1460 the word "consume" took on a slightly different meaning, almost as though someone had a vision that North America was about to be discovered. At that time it came to mean *squander* and *waste*. The opposite of consume is to produce. For humans to survive they must consume and produce in balance.

After reading the following two descriptions of consumption, consider and discuss the questions at the end. The value of this exercise is for you to realize how differently these questions can be answered, and hence, the need for clarifying questions (as in Exercise 3) and for choosing explicitly one of the three explanatory paradigms presented in this book. After reading the book it might be worthwhile to reconsider your answers to the questions in this exercise.

A Canadian

BILLY BUYER may not be a typical Canadian (typical Canadians come in different sexes, shapes, and colors) but he is a typical Canadian consumer. Billy consumes far more than he produces; he is out of balance, as are many others in North America.

On a typical day, Billy awakens, his clock radio goes on and his electric blanket goes off. He brushes with an electric toothbrush; the bristle part is replaced every three months. He squeezes out a last glob of toothpaste and tosses out the tube. A few squirts of deodorant from a disposable aerosol; empty! out it goes. Now for some mouthwash (out goes another bottle). Down to breakfast. Two eggs (throw out the disposable carton), bacon (it takes four pounds of edible grain to produce one pound of pork), two slices of toast (another plastic wrapper bites the dust), and a glass of milk from yet another disposable carton.

In school today, Billy will use 23 pieces of paper, and lose two pencils. He will use textbooks and school equipment designed for use by individual students. He will buy his lunch from a vending machine and throw away the plastic and paper food wrappers.

Exaggerated? Not really. Think about your day and the resources and energy you demand. Here are some facts about Billy Buyer's lifelong consumption habits.

Billy Buyer will own eight cars, four televisions, at least five radios, two stereos, eight toasters, five irons, washing machines, dryers, dishwashers, and a number of other appliances. Each of these takes energy and resources to produce as well as to run. Billy will also consume, in his lifetime, in excess of 10,000 pounds of meat, 42,000 eggs, 15,000 quarts of milk, and more than 78,000 slices of bread.

Canadians consume nearly 50 times more energy, food, and resources in pursuing their lifestyles than the people who live in the poorer nations on this planet. So, although Canada is a nation of only 23 million, it puts a strain on the global environment which is the equivalent of 1.15 billion people!

A Nigerian

EKIM lives in rural Nigeria. His family grows cocoa (used in chocolate bars) and groundnuts (peanuts). Both of these crops are cultivated on land owned by the village. Profits are shared by the community. In addition to his responsibilities in the village-owned fields, Ekim has a garden of his own. Here he cultivates yam, gari (cassava), and spinach. Ekim rises early and tends his crops before he leaves for school.

Ekim uses a firm plant stem to clean his teeth. He does not use aerosols; moreover, no bottle or container is ever thrown out by Ekim's family. His mother takes sacks and bottles to the market where they are refilled with the things she buys.

For breakfast Ekim may eat some gari which, ground up, makes a cereal similar to cream of wheat. At school Ekim does not use pencil and paper; instead he uses a slate and a piece of chalk. If Ekim qualifies for senior school, he will use pencil and paper, but even then, he will share his textbooks with other students. At midday Ekim may have fresh fruit, perhaps a papaya, an orange, or a mango.

Ekim does not own a television, nor does he own a radio or a bike. Villagers gather at night to listen to a community radio and Ekim may use one of the two village-owned bicycles if he is sent on an errand. Ekim's clothes are simple and are not replaced year-in year-out for fashion reasons; his sandals, made from an old automobile tire, last a long time.

Ekim is not poor—his father has a job, he has a home, and is never without food. Ekim's family, like other villagers, must grow more food than they actually eat. This surplus food—known as a "cash crop"—is then sold to people in a nearby city. With this money the villagers buy powdered milk, sugar, cloth, and tools.

Questions

(1) Compare Ekim's use of natural resources with Billy Buyer's.

(2) What kind of a consumer are you? Make a consumer's diary of what you used, ate, and threw away yesterday. Multiply by 365 (days in a year) and multiply this figure by the average life span in your nation. How much will you consume in your lifetime?

(3) Are there enough resources in the world for everyone to live the way middle-class North Americans do?

(4) When you think of things you want, where do you get your ideas from?

(5) Do you want things because you know about them from radio or television? From billboards? In stores?

(6) How much of what you think you need do you *really* need?

(7) Do you think Canada or the U. S. might be overdeveloped? Do you think the rest of the world might be "right-on-course?"

(8) What are some of the problems with being *overdeveloped?*

(9) How would you define underdeveloped countries?

(10) When people in underdeveloped countries have the things they need, will they want the luxuries North Americans have?

(11) Do people in underdeveloped countries have some things that people in overdeveloped countries might need or want?

(12) What does "priority" mean? Do you have priorities in your life? In your family? In your community?

(13) One meaning of development is *growth*. Do you think there are other meanings?

EXERCISE 5
WISHING

In this exercise we invite you to use your imagination. Try not to think of standard answers. Truly let your imagination roam widely because it will make the exercise more rewarding. When responding to the four questions below think about the *values* that underlie each of your answers.

People have different value-sets. Their particular values shape the way they see and understand the world. The purpose of this exercise is to get you in touch with what you value and your assumptions about what other people value. These values and assumptions determine in part our understanding of world problems (expressed in Exercise 1) and our proposals for solutions.

Answer each question before reading the next one.

(1) If you were given three wishes, what would you wish for?

(2) If you were given three wishes to help poor people in underdeveloped countries—in Africa, Asia, Latin America—what would you wish for?

(3) Is there a difference between the kinds of things you wish for and the kinds of things you want for poor people in underdeveloped countries?

(4) Do you think that poor people in underdeveloped countries could wish for different things than you wished for them? Where might you look to find possible answers to this question?

EXERCISE 6
MAJORITARIAN IDEOLOGY[7]

DIRECTIONS: Indicate your agreement or disagreement with each statement and then answer the questions at the end of the exercise.

(1) If the majority of social scientists believe that development depends on free enterprise, then the free enterprise system should be preserved around the world.

        Agree_____   Disagree_____

(2) If the majority of Americans reject socialist ideas, then those ideas should be omitted from development studies courses.

        Agree_____   Disagree_____

(3) If the majority of the world's people want to emulate the American way of life, then the U.S. has an obligation to help them to achieve this goal.

        Agree_____   Disagree_____

(4) If most scientists agree that the hot and wet tropics present insurmountable barriers, then U.S. foreign aid should be directed towards countries with temporate climates.

        Agree_____   Disagree_____

(5) If the majority of Americans think Third World people are lazy, then transnational corporations should avoid locating their factories in Latin America, Africa, and Asia.

        Agree_____   Disagree_____

(6) If the majority of economists believe that land owned communally rather than individually is wasteful, then groups who still hold land collectively should be encouraged to abandon this inefficient practice.

        Agree_____   Disagree_____

(7) If the majority of tractors are operated by men, then Third World women should not be trained to run tractors.

        Agree_____   Disagree_____

(8) If most British administrators said that colonialism brought civilization to backward people, then the British Empire was justified in expanding its influence.

        Agree_____   Disagree_____

(9) If the majority of scientists believe that the Green Revolution will solve world hunger, then the first priority of U.S. aid should be the export of high-yielding seeds.

Agree_____   Disagree_____

(10) If most Americans believe rapid population growth is the cause of major global problems, then population control should receive highest priority.

Agree_____   Disagree_____

(11) If the majority of scientists think multinationals are beneficial for economic progress in the underdeveloped world, then the proliferation of multinationals should be facilitated.

Agree_____   Disagree_____

(12) If most Americans oppose foreign aid, then foreign aid should not be given.

Agree_____   Disagree_____

(13) If the majority of middle class North Americans and Europeans want to vacation in exotic tropical islands, then luxury tourist hotels should be built.

Agree_____   Disagree_____

Questions

How many times did you disagree with the majority?
What kinds of reasons did you have when you *disagreed* with the majority?
What kinds of reasons did you have when you *agreed* with the majority?
Does the majority usually get its way?
Is the majority usually right?
Can you think of examples when a minority was right?
Is the majority right in the examples given above? How do you know?
Who would you support, the majority or those in the right?

People in any society are prone to accept the world view presented to them by the majority. Indeed, the principle of democratic rule is based on the assumed wisdom of the majority. However, everyone's view, including that of the majority, is influenced by the ideological context in which it develops. After reading the articles in this book, try to determine how a conservative, liberal, and a radical would respond to these statements.

NOTES AND REFERENCES

1. Paul A. Laudicina, *World Poverty and Development: A Survey of American Opinion.* (Washington, D.C.: Overseas Development Council, 1973), Monograph No. 8.

2. This exercise is based, in part, on a quiz developed by the Information Division, Canadian International Development Agency, 122 Bank St., Ottawa, Ontario, K1A OG4, Canada. Answers to quiz: (1) A) e, (1) B) c, (1) C) b, (1) D) e, (2) e, (3) b, (4) A) d, (4) B) e, (4) C) d, (5) a, (6) A) a, (6) B) a, (6) C) a, (7) d, (8) b (The U.S., Canada, and Australia), (9) b, (10) e, (11) c, (12) c, (13) c, (14) d, (15) c, (16) a, (17) c (Sweden and the Netherlands), (18) b, (19) c, (20) c, (21) b.

3. Adapted, by permission, from "Ideology and Oppression: Ideological Barriers to Learning in Human Relations," an unpublished paper by Alan Downes, St. Cloud State University, copyright 1978 by Alan Downes.

4. Refer to William Ryan's article in this reader.

5. Willard A. Mullins, "On the Concept of Ideology in Political Science," *American Political Science Review,* 66 (June 1972): 510.

6. Based on *Shake-Em-Up Comics*. Information Division, Communications Branch, Canadian International Development Agency.

7. Adapted, by permission, from "Ideology and Oppression: Ideological Barriers to Learning in Human Relations," an unpublished paper by Alan Downes, St. Cloud State University, copyright 1978 by Alan Downes.

About the Editors

Ingolf Vogeler is a rural cultural geographer at the University of Wisconsin-Eau Claire. Born in Germany, he received his undergraduate education at the University of Toronto and his doctorate at the University of Minnesota, Minneapolis. He has published extensively on the underdevelopment of rural areas, particularly in the United States. His fieldwork includes studies in Central America and West Africa.

Anthony R. de Souza is an urban-economic geographer at the University of Wisconsin-Eau Claire. Born in England, he received his undergraduate education and his Ph.D. at the University of Reading. He has taught at several universities, among them the University of Dar es Salaam where his teaching and research were supported by the Rockefeller Foundation. He is the coauthor of *The Underdevelopment and Modernization of the Third World* and *World Space-Economy*. In addition, he has written articles published in journals of geography, planning, and development.